D1500190

The Center for Chinese Studies

at the University of California, Berkeley, supported by the Ford Foundation, the Institute of International Studies (University of California, Berkeley), and the State of California, is the unifying organization for social science and interdisciplinary research on contemporary China.

Publications

Potter, J. M. *Capitalism and the Chinese Peasant: Social and Economic Change in a Hong Kong Village*

Schurmann, Franz. *Ideology and Organization in Communist China*

Townsend, James. *Political Participation in Communist China*

Van Ness, Peter. *Revolution and Chinese Foreign Policy: Peking's Support for Wars of National Liberation*

Wakeman, Frederic, Jr. *Strangers at the Gate: Social Disorder in South China, 1839-1861*

Sun Yat-sen
and the Origins of the Chinese Revolution

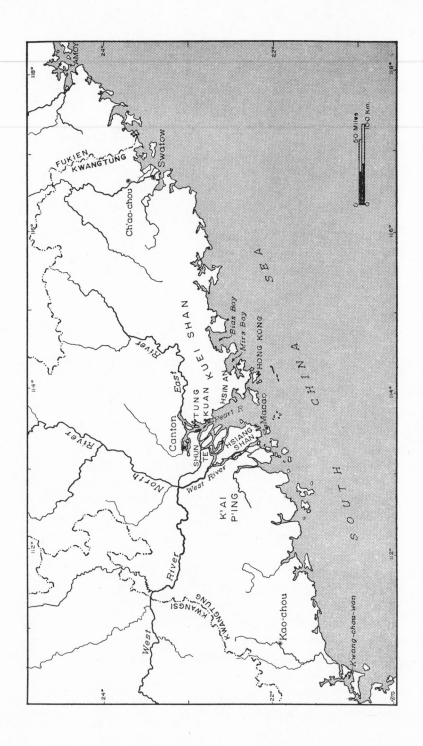

Sun Yat-sen

and the Origins of the Chinese Revolution

Harold Z. Schiffrin

UNIVERSITY OF CALIFORNIA PRESS
BERKELEY, LOS ANGELES AND LONDON • 1970

University of California Press
Berkeley and Los Angeles, California
University of California Press, Ltd.
London, England
Copyright © 1968, by
The Regents of the University of California
Second printing
First paperbound edition
International Standard Book Number 0-520-01752-8 (paperbound edition)
0-520-01142-2 (clothbound edition)
Library of Congress Catalog Card Number: 68-26530
Printed in the United States of America

To Ruth, Meira, and Yael

Foreword

This study of the rise of Sun Yat-sen during the decade from 1895 to 1905 fits him into the revolutionary process in China more intelligibly than any previous work. Harold Schiffrin has done more than use the accumulated wealth of Chinese materials to tie down the details of Sun's early career; he has used the skills of a sociologist and political scientist, as a historian should, to analyze the changing Chinese society in which Sun was finding his upward way. The resulting account shows Sun in action, responding to the chances of day to day, but at the same time it enables us to see those larger forces that set the trends he followed. Since Lyon Sharman wrote her pioneer study *Sun Yat-sen, His Life and Its Meaning* (1934), new Chinese and Japanese sources as well as Western archival materials have become available. One can now delineate more precisely Sun's remarkable personality and the circumstances of his rise.

Looking back after two generations on this first phase of China's still unfinished revolution, we can penetrate a bit further into the scene than Western observers could at the time. Where they saw in 1898 the imminent "breakup of China," we can now see the rise of Chinese nationalism as a cohesive force more powerful than Western imperialism. But we can really appreciate the stress and pace of those times only if we try to imagine ourselves as members of the Confucian-trained scholar elite, who in that era still assumed that only they could be the saviors of China.

Only by such an imaginative tour de force can one today begin to appreciate the disaster that struck China in the late 1890's. The structure of Chinese life had stood self-sufficient and preeminent for many centuries. Suddenly its very foundations were rocked. Japan's victory in the Sino-Japanese war of 1894–95 shook the Chinese world much more violently than the imposition of the treaty system had in 1860. In the decades after 1834, Britain had humbled the Ch'ing dynasty and ended its claim to ritual superiority over all foreign powers that might seek contact with China. But once the Westerners had been given their special privileges—extraterritoriality, treaty port residence, interior travel and proselytism, steamship enterprise on China's coasts and rivers, trade under a limited treaty tariff, and so on—the foreign presence was accepted as part of the established order. After 1860 a Ch'ing emperor continued to reign, the mid-century rebellions were one by one suppressed, and the classical examinations reaffirmed the Confucian orthodoxy. Western arms and material culture gained increasing acceptance, but in theory they were only means to strengthen the Ch'ing establishment against foreign aggression.

When the cataclysm of 1895 showed that the established order itself must go or China would perish, many scholars of the younger generation looked for a new leader. They found him in the modern sage K'ang Yu-wei, who in 1898 became the young Kuang-hsü Emperor's chief adviser on reform. If they had heard of Sun Yat-sen at all, it was only as a plotter of secret society violence in the lower-class peasant tradition, a man active on the fringe of Chinese life—in the foreign ports of Hong Kong and Macao and among the Chinese merchants overseas.

Except that both came from Kwangtung and hated what the old Empress Dowager stood for, K'ang Yu-wei and Sun Yat-sen were each what the other was not. It is an index of the pace of change to find such antithetical personalities becoming rival organizers of rebellion after 1899. K'ang was a brilliant and creative scholar, and he did all that could be done to reinterpret the Confucian teachings to meet China's modern needs. But after 1898, when he had his hundred days of opportunity to restructure the Chinese polity by imperial decree, K'ang could not transform himself into a leader of violent rebellion. He was still an insider from the Confucian scholar tradition, a sage prepared to advise his emperor but unable to make himself a hero. His younger rival, Sun Yat-sen, was a commoner and a rank outsider, yet by 1896 he had already become something of a hero in the world press. By 1905 he had begun to assume a sage-like posture. His rise to leadership at a national level thus dramatized the bankruptcy of the specifically Confucian political tradition represented by K'ang Yu-wei.

For Americans of the late 1960's, Sun's rise to leadership has a peculiarly nostalgic significance. Here was a major Chinese leader who spoke English and knew his way around San Francisco, New York, and London. (Chiang and Mao in their day have seen Moscow but not Western Europe or America.) In short, Sun represented the generation in China that turned to us in the then dominant West for help and inspiration, not once but many times. From us he got Christian teachings and moral support, doctrines of democracy and individualism, and techniques of science and industry; what he did not get was the key to a political reorganization of China. At the end of his life he felt that America had failed him, but during his early travels through the United States, in 1895–96 and again in 1903–04, his mood was one of hope and expectancy. The West, like Japan, was a primary factor in his rise to leadership. Indeed, Sun Yat-sen in himself represented much that was positive in the outside world's impact on China, and this, no doubt, makes it more feasible for Harold Schiffrin as a Western historian to depict his early career with such illuminating insight.

Harold Schiffrin received his B.A. in 1945 and his M.A. in 1956 from the University of California at Berkeley and his Ph.D. in 1961 from the Hebrew University in Jerusalem, where he is now teaching. He began this study at Berkeley, continued it in Jerusalem, and completed it during some nine months at Harvard after trips to London, Hong Kong, Taipei, and other places in the course of his research. The East Asian Research Center at Harvard has thus taken a special interest in this study, and we appreciate this opportunity to express our admiration for a basic contribution to the understanding of the Chinese revolution.

John K. Fairbank

Acknowledgments

In preparing this book I have benefited from the help and encouragement of numerous individuals and institutions throughout the world. It is a pleasure to acknowledge this cooperation, which has often gone beyond the normal demands of academic courtesy. I alone of course am responsible for errors committed and views expressed.

Over ten years ago Mr. Fang Chao-ying, then associated with the East Asiatic Library of the University of California, introduced me to the bibliographical maze surrounding Sun Yat-sen. He not only showed me the sources but often steered me safely through difficult passages. I am grateful to Mr. Fang for his generous assistance and patience in launching me upon my research. For help in the earliest stages of my work I am also in debt to Professor Albert E. Dien, then at the East Asiatic Library, and to Professor Robert A. Scalapino of the University of California.

I wish to express special thanks to Professor John K. Fairbank of Harvard University. For the past five years he has been an unflagging source of encouragement and help, both intellectual and practical. He and Mrs. Wilma C. Fairbank read the book in manuscript, and I am grateful for the many improvements which they suggested. I also want to thank Professor Fairbank for consenting to preface this book with his own remarks.

The hospitality of the East Asian Research Center at Harvard, extended frequently since 1962, enabled me to undertake much of my research under ideal conditions. Associates at the Center provided scholarly advice and allowed me free run of their private libraries. My thanks are due to Mr. Winston Hsieh and Mr. Leong Sow-theng, who assisted me in preparing the Glossary. I am also in debt to Professor Chow Tse-tsung, Dr. Ellis Joffe (now my colleague at the Hebrew University), Dr. Harold L. Kahn, Mr. Winston Wan Lo, Professor Maurice Meisner, Don C. Price, and Professor David Roy.

Friends and colleagues in Hong Kong gave me strong assistance during my visit in 1963 and through correspondence. In particular I wish to thank Dr. T. C. Lau, Sun Yat-sen's dentist in Canton in the 1920's, for his prompt and illuminating replies to my questions and for sending me pertinent clippings from the Hong Kong press; Mr. J. M. Braga, who graciously shared his vast knowledge of Hong Kong and Macao; and Mr. Geoffrey W. Bonsall of the University of Hong Kong Library. I am also grateful to Miss Mary Man-yue Chan, Mr. Henry D. Talbot of the Geography Department of the University of Hong Kong, Mr. Tse Shu-man, son of Tse Tsan-tai, Dr. Tseng Yu-hao, and Mr. Karl Weiss.

I wish to thank Dr. Antonio Nolasco, head of the Information and Tourism Department, for his warm hospitality during my visit to Macao, and Mr. Fung Han Shuh, who guided me through the Sun Yat-sen Memorial House in Macao.

In Taiwan I was fortunate in having the unstinting cooperation and advice of Mr. Chang P'eng-yüan of the Institute of Modern History, Academia Sinica. I also wish to acknowledge with thanks the help of Mr. Lo Chia-lun of the Kuomintang Archives, the late Mr. Fu Ping-ch'ang, and Mr. George C. Chen, son of Ch'en Shao-pai.

In Tokyo, Professor Ichiko Chūzō of the Tōyō Bunko did everything possible to make my stay fruitful. Invaluable assistance and contacts were also provided by Mr. Rōyama Michio of The International House of Japan and his assistant, Mrs. Tamada Noriko, who acted as my interpreter on several occasions. My interviews with Mr. Miyazaki Ryūsuke, son of Miyazaki Torazō; Professor Nozawa Yutaka; Professor Satō Shini-chirō, nephew of Yamada Junsaburō; and the late Mr. Kuhara Fusanosuke were especially useful. I am grateful to Mr. Iwano Ichirō and Mr. Ōtsuka Kinjirō, who acted as interpreter and translator respectively. Dr. Avraham Altman of the Hebrew University and Professor Etō Shinkichi checked a number of Japanese names and titles for me.

I would like to pay tribute to the late Professor Shelley H. Cheng, who generously shared his expert knowledge and enlightened me on several points concerning the early revolutionary movement.

In addition to those already mentioned, I wish to acknowledge with thanks the hospitality of the following institutions: the Public Record Office and the British Museum Library in London; the Supreme Court Library of Hong Kong; the American Geographical Society; the Chinese-Japanese Library of the Harvard-Yenching Institute; the Department of Anthropology and the East Asian Library of Columbia University; and the Hoover Institution of Stanford University, where Mrs. Marina Tinkoff was particularly helpful.

For financial assistance which enabled me to follow Sun Yat-sen's career on three continents, I am indebted to the East Asian Research Center of Harvard, the Harvard-Yenching Institute, the American Council of Learned Societies, and the Social Science Research Council.

Despite the difficulties imposed by intercontinental communication, the University of California Press fulfilled the publisher's obligation with efficiency and consideration. Miss Martha Ricketts provided intelligent editing, which made for improvements in style and clarified numerous questions of substance. Mr. John S. Service of the Center for Chinese Studies, the University of California, also read the book in manuscript. I am most grateful for his helpful criticism and comments. Finally, my task was lightened by Mr. Ronald Splitter, who prepared the index.

Jerusalem, January 1968   H. Z. S.

Contents

Map follows page 225

Sun Yat-sen
and the Origins of the Chinese Revolution

I

Introduction

In a political career that spanned thirty years, Sun Yat-sen never led a united China. His capacities for statesmanship and policy making were thus never tested, but this made it that much easier for him to become a legend after his death. Unlike most politicians of his time, he had not used politics to build a personal fortune. He had spoken for the big goals—a modern, powerful, independent, democratic, and socialist China. As slogans, untranslated into coherent policy commitments, these aims won widespread support. The failure of Sun's long quest for power also assumed a symbolic quality; in retrospect, he came to epitomize the frustration of Chinese nationalism. He had been betrayed by everyone identified with China's weakness and backwardness: the literati, the bureaucrats, the warlords, and most of all the foreign powers.

The legacy of Sun's "unfinished revolution" attracted numerous claimants. These included members of various Kuomintang factions, Communists, "good" warlords, and even the Japanese invaders of World War II. Today, Peking and Taipei quote Sun to perpetuate their respective versions of his legend; and Moscow, in a rebuke to Peking, has called him a "true Chinese internationalist" who sought "friendship with the Soviet Union."[1]

[1] Delusin, *Sun Yat-sen* [31], p. 19. Complete authors' names, titles, and publication data are given in the Bibliography, pages 379 to 393. Short forms of Chinese- and Japanese-language titles are cited in English and are keyed to the Bibliography by bracketed numbers: thus [31] refers to the Bibliography entry numbered [31].

Famous leaders and great thinkers tend to leave disputed legacies, as is well-known in Moscow and Peking, where the Sun Yat-sen legend is after all only a side issue.

The search for Sun Yat-sen's "true" doctrine is the less rewarding because he was not a great thinker. He was an improviser, not a political philosopher. But neither his role in history nor his personal heroism need be diminished by our recognition that it was his political style, not his ideas, which made him unique.

His improvised tactics can be explained first of all as practical responses to unprecedented political problems, to crises raised by foreign aggression and domestic institutional obsolescence; these invited solution by emergency-oriented techniques. More important, however, are the human and sociological dimensions of Sun's behavior. His particular way of improvising reflected his temperament as well as his social and educational background. He was irrepressibly optimistic, convinced that he could do no wrong, and he had that audacity to act which is the indispensable ingredient of the revolutionary spirit. He was thus able to keep in step with Chinese history. More gifted contemporaries made their bids for power, failed, and fell by the wayside, but Sun always came back from defeat, ready to adjust to a new situation.

Nevertheless, Sun's social antecedents handicapped his claim to leadership. He was a Westernized ex-peasant, an outsider who throughout his life encountered the prejudice of the Chinese elite, both in its traditional and modern forms. He tried to compensate for this social disability by soliciting foreign support. He lived at a time when foreign ability to intervene in China was considered limitless, but there was more than expediency behind his foreign orientation. He honestly believed that the entire world would benefit from the creation of a strong and modern China, and he tried his best to convince foreigners of this.

Approval by the Chinese literati (and their offspring, the modern intellectuals) and receipt of foreign support were the two main goals of Sun's pragmatic efforts. In pursuing these goals Sun often resorted to compromises and maneuvers which now seem incompatible with the nationalist, democratic impulse he came to represent. He was forced into humble, even humiliating postures. There were, then, two faces to Sun Yat-sen: the vulnerable aspirant and the confident manipulator. The aspirant had to seek compromises; the manipulator was convinced that he could turn them to his advantage.

In this study, which deals with the first decade of his career, the period 1894–1905, these two faces of Sun Yat-sen come into sharp focus. In the background is traditional China entering her final period of decline. Her oligarchic rulers were bankrupt and ineffective; her scholarly elite became indecisive and divided; and her peasant masses became more unruly. Each of these traditional groups—the oligarchs, the literati, and the peasants—perceived the crisis in a different way, but their respective solutions were essentially tradition-bound. The court tried to manipulate traditional forces to restore dynastic power and prestige. The progressive literati tried to make innovation compatible with Confucianism, but the conservative majority realized that institutional change would endanger the elitist prerogatives of the entire group. The peasants, if they had any large political goal, were anti-dynastic and hoped that a Ming restoration would usher in a benevolent, utopian version of the Confucian state.

Western penetration, however, created new focal points for non-Confucian nationalism. In Hong Kong and the treaty ports, Chinese businessmen grew accustomed to European institutions, to such conceptions as the rule of law and the sanctity of contractual relations. Clerks and professionals, mostly missionary protégés, could boast of a more modern education than the Confucian elite, and as Christians they also claimed a moral superiority. There were also the overseas Chinese, the *hua-ch'iao*. Neglected emigrants, usually scorned by their home government, they became increasingly receptive to political agitation. If as minorities they were persecuted or discriminated against abroad, they wanted a powerful home government for protection. And to the extent that economic success overseas could not be translated into comparable opportunities and prestige at home, they likewise favored change. Both the treaty port Chinese and the *hua-ch'iao* thus tended to admire European institutions and to resent European social and political privileges. As residents of Western outposts they were also highly impressed with Western power, which seemed an invincible global force. This gave rise to an ambiguous nationalism in which admiration, resentment, and fear of Europe were intermingled.

Sun Yat-sen was a product of these new peripheral groups. He grew up among the Hawaiian *hua-ch'iao* and studied in foreign schools in the Islands and in Canton and Hong Kong. His brother was a successful overseas entrepreneur, and Sun himself was a Christian and a modern physician. When the Confucian establishment showed no interest in his talent, he turned to his marginal groups as a revolutionary. He and his friends, also ex-peasant graduates of missionary schools, formed a conspiratorial society, the Hsing Chung Hui. Based in Hong Kong and backed by Hong Kong and Hawaiian *hua-ch'iao* funds, its immediate goal was to unleash secret societies and peasant bandits against the Canton government.

But this was not to be a typical peasant rebellion. The society's political goals were not defined by ideals of the Confucian order as interpreted by secret society elders. The Hsing Chung Hui leaders wanted their country to have the kind of institutions they had learned to respect in foreign schools and communities. They assumed that they, and not the literati, who were discovering the West only through translations, were best equipped to save China. Though not insensitive to the danger of imperialism, they felt that a China fashioned after Europe would be strong and inviolable and could also satisfy the commercial and religious interests of foreign powers. This larger, ultimate goal—the overhauling of Chinese government along European lines—was held only by the tiny leadership group and only vaguely explained. This was strictly an action-oriented conspiracy, a framework for exploiting but not organizing peasant dissent—that weapon as old as the Chinese bureaucratic empire itself. The Hsing Chung Hui was therefore a hybrid creature. It fed upon traditional lower class anti-dynasticism and served the political ambitions of a small Western-oriented counter-elite.

Though Sun was not at first the undisputed leader of the Hsing Chung Hui, the society's modus operandi largely reflected his style and inclinations. He knew his peasants, and as a child had been fascinated by stories of Taiping valor. He had a ready-made overseas base, well-stocked with relatives and fellow-townsmen, in Hawaii. He had spent years in Hong Kong, Macao, and Canton, and even had a few contacts in Shanghai. All these cities were rich breeding places for Westernized and semi-Westernized fringe elements. He was also on excellent terms with missionaries and native pastors, who were influential rivals of mandarin rule and potential links to foreign power.

Yet the groups Sun represented were indeed on the fringes of Chinese society, both structurally and geographically. Modernization had proceeded too slowly to produce a true bourgeois class. Real versatility was necessary to secure revolutionary footholds inside or outside the Chinese power-structure. Convinced that delay in changing China would invite disaster, Sun preferred fluid tactics that promised quick results. Matters of principle were less important; he always felt that he could properly use others to achieve his own patriotic ends.

At Canton in 1895 Sun's contacts and flair for conspiracy dictated the formula for the Hsing Chung Hui's first revolutionary attempt. After the plot failed Sun became a hunted exile. As China's first professional revolutionary, he began circling the globe in pursuit of money for the revolution that he always believed was just around the corner. Too often, however, fund-raising barely provided his food, lodging, and the price of a ticket to his next station. He might even have been doomed to a long period of obscurity had not the Manchus made their fantastic attempt to spirit him out of London in 1896.

Sun returned to the East the following year as a notorious and even more confident enemy of the throne. He now displayed his special gift for being in the right place at the right time. Though he had accidentally chosen Japan as a refuge, circumstances were to turn it into a flourishing center for Chinese nationalism, and Sun was in on the ground floor. First, Japanese pan-Asian nationalists were looking for someone to help realize their plan of saving China through Japanese tutelage. Sun convinced them that he was their best candidate and obtained their warm support and collaboration. A year later, when K'ang Yu-wei's reform movement failed, several illustrious reformers also became political refugees in Japan. This gave Sun a chance to renew his quest for cooperation from the gentry. Assisted by the Japanese, he made close contact with the influential reformer, Liang Ch'i-ch'ao. But just when it seemed that Sun had succeeded in splitting the reformers, Liang renewed his allegiance to his mentor, K'ang Yu-wei. Ultimately Liang shared some of the disdain which the literati, even as radical reformers, held for Westernized upstarts who knew little of real Confucianism.

The Boxer troubles of 1900 soon provided a classic test for Sun's pragmatic style, and he responded with ingenious formulas for exploiting Peking's war with the foreign powers. He tried various gentry-oriented combinations and even contemplated Li Hung-chang as a prospective ally. Frustrated, he tried to compensate by making foreign alliances. But in the end, even the Japanese government decided not to go along with its adventurous pro-Sun agents. Meanwhile the active part of the conspiracy proceeded under its own momentum. The feeble spark that Sun's agents had tossed into the Kwangtung countryside produced a major armed uprising in Waichow. This campaign was an impressive display of revolutionary potential, and despite the failure of Sun's grand stratagems, his reputation as a revolutionary was enhanced.

Waichow also demonstrated the limits of the old techniques. It showed that even under optimal conditions the Hsing Chung Hui lacked the thrust and staying power to achieve a successful revolution. By definition, Sun's overseas supporters, at this time mainly restricted to the small Hawaiian Chinese community, could not be a main force for revolution. At best they could serve an important but still auxiliary function as revolutionary bankers. The same can be said for the Hong Kong merchants, who, though they never really solved Sun's financial problems, were actually the biggest investors in revolution. At the leadership level, the Westernized and semi-Westernized Chinese of Hong Kong and Canton were still too few in number to play a decisive role in a political upheaval. They were a marginal group, too far removed from the potential sources of indigenous revolution. From these sources, largely peasant in derivation, indirect recruitment through secret societies and bandit gangs had produced an unreliable weapon. The conversion of peasants into politically conscious and disciplined revolutionaries, as we know from more recent Chinese history, requires direct recruitment by an intellectual elite.

In 1900, immediately after the Waichow expedition, Sun was in an extremely precarious position. The literati who shunned him at home threatened to eliminate him abroad. Preaching in a vein rather similar to his own, the exiled K'ang and Liang successfully invaded Sun's financial base. As prestigious imperial retainers, they promised to share the emperor's benevolence with overseas merchants. Their easy seduction of the *hua-ch'iao* revealed the strength of traditional prestige symbols. Though a bourgeois ethos had been sprouting in these outskirts of Chinese society, it was not yet strong enough to stand on its own. Even secret society fighters proved susceptible to the financial blandishments of the reformers.

However, while Sun was in Japan, preparing to meet this threat on his own ground, some of these same literati became potential recruits for revolutionary action. After the Boxer disaster hundreds and then thousands of Chinese students went to Japan, many of them at government expense. Aroused by nationalism and an intoxicating dose of Western political thought fed through Japanese sources, militant students rejected the Confucian officialdom which had sent them. Many also became skeptical of the pro-emperor reformism advocated by K'ang and Liang. The emergence of this group, which came from the best families of almost every province in China, established one of the universal preconditions of revolution: a disaffected intellectual elite.

The political fortunes of Sun Yat-sen depended upon his adjustment to this new elite. Compared with his original followers, these students were political sophisticates. They were more aggressively nationalist and anti-imperialist because they were culturally more Chinese, more responsive to traditional feelings of superiority. They were also less accustomed and less reconciled to the foreign presence which had only recently been felt in the interior of China. And since their social origins lay mainly in the scholar-bureaucrat elite, they still valued the form and style if not the substance of literati competence. This meant that an ideal leader would have to offer them some proof of his intellectual and moral superiority.

First considered an uncouth conspirator, Sun gradually improved his image in these new student circles. Actually, Sun's political personality had matured considerably since 1896. His travels, his studies in London, and especially the stimulating contact with Japanese intellectuals and Chinese émigrés, had enriched his thinking. In political vision and commitment to revolution, he had gone far beyond his Hsing Chung Hui supporters. Now, freed from his limited social orbit, Sun showed his remarkable capacity for adaptation. He developed expository skills, used the right nationalist metaphors, and displayed familiarity with the latest trends in European political thought. By 1905 he was able to form a new revolutionary organization based on the overseas students. This was his great breakthrough, the chance he had been seeking ever since he had become politically ambitious. Ten years of activism at the periphery, juggling meager resources, had finally enabled him to move into the mainstream of Chinese nationalism.

The new movement, the T'ung Meng Hui, was an important innovation. Organizationally, it was the prototype of a modern political party. Geographically, it shifted the fulcrum of revolutionary activity from the treaty ports and overseas communities to the heart of China, where returned students would act as revolutionary agitators and leaders. In contrast to the Hsing

Chung Hui, which had been overwhelmingly Cantonese, the new organization commanded multi-provincial, national support. It was also multi-class, bringing intellectual disaffection into closer coordination with peasant turbulence and offering Sun's peripheral elements a voice in Chinese politics. Above all, the T'ung Meng Hui gave substance to the deepening rift between Chinese intellectuals and the traditional government. The students demonstrated their diminished faith in Confucian leadership by choosing a leader from outside it.

This was the historical significance of Sun's achievement in 1905. He was the first non-gentry leader of a political movement composed mainly of Chinese intellectuals. The purpose of this study is to explain how and under what conditions Sun attained this position of leadership.

II

Sun Yat-sen: Early Influences

Because of its proximity to Hong Kong and Macao—two early European enclaves in East Asia—the district of Hsiang-shan in Kwangtung province produced a large share of those Chinese who pioneered in introducing Western ways and institutions. The best known of them all is Sun Yat-sen, after whom the district was given its present name, Chung-shan. Sun was born in the Hsiang-shan village of Ts'ui-heng in the delta of the Pearl River on November 12, 1866. His given name (*ming*) was Wen, and his courtesy name (*tzu*) was Ti-hsiang.[1]

Most of Ts'ui-heng's hundred or so families were engaged in agriculture and fishing, and, since the rocky and mountainous terrain placed limits upon farming, some of the men found supplementary work in the nearby cities of Macao and Canton and others went in for trade. Ts'ui-heng was therefore not an isolated hamlet; even wealthy town-dwellers built summer villas there. Like countless other villages on the Kwangtung and Fukien coast, Ts'ui-heng produced emigrants for Southeast Asia and the West, and contact with these emigrants tended to broaden the villagers' outlook and raise their expectations.

For the Sun family in particular, emigration proved of crucial importance. Originally they were quite poor and the father, Sun Ta-ch'eng, who held little land of his own, tried earning a living

---

[1] Lo Chia-lun, *Biography* [192], I, 1, 6.

as an agricultural laborer, a petty trader, and a tailor in Macao.[2]
After Sun Wen was born, he found additional work as the village
watchman. He was then fifty-four years old and the family's prospects were unusually gloomy. Five years later, although aware
of the hazards of emigration—two of his younger brothers had
died seeking gold in California—he decided to let his oldest son,
Sun Mei, go to Hawaii with an uncle who was in business there.[3]
Sun Mei, though energetic, was a restless, pleasure-loving sort,
and one report has it that his father was glad to see him leave.[4]

Hawaii offered a suitable challenge to Sun Mei's enterprising
spirit. During this period Chinese-style rice cultivation was in
vogue there, and he first hired himself out as an agricultural
laborer to other Hsiang-shan emigrants.[5] Later, helped by his
uncle, he formed an agricultural partnership and also opened a
store in Honolulu.[6] As remittances began flowing home, his
younger brother, enthralled by Sun Mei's accounts of his exploits and his descriptions of the Islands' wealth and liberal government, began to think of joining him.

In 1878, Sun Mei, by now the family benefactor and a village
hero, made a triumphant return to Ts'ui-heng where his father
had arranged a marriage for him. The twelve-year-old Sun Wen
was anxious to return with his brother, but he had to wait until
the following year, when his mother took him on a visit to Honolulu and left him in the care of Sun Mei.[7]

[2] Ch'en Hsi-ch'i, *Before the T'ung Meng Hui* [151], p. 6; Ch'en Shao-pai,
Hsing Chung Hui [152], p. 1.

[3] Linebarger, *Sun Yat-sen* [81], pp. 28–29. Lo Chia-lun, *Biography* [192],
I, 2.

[4] Ch'en Shao-pai, *Hsing Chung Hui* [152], pp. 1–2.

[5] Coulter and Chun, "Chinese Rice Farmers" [28], describe the development of rice farming in the Islands during the latter half of the last century.
After 1900 the industry declined due to competition from modern, large-
scale farming in the United States and the application of anti-Chinese
exclusion laws.

[6] Chen Shao-pai, *Hsing Chung Hui* [152], p. 2. For a short biography of
Sun Mei, see Feng Tzu-yu, *Reminiscences* [160], II, 1–9.

[7] Lo Chia-lun, *Biography* [192], I, 20–21. Another biography states that
Sun's mother stayed in Honolulu until 1883. See Hsu Pao-chu, "Biography
of Sun Yat-sen," [64], p. 71.

In the village Sun had acquired only a rudimentary education. Although he had read the traditional primers and continued with the Four Books and Five Classics, his formal schooling had suffered because of the family's poverty and he lacked a thorough preparation in classical studies.[8] His systematic education began in Hawaii. Because there was no Chinese school in the Islands at this time, the only alternative was one of the foreign institutions. Even these were not well attended by Chinese children, but Sun Mei was determined that his brother should receive a good education and hoped that he might surpass even his own commercial success.[9] Sun Wen did a short stint in his brother's shop, where he became familiar with the abacus and with bookkeeping, but the work repelled him.[10] He then entered Iolani School, an Anglican institution in Honolulu which accepted a limited number of Chinese, although it catered chiefly to Hawaiian and part-Hawaiian children. Some of the students, including Sun, were boarders.[11]

The arrangement which placed Sun in the school proved to be practical, for in a few years—by 1881 or 1882—Sun Mei had accumulated enough capital to undertake a more ambitious enterprise. Leasing land on the island of Maui from the Hawaiian government, he established himself as a planter, cattle grower, and purveyor of farm equipment in Kahului. There his generosity and leadership earned him the respect of the islanders, who dubbed him "King of Maui."[12]

His departure to Maui increased the family's affluence, but it also enabled his younger brother, like many students far from home, to take a more sympathetic view of the foreign influences to which he was being exposed at school.

Hawaii was then under American influence, but Iolani School,

8 Lo Chia-lun, *Biography* [192], I, 15. Ch'en Hsi-chi, *Before the T'ung Meng Hui* [151], p. 8.

9 According to the *Hawaiian Almanac, 1881* [54], p. 29, the Islands' schools were not well attended by Chinese children.

10 Lo Chia-lun, *Biography* [192], I, 21–22.

11 Sharman, *Sun Yat-sen* [107], pp. 11–12. Restarick, *Sun Yat Sen* [94], p. 12. There were nine other Chinese boys who registered at Iolani that fall. See Chung Kun Ai, *My Seventy Nine Years* [26], p. 53.

12 Ch'en Shao-pai, *Hsing Chung Hui* [152], p. 2.

directed by the Anglican prelate, Bishop Willis, was a stronghold of anti-American, anti-annexationist sentiments. With the
exception of one Hawaiian, all of the teachers were British, and
English was the language of instruction. As a result, Sun's first
taste of Western history and institutions had a decidedly British
flavor. In fact, far from taking any credit for Sun's subsequent
espousal of republicanism, the Bishop, who was a spokesman for
the pro-Hawaiian monarchical movement, later vigorously denied that Sun's stay at Iolani had bequeathed to him a "tradition
of hatching plots against magisterial authority."[13]

Despite the Bishop's disclaimers, if Sun was exposed to Anglo-
Saxon ideals of constitutional government and to the story of the
English people's long struggle against the autocratic power of the
throne, his stay at Iolani during this impressionable period was
not unrelated to his eventual commitment to revolution at home.
By championing the cause of Hawaiian independence and attacking the designs of pro-American annexationists, Iolani may perhaps be held responsible for suggesting yet another of Sun's future political concerns: the Asian's need to resist the Westerner's
aggression.[14]

[13] Restarick, *Sun Yat Sen* [94], p. 14.
[14] Ch'en Shao-pai, *Hsing Chung Hui* [152], p. 5, claims that Hawaiian
opposition to American encroachment stimulated the political thinking of
Sun and other Chinese, and encouraged nationalist, anti-Manchu sentiments. A native Hawaiian nationalist movement had emerged in the wake
of the Reciprocity Treaty of 1875 which gave America a political and
economic hold over the Islands. See Stevens, *American Expansion* [112],
p. 149. The Chinese could be expected to share the natives' fear of annexation since it would mean the extension of America's exclusion policy to
Hawaii. Exclusion had been inaugurated in the States in 1882, and in
1902, three years after annexation, was applied to the Islands. See Griswold,
Far Eastern Policy of the U.S. [48], p. 337. Fear of Oriental domination,
especially by the Japanese, was one of the major arguments advanced on
behalf of annexation. In 1887, pro-American annexationists succeeded in
passing a law which restricted voting rights to Hawaiian citizens and
threatened to confiscate the property of aliens and deport them. The
Chinese, who now took an interest in local politics, formed a Self-Defense
Society and the anti-alien proposal was shelved. See Chung Kun Ai, *My
Seventy Nine Years* [26], p. 175. On the other hand, many of the American
planters opposed annexation because it would deprive them of cheap labor.
There was also considerable anti-Chinese sentiment among the natives,
who saw their own numbers dwindle while the Oriental population in-
creased. See Kuykendall, *Hawaiian Kingdom* [72], pp. 184–185.

Sun's association with Christianity—which was to exert a powerful influence in shaping his political career—also began at Iolani. Bishop Willis, who taught the classes in Christian doctrine, later suggested that Sun would have been baptized if not for the opposition of his "heathen relatives."[15] According to a fellow student, the Bishop was eager to see that the seven Chinese who were boarders became Christians, and he hired a young Chinese evangelist to instruct them in biblical literature every afternoon. When the youngsters threatened to boycott this class if religion were taught and forced the evangelist to tell them stores about Chinese history, the Bishop declared that he would not compel them if they did not want to hear the Good Word.[16] All boarders, however, including Sun, had to attend services on Sunday at St. Andrew's Cathedral, and gradually the young Chinese were drawn toward Christianity.[17]

Most significantly, this stay at Iolani introduced Sun to Western learning. He had entered school without knowing a word of English. Three years later at graduation exercises he was awarded second prize in English grammar; the King of Hawaii, David Kalakaua, made the presentation.[18] Moreover, Iolani led him to want more Western education—more than that required to assist in his brother's business.

Thus, after another brief stay in his brother's store, Sun entered Oahu College (Punahou School), then the highest center of learning in the Islands.[19] The American Congregationalist school, located at Punahou in Oahu (two miles from Honolulu), was attended by the children of missionaries connected with the Hawaiian Evangelical Association (Congregationalist and Pres-

15 Restarick, *Sun Yat Sen* [94], p. 17.

16 Chung Kun Ai, *My Seventy Nine Years* [26], pp. 55–56.

17 *Ibid.*, pp. 60, 312; Lo Hsiang-lin, "Sun and Bishop Willis" [194], IX, 184.

18 Restarick, *Sun Yat Sen* [94], p. 16.

19 Lo Chia-lun, *Biography* [192], I, 26. Linebarger, *Sun Yat-sen* [81], p. 131, has Sun first attending St. Louis College, a high school, for a term before going to Oahu. Ch'en Hsi-ch'i, *Before the T'ung Meng Hui* [151], p. 11, mentions St. Louis and omits Oahu. The former was a Roman Catholic institution in Honolulu. See Kuykendall, *Hawaiian Kingdom* [72], p. 105.

byterian).[20] At Oahu Sun developed interests in both government and medicine and even thought of going to America for
advanced studies. In this environment, his feeling for Christianity grew even stronger.[21]

This attachment to the foreign religion put a sudden end to
his Hawaiian education. Sun Mei had been quite pleased with
his younger brother's progress and had even registered a piece
of his property in his name,[22] but he had not subsidized Sun's
education in order to alienate him from the Chinese tradition.
Although Sun Mei himself had never shown any scholarly aptitude, he was nonetheless loyal to traditional concepts of learning
and religion. The religious issue was a thorny subject among the
Hawaiian Chinese and had already split the community; Sun
Mei had joined the conservatives. In 1883, when Sun Wen's conversion appeared imminent, the infuriated Sun Mei sent him
back to Ts'ui-heng with no return ticket.[23]

Sun's behavior at home substantiated his brother's fears. The
secular and religious education Sun had acquired in Hawaii
proved incompatible with peasant mores and beliefs; soon he
and his friend Lu Hao-tung shocked their families and the entire village by deliberately desecrating the wooden image of the
local deity. Branded as iconoclasts, the two were expelled from
the village. Even before this incident, Sun had gained a reputation for his intense political interests; he talked enthusiastically
about the Taipings—childhood heroes glorified by village legend
—and about Napoleon and Washington, romantic figures from
his Hawaiian textbooks.[24]

[20] Kuykendall, *Hawaiian Kingdom* [72], pp. 105, 110. Oahu offered in-
structon on the college level but never became a full-fledged college.
[21] Lo Chia-lun, *Biography* [192], I, 26. Lo Hsiang-lin, *Sun's University
Days* [195], p. 28. According to Feng Tzu-yu, *Reminiscences* [160], II, 10,
Sun became friendly with Reverend Frank Damon—whom Feng and other
Chinese sources identify as "Fu-lan-ti-wen"—while he studied at Oahu, but
there is Chung Kun Ai's testimony that Damon returned to Honolulu in
1884 and therefore could not have met Sun until Sun's return to the
Islands in 1885. See *My Seventy Nine Years* [26], p. 314.
[22] Chung Kun Ai, *My Seventy Nine Years* [26], p. 106.
[23] *Ibid.*; Feng Tzu-yu, *Reminiscences* [160], II, 2. Ch'en Shao-pai, *Hsing
Chung Hui* [152], p. 2, writes that Sun Mei gave his brother a beating and
forced him to leave school by withdrawing financial support.
[24] Lo Chia-lun, *Biography* [192], I, 29.

The opportunity to escape provincial life and resume his studies was welcome to Sun Wen. He went to Hong Kong and enrolled in another Church of England school, the Diocesan Home.[25] At the same time, either as a concession to the family or from a personal desire for further Chinese learning, he began studying the classics with Ch'ü Feng-ch'ih, a Christian minister associated with the London Missionary Society.[26] In April of the following year, 1884, Sun transferred to Government Central School, a well-known Hong Kong secondary school attended by middle class children of all nationalities.[27] Sun's father, being of a forgiving nature, probably gave him financial assistance.

Sun now decided to formally embrace Christianity. He was baptized in 1884 by Dr. Charles Hager, an American Congregationalist missionary who had recently arrived in China.[28] At the same time Hager baptized Sun's friend, Lu Hao-tung, who later became his devoted follower. Sun felt a close attachment to Hager and to two other Christian ministers as well—Ch'ü Feng-ch'ih, and Wang Yü-ch'u.[29] After the baptism, Pastor Ch'ü gave Sun a new name, Yat-sen, the Cantonese pronunciation of I-hsien.[30]

With respect to one tradition, however, Sun remained an obedient son. On May 7, 1884 (or 1885), he returned to Ts'ui-heng to consummate the marriage which his parents had arranged for him. His bride, Lu Mu-chen (1867–1952), the daugh-

[25] *Ibid.*; Linebarger, *Sun Yat-sen* [81], p. 139.

[26] Feng Tzu-yu, *Reminiscences* [160], II, 11. Ch'ü went to Berlin in 1889 as a teacher of Chinese and later returned to China, where he joined Sun's early revolutionary activities. See *ibid.*, I, 12.

[27] Government Central School, called Queen's College since 1894, offered instruction in both Chinese and English. A number of graduates found posts in the Chinese government. See Endacott, *Hong Kong* [36], pp. 209–210; 237–238; and G. H. Bateson Wright, "Education," [135], p. 125.

[28] Lo Chia-lun, *Biography* [192], I, 31, dates Sun's conversion in 1885. According to Hager's recollection, however, this took place earlier, probably in 1884 or toward the end of 1883. See Hager, "Doctor Sun Yat Sen" [50], pp. 382–383.

[29] Lo Hsiang-lin, *Sun's University Days* [195], p. 30. For an account of Sun's position in regard to Christianity, see Feng Tzu-yu, *Reminiscences* [160], II, 10–18.

[30] Lo Chia-lun, *Biography* [192], I, 31.

ter of a merchant, remained in the village while Sun returned to his studies in Hong Kong.[31]

In the meantime, news of Sun's scandalous behavior at home had reached Sun Mei. The elder brother's antipathy to Christianity, which one of Sun's intimates described as "irrational,"[32] had not abated, and he ordered Sun to return to Hawaii. This was the first time Sun had heard from his brother in two years, and he dutifully reported to Kahului. But if Sun looked for reconciliation, his brother did not. Sun Mei demanded that Sun return the property previously given to him, and according to one account told him to "go out and earn a living by the sweat of his brow."[33] Another story has it that Sun Mei tried to purge Yat-sen of his heresies by putting him to work in the store and training him for business.[34]

Whatever the details, this was a critical moment in Sun's life. Nevertheless, his spirit did not break and he went on to Honolulu to seek the support of his Christian friends. He stayed with Chung Kun Ai (Chung Kung-yü), a classmate at Iolani, and met the Reverend Francis Damon, the Cantonese-speaking superintendent of the Hawaiian Board of Missions. When Damon learned of Sun's desire to return to China and pursue advanced studies, he raised the necessary $300 among his friends, whose number included some influential American businessmen. Chung Kun Ai donated his entire monthly income—five dollars —and allowed Sun to choose whatever clothes he wished from his

[31] Sharman, *Sun Yat-sen* [107], p. 23, gives the earlier date, relying upon the testimony of the bride. Lo Chia-lun, *Biography* [192], I, 31, citing Sun's son, Sun Fo, dates this on May 7, 1885, but this does not correspond with the date given in the lunar calendar, thirteenth day of the fourth moon. The 1884 date, however, does correspond and is probably correct. Wu Shou-i, *Sun's Youth* [225], p. 55, agrees with Sharman.

[32] Ch'en Shao-pai, *Hsing Chung Hui* [152], p. 2.

[33] Chung Kun Ai, *My Seventy Nine Years* [26], pp. 106–107. Lo Chia-lun, *Biography* [192], I, 32, 34, has Sun leaving Hong Kong for Hawaii in November 1885 and returning the following April. According to Sharman, *Sun Yat-sen* [107], pp. 25–26, Sun left in the beginning of 1886 and returned in the summer. Ch'en Hsi-ch'i, *Before the T'ung Meng Hui* [151], p. 81, and Feng Tzu-yu, *Reminiscences* [160], II, 11, have Sun leaving in October or November of 1884. Ch'en dates his return in April 1885.

[34] Feng Tzu-yu, *Reminiscences* [160], II, 11.

tailor shop.[35] Newly attired and with a few dollars in his pocket, Sun returned to China in the spring of 1886.

Finally convinced of his brother's determination to choose his own path, Sun Mei decided to heal the rupture and renewed his assistance by sending remittances through their father. When the father died in 1888 the brothers were fully reconciled.[36] Henceforth, Sun Mei's faithful support would be of vital importance in the career of Sun Yat-sen. It subsidized his professional training and gave the first impetus to his revolutionary political activities. Sun's fellow Chinese Christians and his Western friends—the missionaries and teachers who had engendered Sun Mei's suspicions—provided additional aid. Time and again Sun Yat-sen would turn to these personal sources when all other doors were shut.

After completing two and a half years at Central School, where he did not receive a diploma, Sun considered a military or naval career;[37] perhaps he was influenced by the Sino-French War of 1883–1885. But peasant youngsters were not welcome in the few modern institutions, and the most prominent of these, the Foochow Naval Academy, had been damaged by the French during the war.[38] Another possible profession, the law, likewise could not be pursued in China. The remaining alternative was medicine, a field which had interested Sun earlier in Hawaii. In 1886 Dr. Hager helped him to enroll in the Canton Hospital Medical School, an Anglo-American missionary institution headed by an American, Dr. John Kerr.[39]

At the time Sun began his medical studies, he was becoming increasingly aware of China's political difficulties. According to one of his reminiscent accounts, he had decided as early as 1884 to work for the overthrow of the dynasty. During the Sino-French War, he had been impressed with the patriotism of Chinese dockworkers, who refused to repair a damaged French vessel

[35] Chung Kun Ai, *My Seventy Nine Years* [26], pp. 107, 314.
[36] Feng Tzu-yu, *Reminiscences* [160], II, 2.
[37] Sharman, *Sun Yat-sen* [107], p. 23.
[38] Biggerstaff, *Earliest Modern Schools* [5], pp. 49, 51.
[39] Lo Chia-lun, *Biography* [192], I, 34; Linebarger, *Sun Yat-sen* [81], p. 196.

which had arrived in Hong Kong from Taiwan. He contrasted
their resistance with the Manchu regime's surrender of Chinese
rights in Annam.[40] But if this had been a firm decision on his
part, why did he start medical studies in 1886? Sun himself ex-
plains that he planned to "use the school as a place for propaganda and to exploit the medical profession in order to reach
people."[41] It is true that Sun's family background limited his
range of influence, and the prestige of modern professional status
might presumably enhance his authority among the elite. Yet it
is difficult to accept his statement, made some thirty years after
the fact, that enrollment in medical school was a deliberate step
in the direction of revolution. Like many educated Chinese, Sun
was concerned with his nation's plight, but his decision indicates
that he had not yet discovered how to reconcile the pursuit of a
professional career with his new political consciousness. During
this transitional phase, professional and political ambitions remained in flux.

A new acquaintance at the medical school, Cheng Shih-liang,
one fellow student who shared Sun's strong anti-dynastic feelings, was destined to play an important part in Sun's political
activities. Cheng was a Hakka from Kwangtung who had developed an interest in the local banditti (*lü-lin*) and the Triads,
the pervasive secret societies of South China. Despite his talent
for classical studies, Cheng had entered a German missionary
institution in Canton, where he was baptized, and then went
to medical school. He and Sun became fast friends and it was
through Cheng that Sun recognized the anti-dynastic potentialities of the secret societies.[42]

Sun continued to study Chinese history and engaged a private

---

[40] Sun Yat-sen, *Collected Works* [205], II, 80. This autobiography, written
by Sun in 1918, appears as Chapter Eight of his *Psychological Reconstruction*. See also Linebarger, *Sun Yat-sen* [81], pp. 180–181, and Endacott,
Hong Kong [36], p. 208, for accounts of this incident which took place in
1884.

[41] Sun Yat-sen, *Collected Works* [205], II, 80.

[42] Lo Chia-lun, *Biography* [192], I, 35; Feng Tzu-yu, *Reminiscences* [160],
I, 24–25, for a short biography of Cheng. See also Ch'en Shao-pai, *Hsing
Chung Hui* [152], p. 4.

teacher to help him reduce deficiencies in his classical education.[43] The other students assumed that the twenty-four dynastic
histories which lined his shelves were meant for display only, but
Sun had occasion to demonstrate his familiarity with them.[44]
The ancient period, and the Han dynasty in particular, especially attracted him.[45] This extracurricular interest is a further
indication of Sun's growing sensitivity to political affairs.

After a year in Canton, Sun decided to transfer in 1887 to the
newly opened College of Medicine for Chinese in Hong Kong.
He was, no doubt, equally challenged by the superiority of the
new school and by the more liberal scope for his political views,
now often verging on the subversive, which British territory
afforded.[46] As a source of intellectual stimuli and personal contacts, the five years spent in Hong Kong, 1887–1892, were among
the most fruitful in Sun's life. The College was a British institution which set a new standard for medical education in East Asia.
English was the language of instruction and most of the teachers
were British, some of them scientists of international repute.

The College had been established chiefly through the efforts of
Dr. Ho Kai (Ho Ch'i, 1859–1914), who was probably Sun's first
contact among those attempting to modernize China along Western lines.[47] Ho Kai, like Sun, was a product of European-Chinese
culture contact. His father, Ho Fu-t'ang, had been associated
with the London Missionary Society in Malacca and in 1843 had
begun preaching in his native Kwangtung. Later, he gave up
missionary work and became a successful businessman. The elder
Ho was well trained in both Chinese and Western learning and
wrote several books in Chinese. His son, Ho Kai, studied at the
Government Central School in Hong Kong (which Sun also attended) and then studied in Britain, where he qualified in med-

[43] Feng Tzu-yu, *Reminiscences* [160], I, 13–14.

[44] Lo Chia-lun, *Biography* [192], I, 35.

[45] Lo Hsiang-lin, *Sun's University Days* [195], p. 29.

[46] Ch'en Shao-pai, *Hsing Chung Hui* [152], p. 4.

[47] For a biographical sketch of Ho, see Ride, "The Antecedents" [97],
pp. 11–12. See also Arnold Wright, (ed.), *Treaty Ports* [132], p. 109; Lo
Hsiang-lin, *Sun's University Days* [195], pp. 9–10. Endacott, *Hong Kong*
[36] also has various references to Ho's business and civic activities in
Hong Kong.

icine at Aberdeen and became a barrister as well.[48] After returning to Hong Kong, Ho found that the Chinese were not yet willing to pay for Western medical treatment. It was acceptable if offered free of charge, as in the missionary institutions, but those possessing the means to pay preferred traditional practitioners (which perhaps influenced Sun's subsequent decision to forego a medical career). His law training, however, enabled Ho to become one of Hong Kong's most distinguished civic leaders. He served on almost every public board appointed during his time and was a senior unofficial member of the Legislative Council for three terms.

In 1882, soon after returning from Britain, he helped organize a committee advocating a free hospital for Chinese patients, and, upon the death of his English wife, the former Alice Walkden, he decided to undertake the project himself.[49] Named the Alice Memorial Hospital, in memory of his wife, the institution was completed in 1887 and its administration was turned over to the London Missionary Society. Anxious to educate his countrymen in modern medicine, as well as to provide modern care, Ho proposed that a medical school for Chinese students be attached to the hospital. Colleagues instrumental in founding the College of Medicine were Dr. Patrick Manson, the school's first dean, and Dr. James Cantlie, who later succeeded Manson.[50] Like other

[48] He studied law at the insistence of his British wife, who felt that a medical career would interfere with his home life. (Interview with Mr. Fu Ping-ch'ang, Ho's son-in-law, in Taipei, November 1, 1963).

[49] Endacott, *Hong Kong* [36], pp. 249–250. He stipulated that the hospital be managed and controlled by the missionaries of the London Missionary Society residing in Hong Kong. See the *China Mission Handbook* [24], Part II, 8. According to Ch'en Shao-pai, *Hsing Chung Hui* [152], p. 3, Mrs. Ho left her husband a large inheritance, which he donated for building the hospital.

[50] Lo Chia-lun, *Biography* [192], I, 39, erroneously names Cantlie the first dean of the medical school. See the *China Mail*, October 3, 1887, for an account of the opening ceremonies and texts of speeches by Manson, Ho, and others. Lo Hsiang-lin, *Sun's University Days* [195], p. 3, writes that Sun began his studies in January 1887, but the *China Mail* account shows that the school opened in October. Ch'en Hsi-ch'i, *Before the T'ung Meng Hui* [151], p. 11, note 4, points out Lo's error. See also Cantlie and Jones, *Sun Yat-sen* [17], pp. 37–38.

members of the faculty, both were residents of the colony who freely contributed their services as lecturers. Ho Kai's brother-in-law, Wu T'ing-fang, likewise prominent in Hong Kong civic affairs, also lent his support.[51] All of these men, especially Ho, Cantlie, and Wu, were to play leading roles in several phases of Sun's career.

Reform or Revolution?

Sun's dual interest in medicine and in politics continued and deepened during his stay in Hong Kong. But, in seeking a mode of political expression, he was disturbed by an additional conflict. Should he rely upon the Taiping anti-Manchu tradition, which he had inherited from his village and which Cheng Shih-liang's introduction to the secret societies had further stimulated, or should he pursue the more respectable course of reformism?[52]

Among his contemporaries, he repeatedly voiced his opposition to the Manchu regime. At Canton he had only Cheng Shih-liang as a confidant; in Hong Kong he added others. The most important of these was the colorful Ch'en Shao-pai, destined to remain Sun's chief lieutenant for almost a decade.[53] Ch'en, a Cantonese Christian and an excellent stylist in the classical language, had a sharp tongue and often antagonized his associates. He had studied at Canton Christian College (Ko-chih Shu-yüan or Science Academy), a missionary institution that played a pivotal role in the early years of the revolutionary movement. (Later it became better known as Lingnan College.)[54] After being in-

---

[51] Lo Hsiang-lin, *Sun's University Days* [195], p. 9.

[52] Kuomintang historians tend to agree that Sun was a confirmed revolutionary after the Sino-French War. Mainland scholars, however, do not take a uniform stand, some of them attaching more importance to Sun's reformist leanings before 1894. Compare, for example, Chin Ch'ung-chi and Hu Sheng-wu, "Sun's Revolutionary Ideas" [154], pp. 49–58, and Ch'en Hsi-ch'i, *Before the T'ung Meng Hui* [151], pp. 18–21.

[53] Ch'en's original name (*ming*) was "K'uei-shih." Because of his admiration for the Ming scholar Ch'en Pai-sha, he changed it to Shao-pai (young "pai"). (Interview with his son, George C. Chen, in Taipei, November 8, 1963.)

[54] Feng Tzu-yu, *Reminiscences* [160], I, 8. In this, as in many other in-

troduced to Sun by mutual Chinese Christian friends, Ch'en decided to join Sun at medical school. They became sworn brothers and shared a room, though Ch'en soon dropped out of school.[55]

Besides Ch'en, two other young men became intimates of Sun. The first, Yang Ho-ling, the scion of a wealthy family from Sun's village, was in business in Hong Kong. Earlier, while studying draftsmanship in Canton, he had become friendly with a fellow apprentice, the Cantonese Yu Lieh, who was now working as a clerk in Hong Kong. Through Yang, Yu was brought into Sun's circle, and as a Triad devotee, further stimulated Sun's interest in the political potential of secret societies.[56]

These three (Ch'en, Yang, and Yu), dominated by Sun Yat-sen, spent hours in Yang's store discussing politics and condemning the Manchus in a rather amateurish and romantic fashion. Outsiders did not take them seriously and called them the "Four Great Bandits." Sun himself was dubbed "Hung Hsiu-ch'üan" because of his admiration of the Taiping leader.[57] His old Canton friends, Lu Hao-tung and Cheng Shih-liang, now based respectively in Shanghai and Canton, would join the gatherings when they passed through the colony.[58] The final touch to this portrait of a budding radical is the revelation that Sun Yat-sen secretly experimented with bombs in the school's chemistry laboratory.[59]

---

stances, I am indebted to Dr. T. C. Lau of Hong Kong, himself a Lingnan graduate, who confirmed the connection between the Ko-chih shu-yüan and Lingnan. The Chinese title does not appear in any of the Western sources I have seen, but I assume this is the boarding-school for boys mentioned in the *China Mission Handbook* [24], p. 184. The Reverend O. F. Wisner, later head of this school, also became President of Lingnan (Christian College of China). These institutions were founded by the American Presbyterian Mission (North). See the *Directory of the Educational Association of China* [33], p. 17.

[55] Feng Tzu-yu, *Reminiscences* [160], I, 3–4; Ch'en Shao-pai, *Hsing Chung Hui* [152], pp. 4–5.

[56] Feng Tzu-yu, *Reminiscences* [160], I, 4–6, 8, 26; the eighty-year-old former secretary of Lin Tse-hsü, named Cheng An, is said to have impressed upon Sun and his comrades the importance of joining with the secret societies if they wanted to overthrow the Manchus.

[57] Ch'en Shao-pai, *Hsing Chung Hui* [152], p. 4.

[58] Feng Tzu-yu, *The Overseas Chinese* [161], p. 2.

[59] Lo Chia-lun, *Biography* [192], I, 40.

Yet the picture becomes distorted by overemphasis of his back-room enthusiasm for radical anti-dynasticism. As a recipient of an almost entirely Western education and as a potential pioneer in modern medicine, Sun had qualifications which would not appeal to the Triads as much as to progressive supporters of the dynasty. His experience in Hong Kong made him aware of this alternate possibility. It gave him a broader view of China's problems and gave him hope that he might contribute to reform without necessarily assuming rebel status.

A primary support for this hope was Dr. Ho Kai, whose career up to this point could serve as a model for Sun Yat-sen. Since there were only twelve students in the first-year class and since Ho taught at the school in addition to being its honorary secretary, there was ample opportunity for the two to become acquainted.[60] The launching of the school closely followed Ho's decision to express his views on Chinese political affairs. Later, with the assistance of a collaborator, he would try to reach the Chinese-reading public.[61] In the meantime, he began using the Hong Kong English-language press to argue the need for basic institutional reform instead of the government's one-sided concern with military defense.[62] His first essay, written under a penname in response to an article by Tseng Chi-tse, a former Minister to London and eldest son of Tseng Kuo-fan, represented the viewpoint of a man whose influence upon Sun continued long after these formative years in Hong Kong.[63]

[60] For a list of Sun's contemporaries at medical school, see Lo Hsiang-lin, *Sun's University Days* [195], pp. 35–36.

[61] *Ibid.*, pp. 9, 114, note 10. Ho's collaborator was Hu Li-yüan, also known as Hu I-nan, a Hong Kong merchant and another alumnus of Government Central School. Ho probably supplied the ideas while Hu rendered them into classical Chinese. One of their reformist essays, "Modern Government" [164], appears in [178], IX, 149–173.

[62] For a partial list of Ho's articles, including his criticism of K'ang Yu-wei (1898) and Chang Chih-tung (1899), see Arnold Wright (ed.), *Treaty Ports* [132], p. 109. They were usually written under the pseudonym, "Sinensis." For his publications in Chinese, see Hsiao Kung-ch'üan, *Chinese Political Thought* [166], VI, 795–796.

[63] See Teng and Fairbank, *China's Response* [121], p. 102, for an appraisal of Tseng's career.

Tseng had maintained in his article, "China: the Sleep and the Awakening,"[64] that after the Anglo-French occupation of Peking in 1860 and similar disastrous conflicts with foreigners, China had finally realized the need for new policies. She was no longer asleep, but fully aware of the outside world. As evidence of this happy development, he pointed to the effort to strengthen China's coastal defenses and the plans for modernizing the armed forces. He approved of this priority on military strength, arguing that "the changes which may have to be made when China comes to set her house in order, can only profitably be discussed when . . . she can rely on the bolts and bars which she is applying to her doors."[65]

Ho Kai's rejoinder amounted to a thorough denunciation of the "self-strengthening" program. Not denying that China had been victimized by foreigners, he argued that the cause of her troubles was not military weakness, but "loose morality and evil habits, both social and political." Foreigners demanded and obtained extraterritoriality, he continued, not because China's army and navy were weak, as Tseng implied, but because Europeans distrusted "the Chinese system of law, and especially its administration." Ho therefore reversed Tseng's order of priority: "Get an efficient navy by all means, but before all, get reform." Citing numerous examples of how modern military equipment was rendered useless by the lack of men trained to handle it, Ho contended that it was senseless for China to apply "bolts and bars" to her doors before setting her house in order. In particular, he demanded a new basis for recruiting officials. The literary examinations, he charged, were worthless because no modern knowledge was required to pass them, and because the traditional system deprived Chinese who had been trained abroad of the opportunity to serve their country.

Ho also ventured an opinion concerning China's economic

[64] The article, phrased in highly polished English, was drafted by Sir Halliday Macartney, Secretary to the Legation, and appeared in the *Asiatic Quarterly Review* published in London, January 1887. See Boulger, *Life of Macartney* [10], pp. 431–432.

[65] Reprinted in the *China Mail*, February 8, 1887.

development which represented the views of a new social stratum—the Westernized bourgeoisie. Warning against the dangers
of foreign loans, he suggested that domestic borrowing, as practiced in most countries, would be possible if there were more
confidence in the government. He felt that with governmental
encouragement, private enterprise offered the best means for industrial development.[66]

Even if he were anti-Manchu, Ho as the "leading Chinese of
Hong Kong" could not enter into such polemics under his own
name.[67] Yet his commentary on the mandarin system and his
sweeping condemnation of Chinese traditional institutions must
have appealed more to Sun's practical interests than did secret
society talk of Ming restoration.[68] The foremost concern was
whether people like Ho and Sun would be given a chance to
help modernize their country.

The hope that Sun would have this chance brightened in 1889
when Li Hung-chang (1823–1901), Governor-General of Chihli
and the most powerful official in the empire, became a patron of
the medical school. In a public letter announcing his support,
Li told of his admiration for British science, and especially for
the practical bent of the Englishman, who differed from "those
who are content with theories."[69] This was not merely polite

[66] Ho's article appears in the *China Mail*, February 16, 1887.

[67] Ride, "Antecedents" [97], p. 12.

[68] In a conversation with Fu Ping-ch'ang, who served under him in the
Canton government in the 1920's, Sun acknowledged his intellectual debt
to Ho Kai and said that immediately after the 1911 revolution he asked
Hu Han-min, then Governor of Kwangtung, to consult with Ho on foreign
policy. (Interview with Fu Ping-ch'ang). In his autobiography, Hu relates
that Ho did advise him but that he was not impressed with the latter's
concern with foreign opinion. Ho wanted him to deposit customs receipts
in the Hongkong and Shanghai Bank and earmark them for payment on
foreign loans, but Hu considered this a bad precedent. The clash between
the two is illustrative of the conflicting influences upon Sun Yat-sen. Both
Ho, worried about appeasing the foreigners, and Hu, a staunch anti-
imperialist, were at different periods among Sun's closest associates. See
Hu Han-min, "Autobiography" [171], III, 416.

[69] See Li's letter photocopied from the *China Mail* (October 18, 1889),
in Lo Hsiang-lin, *Sun's University Days* [195], p. 6. (illustrations). See also
Ride, "Antecedents" [97], pp. 8–9.

praise. Ever since his wife had been cured by British missionary physicians, Li had recognized the superiority of Western medicine and had even helped one of those physicians, Dr. John K. Mackenzie, to found a modern hospital in Tientsin. In 1881, the Viceroy's Hospital, as it was called, began teaching medicine and became one of the few modern medical schools in the country.[70] Furthermore, through his patronage of modern technology and his leadership of the *yang-wu* (foreign matters) school of thought, Li was clearly among the most progressive representatives of a class steeped in conservatism.

The pioneer journalist, Wang T'ao, in his Hong Kong newspaper, *Hsün-huan jih-pao*, may also have planted reformist ideas in Sun's mind. Though not anti-Manchu, Wang was another advocate of institutional changes which answered China's real needs more directly than the purely military and technological devices promoted by the "self-strengthening" school.[71]

With a new understanding of the reformist posture, Sun Yat-sen began to display the proficiency at focusing simultaneously upon conflicting goals, and the tactical flexibility, which characterized his entire career. Though privately nurturing anti-Manchu sentiments, he gazed longingly in the direction of moderate, gentry-sponsored reform which bore the stamp of prestige and legitimacy. During the years between 1890 and 1892, Sun made reformist proposals to two progressive officials.

One of these men was Cheng Tsao-ju (d. 1894), a distinguished scholar-official, a holder of the *chü-jen* degree, a former Minister to Japan and the United States, and, as Customs *tao-t'ai* in Tientsin in 1880, a subordinate of Li Hung-chang.[72] The exact form of

[70] Biggerstaff, *Earliest Modern Schools* [5], pp. 68–69; and Bland, *Li Hung-chang* [6], pp. 66–67.

[71] Ch'en Hsi-ch'i, *Before the T'ung Meng Hui* [151], p. 26. Wang T'ao (1828–1897), who had had brief contact with the Taipings and then helped James Legge translate the Chinese classics, visited England and became famous as a journalist in Hong Kong and Shanghai. An admirer of Victorian England, though in personal behavior not a shining example of Victorian morality, Wang was a vigorous advocate of reform. See Teng and Fairbank, *China's Response* [121], pp. 135–137; and de Bary, Chan, and Watson (eds.), *Sources* [30], pp. 717–718.

[72] See Hummel (ed.), *Eminent Chinese* [68], I, 61.

his connection with Sun is unknown, but their common roots in the Hsiang-shan district may have provided a link. Sun's letter to Cheng in 1890 was a model of humility and moderation. Claiming that he "raises his head in the hope of being of some use in the world," Sun goes on to propose that Western practices be studied and that improvement associations be formed to advance agriculture and sericulture and combat the opium habit. He stresses familiar reformist themes such as the diffusion of education, the alleviation of economic distress, and the development of institutions which would promote the flowering of "men's talents." Education, and in particular the spread of literacy, are held to be of crucial importance. Even women and children must be literate. "If human talent is not in abundance and if customs are not good," Sun admonishes, "then the nation cannot be strong."[73]

The second eminent man whom Sun approached was Cheng Kuan-ying, an influential comprador and another Hsiang-shan native. Sometime during his medical studies, Sun is said to have sent two essays to Cheng which were incorporated in the latter's famous reformist tract, *Sheng-shih wei-yen* (Words of Warning to a Prosperous Age).[74] One of those essays has been identified as the chapter entitled "Nung-kung" (Agricultural Operations), which again calls for the improvement of agriculture, and specifically sericulture. Whether Sun was the original author or not, a reference in the text to a "fellow townsman, Sun Ts'ui-ch'i," who was interested in botany and wished to study European agri-

[73] Ch'en Hsi-ch'i, *Before the T'ung Meng Hui* [151], pp. 7, 24–25. This letter was reprinted in *Chung-shan wen-hsien chou-k'an*, no. 41, 1948.

[74] Lo Hsiang-lin, *Sun's University Days* [195], p. 61. Tai Chi-t'ao reports that Sun once told him that he drafted two chapters of the revised version of *Sheng-shih wei-yen* which appeared in 1892. An earlier version of Cheng's work had been called *I-yen*. See Chou Hung-jan, "Sun's Letter to Li Hung-chang" [156], IX, 274–275. This excellent piece of research, originally in *Ta-lu tsa-chih*, 23.5 (September 15, 1961), is the most informative comparison of Sun's earliest political thinking and that of late nineteenth century reformers prior to K'ang Yu-wei. Sun's reputed contribution to *Sheng-shih wei-yen* was mentioned as early as 1904 in *Kuo-min jih-jih-pao*. See Chang Nan and Wang Jen-chih (eds.), *Selected Articles* [143], I, *ts'e* 2, 741.

cultural innovations, indicates that Cheng had some acquaint-ance with Sun.[75]

The response to these, and other attempts at achieving recog-nition, was negligble and left Sun in his obscure status as a medical student. Yet his awakened interest in reform was not dampened. Above all, living in Hong Kong for five years con-vinced him that China had to change. As he later recalled, the relatively honest and efficient administration of the Crown Col-ony delineated more sharply the backwardness and corruption of his native province, which he visited during vacations.[76]

Sun's energetic pursuit of knowledge and his diverse interests were displayed during the course of his medical studies. He brought his tutor, Ch'en Chung-yao, from Canton and kept up with his Chinese studies,[77] and he learned cricket from Cantlie.[78] He delved into Darwinism, the French Revolution, Chinese ge-ography, and scientific agriculture—subjects which might later help him contribute to the modernization of China.[79] Yet medi-cine dominated other interests, and Sun continued to be a dedi-cated, if not a brilliant, medical student. None of his political concerns—neither his sessions with the other three "bandits" nor his interest in reformism—distracted him from his major object in Hong Kong.

He was one of Cantlie's favorite students, and the doctor took him along as translator when he visited Chinese leper villages in the course of his prize winning research.[80] Sun did so well, in

[75] Quoted in Lo Hsiang-lin, *Sun's University Days* [195], p. 63.

[76] Sun Yat-sen, *Collected Works* [205], III, 242. These remarks were made while addressing an audience at the University of Hong Kong in 1923. Sun's praise of British administration and justice in Hong Kong has not escaped the critical eyes of Chinese Marxists. A mainland historian, who is generally very sympathetic to Sun, criticizes him for forgetting that Hong Kong is an "inseparable part of the homeland" which, in the hands of the British, became a "springboard for imperialist aggression against China." He takes Sun to task for his ignorance of the true nature of imperialism and for expressing unpatriotic sentiments. See Ch'en Hsi-ch'i, *Before the T'ung Meng Hui* [151], p. 30.

[77] Feng Tzu-yu, *Reminiscences* [160], I, 14.

[78] Cantlie and Jones, *Sun Yat-sen* [17], p. 35.

[79] Lo Hsiang-lin, *Sun's University Days* [195], p. 28; Lo Chia-lun, *Biog-raphy* [192], I, 42.

[80] Cantlie and Seaver, *Sir James Cantlie* [18], p. 73.

fact, that he was awarded a scholarship which defrayed his expenses.[81]

This promise as a student was realized in 1892 when only Sun and one other of the original twelve successfully completed the course. Sun, moreover, achieved the most distinguished grades and carried off the most prizes.[82] At this moment of success, however, Sun faced a further difficulty which prevented the complete suppression of his political ambitions. Was there really any scope for modern medicine in China?

Even when the school was founded there had been some skepticism in missionary circles. In 1887, for example, the *China Medical Missionary Journal* questioned the premise that there were enough Chinese students with the knowledge of English required for medical study. The few who knew English, the paper contended, could command a better income in business or in the diplomatic corps or customs service. And the fact that so small a number of the first class completed the course seemed to substantiate this fear.

But an even more important question was, if European trained Chinese physicians were produced, was there a market for their services? "In such places as Hong Kong or Shanghai," the paper argued, "room might be found for a limited number, but where else?" Since most Chinese would not pay for it, some Westerners felt that foreign medicine would for many years be administered best under missionary auspices.[83]

Furthermore, the medical school's curriculum did not fully comply with British standards and its diploma was not recognized by the Hong Kong General Medical Council. Sun's de-

[81] Wu Shou-i, *Sun's Youth* [225], p. 65.
[82] See Lo Hsiang-lin, *Sun's University Days* [195], pp. 43–53, for a detailed account of the examination records of Sun and his classmates. Four of his fellow students were graduated a few years later and the other six never qualified. See pp. 34–35. By 1901 the school had produced only twelve graduates, and twenty students had either failed or dropped out. The fact that most of the licentiates practiced in Singapore or Malaya is again indicative of the limited opportunities for modern medicine in China. See Endacott, *Hong Kong* [36], p. 282.
[83] Quoted in the *China Mail*, October 5, 1887.

gree, "Licentiate in Medicine and Surgery of the College of Medicine for Chinese, Hong Kong," did not give him the right to issue any birth and death certificates nor did it afford him any protection in law. As a Chinese, however, he enjoyed "the modified protection and recognition allowed to herbalists."[84] In other words, although he had studied Western medicine, his legal status was that of an ordinary Chinese herbalist, who required no diploma at all.

Sun was aware of these obstacles and was reconciled to practicing traditional herbalism. But since his teachers argued that he had been trained for better things, he compromised by combining both kinds of medicine.[85] In Macao, which was close to home, he established the "Chinese-Western Apothecary" with the help of several Chinese gentry. Here he dispensed traditional herbal remedies as well as modern drugs. He had financed the venture by borrowing funds from a traditional Chinese hospital —the Ching-hu Hospital—which had been established in Macao in 1871 with the help of overseas Chinese. Instead of paying interest in cash, Sun gave the hospital drugs and treated its patients without taking a fee.[86] This gave him an opportunity to practice modern surgery, and Dr. Cantlie sometimes came over from Hong Kong to assist him in difficult operations. According to his former teacher, Sun was a skillful surgeon.[87]

Yet if his status as a European-style physician was not fully recognized by the British, Sun found himself on even shakier ground according to Portuguese regulations. He relates that the Portuguese physicians, who monopolized European medicine in their colony, saw in him a professional threat and prevailed upon the Macao authorities to bar him from practicing on the grounds that he lacked a Portuguese degree.[88] The real reason was probably the lack of reciprocal recognition between the medical au-

[84] Ride, "Antecedents" [97], pp. 13, 15.

[85] Ch'en Shao-pai, *Hsing Chung Hui* [152], pp. 6–7.

[86] Lo Chia-lun, *Biography* [192] I, 46. This hospital, now a modern institution, is still in existence and is administered by personnel from the mainland. See also Feng Tzu-yu, *Reminiscences* [160], I, 9.

[87] Cantlie and Jones, *Sun Yat-sen* [17], p. 31.

[88] Sun Yat-sen, *Kidnapped* [115], p. 12.

thorities of the two colonies.[89] Since Portuguese, as well as other foreign degree-holders, were barred from practice in Hong Kong, the Macao government was under no obligation to recognize a Hong Kong medical diploma, especially one that did not even meet British standards. Like the British, however, the Portuguese had no qualms about allowing the practice of Chinese herbalism.

Thus shortly after he began his dual practice in Macao, the local authorities disqualified him from treating Portuguese patients; later they went a step further and forbade all pharmacies to fill prescriptions sent by foreign doctors.[90] This was apparently a general directive and not aimed specifically at Sun, but of course it limited his effectiveness as a European-style practitioner. It is not certain whether he immediately closed his Chinese-Western Apothecary, since no steps were taken to bar him as a herbalist. At any rate, he practiced in Macao long enough to strike up a valuable friendship with a local Portuguese family named Fernandes, in whose home he took refuge when the Canton coup failed a few years later.[91]

The setback in Macao did not discourage Sun from continu-

[89] I am indebted to Mr. J. M. Braga for supplying me with this information. (Interview with J. M. Braga, Hong Kong, October 18, 1963.)

[90] Sun Yat-sen, *Kidnapped* [115], p. 12. The Hong Kong government at one time suggested that Chinese graduates of the school be restricted to practicing their profession among members of their own race, in order to eliminate the injustice to non-Chinese licentiates, who could not even appear in the guise of herbalists. (By 1907 the school had been opened to all nationalities and the name was changed to "Hong Kong College of Medicine.") The school authorities successfully opposed the proposal, and in 1914 graduates were awarded registrable status. See Ride, "Antecedents" [97], pp. 15–17. In view of the Portuguese action against Sun, it is appropriate to point out that when the medical school was founded, the Macao weekly, *Extremo Oriente*, had doubts whether the graduates "would have the privilege of practicing medicine in all and every place out of Hong Kong." See "The College of Medicine and its Critics" in the *China Mail* (October 18, 1887).

[91] Interview with J. M. Braga who was acquainted with the Fernandes family. Evidence of Sun's friendship with the Fernandes' can also be found in the exhibition in the Sun Yat-sen home in Macao where porcelain, which he presented to Miss Sursula Fernandes upon his departure from the colony, is on display.

ing with medicine. In 1893 he moved to Canton, where he again tried to combine herbalism with European medicine. Like any traditional physician, he took space in a store in the center of the provincial capital, and he also established an "East-West Apothecary" in the western part of the city. A former classmate at the Canton Hospital Medical School acted as manager of this enterprise. Soon afterward, in association with Yin Wen-k'ai, a physician and the son-in-law of his old teacher, Ch'ü Feng-ch'ih, he opened yet another branch in the neighboring town of Shih-ch'i, the Hsiang-shan district seat. With Sun concentrating upon surgery and his shops dealing in herbs, the ramified venture started off successfully and Sun quickly gained an excellent professional reputation.[92] Yet, according to Ch'en Shao-pai, Sun expanded too rapidly and encountered financial difficulties.[93]

Though he devoted himself to medicine during these years, Sun did not forget his political ambitions. We note that in 1892, probably at the time of his Macao dilemma, he resumed experimentation with explosives in his village.[94] The following year, he revived his discussion group, which included Yu Lieh, Ch'en Shao-pai, Cheng Shih-liang, and Lu Hao-tung, and even broached the possibility of forming an anti-Manchu organization under the name Hsing Chung Hui (Revive China Society).[95] During the same period of renewed political interest, he assumed the anonymous editorship of a Chinese supplement to the Portuguese weekly published by his friend, Francisco Fernandes, in Macao. The paper circulated among the overseas Chinese, and is said to have carried violently anti-Manchu propaganda.[96] Relying upon these anecdotes, sympathetic biographers have given

92 Wu Shou-i, *Sun's Youth* [225], p. 68; Lo Chia-lun, *Biography* [192], I, 48; Feng Tzu-yu, *Reminiscences* [160], I, 47.

93 Ch'en Shao-pai, *Hsing Chung Hui* [152], p. 7. According to Ch'en, Sun maintained an apothecary in Macao as well, and Mr. Braga informs me that this establishment, located on Rua de Estalagens, was kept open after Sun left the Ching-hu hospital.

94 Ch'en Hsi-ch'i, *Before the T'ung Meng Hui* [151], p. 24.

95 Feng Tzu-yu, *Reminiscences* [160], I, 26.

96 The Portuguese weekly was *O Eco Macaense* and the Chinese supplement was called *Ching-hai ts'ung-pao* (Macao miscellany). See "Wu Ya" (pseud.), "Sun's Newspaper in Macao" [226], and interview with Mr. Braga.

credence to Sun's assertion that his primary purpose in practicing medicine at this time was to advance the revolutionary cause.

Yet the many facets of Sun's behavior—concerning which, incidentally, no two accounts are in complete agreement—do not suggest an unswerving, single-minded devotion to the goal of revolution. The conflicting allegiances to medicine and politics persisted from his student days, and even after medicine proved less appealing, the ultimate choice of a specific political path was still deferred. The evidence further suggests that before making a decision in favor of revolution, Sun made a final attempt to ally himself with the gentry reformists.

Ch'en Shao-pai, who was closer to Sun than anyone else at this time, recorded that one day (in either late 1893 or early 1894) he received a letter from Sun's apothecary describing an alarming situation: there was no trace of the proprietor and the store's cash was running low. Ch'en went to Canton to take care of the business, and after several days an apologetic Sun turned up carrying a huge stack of papers: he had spent the past few weeks at home composing a lengthy petition to Li Hung-chang. Ch'en read the manuscript and made some corrections. After this time, he wrote, Sun was no longer interested in his medical work. There was nothing for Ch'en to do but settle Sun's business affairs while Sun prepared to visit Li Hung-chang's yamen in Tientsin.[97]

Ch'en's account implies that knowledge of Sun's project came as a complete surprise. There is no mention of its being discussed previously by Sun and his friends. According to another chronicler of the revolutionary movement, Feng Tzu-yu, this was indeed a sudden decision of Sun's, at which he arrived when he realized that the dwindling income from his medical-herbal establishment could not underwrite the revolutionary activities he planned.[98] Other biographers likewise have tried to reconcile the

[97] Ch'en Shao-pai, *Hsing Chung Hui* [152], p 7. According to Lo Chia-lun, *Biography* [192], I, 50, Sun gave over his medical practice to his associate, Yin Wen-k'ai.

[98] Feng Tzu-yu, *History of the Revolution* [159], I, 3. According to Chin and Hu, "Sun's Revolutionary Ideas" [154], p. 53, Sun had been contemplating writing to Li while still in medical school.

northern trip with a revolutionary motive. Some say that Sun was trying to probe the defenses of the Ch'ing regime.[99] Others claim that Sun, far from having any intention of cooperating with the Manchu government, was encouraged by Li's progressive record, and wanted to discover whether Li could be used in some way that would support the revolutionary cause.[100]

My own conclusion is that Sun sincerely hoped to join the gentry reformers. Certainly Li Hung-chang's enthusiasm for modern medicine and his patronage of the Hong Kong school could have planted this hope years earlier. When Sun graduated, Dr. Cantlie tried to have him and the other licentiate received by Li, but the meeting could not be arranged.[101] Nevertheless, this was a precedent for the idea of establishing personal contact with Li. Finally, there is the evidence of the petition itself, which reveals a genuine sympathy for reform and a familiarity with reformist literature.

The document which Sun prepared for Li was of the same genre as the earlier writings attributed to him, and was similar in spirit and content to arguments which had been advanced by progressive scholars like Feng Kuei-fen (1809–1874) and Wang T'ao. It also contained views resembling those expressed by Cheng Kuan-ying and by Sun's teacher, Dr. Ho Kai. The crux of Sun's argument was that the source of Western wealth and power was to be found not in its formidable warships and efficient guns, but in the maximum use of human talent, the fullest exploitation of the benefits of land and resources, and the unrestricted flow of commodities. These four things, according to Sun, were the cornerstones of Western success and were necessary for survival in the modern world. If his country were ambitious, it could "gallop swiftly" and "ride abreast of the West." But China must pursue the essentials of Western strength in-

---

[99] Ch'en Hsi-ch'i, *Before the T'ung Meng Hui* [151], p. 28. Sun's sole recollection is the remark that "Lu Hao-tung and I travelled to Peking to examine the strength of the Manchu dynasty." Sun Yat-sen, *Collected Works* [205], II, 81.

[100] Lo Hsiang-lin, *Sun's University Days* [195], p. 67.

[101] Cantlie and Seaver, *Sir James Cantlie* [18], p. 79.

stead of being satisfied with the acquisition of guns and ships.[102]
(This assertion was precisely the basis of Dr. Ho Kai's refutation
of Tseng Chi-tse in 1887.) Sun's prime concern was with education—the recruitment and encouragement of men of talent—and
with basic technical and scientific innovations, particularly in
the field of agriculture. This theme, too, had appeared in his
earlier letter to Cheng Tsao-ju.

There was nothing particularly new or revolutionary in Sun's
four themes. Thirty years previously Feng Kuei-fen, in enumerat-
ing the major differences between the Chinese and the "barbarians," had written that the barbarians were superior in not
neglecting human talent and in not wasting the benefits of the
soil. (Feng had listed two other points—the success of foreigners
in eliminating the barrier between ruler and subject, and in
reconciling "the nominal with the real.")[103] And turning to the
writings of Cheng Kuan-ying, we find a striking resemblance,
not only in subject but in style as well. In the preface to his
Sheng-shih wei-yen (1892), Cheng, like Sun, had introduced
himself as a person conversant with Western ideas and familiar
with foreign institutions. Like Sun, he then argued that the
"sources of foreign wealth and power do not altogether lie in
solid ships and effective guns" (the phrasing of the quoted passage is virtually identical with that in Sun's petition). Although
he included other points as well, Cheng listed three of Sun's
themes, and again with a remarkable similarity of expression:
"Let human talents be fully used; let the land be fully used; and
allow for the free flow of materials."[104]

Sun's petition, then, can hardly be called original. What was
unusual was the fact that he approached the Grand Secretary
with it. Essentially, he was seeking acceptance into the ranks of
China's elite. But what qualifications did he present? Admitting
his inability to write an "eight-legged" essay or qualify for a

---

[102] The text of Sun's petition is in Sun Yat-sen, *Collected Works* [205], V,
1–12. Parts are translated in Teng and Fairbank, *China's Response* [121],
pp. 224–225.

[103] Chou Hung-jan, "Sun's Letter to Li Hung-chang" [156], pp. 275–276.
[104] *Ibid.*, p. 275.

literary degree, he had different accomplishments to offer.[105] "I have already passed the English medical examinations in Hong Kong. When I was young, I tasted the experience of overseas study. Western languages, literature, politics, customs, mathematics, geography, physics, and chemistry—these I have had an opportunity to study in a general sort of way. But I paid particular attention to their [the West's] methods of achieving a prosperous country and a powerful army and to their laws for reforming the people and perfecting their customs."[106]

When Sun praised Li Hung-chang as one who believed in recruiting men of talent, he could have been thinking of a number of former overseas students who had received positions under Li after their return to China.[107] But most of these students were not peasants educated by foreign missionaries; they were young men from gentry families who had been sent abroad under official auspices. They were experts in "foreign matters" with a thorough grounding in classical studies, not unalloyed products of foreign education.

Sun was suggesting that expertise in Western learning was an accomplishment in its own right. Whereas other reformers had hoped to infuse the new learning and techniques into the tiny circle of traditional literati, Sun—like Ho Kai—was now proposing that the circle be enlarged to include those who had mastered the new learning alone. This is clear from his closing passage, in which he offers himself as a candidate for Li's tutelage and humbly asks the Grand Secretary to support his plan to study sericulture in France so that he can help develop the less productive regions of the empire.[108]

Sun's plea to Li Hung-chang was conceived in the same spirit as his earlier approaches to reformers, as we can see from the route he took to Tientsin. Early in 1894, accompanied by his old

105 Sun Yat-sen, *Collected Works* [205], V, 10.

106 *Ibid.*, p. 1.

107 Bland, *Li Hung-chang* [6], p. 258, lists some of these Western-trained protégés of Li. Yet Yen Fu's experience indicates Li's reluctance to entrust power to the hands of these Western experts. See Schwartz, *Yen Fu and the West* [105], pp. 30–32.

108 Sun Yat-sen, *Collected Works* [205], V, 12.

friend Lu Hao-tung, Sun went to Shanghai, where he sought the assistance of Cheng Kuan-ying, whom he had previously contacted.[109] Cheng was sympathetic and put Sun in touch with Wang T'ao. Although still persona non grata in official circles because of his overture to the Taipings in 1861, Wang nevertheless had official contacts. After reading Sun's manuscript and making some changes, he gave him an introduction to his friend Lo Feng-lu, who worked in Li's secretariat.[110] Through Lo, Wang hoped that Sun might be received by the Grand Secretary.

Elated over his prospects, Sun proceeded to Tientsin. Wang's friend was encouraging, but just at this juncture, Sino-Japanese relations took a turn for the worse. With war imminent, it is doubtful whether Li Hung-chang ever took the time to read Sun's proposal. To Sun's disappointment, the eagerly anticipated interview was never granted. Though his proposal was printed in the September-October issue of *Wan-kuo kung-pao* (Review of the Times), a missionary-sponsored reformist monthly patronized by Cheng Kuan-ying, this was not enough for Sun Yat-sen.[111] After closing down his medical practice, he had counted heavily upon the trip to Tientsin. Its failure, however, finally resolved his indecision. The reformist possibility had eliminated itself. His sole object henceforth was to be the overthrow of the Manchu regime, and historians may justifiably conjecture that "had he been employed by Li Hung-chang as a secretary or in some other capacity he might well have developed into a different person, and had a different career."[112]

While in Tientsin, Sun is said to have procured a permit from Li's yamen to organize an association for the improvement of agriculture.[113] Thus he may already have had in mind a method

109 Ch'en Shao-pai, *Hsing Chung Hui* [152], p. 7.

110 Lo Chia-lun, *Biography* [192], I, 50.

111 Sharman, *Sun Yat-sen* [107], p. 35. Teng and Fairbank, *China's Response* [121], p. 113, cite Cheng's connection with the *Wan-kuo kung-pao*.

112 Teng and Fairbank, *China's Response* [121], p. 225.

113 Lo Chia-lun, *Biography* [192], I, 51. Ch'en Shao-pai, *Hsing Chung Hui* [152], p. 8, claims that Cheng Kuan-ying helped Sun obtain the permit to raise funds for his agricultural association. Or was this a passport for traveling abroad? According to Tsou Lu, *History of the Kuomintang* [216], p. 16, Li did read the manuscript and issued the permit. This seems doubtful, but in any case Li's reaction fell short of Sun's expectations.

of camouflaging a future underground network. Returning to Shanghai after visiting Peking and the Yangtze Valley, he visited Cheng Kuan-ying, and then, in the latter part of the year, left for Hawaii.

The failure of Sun's mission to Tientsin brought to a close the first stage in the shaping of a new type of Chinese political personality. It is clear that the location of Sun's birthplace, and especially his thirteen years of foreign schooling and professional education, pushed him toward the Westernized fringes of nineteenth-century Chinese society. There were perhaps other Chinese of his generation who were more conversant with Western thought, languages, and institutions. In Sun's case, however, Western learning alone constituted his claim to intellectual status. Others studied Confucius and Chu Hsi and then expounded upon Darwin and Mill. For Sun, as we have seen, the reverse was true. He must have perceived this inversion, and its implications, at the very time he began thinking about politics. He might have tried to squeeze the dynastic histories in with his physiology and chemistry texts, but he could never assume the guise of the gentleman-scholar or be accepted as such by the Chinese elite. He would always be merely an ex-peasant with a foreign diploma.

If Sun had not become preoccupied with political matters he might have made his mark in one of the treaty ports or in a British Southeast Asian settlement, as did other early graduates of the medical school. Or if the practice of medicine had continued to present obstacles, he could have turned to commerce. His education and missionary connections and Sun Mei's sponsorship would have made such a career more than feasible. He could then have contented himself with writing letters to the local English-language press, perhaps campaigning against opium and footbinding, and loosely identifying himself with the "modernization" of the homeland.

But Sun was not cut out to be a comprador or a member of the "King's Chinese." His vision of a strong and modern China required that Sun Yat-sen play a major role in its creation. Lacking gentry status, he explored the perimeter of the reformist movement from the outside, first using fellow-district ties, as in the

cases of Cheng Kuan-ying and Cheng Tsao-ju, and enlisting the
interest of the outcast scholar Wang T'ao, and then making his
direct overture to the leaders of officially sponsored reform. His
reasoning appeared logical: if progressive officials styled themselves the *"yang-wu"* group, why shouldn't their spokesman, Li
Hung-chang, welcome a genuine foreign product? But to accept
reformism was not the same as to be accepted by reformers. A
diploma from a Western medical school was still not the equivalent of an elegantly composed eight-legged essay. To hope so
was the first display of naivete in a career that would founder on
naive political hopes.

To return to 1894: rejected at the heights of Chinese society,
Sun turned back toward the lower rungs, the overseas Chinese
and the secret societies, with whom he shared social status. Leading these forces, he could employ shock tactics instead of the
essays and petitions which had proved ineffective. It was natural
that when Sun decided to take the plunge and organize a revolutionary network, he would turn first to that quarter from
which he could best elicit support—the overseas Chinese of Hawaii. Here he could rely upon his brother's influence and wealth;
here he would find a Cantonese, and in particular a Hsiang-shan,
community with which he had first-hand acquaintance.

III

The Founding of the
Hsing Chung Hui

After the Tientsin episode Sun Yat-sen never returned to medicine. Until the end of his life he searched for the combination of forces—within China and without—that could bring him to power so that he might lead his country to a position of strength and honor among the nations of the world.

On November 24, 1894, he took the first steps to form the organization he had contemplated, the Hsing Chung Hui (Revive China Society), but political apathy and the members' fears of reprisals against their families at home seriously hampered his efforts.[1] After several months, Sun was able to enlist only some twenty-odd members, and their interest was largely due to the influence of his brother, Sun Mei,[2] whose conversion to the cause of republicanism may have been facilitated by the Hawaiian revolution of the preceding year. The membership included Ho K'uan, a teller at Bishop's Bank, the merchant Teng Yin-nan, and Li Ch'ang, an interpreter for the Hawaiian government, who, like Sun, had been a former student at Central School in Hong Kong. Ho and Li were both natives of Hsiang-shan. Among the other early joiners were a former classmate at Iolani School, now a wealthy lumber manufacturer, an employee of Sun Mei, and a family relation.[3] After Sun left in

---

[1] Sun, in *Collected Works* [205], II, 81: Feng in *Documents of the Revolution* [179], III, 313. See also Yu, *Party Politics* [140], p. 13.

[2] Lo Chia-lun, *Biography* [192], I, 51–52; "Sun's Activities in Hawaii" [204], III, 281.

[3] Lo Chia-lun, *Biography* [192], I, 52; Feng in *Documents* [179], III, 336–339.

January, recruitment and fund-raising were carried on by this core group and over a hundred members were registered with the Hawaiian branch by the time of the Canton uprising in October 1895.

The regulations which Sun prepared at this time consisted of nine paragraphs, dealing largely with procedural matters, and a preamble that warned against foreign designs upon Chinese territory and decried the weakness and corruption of the Chinese government.[4] The members were exhorted to "revive China" and save her from disaster, but no anti-dynastic purpose was revealed in this document; this will be discussed in greater detail in connection with the Hong Kong Hsing Chung Hui, under whose aegis an expanded version of the regulations was issued. There is no doubt, however, that Sun's real intention was to gain support for armed revolt against the Manchu government. If not made explicit to the Hawaiian *hua-ch'iao* community at large because of security reasons, it was certainly confided to the smaller group of intimates, some of whom accompanied Sun back to Hong Kong. It would not seem likely that a Chinese businessman would sell his property and join Sun in Hong Kong merely to engage in agricultural improvement. It is less certain, however, whether the Hawaiian organization was at this time committed to establishing a republican form of government, since its regulations (later called "the manifesto") omitted any mention of this point.[5]

This leads us to the problem of the Hsing Chung Hui oath. Most sources report that all members submitted to a solemn pledge at the inaugural meetings in Hawaii as well as in Hong Kong. As described in a Hawaiian Chinese account, Li Ch'ang, one of the better educated members, read the oath while the inductees, led by Sun, placed their left hands upon an open Bible while raising their right hands.[6] Unfortunately there is no record of the text of this Hawaiian oath, although some investigators assume that it was the same as the traditionally accepted Hsing

---

[4] *Documents* [179], III, 274–275.
[5] Feng, in *Documents* [179], III, 315.
[6] "Sun's Activities in Hawaii" [204], III, 281.

Chung Hui pledge, which called for the "overthrow of the Manchus, the restoration of China to the Chinese, and the establishment of a republican government."[7] There is no doubt that in the course of the organization's development these three planks provided the basis of its program, but, in view of the lack of documentary evidence, it has been suggested that this particular oath was only gradually introduced, and then given "retroactive effect" by historians. According to this view, it is unlikely that the oath was administered in Hong Kong and even less probable that it was used in Hawaii.[8]

There are, however, certain reasons why the origins of this particular oath may very well be traced back to Hawaii. First of all, during the months when the Hsing Chung Hui was being organized, Hawaii became a republic. The new constitution took effect in July 1894, and Sun and the politically conscious among the *hua-ch'iao* could not have been oblivious to the political changes which accompanied the birth of the republic.[9] Furthermore, the Chinese term for "republican government" or "republic" which appears in the oath is *ho-chung cheng-fu* and not *min-kuo*, which Sun began using in 1903. The term *ho-chung* actually means "federation" or "union" and it appears in the Chinese expression for the "United States of America"— "Mei-li-chien ho-chung-kuo." This suggests that the model was the American republican form of government, and it seems reasonable to assume that the American influence was first felt by Sun in Hawaii.[10] But even if Sun's sympathies were republican, they were probably shared only by the few relatively educated *hua-ch'iao*. In dealing with this community, Sun preferred to

[7] Ch'en Hsi-ch'i, *Before the T'ung Meng Hui* [151], p. 33; Feng Tzu-yu, *Overseas Chinese Revolutionary Organizations* [162], p. 26.

[8] Hsüeh, *Huang Hsing* [66], p. 29.

[9] Ch'en Hsi-ch'i, *Before the T'ung Meng Hui* [151], p. 33, note 6; see Russ, *The Hawaiian Republic* [98], pp. 16–25, for a description of the founding of the republic and its constitution.

[10] Feng, in *Reminiscences* [160], III, 205, writes that "*Ho-chung cheng-chih*" was at this time a translation of "republic," but if so, I suspect that it was inspired by the American model. This is suggested by Ch'en Hsi-ch'i, cited above, and by Wu Yü-chang, an early follower of Sun Yat-sen who subsequently joined the Chinese Communist Party. Wu writes: "In 1894 (the)

appeal to its sense of patriotism rather than to try to promulgate specific policies.

Income consisted of membership fees—five dollars per head—and contributions in the form of shares which were to be redeemed when the revolution succeeded. The response was not as strong as expected, although Sun Mei is said to have made a handsome contribution. By the end of 1894, when Sun was ready to leave, the treasurer could give him only one hundred dollars. More was forwarded later as the membership increased and more shares were sold.[11]

Sun had intended to solicit the American *hua-ch'iao*, but when news arrived of further Chinese setbacks in the war with Japan in southern Manchuria, the time seemed ripe for a rising, and encouraged by a letter from a friend in Shanghai, Sung Yüeh-ju (better known as Charley Soong), Sun departed for Hong Kong in January 1895.[12]

Although the financial response of the Hawaiian *hua-ch'iao* had been discouraging, the trip had not been in vain. The political activization of even a small fraction of the overseas community was a significant innovation. As merchants, clerks, peasants, and artisans, they were outside the arena of traditional Chinese politics. Some were Christian idealists and others were stirred by personal ambitions. Most were satisfied to pay their dues and perhaps gamble a few dollars on the chance of a revolutionary success. Linking their names with Sun's cause demanded

---

Hsing Chung Hui . . . included a call for the establishment of a 'united government' (*ho-chung cheng-fu*) in its program. What was meant by this 'united government'? It may have been derived from the term 'the United States of America'. If so, it would mean a federated government which was of course a form of bourgeois republican government." See Wu Yü-chang, *The Revolution of 1911* [137], pp. 16–17. See also Wu's original Chinese version [227], p. 15.

[11] *Documents* [179], III, 289–290; Feng, in *Documents* [179], III, 313.

[12] Lo Chia-lun, *Biography* [192], I, 53; Sharman, *Sun Yat-sen* [107], pp. 38–39; Sung Yüeh-ju is not listed as a Hsing Chung Hui member, but Feng, *Reminiscences* [160], III, 19, under the name "Sung Chia-shu," has him among Sun's "good friends and comrades," and reports that they first met in 1894, when Sun passed through Shanghai. See also Hahn, *The Soong Sisters* [51], pp. 24–25.

tremendous courage because of their families' vulnerability, yet several were willing to take even greater risks and plunge into the thick of the conspiracy back home.

Among these was Teng Yin-nan, a generous, adventurous merchant-farmer who had been active in the Triad Society in the Islands. After bringing another fourteen members into the fold (including four other Tengs from his native district of K'ai-p'ing), Teng sold his business and property and joined Sun in Hong Kong. Thus, in his first attempt to tap the resources of an emigrant community, Sun revealed that personal magnetism which became his strong point, especially among Chinese of similar social origin and background. He was able to inspire confidence in himself as a disinterested patriot, the kind of legendary hero whom the Chinese peasant associated with a *ch'i-i*, a "righteous uprising." Perhaps, too, Teng saw in Sun a "man of destiny" who was bound to succeed and enable his followers to overcome the barriers that separated them from prized positions at home. And after playing an active part in several of Sun's conspiratorial adventures, Teng eventually reaped his reward. In the republican period he was appointed magistrate of two Kwangtung districts.[13] The original Hawaiian nucleus also supplied another district magistrate in Kwangtung after the revolution.[14] Besides Teng and other Hawaiian *hua-ch'iao* who were to participate in Sun's Canton plot,[15] several Western "specialists" and military men in Hawaii were also recruited.[16] Sun always liked to use foreign "experts"; this was another characteristic of his mode of operation which first emerged from the trip to Hawaii.

The long voyage back across the Pacific gave Sun a further opportunity for anti-Manchu agitation. When the ship stopped at Yokohama, his attempted conversion of *hua-ch'iao* fellow-passengers came to the attention of Ch'en Ch'ing, a peddler who

[13] For a short biography of Teng Yin-nan, see Feng, *Reminiscences* [160], I, 42–45.

[14] This was Hsü Chih-ch'en, a native of Hsiang-shan who was a teacher in Hawaii. See Feng, in *Documents* [179], III, 334.

[15] Lo Chia-lun, *Biography* [192], I, 53–54.

[16] Tsou Lu, *The Kuomintang* [216], p. 655.

catered to the port trade. Ch'en informed several Cantonese merchants, among them Feng Ching-ju, a bookseller and the father of Feng Tzu-yu, who later became an important emissary of the revolutionary movement and its major chronicler. The elder Feng, who had taken refuge in Japan after his own father had been imprisoned by Chinese authorities for associating with Taiping agents in Hong Kong, made no secret of his anti-Manchu opinions. The Chinese community knew him as "Queue-less" since he had removed his pigtail. Feng liked what he heard of Sun, and through Ch'en, invited Sun to disembark and talk over "national affairs." Since the ship was leaving immediately, Sun handed Ch'en some Hsing Chung Hui propaganda and asked that Feng and his friends organize a local branch. Feng circulated the literature and a few months later paid Ch'en Ch'ing's expenses for sailing to Hong Kong, where the peddler joined the Hsing Chung Hui's activist section.[17]

Yang Ch'ü-yün and the Fu-jen Wen-she

The Hong Kong headquarters was formed from members of Sun's circle, which included his oldest friends, Ch'en Shao-pai, Cheng Shih-liang, Lu Hao-tung, and Yu Lieh, some newly arrived Hawaiian enthusiasts, and, in addition, a small number led by Yang Ch'ü-yün (1861–1901).[18]

Yang Ch'ü-yün developed his political interests out of an even more Westernized background than Sun's. Born in Hong Kong, he had studied in an English school there, and after teaching in another Western institution had worked for leading Hong Kong firms. His knowledge of Chinese was scanty, and like Sun, he tried to improve it when he became involved in politics. Little is known about Yang, and for reasons which will be made apparent, Kuomintang historians have not gone to great lengths to portray him in a favorable light. Yet even their sketchy accounts indicate that Yang, whose temperament, ambition, and

[17] Huang Fu-luan, *The Overseas Chinese* [175], p. 94. Feng, in *Documents* [179], III, 322–323. According to Ch'en Shao-pai, *Hsing Chung Hui* [152], p. 13, however, one of Feng's friends, the clothing dealer, T'an Yu-fa, also came to the ship and held a discussion with Sun.

[18] Feng, in *Documents* [179], III, 317–318; Lo Chia-lun, *Biography* [192], I, 56.

education were so similar to Sun's, was a formidable contender for Hsing Chung Hui leadership. His experiences in the British colony had given him a pugnacious nationalism: boxing was one of his hobbies, and he was quick with his fists when he encountered foreigners taking advantage of Chinese. His extensive reading of Western literature allowed him to speak with authority on revolutionary theory and history, and he is said to have dominated discussions of these subjects. He would instinctively assume the seat of honor at social gatherings, and he was not a man to be interrupted during his discourses.

Yang Ch'ü-yün had found in anti-Manchuism an outlet for nationalist pride and political ambitions, and even earlier than Sun—who was his junior by five years—he had formed an association, the Fu-jen Wen-she (Literary Society for the Promotion of Benevolence), which apparently discussed revolution under the guise of pursuing social and literary interests. The motto of the group was "ducit amor patriae."[19] It claimed only sixteen members, several of whom were connected with shipping companies, a trade which required some knowledge of English.

Another prominent member of the group was Tse Tsan-tai (Hsieh Tsuan-t'ai), an Australian-born Cantonese who was employed as a clerk in the Hong Kong Government service. A Christian, Tse had completed his education at the Government Central School of Hong Kong, an institution which proved to be a veritable cradle of anti-dynastic revolutionaries. According to Tse, who glamorized his own role, he had inherited anti-Manchu convictions from his father, and immediately upon arriving in Hong Kong in 1887—at the age of fifteen—he had gathered together a group of young patriots, including Yang, and begun conspiring against the Manchus. Their "Revolutionary Headquarters," he wrote, was established only on March 13, 1892, when the name Fu-jen Wen-she was adopted.[20] That Yang, however, was the central figure in the group, seems beyond

19 For biographical data on Yang, see Hsüeh, "Sun Yat-sen, Yang Ch'ü-yün" [65], pp. 308, 317–318; Ch'en Shao-pai, *Hsing Chung Hui* [152], p. 55; Feng, *Reminiscences* [160], I, 4–6.

20 Tse Tsan Tai, *The Chinese Republic* [122], pp. 6–8. But in his "confidential" biographical record, *Tse Tsan Tai* [123], Tse writes that the Fu-jen Wen-she was formed in 1890.

doubt, and furthermore there is no indication that their secret plotting had been any more realistic than the discussions which Sun and his friends were conducting at the same time.

Sun had already met Yang Ch'ü-yün in 1891, and when he returned to Hong Kong early in 1895, both were prepared to take advantage of the uneasy political situation resulting from the war with Japan.[21] On February 18, Yang, Tse, and one other member of their clique joined Sun's followers in forming the Hong Kong Hsing Chung Hui.[22]

An important new recruit at this inaugural meeting was Huang Yung-shang (Wong Wing-sheung), the scion of a distinguished Hong Kong family, originally natives of Hsiang-shan and related to Dr. Ho Kai.[23] Huang's father, Huang Sheng (Wong Shing), a graduate of the London Missionary Society's Morrison School, had in 1846 been sent to America with two classmates as the first Chinese to be educated in that country. The elder Huang, who was no longer living at this time, had been a naturalized British subject and had once been appointed Chinese representative to the Hong Kong Legislative Council.[24] But despite his family's Western, Christian orientations, Huang Yung-shang was a keen student of the esoteric *I-ching*. According to the cyclical principle enunciated in the appendixes to this classic, all things were subject to an ineluctable law of return after reaching an extreme, and Huang was firmly convinced that the fortunes of the Han (Chinese) people had reached their nadir and were ready to rise.

Huang's faith in the timeliness of the anti-dynastic effort was expressed in the name he chose for the meeting place of the

[21] Hsüeh, "Sun Yat-sen, Yang Ch'ü-yün" [65], p. 308. Sun's friend, Yu Lieh is said to have introduced them. See Lo Chia-lun, *Biography* [192], I, 56.

[22] Lo Chia-lun, *Biography* [192], I, 56. Although Yang's organization is said to have included sixteen members, only three appear on the membership list of the Hsing Chung Hui. See Feng, in *Documents* [179], III, 344–345.

[23] Feng, *Reminiscences* [160], I, 6; Lo Hsiang-lin, *Sun's University Days* [195], p. 118, note 64.

[24] Endacott, *Hong Kong* [36], pp. 204–205; Hummel, *Eminent Chinese* [68], II, 837–838.

conspirators: the Ch'ien-heng Hang (the Ch'ien-heng "club" or "business establishment").[25] The character *ch'ien* according to the *I-ching*, is identified with the *yang* or male principle and represents the positive forces of Heaven; thus the name of the headquarters could be translated as the "Heaven Pervades" or "Heaven Prospers" Club.[26] Outsiders, like the Hong Kong police and Manchu spies, need not have suspected that the name was any more significant than similarly exotic titles adopted by other Chinese business firms or social clubs.[27]

The Hsing Chung Hui oath, possibly introduced in Hawaii, is said to have been used on this occasion in Hong Kong as well, and the earlier regulations and preamble were amplified and given a more overtly anti-Governmental tone. The preamble particularly emphasized the danger of foreign aggression and the corruption and debility of the court:

China has become increasingly weak. . . . Our venerable China is not considered the equal of the various powers. . . . Is it possible for men of determination not to be pained? If our multitude of four-hundred millions . . . could be stirred to militancy no power under Heaven could withstand them. But since the government is derelict, public morality is corrupt. The court sells titles and offices, and bribery is openly practiced. The officials fleece the people and rob them. . . . Famines increase and the homeless crowd the countryside. . . . Now powerful neighbors encircle us, glaring like tigers and staring like falcons. . . . We have already seen the result of earlier precedents—to be dismembered. . . . There are men of heart who cannot resist the urgent cry to save the people from disaster. . . . Our descendants may become the slaves of other races! China can only be restored by assembling men of determination.[28]

The second paragraph of the revised regulations (now numbering ten) continued in the same vein. The country and its

---

[25] Feng, *Reminiscences* [160], I, 6; Ch'en Shao-pai, *Hsing Chung Hui* [152], p. 9.

[26] See Fung, *Chinese Philosophy* [44], I, 382–391.

[27] The headquarters at 13 Staunton St. was closed on August 27, 1895, apparently for security reasons. See Lo Chia-lun, *Biography* [192], I, 58, and Tse, *Chinese Republic* [122], p. 9.

[28] *Documents* [179], III, 275.

entire civilization were endangered by foreigners, who were encouraged by Chinese disunity. The circumstances required men of audacity, who would master the modern scientific means of making a country prosperous and its army powerful, men who would seek to rejuvenate China and support the "national entity." By unifying and enlightening the people, they could easily extricate the nation from its current danger, for "the people are the foundation of the country, and if the foundation is secure, the country is tranquil." Another paragraph advocated carrying out any measures which would benefit the nation and the people; among those mentioned specifically were the establishment of newspapers and schools.[29]

The other regulations dealt with procedural matters. The main branch of the organization was to be in China, and others, with a minimum of fifteen members each, were to be established elsewhere. Anyone, Chinese or foreign, was eligible for membership so long as he was altruistically motivated and willing to expend his utmost efforts on behalf of China. All that was required was the recommendation of two members and the payment of the five-dollar membership fee. Officers, to be elected annually, included a chairman, vice-chairman, treasurer, Chinese secretary, foreign language (English) secretary, and a ten-man board of directors.[30]

Members were urged to contribute to the organization's treasury through the purchase of shares, or bonds, each ten-dollar investment to be redeemed for one hundred dollars "when the country is established." In addition to fund-raising, the various branches were to sponsor the discussion of current affairs and develop a strategy to revive China. The usual frivolities associated with fraternal groups were to be eschewed: "there will be no gambling or lounging around." Instead, the members were to engage in serious activities, such as the study of foreign political systems.[31]

The similarity in both content and style between this docu-

---

[29] *Ibid.*, pp. 275–276.
[30] *Ibid.*, pp. 276–277.
[31] *Ibid.*, pp. 277–278.

ment and the one produced in Hawaii indicates the authorship of Sun Yat-sen, or that of the same person who drew up the earlier statement and by-laws. Sun's control of the organizational framework appears to substantiate the prevalent view that it was his initiative which led to the merger of 1895, and that, having already created the organization in Hawaii, he was accepted as its leader in Hong Kong as well. Yet there are no records of officers being elected at these first meetings, and as we shall subsequently discover, the leadership contest which ensued was not won by Sun Yat-sen.[32]

As a political tract, the manifesto is neither weighty nor revealing. Its significance lies in the audience to which it was directed and the mood which it projected. If the leaders of the Hsing Chung Hui refrained from outlining a definite political program, they nevertheless issued a challenge to China's Confucian leadership, which by implication called for a unified national effort at modernization and reform, regardless of the expense to traditional culture and institutions. Even the conventional reformist rhetoric cannot obscure the revolutionary thrust of the statement.

For example, one of the key phrases of the manifesto is "a prosperous country, a powerful army" (*fu-kuo, ch'iang-ping*), a widely circulated slogan in late nineteenth-century reformist quarters.[33] We have already taken note of this theme's appearance in Sun's petition to Li Hung-chang. At that time, in presenting his credentials to the Grand Secretary, Sun had stated that during his sojourn among the foreigners he had "paid particular attention to their [the West's] methods [of achieving] a prosperous country and a powerful army, and their methods for transforming the people and perfecting their customs."[34] And now in the Hsing Chung Hui manifesto, he invited auda-

[32] In Hawaii, however, officers had been elected. A local businessman, Liu Hsiang, was the first chairman. See Lo Chia-lun, *Biography* [192], I, 52; and Feng, in *Documents* [179], III, 312.

[33] As noted by Benjamin Schwartz, the "wealth and power" goals were more in accord with Legalist than Confucian thinking. See his "Confucian Thought" [104], p. 56.

[34] Sun Yat-sen, *Collected Works* [205], V, 1.

cious patriots to join him in seeking the same broad goals. There is a significant link, then, between the position of literati reformism, as represented by the individual petition to Li Hung-chang, and the collective appeal of the manifesto. But the manifesto pursued the implications of reform far beyond these well-worn slogans: it placed the blame for China's vulnerability and her obdurate resistance to change squarely upon the nation's ruling class. It affirmed that traditional leaders were incapable of realizing the goal of "a prosperous country, a powerful army."

In contrast to literati reformers, who limited their educational proposals to gentry ranks, the Hsing Chung Hui called for the diffusion of knowledge among the populace at large. The deliberate invitation to foreigners to join the organization, the stress upon the study of foreign models, the injunction to adopt any measure necessary to benefit the nation and its people—all these indicate a readiness to embrace sweeping reforms which were not necessarily justified by Chinese tradition.[35]

[35] For a most enlightening study of the official effort to introduce education in the latter half of the century, beginning with the T'ung-wen Kuan in the 1860's, see Biggerstaff, *Earliest Modern Schools* [5]. The reformist literati not only hoped to preserve the sanctity of traditional learning while admitting Western studies, but invariably sought recruits for modern institutions from sons of "respectable" or "reputable" families—that is, candidates who already had been raised in the gentry tradition and who were expected to qualify in the traditional examination system as well. See pp. 1–93. Feng Kuei-fen (1809–1874), the champion of the "self-strengthening" school, who anticipated Chang Chih-tung's famous slogan, "Chinese learning for the fundamentals, Western learning for practical use," was especially opposed to the recognition of treaty port Chinese who had become "experts" in the use of Western languages. These were "either unemployed merchants of Canton or Ningpo origin who had picked up a smattering of foreign languages or graduates of missionary schools who had come from poor families of uncertain social status and who had been partially foreignized and in some cases actually converted to Christianity" (p. 13). This last category is precisely where Sun and most of the Hsing Chung Hui leaders fit. The literati suspected, and with some justification, that missionary-sponsored education was inimical to the preservation of traditional Chinese culture. As Mary C. Wright has pointed out, Feng's arguments against the compradors "represented a fusion of the class and cultural interests of the bureaucracy." See her *Tung-chih Restoration* [136], p. 243. Officials were also afraid that the universal diffusion of new military techniques would weaken traditional

Although the manifesto reflected a revolutionary mood, it stopped short of defining the particular political results the organization sought to achieve. Even the anti-Manchu goal was merely implied, not stated categorically; it was part of the secret pledge but not a subject for argument or explication. The same may have been true of the republican aim. The exhortation to study foreign governments and the tone of the statement certainly allowed for an attempted emulation of republicanism as the most promising of foreign models. Yet not a word concerning republicanism appeared in the formal pronouncement.

Security considerations obviously contributed to the leaders' reticence. Since the British were wary of subversive plots against the Chinese government, and because of danger from Manchu informers, subterfuge and camouflage were preferable to a frank exposition of political sympathies. Then, too, the founders of the Hsing Chung Hui seem to have been less interested in the end results of political action than in the action itself. Their tenuous organization offered little scope for indoctrination and the dissemination of ideas. There is no evidence that the procedural provisions were ever carried out or that branches held regular meetings.[36] The discussions in Hong Kong, attended by as few as seven or eight members of the inner circle, centered chiefly upon the practical, immediate problems of fund-raising, logistics, and strategy required for the Canton uprising.[37] Propagandistic efforts were practically nil, and when pursued were aimed primarily at foreigners and undertaken neither by Sun nor Yang Ch'ü-yün, the ostensible leaders, but by intimate sympathizers. Officers had been elected in Hawaii, but there is no record of the election of a full complement of officials in the Hong Kong headquarters. Instead, temporary tasks connected with the uprising were parceled out. Consequently, the Hsing

---

class barriers and warned that "in order to avoid other subsequent evils the common people should still be forbidden to learn about the use of these new weapons." See Fairbank, "China's Response" [39], p. 389.

[36] Hsüeh, *Huang Hsing* [66], p. 30.

[37] Ch'en Shao-pai, *Hsing Chung Hui* [152], p. 10.

Chung Hui impresses one as an ad hoc conspiracy geared for an immediate thrust of regional dimensions rather than as a broadly based political movement with a long-range program.

Just before the scheduled coup, there were only 153 members enrolled in the organization.[38] Of these, 112 had joined in Hawaii, one in Yokohama, eleven in Hong Kong, and twenty-nine in the Canton area. Almost half these members (73) were natives of Sun's home district and almost all were Cantonese, the two exceptions being Yang Ch'ü-yün, whose family was originally from Fukien, and a Hunanese soldier serving in the Kwangtung army. Friendships and village ties, especially in Hawaii, were apparently a more important factor than ideology in bringing these people together.

The preponderance of the overseas merchant element and other non-gentry categories is revealed in the following occupational breakdown of the 153 members. (The merchant category includes not only wealthy entrepreneurs but also the struggling proprietors of one-man establishments; secret society activists are so listed because they indicate no other occupation.)

Merchants	69	Physicians and Dentists	3
Laborers	39	Students	2
White collar workers	10	Christian clergymen (Chinese)	2
Military personnel	5	Bankers	1
Farmers	4	Journalists	1
Teachers	4	Secret society activists	13

Not only did this membership represent the traditional low prestige groups in Chinese society, it also represented a significant number of vocations which required modern, Westernized education and training. These members—Western trained phy-

[38] For biographical data of Hsing Chung Hui members in 1894 and 1895 (prior to the Canton coup) I have used Feng Tzu-yu, in *Documents* [179], III, 331–348; 369–370; and the original membership list of the Hawaiian branch which appears in *Documents* [179], III, 288–289. I have attempted to eliminate duplication and have included only those Hawaiian members who actually paid the membership fee, excluding one individual who appears only on the list of share-purchasers. It should be pointed out too, that "natives," presumably Hawaiians, bought $200 worth of these shares. This outside support was probably the result of Sun Mei's influence in Maui.

sicians, English teachers, clerks and technicians for foreign enterprises, and young cadets of the modern armed forces—provided the leadership. Several, like Sun, Yang Ch'ü-yün, and Tse Tsan-tai, had spent a good part of their lives outside China and were only superficially acquainted with Chinese culture. Some even corresponded with each other in English. Only one member of the organization, Chu Ch'i, possessed a literary degree, and, interestingly enough, his gentry affiliation proved to be one of the chief reasons for the failure of the plot.[39] Among the inner circle, perhaps Ch'en Shao-pai was the sole exception to the prevailing lack of facility in the use of written Chinese. Throughout this period and until 1905, Sun's movement suffered from a deficiency of the literary talent required for editing newspapers and journals.

But the tactics pursued for the capture of Canton assigned only a minor role to propaganda. Sun and his confederates did not try to create a disciplined political movement based upon an indoctrinated following. Instead, they assumed their task to be merely the release of the dammed-up reservoir of anti-dynastic sentiment. In planning to seize power they took the path that seemed to promise the quickest results, namely, reliance upon traditional vehicles of anti-dynasticism—the secret societies and bandits. The organization as such had a dual function: it solicited funds among the *hua-ch'iao* abroad and it tried to act as a catalyst and coordinator of armed uprising at home. The Canton plot was its immediate reason for existence, and the strategic and tactical ramifications of the plot provide an additional dimension for evaluating the political personality of Sun Yat-sen.

[39] According to Tsou Lu, *The Kuomintang* [216], p. 658, Chu, a Cantonese teacher whose role in the plot will be discussed in the next chapter, was a *chu-sheng*, which is the equivalent of the first degree.

IV

The Canton Plot of 1895

Canton, the provincial capital of Kwangtung and the residence of the Kwangtung-Kwangsi governor-general, was a logical target for the revolutionaries. This was their home territory. The people and the terrain were familiar. Linguistic considerations would have made it difficult to operate elsewhere; later the non-Cantonese speaking Swatow contingent was at a disadvantage in the environs of the capital.[1] In addition the Canton delta area was easily accessible from the conspirators' main base, Hong Kong; the success of their operation hinged upon the influx of men and arms from without, in contrast to traditional rebellions, which arose from internally established bases. Furthermore, the province had a long tradition of antipathy toward the dynasty. Bitter fighting had attended its conquest by the Manchus in the seventeenth century and it had been a stronghold of rebels in the mid-nineteenth century.[2] Recently Kwangtung had been rife with Triads and bandit groups including opium smugglers and pirates, who required little urging to take up arms against authorities. The region was also rather

[1] Tsou Lu, *The Kuomintang* [216], p. 657.

[2] Yeh Ming-ch'en (1807–1859), as Governor of Kwangtung and later as Governor-General of the Liang-Kwang provinces (Kwangtung and Kwangsi) used particularly harsh measures in repressing the rebellion in Kwangtung. See Hummel, *Eminent Chinese* [68], II, 904–905; and Ch'en Hsi-ch'i, *Before the T'ung Meng Hui* [151], pp. 15–16. For a stimulating and authoritative analysis of social turbulence in Kwangtung, see Wakeman, *Strangers at the Gate* [125].

isolated from the rest of the country and the tendency toward separatism was strong.

At the end of March 1895, a British political report described Kwangtung as "perfectly quiet" except for one disturbance. Yet this exception, a minor uprising in the south, where a force of one or two thousand men attacked and looted a town, indicated that the province abounded in the explosive ingredients which had upset other parts of the empire during and after the war with Japan.[3] In Manchuria, the major battlefront, rebellion had broken out from the Amur region to Kalgan even while the war was in progress. According to foreign observers, the rebels, apparently squatters from the northern provinces who were affiliated with secret societies, would have defeated the imperial armies had they been better united. Fugitive soldiers, who fled toward Manchuria and away from their own retreating armies, seriously increased the prospects of continued disorder in the northern provinces.[4] The signing of the Treaty of Shimonoseki in April 1895, though it brought some respite to the external front, only heightened the internal danger to the dynasty. Disgruntled troops, who had been hastily recruited and sent north only to find themselves dismissed and stranded without pay at the close of the war, posed an urgent problem.

A report from Hankow in May 1895 described "a very uneasy feeling . . . amongst the Chinese authorities, who are apprehensive of trouble in the future." Hunan and Hupeh were comparatively quiet because a large proportion of the Ko Lao Hui (Society of Brothers and Elders), the major secret association in the Yangtze Valley, had enlisted as soldiers and had been sent to the front. A flare-up was expected as soon as they were disbanded and left to shift for themselves. In Wuchang there had already been a crisis when some Hunan troops refused to be released while their pay was four months in arrears. Some three hundred thousand men had been recruited from Anhwei, Hu-

[3] FO 17/1234, Bourne to O'Conor, enclosed in O'Conor's no. 141, April 16, 1895 [46].
[4] FO 17/1233, O'Conor's no. 78, March 14 [46], enclosed a translation from *Shen Pao* which appeared in the *North China Daily News*.

nan, and Hupeh alone, and these Yangtze Valley soldiers plus the southerners greatly worried the authorities.[5] Many refused to leave the service and others made their way home by looting and terrorizing the countryside. Described as the "dregs of society," and apparently heavily infested with secret society adherents, the disbanded Chinese army was probably more interested in loot than in politics, but the anti-dynastic potential was there, awaiting only suitable coordination and leadership. Disaffection toward the regime mounted among the respectable elements of society as the government proved itself unable to control its troops.

In addition to the bandit menace, the gentry had other complaints. During the war, the government had imposed special levies on home-owners and landowners, compelling them to contribute the equivalent of several months' rent.[6] Gentry reluctance to support the war effort can be attributed not so much to lack of patriotism as to skepticism regarding the true destination of the funds. And even if the money were to be allocated for the purchase of arms, they questioned whether Chinese armies could use them effectively.

Anti-Japanese feeling was not lacking, and in Taiwan the local population took the initiative in resisting the annexation agreed to in the Treaty of Shimonoseki. Under the leadership of the scholar Ch'iu Feng-chia and the ex-Taiping officer Liu Yung-fu, whose Black Flag force had been incorporated into the Ch'ing army during the war with France, the Chinese established a short-lived Taiwan Republic (Taiwan Min-chu Kuo) in the summer of 1895. The "republic" fell in late June when the Japanese landed, but armed resistance was not extinguished until October.[7] Earlier Liu had complained to the

---

[5] FO 17/1233, Warren to O'Conor, May 20, 1895; Cavendish to O'Conor, June 7, 1895 [46].

[6] *Overland China Mail*, March 6, 1895. The *Overland China Mail* was the weekly edition of the *China Mail*.

[7] Liu's black flag is said to have been a symbol of mourning for the fallen Taiping Kingdom. See Li Chien-nung, *The Political History of China* [78], pp. 117–118; Hummel, *Eminent Chinese* [68], I, 171 concerning the "Taiwan Republic"; Lo Hsiang-lin, *History of Liu Yung-fu* [196], pp. 236–266

Tsungli Yamen about the dismissal of veterans from his army and the government's failure to offer his soldiers proper inducements to enter the campaign in Manchuria.[8] But the emerging patriotism of the day, which cut across class barriers, also accentuated the growing cleavage between the people and their rulers in Peking, where corruption and inertia had curtailed the half-hearted attempts at national defense.

During the war, Kwangtung itself heard invasion rumors; Canton would be at the mercy of any small enemy force that could take the defenses of the Pearl River by a flank attack.[9] Cantonese merchants were already expressing a preference for British instead of Japanese rule, apparently placing little hope in their own government's ability to repel the invader.[10]

Kwangtung had other grievances as well. Under the five-year rule of Governor-General Li Han-chang, elder brother of Li Hung-chang, corruption "had attained a degree of notoriety rarely surpassed even in China."[11] Li's reputation resulted from such practices as his acceptance of a million tael birthday gift, ostensibly from his subordinates but actually extorted from the gentry.[12] Illegal dealings in the sale of literary degrees also irritated the gentry, and finally, the postwar demobilization problem, though national in scope, was unusually severe in Kwangtung. After amassing a huge army to support his brother's

on the "Taiwan Republic"; Woodside, "T'ang Ching-sung" [131], pp. 160–191. British Consular dispatches from Taiwan also provide an excellent source for studying this episode. See FO 17/1235, FO 17/1236, FO 17/1237, FO 17/1238, FO 17/1240, covering the period April 1895–November 1895 [46].

[8] *North China Daily News*, January 9, 1895, has a translation of Liu's letter to the Tsungli Yamen.

[9] FO 17/1234, Bourne to O'Conor, enclosed in O'Conor's no. 141, April 16, 1895 [46].

[10] FO 17/1234, O'Conors no. 126, April 10, 1895, encloses Jamieson's intelligence report [46].

[11] FO 17/1234, O'Conor's no. 146, April 19, 1895 [46]. See also article from *Shanghai Mercury* in *Overland China Mail*, May 1, 1895, which described Li's dismissal as a precautionary measure designed to avert rebellion in the south.

[12] Tsou Lu, *The Kuomintang* [216], p. 656.

war effort in the north, Li Han-chang dismissed three-fourths of the men when the fighting ended and left them stranded in Kwangtung ports, where they inevitably contributed to unrest and disorder. Nor were the regular provincial troops any less a menace to public security.[13]

Governor-General Li's misbehavior finally came to the attention of Peking, and though he was cleared of the charges brought against him, he was replaced by T'an Chung-lin in April 1895.[14] In the meantime there was mounting unrest. In June and July of the same year, the new governor-general had to quell an uprising that spread over three districts in eastern Kwangtung. The two to three thousand insurgents, who were mainly members of secret societies and *lü-lin* (bandit gangs), probably included a number of discharged soldiers.[15] In September and October there were three other such secret society disturbances in the province; the last occurred less than two weeks before Sun Yat-sen was scheduled to go into action.[16]

These were the major features of the political situation in Kwangtung which encouraged the launching of the Hsing Chung Hui plot: a growing mood of patriotism expressed in resentment toward the government, which was held responsible both for the military failures in the north and for the humiliating peace terms that affected the south; discontent among the gentry aggravated by bureaucratic exactions and the spread of lawlessness; and increasing turbulence among the lower strata of society, specifically the ex-soldiers and peasants, who flocked to the secret societies. There was no way to gauge the extent or depth of disaffection, but the symptoms justified a prognosis favorable to revolution, at least on a regional level.

The plan to seize Canton began to crystallize in March 1895 during meetings held in Hong Kong.[17] With the overthrow of

[13] *Ibid.* Tsou's account of these events is apparently derived from Sun's description in his *Kidnapped in London* [115], pp. 20–23.

[14] FO 17/1234, O'Conor's no. 146, April 19, 1895, contains a translation of the decree clearing Li of the charges brought against him [46].

[15] Ch'en Hsi-ch'i, *Before the T'ung Meng Hui* [151], p. 34.

[16] See Kuo T'ing-i (ed.), *Daily Record* [184], II, 936.

[17] According to Tse Tsan Tai, *Chinese Republic* [122], p. 9, the first dis-

the Manchu regime as their ultimate goal, the plotters presumably intended first to establish an independent Kwangtung-Kwangsi government which would serve as a springboard for a northern drive or a pawn in high-level bargaining. Anticipating an anti-dynastic chain reaction, they showed little concern for planning beyond this initial stage.

Hong Kong was designated as the rear headquarters where men, arms, and funds were to be assembled. The date set for the coup was October 26, 1895 (the ninth day of the ninth lunar month), the traditional day upon which Chinese offered sacrifices at their ancestors' graves, which provided convenient cover for the planned influx of fighters.[18] A revolutionary flag, a white sun against a blue sky, was designed by Lu Hao-tung.[19]

The plans, which were finally completed by the end of August 1895, had been elaborated to the most minute detail. Some 3,000 Triad members, including recruits from Kwangtung coastal districts, would assemble in Hong Kong and Kowloon and reach Canton by ferry early in the morning of October 26, bringing with them arms and ammunition. Upon landing, this "do or die" spearhead would divide into four companies, distribute the arms—which were to be packed into barrels labeled "cement"— and immediately attack the offices of the governor-general and governor, and the headquarters of the military commandants. The attackers would break into the private apartments of these officials and either kill them or hold them as prisoners, in order to weaken the expected counterattack by choking off its command echelon. Not only the city but also the two provinces were thus to be deprived of leadership.[20]

In addition to this shock force from Hong Kong, supporting

---

cussion of the plan took place on March 13th and March 16th. It seems clear, however, that the Hsing Chung Hui leaders were thinking of such an uprising much earlier and Tse's dating of the formation of the Hong Kong branch is about a month late.

[18] Ch'en Shao-pai, *Hsing Chung Hui* [152], p. 10.

[19] Feng, *Reminiscences* [160], I, 18.

[20] Tsou Lu, *The Kuomintang* [216], pp. 657–658; Lo Chia-lun, *Biography* [192], I, 60; Feng in *Documents* [179], III, 319–320. Feng's history of the Hsing Chung Hui originally appeared in *Reminiscences* [160], IV.

columns were scheduled to converge upon the city by way of
the Pearl River tributaries. Two boats had been purchased for
transporting troops. The fighters, recruited by the hard core
Hsing Chung Hui members, included Triads from the North
River area led by a notorious bandit chieftain, "Big Gun"
Liang,[21] and similar bands from Hsiang-shan, Shun-te, and other
districts. Even Swatow, some 180 miles from Canton, was expected to send a contingent. Some of these forces were to be
stationed at strategic approaches to the city to ambush and
divert loyalist troops, while within the capital a bomb-throwing
squad led by Ch'en Ch'ing, the peddler whom Sun had recruited
in Yokohama, was to further distract and confuse the enemy. As
a means of identification, the rebels were to wear red belts.
They were also given a password, "Ch'u-pao, an-liang" (remove
the tyranny, bring peace to the virtuous).[22]

This plan depended upon secrecy, split-second timing, and
above all, a great measure of audacity. The active participants
probably numbered in the hundreds rather than the thousands, and there is evidence that many among the rank and file
were mercenaries, not indoctrinated supporters of the revolutionary movement. Yet the leaders had reason to believe that
once the shooting had started and they had seized their first
objectives, spontaneous risings of *lü-lin* and secret societies in
the hinterland would be forthcoming. According to one source,
Sun was not concerned about the size of his striking force; he
counted upon audacity and valor rather than numbers. During
the Taiping Rebellion, Sun's fellow townsman Liu Li-ch'uan
was said to have captured Shanghai with seven men; Sun was
confident he could take Canton with several hundred stalwarts
who were not afraid to die.[23] Just as Liu Li-ch'uan had been

---

[21] Lo Chia-lun, *Biography* [192], I, 60. Feng Tzu-yu, *Reminiscences* [160],
347.

[22] Lo Chia-lun, *Biography* [192], I, 60.

[23] Tsou Lu, *The Kuomintang* [216], p. 657, draws the analogy with Liu
Li-ch'uan, although the Triad force which captured Shanghai in 1853 consisted of about 2,000 men and not seven. The comparison, however, is appropriate and one wonders if Sun had Liu's example in mind. Just as Sun
planned to take advantage of a local holiday in order to infiltrate Canton,

assisted by a friend in high office, so Sun hoped to gain cooperation—both active and passive—from leaders among the Cantonese
gentry as well as key military and naval personnel.[24]

Yang Ch'ü-yün, assisted by the wealthy Huang Yung-shang,
by Teng Yin-nan, and by others, took charge in Hong Kong;
Sun personally led operations at the advance base in Canton,
aided by Cheng Shih-liang—the chief link to the Triads—and
the faithful Lu Hao-tung.

To camouflage his activities, Sun established a new association, innocuously named the "Agricultural Study Society," in
Canton on October 6, 1895.[25] The society's manifesto, ostensibly
written by Sun but possibly ghost-written or edited by his
former teacher, Ch'ü Feng-ch'ih, reiterates the familiar themes:
promotion of universal education and of scientific agriculture.[26] "If we want China to change from a state of weakness to
one of strength, from impoverishment to prosperity, we must
promote education." Criticizing the "self-strengthening" program for its emphasis upon military modernization, Sun again
contended that the people's real problems revolved around agriculture, which sorely needed the introduction of scientific
methods. "I am a son of a peasant family," he wrote, "and know
the hardships of life in agriculture. When I was young, I went
abroad and learned about Western government and civilization,
and read extensively and studied everything concerning modern
learning, paying special attention to agriculture and botany. . . ."
And now, through the medium of the new association, he
wished to serve the people with his expert knowledge.[27] Dis-
guised as a reformist, educational enterprise, the society was

---

so did Liu's band strike on a festive occasion—the birthday of Confucius
(September 7th). See Fairbank, *Trade and Diplomacy* [38], pp. 406–408.

[24] Wu Chien-chang (Samqua) was the Shanghai *tao-t'ai* who was strongly
suspected of being in collusion with his fellow Hsiang-shan native, Liu Li-
ch'uan. See Fairbank, *Trade and Diplomacy* [38], pp. 431–432.

[25] Lo Chia-lun, *Biography* [192], I, 58–59; Feng, in *Documents* [179], III,
47.

[26] Feng, *Reminiscences* [160], I, 12.

[27] For the text of the manifesto see Sun Yat-sen, *Collected Works* [205],
V, 13–14.

reportedly well received in bureaucrat and gentry circles, and a number of prominent citizens agreed to help Sun, who had previously attained some local renown as a medical practitioner. But not all these local worthies were ignorant of his real intentions.

Among those who had been admitted to the inner circle was Liu Hsüeh-hsün, an ambitious *chin-shih* (recipient of the highest literary degree) who wielded power in local politics. He was a Hsiang-shan native, like so many other early associates of Sun, and the two probably first became acquainted through Sun's medical practice.[28] Liu's influence stemmed from his management of a lucrative public lottery called *wei-hsing*, the object of which was to pick "winners" in the government examinations. It was an important item in Kwangtung's public revenue and was also profitable for Liu, who amassed a fortune after managing the lottery for several years.[29] In spite of his prestigious degree, wealth, and high connections, Liu aspired to a more exalted position and discussed with Sun the grand strategy of an anti-dynastic plot. Liu saw himself in the role of a dynastic founder like Chu Yüan-chang of the Ming or Hung Hsiuch'üan of the Taipings, and Sun was to be his chief collaborator, a Hsü Ta or a Yang Hsiu-ch'ing.[30] Apparently he pursued a policy of "watchful waiting." According to one source,[31] he informed Sun of the availability of the receipts from the *wei-hsing* lottery, which, according to a report later submitted by the

[28] Feng, *Reminiscences* [160], I, 77.

[29] Proceeds from the *wei-hsing* lottery in Kwangtung were used for soldiers' salaries during the Kuang-hsü period (1875–1908). See *"wei-hsing"* in *Tz'u yüan* (one volume edition, 1947), 1558.4. In 1900 one million taels were collected from the lottery. See Morse, *Trade and Administration* [86], pp. 104–105. J. O. P. Bland, in *Li Hung-chang* [6], p. 204, refers to Liu as the organizer of the "notorious 'White Pigeon' lottery." I assume this is a colloquial designation for the same lottery.

[30] Hsü Ta (1329–1383) assisted the founder of the Ming dynasty. Yang Hsiu-ch'ing (d. 1856) served as the major collaborator of Hung Hsiu-ch'üan, the founder of the Taiping movement, and was considered the Taipings' ablest political strategist.

[31] Feng, *Reminiscences* [160], I, 77.

governor-general, amounted to several million taels.[32] If the plot came off as scheduled and they seized this treasure, there would be more than enough money for buying arms.

Why should Sun have taken Liu Hsüeh-hsün into his confidence? Liu, despite his subversive propensities, was an old-fashioned monarchist who had little in common with Sun and his Western-educated friends. The answer seems to be that in this first venture in high level politics Sun was allowing himself ample room to maneuver. In order to unseat the Ch'ing authorities in Kwangtung, he was prepared to compromise with essentially conservative but ambitious gentry, even if it involved a temporary attenuation of his political goals, which at this time were still hazily formulated. This relationship with Liu, to be renewed in similarly secretive circumstances five years later, was a further indication of the strong pragmatic tendency of Sun's personality. Moreover, his longing for gentry affiliations had not waned. Although his lieutenants recruited followers among the lowest strata of Chinese society, Sun did not consciously assume the role of a lower-class leader. His political outlook embraced all classes, and especially during these early years he viewed the collaboration of respectable and influential citizens as a necessity if he was to obtain power. Throughout his life, he was always ready to attempt diplomacy or a secret understanding as a supplement to, or even a substitute for, direct action. Therefore some credence must be placed in the rumors that hinted at high-level complicity in his plot. (Sun had previously sent Ch'en Shao-pai to Shanghai to contact the influential comprador Cheng Kuan-ying.)[33]

[32] T'an's memorial appears in Tsou Lu, *The Kuomintang* [216], pp. 663–664. T'an's estimate of the funds available from the lottery seems quite high, and perhaps this figure is no more reliable than the 50,000 he used in describing the strength of the Hsing Chung Hui rebels.

[33] Ch'en Shao-pai, *Hsing Chung Hui* [152], p. 9. In the opinion of J. O. P. Bland, "After the Japanese war something approaching to an expression of national sentiment was created, and the revolutionary conspiracies led by Sun Yat-sen and other Cantonese were secretly supported by a very considerable number of officials." See *Li Hung-chang* [6], p. 253.

In the meantime rooms and storehouses for arms were arranged in the vicinity of Canton. Under the guidance of the American chemistry teacher whom Sun had brought from Hawaii, the conspirators even tried making their own munitions.[34] Sun, who had previously carried on experiments with explosives, was reported to have been a frequent visitor at this secret arsenal in a Canton suburb.[35] Within the city, one of their important hideouts was the religious bookstore, Sheng-chiao Shu-lou, whose proprietor, Tso Tou-shan, was a devout Christian with whom Sun had become friendly during his residence in Canton. This was in fact the same store in which he had rented space for his medical office in 1893. The street on which it was located—the Shuang-men-ti (Double Gateway)—was a favorite resort of the literati since it had the largest bookstores in the city. The rear of the premises served as a Presbyterian chapel, where services were conducted on Sundays by Wang Chih-fu, who also acted as manager of the bookstore. Both Tso and Wang joined the Hsing Chung Hui, and their store, which was listed as an office of the Agricultural Study Society, was a meeting-place and arms cache.[36] The all-important casks labeled "cement" which Yang

[34] Tsou Lu, *The Kuomintang* [216], p. 658, transliterates this name as "Ch'i-lieh." This probably refers to one "Crick" mentioned in a British consular despatch after the plot's exposure. Consul Brenan reported that Crick was British, and had been "deported from the Sandwich Islands in consequence of his complicity in the political trouble there." But the Foreign Office had no record of anyone called Crick having been in the Islands. See FO 17/1249, Brenan to O'Conor in O'Conor's no. 26, November 12, 1895 [46]. It will be recalled that Sun was said to have brought several Western "specialists" with him upon his return from Hawaii; see Lo Chia-lun, *Biography* [192], I, 54. Ch'en Shao-pai also reports that "an American chemistry teacher whom Sun had brought from Hawaii" was present at a meeting held by the conspirators in October; Ch'en Shao-pai, *Hsing Chung Hui* [152], p. 11.

[35] FO 17/1249, Brenan to O'Conor in O'Conor's no. 26, November 12, 1895 [46]. It was located in Ho-nan, south of the main part of the city and was known as the "Ch'i-lieh yang-hang" (Ch'i-lieh company). See the account of one of the Hawaiian *hua-ch'iao* participants, Sung Chü-jen, in *Development of the Revolution* [178], IX, 464.

[36] Feng, *Reminiscences* [160], I, 13. For a contemporary decription of the street, see John Kerr, *The Canton Guide* [70], pp. 24–25. Kerr also mentions the chapel, which he considers favorably located because of literati interest in the neighborhood.

Ch'ü-yün shipped from Hong Kong were addressed to Pastor Wang in care of the bookshop.[37]

The plotters also found a few sympathizers in the Ch'ing armed forces. Eventually exploitation of dissatisfaction in this quarter proved to be a potent weapon in the revolutionary arsenal, but at this time success was limited and based largely upon village and kinship ties. Two naval officers, the Ch'eng brothers, K'uei-kuang and Pi-kuang, who were natives of Hsiang-shan and had been in sympathy with Sun and his friends since his earlier Canton period, joined the Hsing Chung Hui. Pi-kuang had received naval training in England and Ch'eng K'uei-kuang, the elder brother, was a flotilla commander serving on one of the warships in the area. The latter was expected to commit his forces to the revolutionary cause once the attack on Canton got underway. Another kinsman, Ch'eng Yao-ch'en, likewise a navy man out of Sun's native district, also joined the movement.[38]

Although the conspirators tried to infiltrate the provincial land forces, which were over ten thousand strong, the only name which appeared on their roster was that of Hu Feng-chang, a Hunanese sergeant in the Liang-Kwang army who was brought into the plot by one of the Triad members. Hu later helped Sun escape from Canton after the plot was exposed.[39]

Another recruit from the armed forces played a less honorable role. Ch'en T'ing-wei, a Naval Academy graduate, had been enlisted by Ch'en Shao-pai in Shanghai after being previously introduced to Sun by Cheng Kuan-ying. When Ch'en T'ing-wei returned to his native Kwangtung, Sun supplied him with funds and commissioned him to recruit *lü-lin* bandits in the North River region. Ch'en began to send glowing reports of his accomplishments and Sun was highly pleased. At the same time, however, it was heard that Ch'en was always at home. Sun refused to

[37] Ch'en Hsi-ch'i, *Before the T'ung Meng Hui* [151], p. 35; Pastor Wang's complicity is also mentioned in Brenan's report, in FO 17/1249, no. 25, November 1, 1895 [46].

[38] Feng, in *Documents* [179], III, 345–346; Feng, *Reminiscences* [160], I, 26; Wu Shou-i, *Sun's Youth* [225], p. 69.

[39] Feng, in *Documents* [179], III, 370. See Hu's biography in *Development of the Revolution* [178], IX, 476.

believe that he was being deceived but sent Ch'en Shao-pai to investigate, whereupon the worst was confirmed; instead of agitating in the countryside Ch'en T'ing-wei had been plying Sun with fictitious reports.[40] The incident not only illustrates Sun's gullibility, but exposes the looseness of Hsing Chung Hui recruiting techniques. Although this episode ended Ch'en T'ing-wei's connection with the Canton coup, a few years later he tried to inveigle the movement's leaders into coming to terms with the Manchu government, and he eventually turned traitor to the revolution.[41]

Yet despite the weak strands inevitable in every subversive network, there is no doubt that Canton and its adjoining districts had become a hotbed of conspiracy. And this was almost altogether the result of Sun's leadership. His extensive contacts in the city had enabled him to set up operations right under the noses of the Ch'ing authorities. His own recruits and personal followers were the emissaries to the Triads and the local banditti. His Christian friends provided a sanctuary for storing arms and planning. His imported foreign expert dabbled in the manufacture of munitions. Two fellow villagers whom he had brought with him from Hawaii—Hou Ai-ch'üan and Li Ch'i—were assigned the leadership of the Hsiang-shan column;[42] as already noted, his personal recruit from Yokohama, Ch'en Ch'ing, was given a similarly strategic assignment, and it was largely his connections which led to the infiltration of the Ch'ing naval forces.[43]

Yet neither in name nor in fact was Sun the undisputed leader of the Canton plot. This position was held by Yang Ch'ü-yün. Sun was the key figure in the activist phase of the conspiracy, and his personal followers comprised the numerically larger faction, especially if the comparatively quiescent Hawaiian branch is taken into consideration; but Yang, whose background and personality were so similar to Sun's, commanded sufficient prestige and influence to assume titular leadership of the movement on the eve of its launching.

[40] Ch'en Shao-pai, *Hsing Chung Hui* [152], pp. 9, 47–48, 55–56.
[41] *Ibid.*, p. 56; Ch'en Hsi-ch'i, *Before the T'ung Meng Hui* [151], p. 36.
[42] Feng, in *Documents* [179], III, 319.
[43] Lo Chia-lun, *Biography* [192], I, 60.

Apparently the election of a leader had been a delicate issue, for it was inexplicably postponed until October 10, a little over two weeks before the day set for the coup. What was at stake was more than the chairmanship of the organization; it was the presidency of the future Chinese Republic which the conspirators were deciding.[44] The choice of the term *"Po-li-hsi-t'ien-te,"* a transliteration of the English "president," indicates their attraction to a Western republican model.[45] There is evidence too that Yang, rather than Sun, was more insistent upon republicanism at this time.[46]

The "presidency" of what one of the participants called the "provisional government" was bitterly fought over and almost led to murder. According to Ch'en Shao-pai, Sun was first elected but Yang Ch'ü-yün demanded that the office be his at least until Canton was secured, after which it would revert to Sun. The challenge to Sun's leadership apparently came as a surprise to him and his supporters. Cheng Shih-liang wanted to "eliminate" Yang on the spot while Sun's other confidant, Ch'en Shao-pai, advised temporary appeasement, arguing that killing Yang would create an incident and involve the authorities, and that he was still needed for handling the Hong Kong end. Once the plot succeeded Sun would be in control in Canton anyway, and if it failed, the title would have no meaning. According to Ch'en, Sun saw the logic of this argument and grudgingly deferred to his rival. Although unity was thus maintained, mistrust and suspicion had been planted in the midst of Sun's faction, and they

[44] *Ibid.*, p. 59; Hsüeh, *Huang Hsing* [66], p. 30.

[45] It should be noted that in both the Hawaiian and Hong Kong versions of the Hsing Chung Hui regulations, this transliterated term was not used. Instead the head of the organization was designated as "chairman" (*chu-hsi*) or "director" (*tsung-pan*). This might be explained by the fact that the regulations were designed to conceal the revolutionary purpose of the organization. (See Lo Chia-lun, *Biography* [192], I, 58.) There is also the possibility that Chinese historians—Lo and Feng—merely transliterated Tse Tsan-tai's "president" while Tse, who wrote his book in English, had in turn translated one of the Chinese terms as "president." Ch'en Shao-pai, who was also present at these meetings, does not mention *"Po-li-hsi-t'ien-te"* but refers to the movement's leader as *"tsung-t'ung,"* which might be translated as "president." See Ch'en Shao-pai, *Hsing Chung Hui* [152], p. 10.

[46] See Hsüeh, *Huang Hsing* [66], p. 29.

never forgave Yang for what they felt to be a usurpation of their leader's authority.[47]

Ultimately they had to comply with Yang's demand because of his control of the movement's finances. Although fund-raising had been one of Sun's major objects in going to Hawaii, his effort in the Islands had produced only a tiny dribble of cash. The big contributors, like Huang Yung-shang, were from Hong Kong.[48] Huang, who had sold some property and contributed $8,000 to the Hsing Chung Hui treasury, appears to have been Yang Ch'ü-yün's man.[49] Yang, Huang, and the Fu-jen Wen-she co-conspirator, Tse Tsan-tai, formed the triumvirate which managed the financial and other aspects of the Hong Kong phase of the plot.[50] But if Yang forced Sun to back down during their tense confrontation of October 10, there was yet a third figure to whom they both deferred in matters of policy and program: Dr. Ho Kai.

Ho Kai reappeared in the life of his former student in March 1895 and acted as a sort of "grey eminence" to the merged forces of Sun and Yang.[51] Without formally enrolling in the organiza-

47 *Ibid.*, pp. 10–11. Tse's criticism of Sun's "recklessness" (*Chinese Republic* [122], p. 4) reflects the deep antagonism between the two factions.

48 Lo Chia-lun, *Biography* [192], I, 59; Feng, *Reminiscences* [160], I, 6; Ch'en Shao-pai, *Hsing Chung Hui* [152], p. 29. According to Feng Tzu-yu, Huang turned this money over to Yang in the spring of 1895. He also reports that another Hong Kong businessman, Yü Yü-chih, gave Yang over $10,000 at a secret meeting in a cemetery. (Feng, *Reminiscences* [160], I, 45; and *Documents* [179], III, 345). Prior to the Canton rising, the Hawaiian branch had forwarded a little over $1,000 to Sun. See *Documents* [179], III, 290, which is based on Hawaiian Chinese records; cf. Hsüeh, *Huang Hsing* [66], p. 27.

49 This sum was in Hong Kong dollars, each worth approximately $.50 in U.S. currency; unless otherwise noted, all future references to funds represent Hong Kong dollars. I am indebted to the late ·Professor Shelley H. Cheng for enlightening me on this point. On Huang's relations with Yang, see Hsüeh, *Huang Hsing* [66], p. 30, and Tse, *Chinese Republic* [122], pp. 9–10; but according to Feng, *Reminiscences* [160], I, 6, Huang was introduced to Sun by Ho Kai.

50 Feng, in *Documents* [179], III, 318.

51 According to Tse, *Chinese Republic* [122], p. 9, Ho first undertook to help the plotters on March 16th. Many Chinese accounts rely upon Tse for this phase of Hsing Chung Hui activities in Hong Kong, although he is not

tion, he attended meetings of the high command and pledged his secret support. That two Hong Kong journalists, Thomas A. Reid and Chesney Duncan, editors of the *China Mail* (hereafter referred to as the *Mail*) and *Hongkong Telegraph* respectively, also promised to help can undoubtedly be attributed to his influence.[52] Ho had already favored the *Mail* with his anonymous articles on Chinese reform and apparently enjoyed a special relationship with the paper.

Ho's support, however surreptitious, opened new vistas for the conspirators. Here was a man of wealth and standing in the British colony, eminently qualified to provide the movement with respectable standing when it shook off its conspiratorial cloak and emerged into public view. Sun was only a young physician and Yang a mere clerk. Once a foothold was secured in Canton, the plotters would need a spokesman to present their case to the foreign powers, of which Britain was the most important; who was better suited than Ho?

Yet there was no reason to assume that Ho Kai would have been content to remain behind the scenes had the revolutionary plot succeeded in attaining its initial objectives and taken on larger dimensions. He was more than an influential sympathizer. Of all those connected with the Hsing Chung Hui at this time, his was the only name linked to a definite political program, and it is hard to believe that he did not anticipate having a hand in its realization. For obvious reasons he could not expose himself, and at this stage he only took on the responsibility of "drafting proclamations, etc." Thus while Yang Ch'ü-yün and Cheng

---

always accurate. Feng, *Reminiscences* [160], I, 6, reports that when the Hsing Chung Hui was established, Sun consulted a great deal with Ho on legal and foreign policy matters.

[52] According to Tse, *Chinese Republic* [122], p. 9, Reid was interviewed on March 16th and Duncan on the 18th, but Reid was already privy to the plot several days earlier as evidenced by his favorable editorials on March 12th and March 16th. Duncan and Tom Cowen, a sub-editor of the *Telegraph*, who also helped the conspirators, were both described as champions of foreign interests who received Japanese support in publishing the *Shanghai New Press* after the turn of the century. See Arnold Wright, *Treaty Ports* [132], p. 365.

Shih-liang operated at one level, recruiting freebooters in Kowloon and the Canton delta, and while Sun, on a different level, tried to ensnare Cantonese gentry via his Agricultural Association, Ho Kai, working through foreign journalists, sought endorsement from the aggressive foreign merchants of the treaty ports and the more restrained British policy makers in London.[53]

The *Mail* in particular was used to broadcast Ho's version of the aims of the Canton plot. Yet the progress reports of the conspiracy which appeared in the paper attribute to the Hsing Chung Hui quite different goals from those which are usually accredited to it. Whether this was a genuine version of the revolutionists' political aims is another question; it was undoubtedly the profile they tried to show foreign viewers. Moreover, the columns of this friendly paper revealed what treaty port interests hoped to gain by an upheaval and why they trusted the Hsing Chung Hui.

On March 12, 1895, the *Mail* first hinted at the existence of the Canton plot. After discussing the general feeling of unrest in the wake of the latest Ch'ing military fiasco, an editorial critically appraised the prospects of traditional secret society uprisings. While other sources made much of the revolutionary potential of the Ko Lao Hui in the Yangtze Valley and the government rushed armed vessels to the waterways of the central provinces, the *Mail* asserted: "When the rising does come, it will be on the part of a large section of the population in the Provinces south of the Yangtse, although it may include the people of that locality. Quietly . . . the inhabitants of South China have been fairly well organized, and all that is needed to kindle the flame of popular revolt is a leader of outstanding merit."

After intimating that this Reform Party (the name Hsing Chung Hui never appeared in Reid's articles) had contacts with Yangtze Valley insurgents, the editorial went on to establish the southerners' bona fides as moderate constitutional reformers, who, in contrast to the lowly secret societies, were worthy of European support and tutelage:

[53] It appears that Tse too enjoyed a close relationship with these foreign journalists. At least that is the impression gained from his account.

It is the intention of the revolutionists, who belong to no secret society and are banded together for the sole purpose of reforming the government . . . to effect a coup d'etat by peaceful means if possible. What they desire . . . although it seems impossible to realize any such feeling amongst a body of Chinamen, is a constitutional upheaval, to rid their country of the iniquitous system of misrule which has shut out China from Western influences, Western trade, and Western civilization.

The editor anticipated a temporary blocking of foreign trade should civil war ensue, but accepted it as a necessary prelude to the reorganization of the country for the improvement of the lot of the peasantry and the "opening up of the Empire to the advantages of international intercourse." He hoped that the foreign powers would not support the Manchus as they had during the Taiping Rebellion, asserting that "it is a moot point yet whether China would not have been in a better position today had it not been for the personal efforts of Chinese Gordon."

While much of the reformers' program could only be described as "nebulous," the editor was nevertheless encouraged by specific proposals such as the modernization of the judicial system and the civil service. Most important of all, he could assure his readers that "the whole of China's obligations will be recognized and accepted by the new Government . . . and the Imperial Customs will be given, as at present, as a security for all loans." Furthermore, "as in the case of Japan, and, more forcibly perhaps, in the case of Egypt," the use of foreign advisers would give the new regime every likelihood of succeeding.

Prospects for foreign commercial interests were glowingly portrayed. Railways and mines would be developed and "the reputed mineral wealth of China would be brought to the surface and utilized for manufactures on the spot, a fresh outlet would be provided for British enterprises and capital, and the long-deferred but frequently predicted opening up of China would at last be an accomplished fact."[54]

The type of reforms envisioned in the editorial shows Ho Kai's

[54] *China Mail*, March 12, 1895.

inspiration, and in fact, Tse Tsan-tai has recorded that Dr. Ho Kai's reform article was published in this same issue of the *Mail*.[55] It is doubtful, however, whether Ho did the actual writing since the style and tone are inconsistent with Chinese authorship: in this and subsequent editorials as well, laudatory expositions of the plotters' cause were heavily laced with the contemptuous gibes which old China hands reserved for China and things Chinese. It was obvious that the "un-Chineseness" of the Hsing Chung Hui leaders and their apparent eagerness for European tutelage attracted the support of the paper.

On March 16 the *Mail* again described the prevailing mood of unrest which gripped the country, and it announced that many of the leading Chinese merchants in Hong Kong looked forward to an upheaval which would destroy the mandarin system and open up their homeland to foreign trade. Preparations for the coup, the paper disclosed, were not yet complete, nor had the leadership issue been decided. In fact it was suggested that the real leader might not emerge until the people were in open revolt after the initial success. At that time, the paper disclosed, prominent Chinese officials already aware of the plot would be prepared to join the rebels. Concerning the revolutionists' program, the paper asserted that there was now "neither dubiety or indistinctness."

Two days later, on March 18, the *Mail* printed a statement of the conspirators' political goals, which is not only more explicit than any of the Chinese sources for this period, but which casts strong doubt upon the belief that the Hsing Chung Hui was committed to establishing a republic. The Manchus were to be overthrown, and in the words of the editor, "the stupid pigtail, in itself a sign of servility, will disappear." That much at least corresponded to the official secret version of Hsing Chung Hui aims. But as to the future form of government there was this categorical statement: "For State purposes, it is not proposed to set up a Republic. The Central Government, as proposed by the Reformers, will comprise the Emperor, with three principal

[55] Tse, *Chinese Republic* [122], p. 9.

Ministers of State. Which ancient family will provide the Emperor is evidently a matter of after consideration."

The specific reforms to be adopted, previously mentioned in general terms, were now given in detail. The bureaucracy would be revamped through the use of professional examinations, the elimination of the purchase system, and generous salary increases so as to reduce bribery and corruption. There would be judicial reforms, diffusion of modern education, religious tolerance, economic development, and improvement of local government. The pronounced Western orientation of the rebels was further emphasized by the promised opening of more trading centers and ports and "repeal of all laws that have a retarding effect upon trade." It was even proposed that the collection of inland revenue be placed in the hands of foreigners, under an arrangement similar to that of the Maritime Customs Service "until China is in a position to dispense with all foreign assistance."[56]

That this program, as well as all the other disclosures of the rebels' intentions, had been Ho Kai's idea was substantiated a few months later, on May 23, when the *Mail* printed a plan for constitutional reform which was openly acknowledged as Ho's work. It had been first printed in the Hong Kong Chinese daily, *Wah Tsz Yat Pao (Hua-tzu jih-pao)*, known as *The Chinese Mail*, and was said to have been widely circulated as a pamphlet in China.[57] The scheme omitted any reference to anti-dynasticism, but as an outline of a constitutional monarchy it coincided with the aims previously ascribed to the plotters.[58]

The more elaborate adumbration of the reformed political structure was new, however. In addition to the emperor, a prime minister and cabinet were to assume the highest policy making and administrative functions. The country would be divided into four administrative divisions, whose councils and sub-councils

[56] *China Mail*, March 16, March 18, 1895, reprinted in the *Overland China Mail*, March 20, 1895.

[57] *Wah Tsz Yat Pao* used the printing press of the *China Mail*. See Britton, *The Chinese Periodical Press* [13], pp. 46–47.

[58] *Overland China Mail*, May 23, 1895.

would exercise autonomy in local matters, subject to the approval of the central authorities. In the smallest territorial division, the district council members were to be elected directly by the people. This local assembly would then choose from among its own members representatives to the prefectural council, and so on upwards until a national parliament was elected. There would be no need for frequent meetings of this national assembly, however, since the emperor and cabinet would handle important state affairs and other matters would be disposed of locally. Local officials would be recommended by the people with the final power of appointment vested in the emperor. Both elected representatives and appointed officials would have to pass qualifying examinations, and the examination system itself was to be modernized along the lines previously suggested.

The *Mail* saw little chance of this plan being accepted "unless the Central Government, prompted by the Empress-Mother and Li Hung-chang . . . takes upon itself, either single-handed or with the aid of foreign officers, to crush the present deep-seated system of mandarin rule."[59] That Ho Kai was not counting upon any such miracle but was preparing the ground for a favorable reception of the Canton rising was incautiously revealed by the same paper only a few weeks before the impending attack: "Early this year, there was a great stir over the publication of Dr. Ho Kai's reform pamphlet, the foundation-stone of Chinese regeneration; and there were rumours of a violent upheaval to overthrow the dynasty and establish a new Constitution *on Dr. Ho's lines*. That was one method of reform that seemed to promise well, but the promise shows no sign of fulfillment yet [emphasis inserted]."[60] What deserves consideration is the obvious contradiction between the conspirators' aims as ascribed to Ho Kai in the *Mail* and the accepted historical version of their political orientations at this time.

First, how can we explain the constitutional monarchist label which the conspirators publicly assumed? We can only em-

59 *Ibid.*
60 *Ibid.*, October 16, 1895.

phasize, as in the previous discussion of Sun's dealings with Liu Hsüeh-hsün, that the Hsing Chung Hui leaders had no idea how far the proposed Canton coup could take them. Would the seizure of the southern provinces enable them to overthrow the Manchus and establish a liberal monarchy through collusion with high officials, or would it ignite a truly revolutionary conflagration which would obviate the need for gentry allies and allow them to destroy the monarchical system itself? Perhaps the Napoleonic maxim "On s'engage, puis on voit" would best describe their mood. It is probable that Ho Kai exercised a moderating influence upon Sun and Yang Ch'ü-yün and persuaded them to defer the republican goal, or at least to conceal it from the foreign community, which might have been disturbed by a radical program. Above all, the political isolation imposed by Sun's inferior social status required flexibility. He could ill afford dogmatism, and at any rate, who was he to question the authority of Ho Kai in matters political and constitutional?

Nationalists or "Running Dogs of Imperialism"?

Even less consistent with the accepted image of Sun Yat-sen is the foreign policy of the Hsing Chung Hui presented in Ho's program. It seems hardly credible that any Chinese nationalist movement, not to mention one connected with the name of Sun Yat-sen, could invite even greater foreign interference, as for example, in the proposition concerning the Maritime Customs.[61]

---

[61] It is true that the Imperial Maritime Customs, which had been managed under foreign auspices for almost fifty years, facilitated the foreign exploitation of China, and its imperialist function would be more obvious after the Boxer settlement. But it can also be argued, and this is apparently what Ho and the others felt, that this imperialist institution was not only an efficient collector of revenue for the Chinese government, but also a major instrument for the modernization of China. If nothing else, it gave the Chinese a yardstick for measuring the inequities of their own fiscal administration. (See Fairbank, *Trade and Diplomacy* [38], p. 462.) As two leading Chinese officials would later point out bitterly, "delighted at the fair play of the Maritime Customs Service, they [the Chinese people] hate the *likin* (transit tax) offices which purposely cause them trouble." (From the Joint Proposals of Liu K'un-i and Chang Chih-tung, 1901, in Teng and Fairbank, *China's Response* [121], p. 199.)

This is nevertheless compatible with our understanding of the social origins and intellectual orientations of the Hsing Chung Hui leadership, which was preeminently a non-literati, nationalist-reformist movement. The Hsing Chung Hui leaders sought to overthrow the dynasty not because they hated the Manchus more than did the literati reformers, such as K'ang Yu-wei and Liang Ch'i-ch'ao, but because the capitulation of the dynasty —any traditional dynasty—was essential for their accession to power. Neither Sun's medical degree nor the chivalric honors bestowed upon Ho by Queen Victoria in 1892, could compensate for the political and social liabilities which burdened them in traditional China. Their only means of becoming a force in politics was to crash through at the top by means of a coup like the one aimed at Canton. But a bid for power at the pinnacle of the Chinese political hierarchy was inconceivable at the time without the promise of foreign support. Not yet awakened to the possibility of welding their lower class allies into an independent political movement, they needed help from the outside and were prepared to offer a quid pro quo.

But the conspirators were not willing to sacrifice Chinese sovereignty merely to satisfy their political ambitions. For their other distinguishing trait was that they were intellectual and spiritual products of the Western, Christian tradition. They were Chinese who critically appraised their country's institutions through eyes which had already been accustomed to Western criteria of evaluation. They sincerely felt that it was necessary to impose upon China European standards of administration and justice with the help of foreign advisers, at least in the beginning stages. If China was abused by Europeans, then the Hsing Chung Hui leaders could argue that Chinese incompetence and mandarin cupidity invited such violations of her sovereignty. Let China remake herself in the image of Europe, the argument might continue, and she would be treated as an equal in the family of nations. Although the Manchus had been propped up by Western power since the 1860's, their regime had resisted the influx of Western ideas and institutions, and especially the presence of Western-trained personnel, which could eventually guide it to a full recovery of sovereign rights. A new regime, sincerely dedicated to modernization, could more easily dispense with foreign intervention by putting into positions of leadership indigenous talent which had already mastered Western knowledge and techniques. This, it would seem, was the nationalist rationale for the Hsing Chung Hui's pro-Western orientation.

There is some evidence that the plotters attempted to solicit the aid of other foreign powers besides the British. An unconfirmed report had it that the "secret support" of the Japanese government was obtained through its Hong Kong consul.[62] Germany also may have been an object of Sun's attentions, since he was reported to have been acquainted with her consul in Hong Kong, Dr. Knappe.[63] Given the elasticity which characterized Hsing Chung Hui policies, a multilateral approach to the powers could very well have been contemplated. Nor is it possible to determine precisely how far they were prepared to go in seeking foreign approbation. It is a safe assumption, however, that no group in modern Chinese history had ever been more closely identified with Western, and especially British, interests.

It was only such a pro-Western orientation, argued the *Mail*, that could ensure the success of a Chinese reform movement. "Familiarity with Chinese incompetence" made the paper skeptical of any proposal emanating from "purely Chinese sources,"[64] for "if left to their misguided selves, it will take an eternity of time to move this huge lethargic mass of humanity."[65] But the Hsing Chung Hui, which admitted Reid to its secret meetings and sought his counsel as well as that of the Anglicized Ho Kai, could not be considered a "purely Chinese" movement.[66] Although the paper felt that "there is little or nothing ennobling

[62] Tse, *Chinese Republic* [122], p. 9; and *China Mail*, December 3, 1896.

[63] Extract from Fraser's Intelligence Report, October, 1896, in MacDonald to Salisbury, October 19, 1896, in CO 129/274 [46]. At this time, the Chinese government raised the alarm over another purported plot involving Sun.

[64] *Overland China Mail*, September 26, 1895.

[65] *Overland China Mail*, May 23, 1895.

[66] On August 29th, Reid was present at a meeting attended by Sun, Yang, and the other Hsing Chung Hui leaders. Ho Kai acted as spokesman and the policy of the "Provisional Government" was outlined. Reid agreed to "do his best to work for the sympathy and support of the British Government and people of England." Tse, *Chinese Republic* [122], 9.

about the Chinese character, speaking of the race as a concrete mass,"[67] it was impressed by that "class of Chinese" who had acquired some "enlightenment through residence among foreigners."[68] In circles where it was assumed that "religion is the pioneer of trade, and trade is the pioneer of civilization," the Christian affiliation of the leading conspirators was an additional point in their favor.[69]

There is no evidence that journalistic support in Hong Kong made any impression upon official British opinion. The Hong Kong Colonial Secretary is said to have reprimanded Duncan of the *Hongkong Telegraph* for using the paper to incite Chinese against what was considered a friendly government.[70] Although British policy became more fluid under the impact of the Sino-Japanese War, the Foreign Office had always been more cautious than the treaty port hotheads, and was much less anxious for further involvement in internal Chinese affairs.[71] Indicative of the mood of the local British officials, who called for making the best of a hopeless China situation, was an evaluation submitted to London from its vice-consul in Canton during the height of Reid's campaign on behalf of the impending uprising:

There is no sign whatever of revolution in the Western sense, viz.: a change of Government at the instance of the upper or middle classes with particular aims in view. The bold prophecies of one

---

[67] *Overland China Mail*, May 23, 1895.

[68] *Ibid.*, October 16, 1895.

[69] *Ibid.*, August 29, 1895.

[70] Tse, *Chinese Republic* [122], pp. 8–9.

[71] At this time, when the *Hongkong Telegraph* urged that Hong Kong's boundaries be extended, the Colonial Office "advised that this was not a reputable paper and could be ignored." The Hong Kong Chamber of Commerce entered a similar expansionist plea which was enclosed in a "vaguely phrased" telegram sent to London on September 18th by Sir William Robinson, governor of the colony. The Foreign Office remarked that Robinson "seems a somewhat impulsive gentleman," while the Colonial Office commented, "Can he so far have lost his head that he wants to annex Canton?" See Endacott, *Hong Kong* [36], p. 261. For earlier clashes between treaty port expansionists and British policy makers, see Mary C. Wright, *T'ung-chih Restoration* [136], p. 226; and Fairbank, *Trade and Diplomacy* [38], p. 464.

of the Hongkong papers in regard to such a rising are simply moon-shine. It appears indeed that the Chinese Government, though practically unarmed and helpless against a serious foreign foe, is strong enough to keep peace at home—to keep the great Chinese cow steady while foreigners extract the milk of which it is to be hoped the Japanese will only be allowed their fair share.[72]

The difference between this position and that represented by the *Mail* did not reflect a conflict between contending interests so much as a difference in perspective. Both were concerned with British trade and investment in China. But while official circles were reluctant to upset the status quo and gamble for higher stakes which would entail further responsibilities in China, the treaty port community, in whose name the *Mail* spoke, was clamoring for increased intervention as the only means of open-ing China completely and converting it into the Eldorado of which British traders had been dreaming for fifty years. The paper's unique patronization of the Hsing Chung Hui as an instrumentality for achieving this aim with minimal interven-tion was nevertheless part of its belligerent policy, which matched the general tenor of treaty port demands: should the Canton plot fail, the *Mail* saw no alternative but foreign interference without any Chinese collaboration. The British friends of the Hsing Chung Hui, who in another context recommended an-nexation of Chinese territory for the protection of picnickers and shooting parties straying out of Hong Kong, explained this alternative with brutal frankness:[73]

. . . This is no question of regeneration or improved government of the people. The available markets of the world are getting more and more restricted. China is the largest unopened market in the world, and increased competition elsewhere renders it imperative upon the Western nations . . . to insist upon a thorough change in China's attitude toward foreign trade. . . . It is therefore the duty of the Powers to enforce their demands upon China even to the partition of the Empire if their object cannot be obtained. . . .

---

[72] FO 17/1234, Bourne to O'Conor, in O'Conor's no. 141, April 16, 1895 [46].

[73] *Overland China Mail*, October 24, 1895.

There need be no unjust oppression of the people. . . . If there is no sign that China is to undergo internal regeneration, for the sake of civilisation and the Chinese people themselves, it become the imperative duty of the Western powers to interfere, in order to secure some slight glimpse of reform.[74]

The *Mail* thus proposed two methods of opening the China market: "the moral influence of a naval demonstration" and support of the Hsing Chung Hui.[75] As D-Day in October drew near, Reid and a *Hongkong Telegraph* sub-editor, T. Cowen,[76] are said to have drafted a proclamation to the foreign powers which was revised by Ho Kai and Tse Tsan-tai.[77] Whether it was published or held in abeyance pending the outcome of the rising is not clear, but the *Mail* did make a final editorial appeal on behalf of the plotters:

We want no repetition of the Taiping blunder. If there are men willing to come forward and lift China from the Slough of Despond in which she at present grovels, so long as the ordinary dictates of humanity are obeyed and the rights of Foreigners recognised and the whole country thrown open to the civilising influence of trade and commerce, we hope Great Britain will not be chary of the co-operation she has already tendered to Egypt. . . . There may be some few excesses at the outset, but that is probably inevitable, and it will be the duty of the Foreigners on the spot to guide the new impulse into the right channel. It will be a grievous mistake if Great Britain or any of the other Foreign Powers interfere to thrust China back into the arms of the gang of incompetents who at present rule. . . .[78]

[74] *Ibid.*, May 23, 1895.

[75] *Ibid.*, October 16, 1895.

[76] Lo Chia-lun, *Biography* [192], I, 59, identifies him as "J. Cowen" but Tse, *Chinese Republic* [122], p. 9, is apparently correct. There was a John Cowen, who was a correspondent of the London *Times* during the Boxer Rebellion and later founded *The China Times* in Peking; but his brother Tom Cowen worked for the *Hongkong Telegraph* and was later associated with Duncan in Shanghai. See Arnold Wright, *Treaty Ports* [132], pp. 359 and 365.

[77] Tse, *Chinese Republic* [122], p. 9. Tse himself wrote an "Open letter to the Emperor" warning him to reform along Western lines or face the consequences. See text in *Overland China Mail*, June 6, 1895.

[78] *Overland China Mail*, October 24, 1895.

Years later Sun Yat-sen would draw his own conclusions from the "cooperation" Britain had tendered to Egypt. But now, through that curious confluence of interests, the logic of which I have tried to explain, the Hsing Chung Hui prepared to storm the yamens of Canton while its foreign allies looked forward to a Lord Cromer in Peking.

Sun's loosely knit conspiratorial apparatus of 1895 could not maintain secrecy in an undertaking as elaborate and far-flung as this. If nothing else, the ominous prognostications of the pro-revolutionary Hong Kong press were sufficient to alert provincial officials, and according to one report, they had been prepared for an outbreak for several weeks prior to the denouement.[79] Curiously, the reaction of the highest official, Governor-General T'an, had been to discount evidence of the planned uprising, and it was only after being overwhelmed by incontrovertible proof that he took action.

There were security leaks in both Canton and Hong Kong. The plotters, faithful to anti-dynastic tradition, had planned to post a "declaration of war" (*hsi-wen*) throughout Canton and its suburbs once the shooting started on October 26. This proclamation had been drawn up on October 9 by Chu Ch'i, the only degree-holder on the Hsing Chung Hui roster. But according to the Chinese principle of collective punishment, Chu's complicity jeopardized his family; his elder brother, Chu Hsiang, a *chü-jen* (holder of the second literary degree) and local official, decided to protect himself and the family by divulging the plot to the authorities. A day or so before the 26th, he forged his brother's name to a confession which he sent to the assistant prefect. The latter, one Li Chia-ch'ao, immediately ordered a watch on Sun Yat-sen and reported to the governor-general.[80]

Instead of being alarmed, T'an broke out in laughter when

---

[79] FO 17/1249, Brenan to O'Conor in O'Conor's no. 25, November 1, 1895 [46].

[80] Lo Chia-lun, *Biography* [192], I, 60; although the party held Chu Ch'i responsible for this episode, Ch'ü Feng-ch'ih later proved that Chu Ch'i had nothing to do with his brother's betrayal of the plot. See Feng, in *Documents* [179], III, 346.

told that the suspected rebel was Sun Yat-sen. He knew of Sun as a harmless "wild man" who "would not dare revolt!" Besides, had not his Agricultural Study Society been given official sanction?[81] Since his superior was unperturbed, Li Chia-ch'ao let the matter drop. In the meantime his patrol had found Sun at a wedding banquet in a suburb. Aware that he was under surveillance, Sun nevertheless remained calm and no move was made to detain him.[82]

There were several reasons for the authorities' hesitation. In the first place, with the exception of Li Chia-ch'ao, Governor-General T'an's subordinates were afraid of being held responsible should a large-scale plot be uncovered, and so they kept T'an in the dark.[83] That Sun was a Christian also gave him some immunity. T'an hesitated to accuse a known protégé of the missionaries without firm proof.[84] And finally there was Sun's reputation. Paradoxically, his recklessness and unrestrained enthusiasm made him appear harmless. His political ambitions, his thirst for official recognition, and his grandiose reformist schemes were well-known in Canton, but the image he projected was that of an effervescent political tyro, and not that of a cold-blooded conspirator capable of making real trouble. Both as a revolutionary and as a reformer, Sun had found it difficult to make people take him seriously. In the past, this had been a source of frustration, but when his interest in explosives had passed the experimental stage, his reputation for eccentricity provided an unexpected shield.

Nevertheless, suspicions had been aroused and it was all the more important to keep on schedule. But Yang Ch'ü-yün had

---

81 Lo Chia-lun, *Biography* [192], I, 60. T'an, apparently referring to Li Hung-chang, is reported to have said that "Junior Preceptor Li" endorsed Sun's society. While this report may have resulted from the Tientsin trip of the previous year, it could also have been planted by Sun in order to strengthen his position in Canton. See also Feng, in *Documents* [179], III, 320.

82 Lo Chia-lun, *Biography* [192], I, 60.

83 FO 17/1249, Brenan to O'Conor in O'Conor's no. 25, November 1, 1895 [46]. Li Chia-ch'ao, identified in Chinese sources as the *"Ch'i-pu wei-yüan,"* was probably the "Superintendent of Police" referred to by Brenan.

84 Tsou Lu, *The Kuomintang* [216], p. 659.

not been able to complete his arrangements in Hong Kong on time, and in the early hours of October 26, he sent a telegram to Sun reporting that the "goods" could not arrive on schedule but would be sent a day later, on the evening of the 27th.[85] This message brought the Canton plotters close to panic. On the night before, the bandit leaders and other fighters had assembled in Canton and were standing by to receive the morning ferry from Hong Kong. Sun and Ch'en Shao-pai realized that if the attack could not go off on schedule, indefinite postponement was their safest course. A telegram was sent to Yang ordering him to cancel "the shipment" until further notice, and the fighters were sent home to await orders. That they were not entirely motivated by idealism is indicated by the fact that Sun had to pay them off with precious funds.[86]

It was too late, however, to prevent disaster. On the same day, the Canton government was fully apprised of the plot, either by informers in Hong Kong or by the British authorities, and began seizing the conspirators in their local hideouts.[87] Sun still evaded arrest, but to his great dismay, he received a telegram from Yang Ch'ü-yün reporting that his message had come too late—the goods were already on board and would Sun "please receive them."[88] Though Yang's role in Hong Kong later became a subject of internecine dispute, a detailed British account of events is ample proof of his conscientious effort to carry out a most difficult assignment.

A few weeks earlier the Hong Kong police had received word that the Triads were recruiting a force for a rising in Kwangsi. Though their investigation proved fruitless, on October 27 Inspector Stanton learned that about four hundred fighters had been engaged in the colony and were scheduled to depart for Canton on the evening voyage of the S. S. *Powan (Pao-an)*. At

[85] Ch'en Shao-pai, *Hsing Chung Hui* [152], p. 11; Lo Chia-lun, *Biography* [192], I, 60.

[86] Ch'en Shao-pai, *Hsing Chung Hui* [152], p. 11.

[87] Tsou Lu, *The Kuomintang* [216], p. 659; Lo Chia-lun, *Biography* [192], I, 61.

[88] Lo Chia-lun, *Biography* [192], I, 61.

the wharf he found some six hundred coolies, "all of the poorest class," who had been turned off the ship because they lacked the fares. They claimed that they had been engaged as "government soldiers" at $10 per month by one Chu Ho, acting on behalf of Sassoon's comprador. Their final destination, they said, was Wuchow, in Kwangsi. They had in the meantime received five cents for rations during the previous two days and had been promised one dollar each for their fares.

During the inquiry at the dock, Chu Ho arrived accompanied by two men carrying bags of money, the total amounting to nine hundred dollars. The newcomers declared that they had been sent by Yang Ch'ü-yün, who worked for Sassoon's comprador and had given them instructions to pay the coolies' passage. Though a police party searched the men and the ship for arms, nothing was found and the captain raised no objection to their sailing. Later in the evening, Inspector Stanton learned that Yang had purchased a large quantity of arms and managed to ship them on the *Powan*. This information was telegraphed to Canton, where the initiative passed to the Chinese authorities.[89]

The governor-general called in 1,500 soldiers to reinforce his garrison and then sent a party to intercept the steamer when it arrived on the morning of the 28th.[90] Thus the fighters were greeted as they stepped off the boat not by their fellow conspirators but by this reception committee led by the district magistrate. The police force was, however, too small to hold the entire group and most got lost in the crowd. Only forty or fifty, including the two leaders, Ch'iu Ssu and Chu Kuei-ch'üan, were apprehended. Still another search at this time did not immediately

89 Memorandum by F. J. Badeley, Acting Assistant Colonial Secretary (Hong Kong), March 11, 1896, enclosed in Robinson to Chamberlain, March 11, 1896 in CO 129/271 [46]. The governor-general's report agreed with this British estimate of the number of men sent from Hong Kong, while Chinese secondary sources give the figures as 200 or 300. Sun, in confronting Yang two years later, accused him of sending 600 men after having been told to call off the expedition. (See Ch'en Shao-pai, *Hsing Chung Hui* [152], p. 35.) According to the British, this was the number of those who first turned up at the dock but only 400 actually boarded.

90 Lo Chia-lun, *Biography* [192], I, 61.

disclose the arms. Only after the consignee failed to claim them was suspicion directed at seven barrels labeled "Portland Cement."[91] These were found to contain over two hundred revolvers which were to have been distributed among the coolies. The Hong Kong police were informed and began looking for Yang Ch'ü-yün, who by virtue of his local birth was a British subject. By this time he was in hiding and would soon be on the run.

Raids on the secret premises of the Canton plotters yielded six prisoners as well as flags, arms, uniforms, and hatchets.[92] Fleeing for his life, Sun took refuge in the home of Wang Yü-ch'u, the Christian minister he had known in Hong Kong, and then escaped to Macao by sedan chair. There his Portuguese friends, the Fernandes', took care of him,[93] and on October 29 he reached Hong Kong, where he was anxiously awaited by Ch'en Shao-pai, Cheng Shih-liang, and others who had preceded him out of Canton.[94]

Six months of intensive plotting thus went to waste as the uprising was aborted before the conspirators could raise their flags and fire a shot. Yet despite its farcical aspects, this was not opéra bouffe. Along with the mercenaries and traitors, the plot had attracted men of principle who were prepared to die so that their country might be revived. One such hero was Sun's boyhood friend, Lu Hao-tung. Lu might have escaped had he elected to remain in hiding or to flee immediately. Instead he overrode the objections of his comrades and returned to the bookstore hideout in order to destroy the party's membership list before it fell into the hands of the authorities. While carrying out this task he was caught by the police on October 27.[95] Despite his subjection to the usual tortures accompanying Chinese police interrogations, Lu refused to cooperate with his captors. What they elicited was

[91] *Hongkong Telegraph*, August 27, 1900.

[92] Lo Chia-lun, *Biography* [192], I, 61.

[93] I have received this information from Mr. J. M. Braga to whom it was told by Francisco Fernandes, who had known Sun since 1892. See also, Wu Ya, "Sun's Newspaper in Macao" [226].

[94] Lo Chia-lun, *Biography* [192], I, 61. Ch'en Shao-pai, *Hsing Chung Hui* [152], p. 12.

[95] Lo Chia-lun, *Biography* [192], I, 61–62.

not a confession but a defiant statement in which he proudly described the motivation and broad objects of the attempted attack on the Canton government.

He told how he and his fellow villager, Sun Wen, had been stirred to anger by "the decadence and despotism of the alien government, the greed and ineptness of the officials, and the dark designs of the foreigners." After several years spent in Shanghai, he had returned to Canton where he, Sun, and other friends spent long hours in discussion. Seeing the foreigners' encroachment as the greatest threat, Lu "wanted to cure the symptom," but Sun, who gave highest priority to exacting revenge from the Manchu enemy, "wanted to cure the source" of China's affliction. This difference in emphasis had been resolved only after a long debate; Sun's view had prevailed and anti-Manchuism became their common goal. They had sought to awaken the Chinese spirit and bring about a national revival, a restoration of Chinese rule. Avaricious officials, evil gentry, and corrupt scholars willingly served the Manchus, who perpetrated countless atrocities against the Chinese. Among the Manchu crimes, Lu listed the ten-day massacre at Yang-chou and the ruthless slaughter at Chia-ting—two episodes in the seventeenth century conquest of China which had rankled in Chinese breasts for over 200 years.[96] His final words contained a warning to Chinese officials as well as to the Manchu rulers:

Without destroying the Manchus there can never be a revival of the Chinese. And without exterminating Chinese traitors (*han-chien*) the Manchus can never be removed. Therefore we wanted very much to kill one or two contemptible officials and thereby arouse our Chinese people. That this present affair unfortunately did not suceed is a source of deep regret. But though I, one individual, can be killed, those who will rise and follow me cannot all be killed.[97]

---

[96] For example Liang Ch'i-ch'ao wrote "I have no affection for the Manchus. Whenever I read the 'Ten Days of Yang-chow' and the 'Massacre of the City of Chia-ting' by the Manchu conquerors, my eyes overflow with warm tears." Quoted by Li Chien-nung, *Political History* [78], p. 207.

[97] Lu's confession is reprinted in Tsou Lu, *The Kuomintang* [216], pp. 659–660.

The American consul protested Lu's arrest, informing the district magistrate that the prisoner was a Christian who had been harmlessly engaged as a translator for the Shanghai telegraph office and was in no way connected with "terrorist bands." Although he personally vouched for Lu's innocence, the appeal fell flat when he was confronted with Lu's brazen statement.

The consul was successful, however, in gaining the release of another Protestant, Tso Tou-shan, the bookstore proprietor; Wang Chih-fu, who officiated at the chapel in back of the store, evaded the police dragnet with the help of a timely warning from a foreign missionary. Another minister who belonged to the Hsing Chung Hui, Sun's close friend and classics teacher Ch'ü Feng-ch'ih, prudently removed himself to Hong Kong.[98]

Such a prominent display of Christian participation—most of the leading plotters were Protestants and they had turned a chapel into one of their main hideouts—alarmed both the Chinese authorities and the foreign community. Since the Taiping movement had fed upon Christian influences in the same southern coastal area, it is reasonable to assume that Peking saw in the plot signs of a potential repetition of the religiously inspired movement which had almost toppled the empire less than half a century earlier.[99] However, it was not Western religion but Western political influences which motivated the Hsing Chung Hui leaders; their Christianity was merely the religious aspect of their generally Western orientation. Furthermore, only through missionary channels could foreign ideas reach lower-class Chinese at this time. Thus religious and political motives appeared to be

[98] Feng, in *Documents* [179], II, 321; Feng, *Reminiscences* [160], I, 13. According to Sung Chü-jen, an American medical missionary named Chia [Kerr?] obtained Tso's release. This may have been Dr. John Kerr, Hager's colleague and Sun's former teacher at the Canton Medical School. See "Sung Chü-jen," in *Development of the Revolution* [178], IX, 464. Although Pastor Wang was on the "wanted" list, he later returned to Canton and was avoided by the revolutionaries, who suspected him of being in collusion with the authorities.

[99] In requesting Sun's extradition from England in 1896, the Chinese Minister in London, Kung Chao-yüan, claimed that the Canton rebels were the successors to the Taipings, whose stratagems they had emulated. See his protest to Salisbury on October 26, 1896, in CO 129/274 [46].

inextricably interwined. The intervention of a foreign diplomat on behalf of Chinese rebels professing the Christian faith reinforced official suspicions. At the same time, evidence linking rebels with missionary enterprises could be used to advantage by the authorities in their effort to resist the foreigners' demand for greater religious tolerance. Thus on December 3, a little over a month after the Canton episode, Timothy Richard, in an interview with the progressive official Chang Yin-huan, was told that "the documents on rebellion found in the chapel in the Suang Men-to [Shuang-men-ti] in Canton in the possession of a man named Sun would prove a great blow to the settlement of the missionary cause" about which Richard had come to Peking.[100]

This aspect of the revelations at Canton agitated foreigners in the south. The British Consul in Canton, Byron Brenan, felt that Christian involvement in the plot had created "an unpleasant circumstance which cannot but seriously injure Christian Missions in this province."[101] The *China Mail* reported that "the recent conspiracy against the authorities in Canton is just the sort of thing that the anti-Christian literati would gladly fix on as a pretext for persecution and false accusation; and therefore a circular has been issued to all the German missionaries, we believe, by the German consul in Canton, warning them to take special care that none of their converts mix up in any such seditionary movement."[102] Perhaps this fear of being identified with subversive tendencies led missionaries to insinuate that Sun was, after all, not a true believer, and may explain why the British consul was told that while Sun "professed to be a Christian . . . the missionaries with whom he has had to do doubted his sincerity."[103] Yet the evidence of Dr. Hager, who baptized Sun and was undoubtedly closer to him at this time than any other missionary, lends no support to this accusation.[104] He was not a regu-

---

[100] Timothy Richard, *Forty-five Years* [96], p. 237.

[101] FO 17/1249, Brenan to O'Conor in O'Conor's no. 25, November 1, 1895 [46].

[102] *Overland China Mail*, November 7, 1895.

[103] FO 17/1249, Brenan to O'Conor in O'Conor's no. 26, November 12, 1895 [46].

[104] See Hager, "Doctor Sun Yat Sen," [50].

lar churchgoer, but there is reason to believe that he was inspired by Christianity even in later years when his faith in the West was severely shaken.[105]

But whether they felt he was a sincere Christian or not, the Canton authorities now had no doubts about Sun's revolutionary propensities. They realized that instead of a loudmouthed nuisance, they had been entertaining an extremely dangerous conspirator. In classic fashion the governor-general, on the one hand, dealt as severely as possible with those leading conspirators whom he caught, and on the other, he showed restraint and forbearance with their lower-class recruits. Both Lu Hao-tung and Ch'iu Ssu, one of the secret society leaders dispatched from Hong Kong and apprehended on landing, were decapitated. Ch'iu's companion, Chu Kuei-ch'üan, was hacked to death. Two of the young naval officers also paid the supreme penalty: Ch'eng K'uei-kuang died after absorbing 600 strokes of the "military stick," and his kinsman Ch'eng Yao-ch'en did not survive imprisonment.[106] That these products of China's new naval program saw fit to join the rebels should have persuaded the authorities that it was not merely the sinister indoctrination of the Christian church, but exposure to modernizing influences in general that tended to alienate traditional loyalties.[107] The British consul recognized

[105] Feng Tzu-yu was also dubious of Sun's Christianity, pointing out that when he was with him in Japan and the United States, Sun did not attend church except to make revolutionary speeches. See Feng, *Reminiscences* [160], II, 12. And another friend, Chang Yung-fu, declares that he never saw Sun enter a church. Sun was so engrossed in political affairs, he recalls, that he never paid attention to holidays, including Christmas. See Chang Yung-fu, "Notes on Sun's Behavior" [147], p. 96. But Sharman, *Sun Yat-sen* [107], p. 310, quotes Sun as having once declared, "I do not belong to the Christianity of the churches, but to the Christianity of Jesus who was a revolutionary."

[106] Feng, in *Documents* [179], III, 321. According to Feng, Lu Hao-tung earned the respect of his captors and was treated with courtesy during his last days.

[107] I have not been able to ascertain where the other two Ch'engs received their naval training—a third had trained in England—but it seems reasonable to assume that they studied in one of the modern academies in which foreign languages were taught and where foreign teachers were employed. If they attended the Whampoa (Canton) Academy, one might speculate as

this truth and pointed out that "all the names that have come up in connection with the abortive revolution are those of men who have mixed with Europeans and imbibed a taste for change and progress."[108]

The authorities were able to learn the identity of most of the major culprits, either from their prisoners or from other informants. "Wanted" notices with brief descriptions and reward offers were posted throughout the province. Sun's name headed the list; one thousand yüan (dollars) were offered for his capture. Others, including Yang Ch'ü-yün, Ch'en Shao-pai, and Pastor Wang Chih-fu, commanded lesser prizes of 200 and 100 yüan.[109]

In accord with the official opinion that sole responsibility for the projected uprising lay with a small group of troublemakers who "deluded the common people" (*shan-huo yü-min*), a phrase which appeared frequently in the documentary record of the episode, the authorities freed many of the lower ranking participants, and even presented them with one yüan each for "travel expenses." Thus one of the ironic sequels of the attempted uprising was that even though the plot foundered, a good number of the hired fighters did not go home empty-handed: either their revolutionary employer, or the very government they were supposed to overthrow, reimbursed them for their trouble.[110]

There were reasons for the government's magnanimity toward the rank-and-filers. Interrogation of their prisoners had elicited

to whether their revolutionary sentiments were in any way affected by the activities of Kang-i, "one of the most notorious reactionaries of the period," who as governor of Kwangtung (1892–1894) closed the academy and dismissed the foreign staff. During his tenure of office, the modern vessels of the Kwangtung flotilla were tied up. See Biggerstaff, *Earliest Modern Schools* [5], p. 57.

[108] FO 17/1249 Brenan to O'Conor in O'Conor's no. 26, November 12, 1895 [46].

[109] The announcement of the Kwangtung authorities appears in Tsou Lu, *The Kuomintang* [216], pp. 661–662. Hsüeh, in "Yang Ch'ü-yün, Sun Yat-sen" [65], p. 313, is apparently incorrect in stating that Yang, at this time, had the "same price on his head" as Sun.

[110] Feng, in *Documents* [179], III, 321. At least seven society activists however, were killed in clashes with government troops after exposure of the plot. See *ibid.*, 369–370.

the same story that had been told the Hong Kong police, namely that the coolie "shock force" had been recruited by Yang on a purely mercenary basis. They claimed that they had been told only that "braves" were being recruited in Canton and that their duties would be explained upon arrival, that they were merely misguided strong-arm men who did not know what they were getting into.[111] Since many of these fighters from Hong Kong actually were mercenaries, it seemed logical for the authorities to try to win them over by a show of goodwill. It was the ringleaders, and principally Sun, whom they wanted, and they made a point of offering rewards and immunity to the "misguided" rebels who were willing to cooperate in the capture of the leaders.[112]

We can also assume that the governor-general eschewed harsh tactics in order to avoid a confrontation with the accumulated popular resentment which he knew existed. The very fact that hundreds, if not thousands, of malcontents were to be found in the Canton delta region attested to the high level of instability which obtained. Uprisings based upon uprooted peasants, laborers, and ex-soldiers were not unusual during this period. While these risings were local in scope and lacked any cohesive organizational or ideological element, they were more in the nature of riots which could be easily squelched. There was even the possibility of buying off secret society leaders and enlisting their cohorts, as was attempted after the Opium War in 1842.[113] But once an educated leadership with political ambitions appeared in the countryside, there was real cause for concern. This was the danger which Sun and his friends represented. Taking the easiest way out, the bureaucrats struck ruthlessly at the leadership, sending the masses back to their villages with a Confucian admonition to follow better examples in the future.

Yet with Sun, Yang, and fourteen other ringleaders at large, the governor-general had little cause for satisfaction. Well aware

[111] See T'an's account in Tsou Lu, *The Kuomintang* [216], p. 664, and Brenan's dispatch of November 1, 1895 [46].

[112] Tsou Lu, *The Kuomintang* [216], p. 661.

[113] See Fairbank, *Trade and Diplomacy* [38], pp. 88–89.

of his own negligence, T'an's uneasiness was such that he delayed
reporting the episode to Peking, and apparently his superiors in
the capital first heard of it from a brief communication sent by
subordinate officials in Canton.[114] (It will be recalled that Richard's interview in Peking on December 3 disclosed that Peking
was aware of the attempted coup and Sun's role in it.) In response to this intelligence, the Grand Council sent an edict to
T'an on December 2, ordering him to apprehend the chief criminals. T'an then tried to cover his tracks and, in a memorial to
the throne, dramatically described how his vigilant forces had
foiled an attempt by some forty to fifty thousand brigands (*t'u-
fei*) to ransack the provincial capital. T'an had been at his Canton post only since April, and he prefaced his report with an account of the volatile temperament of the Kwangtung populace
and its susceptibility of the lure of booty. The instigators, according to his version, had gathered tens of thousands of ignorant ruffians from as far away as Kao-chou, southwest of the capital, and Hui-chou (Waichow) to the east, and then assembled
them in Hong Kong. He told of the arrests at the rebels' Canton
headquarters, and of the discovery of a crate with fifteen foreign
hatchets, which were to be used to break open the storehouse
where receipts of the *wei-hsing* lottery were deposited. The intention of T'an's memorial was to minimize political aspects and
depict the plot as a predatory bandit venture. Nor did the name
Hsing Chung Hui appear in this or any of the other official documents dealing with the plot. He ended his memorial by describing how justice had been meted out to Lu and other ringleaders
who had "deluded the common people," and how he had acted
mildly toward the minor participants who were "not aware" that
a crime was contemplated. But he promised to devote every effort to apprehending the major instigators, Sun and Yang.[115]

[114] Tsou Lu, *The Kuomintang* [216], p. 663.
[115] T'an's memorial in *ibid.*, pp. 663–664, also mentions the edict from the
Grand Council and the earlier report from Kwangtung. It should be noted
that T'an, in designating the rebels as "bandits," was conforming to the
Ch'ing Criminal Code which "classifies treason and rebellion against the
state as the two leading crimes within the category of 'Banditry' " (*tao-tsei*).
See Sun, *Ch'ing Administrative Terms* [119], p. 221.

T'an's tardiness in reporting to Peking and his effort to de-
emphasize the plot's political implications can be contrasted with
the British Consul's evaluation. Brenan, who gained his information from a source which was certainly available to T'an, saw
the aborted plot as a serious attempt at revolution in which Canton figured only as the springboard. In his dispatch of November
1, he wrote:

With Canton in their possession the rebels were to march north-
wards where they felt confident of gaining support . . . . officials have
ascertained that the movement is very widespread. . . . The Superintendent of Police [Li Chia-ch'ao] has informed me that when the
plot can be sifted to the bottom, many influential men and high
military officials will be involved.[116]

Brenan was convinced that the authorities were unable to
suppress a rising, and that T'an, having been deceived by his
subordinates, did not realize the gravity of the situation. On
November 12 he wrote that "alarm had subsided" and that the
provincial government felt fortunate in having forestalled a
"serious rising." Yet he found that the "general impression
among officials is that a searching investigation would give the
government inconvenient information and compel them to follow up with such drastic measures . . . as would precipitate the
rebellion which has not yet been averted."[117] The contrast between this grave appraisal and the British political report of
seven months earlier attests to the impact of the Canton plot.

The revolutionaries at first glance seemed to have suffered the
ruin of all the financial and organizational gains of the past year.
In October, with a feasible target and a precise plan of action,
they had easily mustered a respectable fighting force. In November they were left with only a general staff, and even this nucleus
had been reduced through internal bickering and the exacting
justice of the enemy. The original leadership clique, never in

[116] FO 17/1249, Brenan to O'Conor in O'Conor's no. 25, November 1,
1895 [46].
[117] FO 17/1249, Brenan to O'Conor in O'Conor's no. 26, November 12,
1895 [46].

full harmony, was divided as Sun and his partisans blamed Yang for the disaster.[118] Not only had they depleted their treasury in buying arms which fell into government hands, but once the plot was smashed, the entire Hsing Chung Hui organization in Kwangtung melted away. It had been recruited for one immediate purpose, the assault on the Canton yamens; when that assault failed, there was nothing to hold it together. No vestige of the Hsing Chung Hui existed on the Chinese mainland until five years later when a second coup was attempted in the province.[119] Organizational work in Hong Kong likewise ended when the leaders were forced to leave.

The evanescent nature of Hsing Chung Hui organizational activity was its major deficiency as an instrument of revolution. Its battle plan was not ill-conceived, but it had little else besides a battle plan. Yet the leaders' obsession with the idea of seizing the Kwangtung capital does not in itself reflect a narrowness of vision or lack of strategic sense. All revolutions evolve from coups, but as Lasswell has phrased it:

Successful violence in revolution depends upon the conjunction of a coup d'etat with a crisis of mass discontent. The coup d'etat can be executed by a small number of storm troops which are well informed, armed and trained; but the chances of securing a loyal conspirative personnel, and of carrying through the action with mass support, depend upon long propaganda preparation in advance of crisis.[120]

Failure to lay this groundwork resulted in the collapse of the Canton plot. The treachery of a few individuals and the malfunctioning of the conspiratorial apparatus were only consequential to the primary neglect of organization and propaganda.

Yet something can be said for Sun's choice of tactics. In drawing together several segments of dissent—secret societies, overseas

---

[118] Ch'en Hsi-ch'i, *Before the T'ung Meng Hui* [151], p. 37, claims that because Yang divided the ammunition unfairly, leaders of the "do-or-die" battalion were not willing to go to Canton on the originally scheduled date. Ch'en relies upon an account by Teng Mu-han.

[119] Feng, in *Documents* [179], III, 321.

[120] Lasswell, *Politics* [74], p. 54.

Chinese, and Westernized intellectuals—and giving them a semblance of unity through a military plot, he found an expeditious and effective way of threatening the government. Organization and propaganda require patience; shortcut tactics were more attuned to Sun's personality and intellectual attributes. What appealed to him was the "propaganda of the deed" which, though it may not result in an immediate grasp of political power, develops "an atmosphere of general expectancy" among the masses and diffuses fear and uncertainty within the government.[121] And such deeds, when their effect becomes cumulative, can bring about a complete breakdown of authority. Thus the Canton plot should not be viewed as an isolated instance that failed, but as the prototype of a series of conspiracies which, enacted over a sixteen-year period, accelerated the overthrow of the Manchus.

To put it simply, the Canton plot, despite its failure, launched the revolutionary career of Sun Yat-sen. Because of Canton he was finally taken seriously not only in Hong Kong and Kwangtung, but in Peking as well. Because of Canton and the unrelenting effort of the Manchu government to hunt him down overseas, Sun would a year later be catapulted into a prominence which was in no way commensurate with the meager organizational resources at his command.

[121] *Ibid.*, p. 55.

V

Kidnapped in London

In Hong Kong Sun and his fellow fugitives, Ch'en Shao-pai and Cheng Shih-liang, were anxious to clarify their status. Anticipating a Chinese demand for extradition, Sun took Cantlie's advice and consulted a British solicitor, who was unprepared with a specific precedent for the case, but advised them to respect the subtleties of the Manchu agents and leave Hong Kong immediately. A chance decision sent them to Japan; the earliest accommodations available were on a Japanese freighter sailing for home the next day.[1] According to the Hong Kong police, who were already interested in his movements, Sun withdrew $300 from the Hongkong and Shanghai Bank on October 31.[2] Sun then evaded the police and made his way to the ship which took him and his friends on a stormy trip to Kobe.

On the day following their departure, the Canton governor-general requested the surrender of Sun and four others suspected of having taken refuge in the colony, but when Governor Robinson's response indicated that the British were not willing to hand

[1] Ch'en Shao-pai, *Hsing Chung Hui* [152], p. 12. Sun Yat-sen, "My Reminiscences" [118]. Although Sun and Cantlie give this lawyer's name as "Dennis," I think he probably was H. L. Dennys, a prominent Hong Kong lawyer who a year later was appointed Crown Solicitor of the colony. Concerning his appointment, see Robinson to Chamberlain in CO 129/273, no. 258, November 10, 1896 [46]; and Norton-Kyshe, *The Laws and Courts of Hongkong* [90], II, 487.

[2] Memorandum by F. J. Badeley, Acting Assistant Colonial Secretary (Hong Kong), enclosed in Robinson to Chamberlain, March 11, 1896, in CO 129/271 [46].

over political criminals, the matter was temporarily dropped.[3]

In Kobe, where they landed on November 12, the three rebels first became aware of the notoriety which their leader had gained from the Canton episode. The phrasing of the news reports they read also gave them cause to reflect upon the historical implications of their anti-dynastic designs. Though none of them understood the language, the Japanese use of Chinese characters enabled them to make out a newspaper item announcing the arrival of "the Chinese revolutionary party leader, Sun Yat-sen." It took Sun and his friends by surprise that the Japanese designation of "revolution," *kakumei*, was in its Chinese reading none other than *ko-ming*, a familiar term but one which they had never associated with their own political goals. To the Japanese the term meant "revolution" in the Western sense, but it had an entirely different connotation in the traditional Chinese lexicon. Though the literal meaning was "remove or change the mandate," it actually denoted dynastic change, the replacement of one dynasty by another of the same institutional makeup. As Ch'en Shao-pai exclaimed, "We had always considered *ko-ming* as applying to the ambition to become emperor," and it is understandable that Sun had not adopted the term which meant only that the "ruler's name was changed."[4]

Instead, they had associated their activities with other traditional terms: *tsao-fan* (rebellion), *ch'i-i* (righteous rising), or *kuang-fu* (restoration). Except for the last, which refers to a Chi-

[3] *Ibid.*, Brenan to O'Conor, no. 26, November 12, 1895, in FO 17/1249 [46].

[4] Ch'en Shao-pai, *Hsing Chung Hui* [152], p. 12; Feng, *Reminiscences* [160], I, 1; Liu Ch'eng-yü, "Sketches of Sun's Character" [189], I.1: 46. See also Levenson, "Confucianism and Monarchy" [77], pp. 259–260. The traditional *ko-ming* is closer in meaning to "rebellion," which is clearly distinguished from "revolution" by Max Gluckman: "In certain types of society, when subordinates turn against a leader . . . they may only turn against him personally, without necessarily revolting against the authority of the office he occupies. They aim to turn him out of that office and install another in it. This is rebellion, not revolution. A revolution aims at altering the nature of political offices and of the social structure in which they function, and not merely to change the incumbents in persisting offices. Aristotle saw this distinction between rebellions and revolutions and pointed out that rebellions do not attack authority itself." *Custom and Conflict* [45], p. 28.

nese rising against ethnically non-Chinese rulers, these terms lack any positive political content; they refer to popular protest movements of local rather than national scope. In the popular tradition, they might be associated with the valorous deeds of brave heroes who take up arms against unjust officials or rapacious landowners. To Confucian literati, a *tsao-fan* was of course a "great perversion and sacrilegious" (*ta-ni pu-tao*), whereas *ko-ming*, the term Sun had avoided, was a valued Confucian expression since its use implied that the literati had given the seal of approval to a new dynasty.

Recalling the locus classicus of *ko-ming*, "The *ko-ming*[s] of T'ang and Wu were in consonance with Heaven and in accord with mankind," Sun was delighted with the Japanese adoption of a modern referent for a traditional Chinese term. He could now appropriate a value-laden expression and put it to effective use. Ancient prestige could adorn the new concept of institutional change. "From now on," he said, "our party will be called the *ko-ming-tang* (revolutionary party)," and Ch'en wrote that these three characters used by the Japanese "made an indelible impression upon our minds."[5]

The trio soon continued on to Yokohama, which had a Cantonese community of several thousand.[6] Relying upon Sun's contacts of the past year, they got settled and established a branch of the Hsing Chung Hui. This was a small group of ten or so

[5] Ch'en Shao-pai, *Hsing Chung Hui* [152], p. 12. In this context it is interesting to note that about nine years later, Sun's future colleague, T'ao Ch'eng-chang, in drawing up a manifesto for a Chekiang secret society argued that a *tsao-fan* was really the same as a *ko-ming*, and that the seditious connotation attached to the former term was arbitrarily imposed by the ruling class, which sought to hide the "revolutionary" teaching of Confucius and Mencius. See *The 1911 Revolution* [167], I, 534–535. And in 1905 Ch'en T'ien-hua would contend that even the traditional *ko-ming* was a progressive instrument in its time, but due to the perfidy of the scholars, the people never came to understand the potentialities of this "divine remedy for mankind." He sought to prove that China's historical legacy of dynastic changes, which originated in the discontent of the masses, equipped her for a ready assimilation of the modern concept of revolution. See *People's Journal* [199], 1:50–52, (November 1905).

[6] According to Sharman, *Sun Yat-sen* [107], p. 60, there were about 2500 Chinese, mostly Cantonese, in the Yokohama area in 1899.

members, including Feng Ching-ju and the clothier T'an Yu-fa. "Queue-less" Feng, who had been an active supporter of Sun for the past year, was elected chairman, and his thirteen-year-old son, Tzu-yu, acted as courier.[7] The negative response of the Yokohama *hua-ch'iao*, however, gave few hopes of immediate expansion. Though anti-Manchu sentiment and personal admiration of Sun were not lacking, the *hua-ch'iao* were much more hesitant to consort with an authentic rebel than with the seemingly inoffensive agitator who had visited them previously. Their reluctance was especially pronounced at this time, when they expected to soon come under the scrutiny of the Chinese consul, returning to Yokohama after the war settlement.[8]

Sun Yat-sen, however, was in no mood to expend his energies in quieting the fears of a rather small emigrant community. He was satisfied to encourage the few militants he found; then he turned toward the larger and more affluent *hua-ch'iao* communities of Hawaii and America. He also hoped to feel more secure from Manchu agents while organizing in these communities. Sun realized that he was a hunted criminal, and in Japan he began to weave the protective web of falsehoods which sometimes ensnared his pursuers and still continues to confound his biographers.

First of all he underwent a change of appearance. He cut off his queue, stopped shaving his head, and began growing a moustache. Having exchanged his Chinese robe for a European suit, he now looked like a modern Japanese, a transformation which both astonished and reassured him.[9] Furthermore, according to his friend Ch'en Shao-pai, he got permission to enter the United States by convincing the American consul in Yokohama that he had been born in Hawaii.[10]

[7] Feng, in *Documents* [179], III, 323.

[8] Ch'en Shao-pai, *Hsing Chung Hui* [152], p. 19.

[9] Sun, "My Reminiscences" [118], p. 303. Sun recalls that he had his queue removed in Kobe, but his companion on this trip, Ch'en Shao-pai, reports this happened in Yokohama. See also Lo Chia-lun, *Biography* [192], I, 63.

[10] It is not clear how Hawaiian birth could entitle Sun to an American passport since the Islands were not annexed until 1898. He might have obtained a visa through this deception, but what kind of passport did he hold?

Together with his capacity for dissimulation, Sun's globe-trotting, conspiratorial jaunts also depended upon his fund raising ability. He never raised as much as was actually needed to finance his military ventures, but he always seemed able to impress enough individuals to keep him moving from one stop to the next. In this case, when the Yokohama Hsing Chung Hui could not raise the 500 yen required for travel expenses, Feng Ching-ju and his brother loaned him the entire sum. Here I may note another characteristic of Sun Yat-sen. He was not greedy and whatever funds he obtained he spent solely on the cause, never forgetting the needs of his fellow conspirators. On this occasion he gave Ch'en and Cheng Shih-liang a hundred yen each. Since the latter's name was omitted from the Manchu wanted list, he was ordered back to Hong Kong where he could lay the groundwork for a future uprising.[11] Five years later this investment paid off, and it was vital for the revolutionary cause.

Although Ch'en Shao-pai had intended to stay in Yokohama, soon even Feng Ching-ju became uneasy over his presence, and he left for Tokyo, where he was helped by Sugawara Den, a Christian minister whom Sun had met in Hawaii in 1894.[12]

Meanwhile Yang Ch'ü-yün had been identified by the British as the chief culprit in Hong Kong and had fled in the opposite direction toward Southeast Asian ports.[13] For the next two years, with Tse Tsan-tai his only link to the original band of plotters, Yang played a quiescent role while the Manchus' feverish concern with Sun Yat-sen helped to establish the latter as the movement's dominant figure.

Arriving in Hawaii in January 1896, Sun found that though Hsing Chung Hui membership had increased since his last visit,

---

The Chinese government would not have given one at this time, but he may have been able to use his passport of 1894. In an article on Sun published in the *China Mail* on December 3, 1896 (and appended to Sun's *Kidnapped in London*) it was stated that he was born in Hawaii, and in 1904 he again used this ruse to enter the United States, See Sharman, *Sun Yat-sen* [107], pp. 79–80.

[11] Lo Chia-lun, *Biography* [192], I, 64; Sun in *Collected Works* [205], II, 82.

[12] Ch'en Shao-pai, *Hsing Chung Hui* [152], pp. 19–20.

[13] Tse, *Chinese Republic* [122], p. 10.

news of the Canton defeat had lowered morale. He tried to revive it through various means.[14] When the Reverend Damon,
always a closely heeded adviser to the Hawaiian Chinese, suggested they take up military training to fit themselves for leading
the Chinese revolution, Sun organized a "Military Education
Association." Victor Bache, a Danish sea captain formerly with
the Chinese navy, began drilling forty young men with wooden
rifles in Damon's schoolyard, but interest soon flagged and the
project was dropped.[15] Sun also tried to gain support through
the "Chinese-Western Discussion Association," a club connected
with the Honolulu Chinese paper, *Lung-chi pao*.[16]

After six months, Sun had done fairly well financially but had
failed to stimulate organizational activity.[17] The reason for his
lengthy stay in Hawaii was probably personal rather than political. After the Canton episode, it was dangerous for his family
to remain in China, and since the latter part of the previous year,
his widowed mother, his wife, and his two small children had
been living with Sun Mei in Maui. A son had been born in
1891, a daughter in 1895, and a second daughter would be born
in November 1896.[18] Thanks to Sun Mei's faithful observance
of the elder son's traditional obligation, Sun Yat-sen was able to
pursue his revolutionary career free of family responsibilities.

While in Hawaii, there was an unexpected reunion with Dr.
Cantlie, who was making a brief stopover on his way back to
England. Whether Sun had previously expected to visit Europe
after his American tour is uncertain, but when he learned of
Cantlies' destination, he promised to see them in England. Cantlie still urged Sun to continue his medical studies and hoped he
would arrive in time to attend classes in the fall.[19]

A less resolute agitator might have taken up Cantlie's offer,

---

[14] Sun, *Collected Works* [205], II, 82.

[15] "Sun's Activities in Hawaii" [204], p. 281. Chung Kun Ai, *My Seventy-
Nine Years* [26], p. 315; Restarick, *Sun Yat-sen* [94], p. 49.

[16] "Sun's Activities in Hawaii" [204], p. 281; Lo Kang, *Errors in Lo's Biography of Sun* [197], p. 54.

[17] "Sun's Activities in Hawaii" [204], p. 282.

[18] Lo Chia-lun, *Biography* [192], I, 44, 64, 65.

[19] Sun, *Collected Works* [205], II, 82. See Cantlie's statement in *The
Globe*, October 23, 1896.

especially since his subsequent three-month sojourn in America proved to be even more disappointing than those in Yokohama or Hawaii. Traveling from San Francisco to New York, and making frequent stops between, Sun covered much ground but gained few converts. Not the least of his obstacles here was the fact that the Chinese Legation knew of his movements and warned off the *hua-ch'iao*, who were in any case politically apathetic.[20] While in San Francisco, Sun foolishly posed for a photograph, and a copy found its way to the legation, thus rendering useless the disguise which had given him so much pleasure and confidence. His every movement was traced, and Chinese officials even resorted to calligraphic juggling in attempts to discredit him. Adding a few strokes to the character "Wen" of "Sun Wen," they appealed to *hua-ch'iao* prejudices by giving his name an odious connotation.[21]

But for the Manchu government, Sun's meager gleanings since Canton in no way detracted from his revolutionary capabilities. Peking saw him as an indefatigable and extremely mobile agitator who threatened to invigorate internal dissidence with overseas wealth, and it was determined to cut him down as fast as possible. Reward notices were posted in Hong Kong, Macao, Saigon, and Singapore, while Chinese diplomats throughout the world were put on the alert.[22] When Sun boarded the S.S. *Majestic* in New York on September 23, the zealous Chinese Minister in Washington, Yang Ju, immediately notified his colleague in Britain, Kung Chao-yüan, to take up the chase when the boat landed.[23]

Sun reached London on October 1 and the next day the Cantlies found lodgings for him in their vicinity. For the first ten days, Sun leisurely took in the sights like an ordinary tourist. He visited the British Museum and the Houses of Parliament, and admired most of all London's quiet efficiency in contrast to

20 Sun, *Collected Works* [205], II, 82–83; Feng, *Reminiscences* [160], I, 136–138.

21 Sharman, *Sun Yat-sen* [107], p. 44; Lo Chia-lun, *Biography* [192], I, 66. The new graph written with the water radical and read "men," means "to defile."

22 Lo Chia-lun, *Sun's Kidnapping* [191], p. 6.

23 Lo Chia-lun, *Biography* [192], I, 66.

the jarring tumult of Eastern cities. He had, after all, been British-educated, and the things he had been taught to respect came to life as he walked the streets of London.[24]

While Sun was meandering, however, the Chinese Legation prepared to act. Slater's Detective Agency had been engaged to follow him from the moment of his arrival, and the Minister, Kung Chao-yüan, gave the matter his complete attention.[25]

The major responsibility, however, was borne by the Secretary of the Chinese Legation, Sir Halliday Macartney (1833–1906). This Scottish military surgeon and kinsman of the famous leader of Britain's first mission to China in 1793, was now nearing the close of a colorful career. After campaigning in the Crimea, India, and Peking, Macartney had in 1862 joined the Chinese army and, like Charles Gordon, fought the Taipings. Later, as the protégé of Li Hung-chang, he held a key post in the Nanking Arsenal, and in 1877 assumed his diplomatic duties in London. During these years Macartney had faithfully carried out a number of important and delicate missions for his foreign employers, but never was it more difficult to be both a British gentleman and a Chinese mandarin than in the episode involving Sun Yat-sen.[26]

Even before Sun arrived, Macartney had asked the British Foreign Office whether he could be extradited and had been turned down.[27] On October 10, 1896, Kung Chao-yüan cabled this information to his colleague in Washington. He also reported that his agents were still on Sun's trail and that he had heard that the rebel's next stop was France.[28]

At this point, when they had apparently given up any idea of legally remanding Sun to China, Macartney and his colleagues

[24] Sun, *Kidnapped in London* [115], pp. 30–31.

[25] Lo Chia-lun, *Biography* [192], I, 66. The Secretary to the Legation, Sir Halliday Macartney, hired the detectives and received their reports.

[26] See Boulger, *Sir Halliday Macartney* [10].

[27] FO 17/1718, Sanderson's memorandum on his interview with Macartney, October 22, 1896, pp. 55–56 [46]. The Chinese had hoped to have Sun extradited according to articles twenty-one and fifteen of the Tientsin (1859) and Burma (1894) treaties respectively. See Lo Chia-lun, *Sun's Kidnapping* [191], p. 11.

[28] Lo Chia-lun, *Sun's Kidnapping* [191], p. 26.

decided upon a much more questionable course. Although the precise circumstances were later heatedly disputed, nonetheless on October 11, 1896, they had Sun under lock and key on the third floor of the legation building and were devising means to transport him back to China, where Governor-General T'an Chung-lin anxiously awaited him.

How was Sun taken prisoner? It is worthwhile to consider the conflicting versions and to draw a conclusion—not in order to judge the legality of the legation's behavior, for they were clearly in the wrong regardless of the manner of Sun's entry—but in order to gain a better understanding of Sun's personality and an appreciation of his talent for dissimulation. This affair became one of the greatest personal triumphs of his entire career, and it was his quick thinking and persuasive manner in dealing with the foreign public that helped make this triumph possible.

The legation, situated on Portland Place, was by a coincidence just around the corner from the Cantlie residence on Devonshire Street. Sun had been on this street several times on his way to the Cantlies from his room at Gray's Inn Place, and he was also in the habit of taking an omnibus from there when he left. Yet he later claimed that he never noticed the legation or knew where it was. However, when Cantlie had jokingly asked whether he planned to visit the legation, Sun had only laughed and replied, "I don't think so"; Mrs. Cantlie strongly warned him not to take any chances.[29] Dr. Manson, another former teacher in Hong Kong, also cautioned him when Sun himself asked whether "it would be wise" to visit the legation.[30] This latter conversa-

[29] Although Sun and Cantlie later published their respective versions of the events surrounding Sun's detention, I am using their earlier testimony which was taken by the Treasury Solicitor, H. Cuffe, who conducted an inquiry on behalf of the Home Office. Since his investigation took place within two weeks after Sun's liberation, I believe the statements he took are more reliable than the subsequent accounts by the same people. Cuffe's report and the appended statements are printed in FO 17/1718 [46], pp. 113–123. The conversation with the Cantlies is reported in the doctor's statement, submitted on November 4, 1896. See FO 17/1718 [46], p. 121.

[30] Manson's statement of November 4, 1896, in FO 17/1718 [46], p. 122. Sun's version of the conversation appears in his statement of that same date, in *ibid.*, p. 119.

tion shows that Sun was weighing the notion. He apparently thought that he had shaken off his pursuers. Moreover he assumed that the Chinese would not dare harm him on British soil. Aside from being tempted by the thrill of infiltrating the legation and haranguing any fellow Cantonese who were available, he simply may have been lonely for Chinese companionship.

His own version, however, omitted any intention of entering the legation on that Sunday, October 11. According to Sun, he was taking his usual route through Portland Place on his way to the Cantlies when he was accosted by a Chinese who inquired whether he was Chinese or Japanese. After a mutual introduction—the stranger was Teng T'ing-chien, later identified as a legation employee—and a short conversation, Sun was maneuvered to the doorstep of the building which he had not yet identified as the legation. Two other Chinese then came out and while Teng disappeared, they invited Sun in "for a talk." Though they pulled him in no real force was used, and it was only when the door was locked behind him that Sun became suspicious. The friendly bantering ceased as he was forced upstairs. There a solemn Sir Halliday Macartney confronted him, told him that they knew who he was and that the legation premises were the same as Chinese soil.

"I know that Sir Halliday Macartney has written to the papers to say that I was there on the Saturday," Sun later related to a British investigator. "I am certain I was not there on the Friday or on the Saturday. I have never been there before."[31] Sun's account has the ring of truth. It seems reasonable to assume that had he wanted to fabricate a strong case against the legation, he could have accused the minister's hirelings of forcibly capturing and imprisoning him. Instead he claimed that he was enticed "in a friendly manner"; "there was no real violence used." The reported conversation with Teng also sounds very credible. And especially if, as he asserted, he had no inkling of the proximity of the legation, the whole episode could have happened in this

[31] *Ibid.*

way. The story is consistent with statements made by Sun when under great stress, and corresponds to the messages smuggled to Cantlie and to his statement to Scotland Yard immediately upon his release. This is the story which Sun repeated to his British friends and immortalized in his *Kidnapped in London*.

In contrast the legation's version, as presented at the time by Macartney, was both inconsistent and implausible. There were actually four accounts attributed to Macartney, one of which is a newspaper report of an interview, the other three more authentic presentations of his case. On October 22 he told British Foreign Office officials that Sun had called at the Chinese legation of his own accord on Friday the 9th. Macartney claimed that on this occasion Sun had been allowed to leave but was detained when he returned.[32] The next day Macartney again visited the Foreign Office and supplied more details concerning the controversial first visit: namely, that Sun had aroused suspicions by his conversation with a Cantonese employee concerning the instability of the Chinese government. Furthermore, after he left they found that some papers which had been prepared for Macartney were missing; the assumption was that Sun had taken them. For these reasons, Sun was held on his next visit.[33]

But on October 24, after Sun had been released and his own version circulated, Macartney wrote to the *Times* contending that the first visit had taken place on Saturday the 10th.[34] This of course is no small inconsistency. In addition there is an interview with Macartney published in the *Times* of the 24th. Again he asserted that Sun first came to the legation on the 10th. But the newspaper also quoted him to the effect that he personally met Sun on this occasion and became suspicious as a result of their conversation.[35] But if he himself had received Sun upon the first visit, why did he not mention it at the Foreign Office

[32] *Ibid.*, p. 57.
[33] *Ibid.*, pp. 73–74.
[34] Macartney's letter is reprinted in Boulger, *Sir Halliday Macartney* [10], pp. 467–468.
[35] London *Times*, October 24, 1896.

or in his letter to the paper? And if Sun did steal documents from the legation, why did Macartney wait until his second interview at the Foreign Office before making this accusation, which would have strengthened his case for holding Sun?

It has been suggested that Macartney was misquoted in his *Times* interview; another inference is that he had no personal knowledge of Sun's alleged first visit but merely repeated what others had told him.[36] These inconsistencies in Macartney's statements and his less than faithful rendering of other aspects of the case (for instance, his denial that Sun was kept a prisoner or that the legation considered removing him by means other than extradition) made a shoddy impression on the British investigator. But what about the detective agency which had been shadowing Sun ever since his arrival? It would seem that the key to the whole mystery lay in the hands of Slater's intrepid sleuths. Surely they could have been expected to know Sun's whereabouts on the 9th and 10th; and what is more important, they should have been able to explain how he entered the legation on the 11th. Unfortunately the activities of these inquiry agents fell far short of the standards set by their fictional counterparts. Slater's detectives were apparently fumbling incompetents, who lost track of their quarry for days on end. After reporting to Macartney on October 6 that there was "nothing of importance" in Sun's movements, their next message did not arrive until October 12.[37] By that time, Macartney wanted to know what Slater's had found out in the past few days, and whether the man they had been following was the same one being detained in the legation. But they could only report that on Saturday afternoon, observation of the subject was renewed and he was followed from his rooming house to the Houses of Parliament. After remaining there for several hours, he had done some window shopping on the Strand and then returned to his lodgings. On Sunday a detective was again on duty outside 8 Gray's Inn Place, "but the party in question was not seen to leave, no doubt owing to the inclement

[36] This is Cuffe's opinion, in FO 17/1718 [46], p. 114.
[37] See Slater's report, appended to Lo Chia-lun, *Sun's Kidnapping* [191].

state of the weather."[38] This, it will be remembered, was the day on which both sides agree that Sun entered the Portland Place legation building. In his statement to the press prior to Sun's release, Macartney implied that Sun had somehow given his watcher the slip—"it is nevertheless a curious fact that he came to the Chinese Legation without the knowledge of the private detective who had been employed to watch him"—but there is no evidence that Sun knew he was being followed, and the gap in Slater's report can be attributed to their agent's bungling.[39]

Nor did the evidence of George Cole, the twenty-nine-year-old legation porter, throw light on the manner of Sun's entry. He knew only that Macartney, who did not usually come in on Sundays, was called to the legation at 10 A.M. on the 11th, and that about an hour later, he, Cole, was told that he had a "nice job for Sunday morning; we have got to clear the furniture out of a room." Within the hour he was assigned to take charge of Sun, who had been brought into the room, one usually occupied by one of the legation employees. Cole and the other British servants were curious as to how Sun had entered the house, but remained unenlightened. Cole only heard one of the Chinese say, "very funny, which way this man come," and Teng, the man Sun claimed accosted him on the street, told him, "I very clever; I knowledge; I getee inside."[40]

Cole's evidence, however, does show that the legation anticipated Sun's visit or some unusual event; otherwise Macartney would not have been called in on a Sunday morning *prior* to Sun's departure from his rooms. (Sun said that he left about 10:30 A.M.).[41] Either Sun had been at the legation previously and was expected again, or the Portland Place conspirators knew that he would be in the vicinity and decided to ensnare him. But Slater's earlier reports made no mention of Sun's route to the Cantlies, and if Macartney obtained this intelligence, it must have been through some other source. Macartney, it should be noted, never stated that an appointment for a second visit had

[38] *Ibid.*
[39] London *Times*, October 24, 1896.
[40] Cole's statement of November 2, 1896, in FO 17/1718 [46], pp. 116–117.
[41] *Ibid.*, p. 119.

been made the first time Sun appeared, and therefore the conclusion of the official British inquiry was that the plan to im-
prison Sun on the 11th did not stem from any previous meeting
with him but was based on the hope that he would somehow
pass by on that particular morning. This is nevertheless one of
the weak points in Sun's account. The translator, Teng, would
never have undertaken the sole responsibility for inveigling Sun
into the legation, and from Cole's evidence as well as Sun's, it
is obvious that his arrival had been anticipated. And if it was
anticipated with such assurance, it might very well have been
arranged previously by appointment.

Yet the official British investigator, the Treasury Solicitor,
was satisfied that the planned detention of Sun was in no way
inconsistent with his denial of an earlier visit. He assumed that
the legation was well enough informed of Sun's general movements to lay their plans in advance. After matching Macartney's
dubious statements against Sun's consistent and detailed account
of his capture, it was the opinion of this official, H. Cuffe, that
"Sun Yat-sen's account of the manner in which he was introduced
into the Legation on the morning of the 11th of October is
substantially correct," and that "Sun is probably speaking the
truth in saying that he did not go to the Legation [previously]."[42]
In addition, by assuming that Macartney had been misinformed
by his Chinese colleagues, Cuffe was "glad to think" that this
conclusion did "not necessarily involve any imputation on Sir
Halliday Macartney's personal veracity."[43]

But Cuffe's conclusions, admittedly tentative because he was
unable to interrogate other legation employees, were based upon
two erroneous assumptions: one, that Slater's were providing
the legation with a much more detailed account of Sun's habits
and activities than they were in fact doing; and two, that Sun,
"with the knowledge that the Chinese Government were anxious
to get him into their hands" would not take such a risk.[44] The
first assumption we have already dealt with, and as for the second,
it did not take into consideration Sun's audacity and love of ad-

[42] *Ibid.*, pp. 113–114.
[43] *Ibid.*, p. 113.
[44] *Ibid.*

venture. Had Cuffe been able to investigate the legation evidence and examine the pertinent Chinese documentary material, he would undoubtedly have formed a different opinion of Sun's behavior on October 10 and 11, and might have discovered what actually took place.

There is in the first place the testimony of Wu Tsung-lien, the legation's French translator.[45] Writing about the incident three years later, Wu related that on October 10 Sun met a student named Sung Chih-t'ien as he strolled past the legation. When Sun asked about Cantonese employees he was taken inside and introduced to Teng T'ing-chien. Calling himself "Ch'en Tsai-chih," Sun inquired about other Cantonese in England and arranged to return for the information the following morning. ("Tsai-chih" was yet another of Sun's given names.) Teng's suspicions were aroused when he noticed the name "Sun" engraved in English on the visitor's watch. Afterward he consulted with his superiors, including Macartney, who realized that this was the man they had been looking for. Plans were made to detain him and on Sunday morning Sun fell into the trap.

The essentials of this account—the Saturday visit, the alias, the unsuspecting return on Sunday when Sun was treated to lunch —were corroborated in a diary kept by the legation's naval attache, a Mongol named Feng-ling.[46] There is also the correspondence between Kung Chao-yüan and his superiors in Peking. On October 12, Kung cabled that Sun had come to the legation using the name "Ch'en" and was being held prisoner.[47] Had Sun been lured off the street, there would have been no reason for the Minister to conceal it from the Tsungli Yamen.

This version is supported by Sun's subsequent confidential revelations. Ch'en Shao-pai, probably the first close friend he saw upon his return to the East, relates how Sun boasted of having visited the legation daily.[48] Later, in a more modest vein, he

[45] The pertinent section from Wu's book, *Sui-yao pi-chi* (Shanghai, 1899) appears in Lo Chia-lun, *Sun's Kidnapping* [191], pp. 31–32.
[46] Lo Chia-lun, *Sun's Kidnapping* [191], pp. 32–33.
[47] *Ibid.*, p. 26.
[48] Ch'en Shao-pai, *Hsing Chung Hui* [152], pp. 14–15.

told both Hu Han-min and Tai Chi-t'ao that he entered the legation of his own accord.[49] His friends admired the daring and the revolutionary fervor which had propelled Sun squarely into the enemy stronghold. They also understood the need for lying in order to blacken the Manchu regime and win the support of world opinion.

That the truth would have to be modified in order to achieve this end was something Sun intuitively grasped when he told his story to the British. There was no opportunity for anyone to advise him. He took this line on his own and maintained it consistently throughout his stay in England. He convinced his friends Cantlie and Manson, who stoutly backed him and vouched for his general truthfulness and trustworthy character.[50] He could have been tripped up had Slater's been more efficient, but when he first spoke to Scotland Yard and the press he probably did not know he had been watched, and by the time he had read Macartney's statement in the papers the following day he knew for certain that no third party could refute him.

From the legal standpoint, however, what happened on the 10th and 11th is not pertinent. Regardless of the manner of Sun's entry into the legation, what Macartney and company did to him once he was there (and what they intended doing to him afterwards) was a flagrant abuse of diplomatic privilege.[51] It seems that when Macartney found that Sun was freely making himself available, he assumed that he could hold him prisoner without

[49] Lo Chia-lun, *Sun's Kidnapping* [191], p. 42; this is further corroborated by another of Sun's old comrades, Teng Mu-han, in a memorandum submitted to the Kuomintang Archives. I am indebted to Dr. Lo for showing me a copy of this document.

[50] Cantlie testified to Cuffe, that "so far as I have found him, Sun has always been perfectly truthful on all occasions." (FO 17/1718 [46], p. 122); Manson found him "trustworthy," and a "decent, honest, good fellow who was anxious to get on." Manson further testified that he questioned Sun twice about the alleged first visit to the legation and Sun denied it distinctly. (FO 17/1718 [46], p. 122.)

[51] The authoritative *Oppenheim's International Law*, H. Lauterpacht, ed. [75], I, 796, states: ". . . an envoy has no right to seize a subject of his home state who is within the boundaries of the receiving State, and keep him under arrest inside the embassy with the intention of handing him over to his home State." In a footnote Sun's detention is cited as a case in point: "An

applying for extradition. His argument was that "if a Chinaman comes into this Legation of his own free will, and if there are charges or suspicions against him, . . . no one outside has any right to interfere with his detention. It would, of course, be quite different if the man were outside of this building, for then he would be in British territory, and we could not then arrest him without a warrant."[52] But the British, backed by authorities on international law, contended that even "if Sun had gone to the legation voluntarily, his detention would [not] have been a proper and lawful act on the part of the Chinese Minister."[53]

The story of that detention as related by Sun was substantially corroborated by the British investigation and the subsequent perusal of the Chinese archives. Macartney kept Sun imprisoned, prevented him from communicating with the outside, and made arrangements to ship him forcibly back to China. Three days after Sun's capture, Macartney was in touch with a Mr. Macgregor of the Glen Line and began negotiating to have a "lunatic" conveyed to China.[54] He also cabled Peking for permission to charter a ship and was subsequently authorized to spend seven thousand pounds for that purpose.[55] This was a measure of the importance which the Court attached to Sun's capture.

Macartney told Sun during their first meeting only that the

---

instance thereof is the case of the Chinese, Sun Yat Sen [sic], which occurred in London in 1896. He was a political refugee from China, living in London, who was induced to enter the house of the Chinese Legation and was kept under arrest there in order to be conveyed forcibly to China. The Chinese envoy contended that, as the house of the legation was Chinese territory, the British Government had no right to interfere. But the latter did interfere, and Sun Yat Sen was released after several days." I am indebted to my colleague, Dr. N. Bar-Yaakov, for calling my attention to this reference in Oppenheim. For a more detailed analysis of the legal aspect of the case, see Gerald E. Bunker, "Kidnapping of Sun Yat-sen" [16]. According to this study, the whole episode created a precedent in international law.

52 Macartney, in the London *Times*, October 24, 1896.

53 Cuffe, in FO 17/1718 [46], p. 116; this was apparently the opinion of the Attorney-General with whom Salisbury discussed the case. See FO 17/1718 [46], p. 55.

54 The report of Chief Inspector Jarvis of New Scotland Yard, who interviewed Macgregor on October 21st. FO 17/1718 [46], p. 94.

55 Lo Chia-lun, *Biography* [192], I, 68.

Tsungli Yamen had been informed of his capture and that Sun's fate depended upon its reply. Sun had a good idea of what could be expected from Peking and realized that he had to get word to his friends. But Macartney appeared to have blocked every route. He installed an extra lock on the door to Sun's room—the windows of which had bars—and posted guards on the outside. Anticipating Sun's attempt to bribe his guards, Macartney instructed them to keep any money the prisoner offered, but to turn over any messages to him. Thus the next day when Sun begged George Cole to deliver a note to a friend in order to "save a fellow creature's life," the message addressed to Cantlie ended up in Macartney's pocket. Cole, who got the impression from the Chinese servants that Sun was a lunatic, tried to humor the prisoner by assuring him that the note had been tossed out of the window.[56]

For almost a week Sun kept pressing messages addressed to Cantlie and Manson upon Cole and the English under-footman who relieved him. He even weighted the papers with coins so they could easily be tossed out the window. Using a pretext, he once had his window opened and threw out a note himself, only to watch Cole pick it up. This one, like all the others, was handed over to Macartney, who then took the additional precautions of nailing down Sun's window and depriving him of writing material.[57]

Soon afterward, Teng T'ing-chien taunted him with the disclosure that all his messages had been intercepted and that he would be sent back to China. "We are going to gag you," Teng said, "and tie you up, put you in a bag, and take you to a steamer we have already chartered." If they could not smuggle him out,

[56] FO 17/1718 [46], pp. 117–118.

[57] *Ibid.*, p. 117. However, one of the notes may have been retrieved by a delivery boy who often brought fish to the legation. Mr. Ernest Wells, now residing in Sydney, Australia, has written the author that he recalls picking up a scrap of paper while passing the legation on October 12, 1896. The paper had floated down from a window and contained a plea for help signed by Sun. Though he gave it to a policeman, there is no reference to the note in British records. I am grateful to Dr. Stuart Schram for referring me to Mr. Wells.

he went on, they would kill him in the legation—"The Legation is China; we can do anything here."[58] (In this case the corpse would presumably be returned to China, where it could be properly beheaded according to the punishment known as *lu-shih*—"beheading of a corpse"—employed when a prisoner dies before execution.)[59]

In the meantime, Sun suffered no bodily harm. He was even offered the sumptuous Hunan dishes prepared for Kung Chao-yüan and his staff, but afraid of poison, he had Cole bring him meals of bread and milk, sometimes with two raw eggs. Cole, at Macartney's orders, also gave him extra blankets when he complained of the cold.[60] He was most afflicted, however, by sheer terror. Should he be returned to China alive, he visualized having his "eyelids cut off, and finally being chopped to small fragments."[61]

He still felt that it was worth cultivating Cole, whom he saw as the weakest link in the legation setup. Although on Friday the 16th, the porter refused to take another note, he had already become convinced of Sun's sanity. The next day, when Sun again begged for help, Cole asked for time to think it over. Exactly how Sun persuaded the Englishman is not quite clear. According to Cole, Sun compared himself with "the leader of our Socialist Party here in London," and claimed that he headed a similar party in China.[62] But when confronted with Cole's statement, Sun insisted that he had said "nothing about Socialists" and that instead he had compared his plight to that of the Armenian Christians whose persecution by the Turks had been widely publicized in Britain.[63] (The first Armenian massacres in Constantinople had occurred on October 1, the day Sun arrived in London.[64] This is a minor discrepancy, but again worth noting as an example of Sun's ability to seize the main chance in manipulating public sympathy. Cole had no reason for lying and

[58] *Ibid.*, p. 120.
[59] See Sun, *Ch'ing Administrative Terms* [119], p. 275, under "lu-shih."
[60] FO 17/1718 [46], pp. 117–118.
[61] Sun, "My Reminiscences" [118], p. 303.
[62] FO 17/1718 [46], p. 118.
[63] *Ibid.*, p. 130.
[64] Langer, *Encyclopedia of World History* [73], p. 744.

it does not seem the kind of story he would have made up. But Sun, when he faced British officials and especially when he wrote his book, was anxious to exploit the religious issue. It is significant that at this time he already had some notion of socialism, but apparently sensed that the analogy with persecuted Christians would have wider appeal in England. To help establish his bona fides in this quarter, he later told Dr. Manson, who had "found him trustworthy," that he was a born Christian and was not a convert.[65]

Whether he appealed to Cole's proletarian or religious sentiments, Sun also struck a more mundane note. He offered him twenty pounds in cash and promised a thousand pounds later if he would take a message to Cantlie.[66] The porter was now definitely wavering and Saturday night he told Sun he would give

[65] FO 17/1718 [46], p. 122.

[66] In his *Kidnapped in London* [115], pp. 103–104, Sun denied offering Cole a bribe or a fee, and he contended that the twenty pounds were given to the servant for safe-keeping only. In his testimony to Cuffe, however, Cole said that Sun promised him more money. According to Sun, *Kidnapped in London*, Cole offered to return the money but Sun felt that the least he could do was urge him to keep it, while he regretted that he could not give him more. Yet on December 31st Sun called upon Cuffe and produced Cole's claim for five hundred pounds, less the twenty which had been paid. At this time Sun admitted promising Cole one thousand pounds and did not wish to dispute the claim, but "wanted to know if anything was being done about the legation." The Treasury official then referred him to the Foreign Office. (FO 17/1718 [46], p. 152). What Sun probably had in mind was to obtain some sort of compensation from the legation which would enable him to meet his obligation to Cole, who left his job on October 24th in anticipation of being fired, since he felt quite sure he would be suspected. Sun was actually quite concerned over Cole who had a family to support and who could not obtain any references from the legation in order to get a new job. Sun told a London *Evening News* reporter that he "would do anything to help" Cole and asked the reporter for assistance. (This interview was later reported in the *South China Morning Post* of August 11, 1934.) There is no official record of how Sun settled Cole's suit for the 480 pounds, but according to one source, he made a number of public addresses after his release and collected several hundred pounds which he turned over to the porter. (Ch'en Shao-pai, *Hsing Chung Hui* [152], p. 18.) Cantlie also announced that he intended asking the public to reward his informants and some money may have been raised in this manner. (See *The Globe*, October 23, 1896.) Sun should have made some money on the sale of his book and this may have given him an opportunity to settle Cole's claim.

him his decision in the morning. On Friday, however, Cole had already sought advice from Mrs. Howe, the legation's English housekeeper, who had only seen Sun briefly the first night he had spent in the building. When told of Sun's pleadings, she had urged Cole to send an anonymous letter to Cantlie.[67]

Cole did not see her again until Sunday, when he had made up his mind to help the prisoner. In the meantime, the lady had taken the initiative and provided Sun's friends with the first word of his plight. On Saturday night, when Cantlie was already in bed, she rang his bell and thrust a note in his letter box. By the time the doctor got downstairs she was gone; like Cole, the housekeeper was probably worried over losing her job and did not wish to be directly involved. Her message itself, however, was enough to stir the doctor to action. It read:

There is a friend of yours imprisoned in the Chinese Legation here, since last Sunday. They intend sending him out to China, where it is certain they will hang him. It is very sad for the poor man, and unless something is done at once he will be taken away and no one will know it. I dare not sign my name, but this is the truth, so believe what I say. Whatever you do must be done at once or it will be too late. His name, I believe, is Lin Yen Sen.[68]

Cantlie had already been concerned over Sun's absence from his room for the past week, and though the hour was late, he decided to act immediately. Assuming that the distinguished Secretary of Legation could not have had a hand in a plot of this order, his first thought was to reach Macartney and enlist his support. No one was at home when he reached the diplomat's residence, but a policeman, who was watching the house because of an attempted robbery a few nights previously, told him that Macartney was out of town and would not return for six months. The doctor's frustration grew as he went first to a police station and then to Scotland Yard without making any headway.[69] The next day he again found Macartney's house empty. He then decided to call on Dr. Manson.

[67] FO 17/1718 [46], p. 118.
[68] Cantlie and Jones, *Sun Yat-sen* [17], p. 60.
[69] See Cantlie's statement in *The Globe*, October 23, 1896.

In the meantime, Cole, whose decision to help Sun had been reinforced by Mrs. Howe's adventure of the previous night, brought a message which Sun had written on two calling cards. The porter, after first going to Cantlie's house around the corner from the legation, caught up with the doctor at Manson's doorstep. Both physicians then read their former student's desperate plea:

I was kidnapped into the Chinese Legation on Sunday, and shall be smuggled out from England to China for death. Pray rescue me quick; A ship is already charter by the C.L. [Chinese legation] for the service to take me to China and I shall be locked up all the way without communication to anybody . . . . O! Woe to me![70]

Sun also asked Cantlie to "take care of this messenger" for him and Cole was now anxious to cooperate. From him they learned the shocking news that far from being kept in the dark, Macartney had actually planned the "kidnapping."

It was Sunday, but these two eminent physicians realized that every hour was precious and began raising the alarm all over London. They contacted Scotland Yard again and even reached the Foreign Office, where they deposited the pertinent information with a duty clerk. Still with no assurance that action would be taken, Manson suggested that if the Chinese legation were bluntly told that their scheme had been exposed, they would hesitate before taking any irrevocable step. He also thought it would be better if he went alone because the legation had been engaged in some counter-intelligence of its own and had already marked Cantlie as an enemy. Two or three days earlier, it seems, when Manson had no inkling of Sun's predicament, a Harley Street colleague, Dr. Thin, who was attending the Chinese Minister, called on him and made inquiries about Sun and Cantlie. For that reason Manson thought he had a better chance of entering the legation than his friend. At Portland Place, however, he was met by Teng T'ing-chien, who denied the presence of any such person as Sun Yat-sen. Without getting much satisfaction from the interview, Manson nevertheless let Teng know that the po-

[70] These two cards are reproduced in Ch'en Hsi-ch'i, *Before the T'ung Meng Hui* [151], fourth photograph in the front part of the book.

lice and the Foreign Office were already informed that Sun was being held.[71]

Exploring every possibility Cantlie decided to give the story to the press. Sunday night he went to the *Times* office and handed in an account of what he had learned. The paper, however, saw fit to exercise its well-known discretion and on Monday it carried no word of the strange activities on Portland Place.[72] The decision to go to the *Times*, nevertheless, was one of the key factors in persuading the Foreign Office to move.

Cantlie also took an additional step before closing his day's work. He decided to get a private detective to watch the legation and raise the alarm should an attempt be made to move the prisoner. And to whom does one turn when seeking private detectives in London? Slater's, of course. But Slater's were never at their best on Sundays and Cantlie found their office closed. After a frustrating search for detectives all over London, he was going to take on the job himself until a man recommended by the police showed up near midnight. Slater's, however, were not to be denied the last measure of profit and on Monday, the 19th, their men put the legation under a 24-hour watch.[73] A subsequent investigation disclosed that on this very day Slater's telegraphed Macartney, "Fresh instructions from doctor to rescue party."[74] Thus the same detectives who had been hired by Macartney to shadow Sun were also commissioned by Cantlie to watch the legation and protect Sun, and at the same time were paid by Macartney to spy on Cantlie. Slater's may not have been good at detecting, but they apparently knew how to make the most out of a case with minimal effort.

By this time the Cantlie-Manson effort had aroused the British bureaucratic machine; the Foreign Office, Home Office, and

[71] FO 17/1718 [46], p. 122.

[72] According to Cantlie's statement to *The Globe* on October 23, he asked the *Times* whether they thought it better to delay publication until "it was seen how things turn out." The paper was in fact waiting to see what action the Foreign Office would take. See Sanderson's memorandum to Salisbury. October 22, in FO 17/1718 [46], p. 34.

[73] Sun, *Kidnapped in London* [115], pp. 75, 83.

[74] FO 17/1718 [46], p. 115.

Scotland Yard had set their sights on the Portland Place premises. With the authorization of Lord Salisbury, concurrently serving as Prime Minister and Foreign Minister, the Foreign Office sent a copy of Cantlie's deposition to the Home Office with a suggestion that the legation be put under surveillance. (Salisbury was not in London at the time but was apprised of Cantlie's evidence in an urgent letter from the Assistant Under-Secretary. The Foreign Minister's telegraphed reply, "Yes," signaled his approval of the communication to the Home Office and launched the British effort to frustrate the legation's plans.)[75]

On the same day Cantlie received further word from Sun, who had been informed by Cole that his friends were alerted. Sun had had time to collect his wits and sent an account of his apprehension and captivity which tallied with his subsequent story. Though relieved, he tried to expedite his release by claiming British nationality: "I was born in Hong Kong. I went back to interior of China about four or five years of age. As legally a British subject, can you get me out by that?"[76] Sun's inspiration made little impression on Sir Thomas Sanderson, the Foreign Office Under-Secretary.[77] It was unnecessary in any case since the government had already decided to prevent his removal to China. Should such an attempt be made, it was suggested that Sun be brought before a magistrate where the affair could be exposed.

At 10 P.M. on October 19, after having interviewed Cole, Chief Inspector Jarvis of Scotland Yard sent six officers to watch the legation continuously in three shifts, and Cantlie was now able to dismiss Slater's.[78] The Inspector also made arrangements with the Thames River police for a watch on all China-bound craft. On the 21st he interviewed Macgregor and got an inkling of Macartney's transportation negotiations.[79]

The special attention they were getting was noticed by the

[75] *Ibid.*, pp. 1–7.
[76] *Ibid.*, p. 113.
[77] *Ibid.*, pp. 34–35.
[78] *Ibid.*, pp. 38–41; *The Globe*, October 23, 1896.
[79] FO 17/1718 [46], p. 94.

legation staff, and on Tuesday, the 20th, one of the servants told Cole, "Policeman stopee outside, I think." He also heard a rumor that Sun was to be released: "Minister no longer keep this man . . . Chinese Emperor no wantee now." Up to the last, Macartney tried to keep his staff in line, and on the 22nd gave Cole and the other English servant a sovereign each with a promise of a better reward when "all this is over."[80] Cole, of course, had already done his damage and was hoping for a bigger prize.

Having checked the legation's transportation plan, the Foreign Office was now ready to deal with the problem of extricating Sun. Salisbury obtained the Attorney-General's opinion that the detention was a violation of diplomatic privilege.[81] In addition, an Old Bailey judge to whom Cantlie and Manson, acting on the advice of the police, had applied for a writ of habeas corpus against the legation, had asserted that the affair required a diplomatic and not a legal solution.[82] By this time, October 22, the Foreign Office decided to take direct action. It was felt that there would be a "great outcry" should Sun be spirited out of the country and the public learn that the government had known of the scheme but done nothing to foil it.

First it was decided to call Macartney for an explanation, but he could not be reached. In the meantime, Salisbury wrote a strongly worded note to the Chinese Minister requesting Sun's immediate release.[83] In the early evening before the letter was dispatched, Macartney finally appeared at the Foreign Office. He readily admitted that Sun was detained, but contended that he had entered of his own volition after an earlier visit on the 9th. He assured the Foreign Office that Kung would comply with Salisbury's request when apprised of it, but stated that the

[80] *Ibid.*, p. 118.

[81] *Ibid.*, p. 55.

[82] With the assistance of Inspector Jarvis, Cantlie and Manson saw a solicitor on October 22 and presented affidavits to Justice Wright at the Central Criminal Court. The judge declined to issue the writ against the legation because of diplomatic privilege, but submitted an opinion that a solution should be sought through diplomatic channels, and encouraged the Foreign Office to exert pressure. See FO 17/1718 [46], pp. 27–32.

[83] *Ibid.*, pp. 24–25.

Tsungli Yamen's confirmation was required. The British then pressed for immediate action, and without contesting Macartney's version of Sun's entry, they warned him that "serious steps on the part of Her Majesty's Government" were justified in view of the Chinese violation of diplomatic privilege. Macartney promised to relay this message to Kung and left. In the meantime Salisbury's letter was dispatched and received at the Legation at 9:50 P.M.[84]

The Foreign Office had warned Macartney that the *Times* was temporarily holding back a story on the affair, but on the 22nd the *Globe*, less concerned about official policy, got wind of the case through the Old Bailey proceedings. The paper interviewed Cantlie and then put out a special edition which broke the case in sensational fashion.[85] Here were all the ingredients of a thriller spiced with a sinister Oriental flavor. As reporters hounded the legation Teng again tried his evasive tactics, but one reporter told him that if Sun were not released in the morning the legation would be ringed by an indignant mob of Londoners.[86]

The reporters finally found Macartney at the Midland Railway Hotel in the evening. (This was apparently where he had been staying when Cantlie was looking for him.) "Incredulous that the story of Sun's arrest had obtained circulation," he admitted that Sun was detained but refused to say what the legation contemplated doing with him. He defended their position with the same argument he had used at the Foreign Office and contended that the case would have to be decided by "professors of International Law."[87]

No one else was waiting for the decision of the professors, and on the following day, October 23, every paper in London carried the story. Overnight Sun's detention had become a cause célèbre and with public sympathy overwhelmingly on Sun's side,

[84] *Ibid.*, pp. 24, 54–60.
[85] The "special edition" of October 22 is not available but the story was reprinted in the October 23rd issue.
[86] Lo Chia-lun, *Biography* [192], I, 71.
[87] *London Daily Telegraph*, October 23, 1896; *The Globe*, October 23, 1896.

the Foreign Office stiffened its attitude. Macartney called at 1:30 to report that, considering Kung's poor health, he had thought it better to wait until that morning before communicating the gist of the verbal message he had received the previous evening. Sanderson then asked him if he knew that Salisbury's letter had been delivered. Macartney replied that it had been brought to him by the Minister's son. He then went on to say that he would try to persuade Kung to release Sun on his own responsibility, and to inform the Yamen that he was doing so; but it would facilitate matters, he said, if he could give an assurance that if Sun returned to Hong Kong, the British would prevent him from engaging in subversive activities. Since the Sino-Japanese War, he pointed out, conspiracies had become frequent and they were in many cases directed from the Crown Colony.

Sanderson said that he had not known of such activities, but that the British would give friendly consideration to any Chinese request for cooperation. Hoping to salvage some honor from what was turning into a diplomatic debacle, Macartney stated that "it would be of assistance that the Minister should be able to telegraph that he had released the man on receiving an assurance to this effect." But the British were in no mood for a quid pro quo. Sanderson replied that the "ground on which Her Majesty's Government required that the man should be released at once was that his detention was illegal," and that he had no authority for giving the assurance Macartney requested. If the Minister did not comply with their demand, he went on, the British would feel justified in requesting his immediate recall. He also aimed a threat at Macartney: they would be prepared to withdraw the diplomatic privilege "from any British Subjects on the staff of the Legation who were concerned in the matter."

Macartney begged that they hold off a further ultimatum until four o'clock, at which time he hoped to have Kung's decision. Sanderson agreed while warning that they would not consent to Sun's remaining another night in the legation. At this time they also discussed the manner in which the release would be carried out. Shortly before four o'clock Macartney returned and announced that the Chinese Minister, while "reserving his rights and privileges," would let Sun go.[88]

The legation was the scene of tremendous excitement.[89] While clerks and interpreters were scurrying about, reporters and spectators swarmed around the entrance, where detectives were still posted. Some of the journalists even got inside and made themselves at home while awaiting the denouement. At 4:30, a Queen's Home Messenger sent by the Foreign Office, Scotland Yard Chief Inspector Jarvis, and the ubiquitous Dr. Cantlie turned up to claim the captive.[90] A few minutes later, Macartney, who had not forgotten to return the coins confiscated with Sun's messages, ordered the prisoner downstairs to the basement and handed him over. Sun was taken in a carriage to Scotland Yard before the stampeding reporters could reach him, and after submitting a statement, went home with Cantlie to recover from the ordeal.[91]

But this was no time for retirement into the shadows. Sun discovered that he was famous and seized the opportunity to rebuke his enemies and glorify the anti-Manchu cause. The next day the reporters clamored for interviews and found Sun "not disinclined to talk of his incarceration." The journalists were favorably impressed and one wrote of his "comely features" and his "diminutive stature."[92] Though tired, he told in an "unfaltering voice" how he had been "decoyed" into the legation, and it was observed that he spoke English "remarkably well" but with a definite foreign accent.[93] Editorial writers mixed indignation with humor in discussing the legation's scheme, and when even the *Times* saw fit to criticize the Chinese, Macartney tried to discredit the "kidnapping" charge, but his arguments were no match for Sun's dramatic story.

[88] FO 17/1718 [46], pp. 69–75.
[89] *London Daily Telegraph*, October 24, 1896.
[90] *The Globe*, October 24, 1896; Inspector Jarvis' report, in FO 17/1718 [46], p. 79.
[91] FO 17/1718 [46], p. 120.
[92] *The Globe*, October 24, 1896.
[93] *Ibid.*; *London Daily Telegraph*, October 24, 1896.

The letter which Sun sent to the *Times* and other metropolitan papers on the day after his release reflected his faith in the British public's sense of fair play, and his own astute handling of public relations. He wrote:

Will you kindly express through your columns my keen appreciation of the action of the British Government in effecting my release from the Chinese Legation. I have also to thank the Press generally for their timely help and sympathy. If anything was needed to convince me of the generous public spirit which pervades Great Britain, and the love of justice which distinguishes its people, the recent acts of the last few days have conclusively done so. Knowing and feeling more keenly than ever what a constitutional government and an enlightened people mean, I am prepared to pursue the cause of advancement, education, and civilization, in my own beloved but oppressed country.[94]

At the request of Professor H. A. Giles of Cambridge, to whom he was introduced by Cantlie, he prepared a short biography, and with the help of an editor, he wrote a stirring account of his recent adventure, entitled *Kidnapped in London*.[95] Published in England in 1897, this little book did more than anything else before the 1911 revolution to spread the name of Sun Yat-sen abroad. In May 1897, *Kidnapped in London* was already on sale in Shanghai. Hirayama Shū, the China-oriented Japanese adventurer who became one of Sun's intimates, bought a copy and was deeply impressed.[96] In Tokyo, Ch'en Shao-pai proudly displayed the book to Miyazaki Torazō, who became a key figure in the

[94] Appended to Sun, *Kidnapped in London* [115], p. 133; Sun also wrote a special letter of thanks to *The Globe* on October 26th.

[95] Lo Chia-lun, *Biography* [192], I, 72; this autobiography was entitled *Life of Sun Yat-sen by Himself*; see also Lo Hsiang-lin, *Sun's University Days* [195], p. 88. In his letter to Felix Volkhovsky, the Russian revolutionary, in March 15, 1897, Sun wrote that he could not write anything "in perfect English without a friend's help." The letter is attached to Volkhovsky's copy of *Kidnapped in London*, now in the Hoover Library at Stanford University.

[96] This was mentioned by Hirayama in a letter to the Kuomintang Committee on the Party's History; see Ch'en Hsi-ch'i, *Before the T'ung Meng Hui* [151], p. 50.

subsequent collaboration between Chinese revolutionaries and the Japanese.[97]

In Hong Kong the *China Mail*, which a year earlier had blamed the Canton failure on the lack of leadership and had demanded Western direction of any future uprising,[98] took a new look at Sun and found an indigenous leader worthy of his nation's cause:

Sun Yat-sen . . . is not unlikely to become a prominent character in history, [for] it may be safely said that he is a remarkable man, with most enlightened views on the undoubtedly miserable state of China's millions . . . . Dr. Sun worked hard and loyally to fuse the inchoate elements of disaffection brought into existence by Manchu misgovernment and to give the whole reform movement a purely constitutional form. . . . His was the mastermind that strove to subdue the wild uncontrollable spirits always prominent in Chinese reactionary [sic] schemes, to harmonise conflicting interests, not only as between various parties in his own country but also as between Chinese and foreigners, and as between foreign Powers . . . . Moreover he had to bear in mind that any great reform movement must necessarily depend very largely on the aid of foreigners . . . while there is throughout China an immense mass of anti-foreign prejudice which would have to be overcome. . . . Dr. Sun was the only man who combined a complete grasp of the situation with a reckless bravery of the kind which alone can make a national regeneration. . . . He is of average height, thin and wiry, with a keenness of expression and frankness of feature seldom seen in Chinese. . . . Beneath his calm exterior is hidden a personality that cannot but be a great influence for good in China sooner or later, if the Fates are fair. . .[99]

In London, Sun did his best to live up to this new image. He attended church under the watchful eyes of the press, and whether it was at his initiative or not, the *Globe* even implied

[97] Lo Chia-lun, *Biography* [192], I, 76; Jansen, *Sun Yat-sen* [69], p. 65.

[98] *Overland China Mail*, October 30, 1895.

[99] *The China Mail*, December 3, 1896; this article, entitled "The Supposed Chinese Revolutionist," is appended to Sun's *Kidnapped in London* [115], pp. 113–120.

that he would stay in England for a while to help Cantlie train Chinese medical missionaries.[100] He also made it a point to visit Timothy Richard soon after his liberation. The endorsement of this well-known China missionary would have been an important achievement, but Richard would not go along with Sun's anti-Manchuism nor was he prepared to jeopardize his work in China by supporting a rebel.[101]

Other Britishers lacked Richard's reservations and Sun received numerous congratulatory letters and a host of admiring visitors.[102] Among his more active sympathizers from this period was Rowland J. Mulkern, the British soldier who later participated in the Waichow campaign of 1900.[103] Sun also had the satisfaction of finding his name mentioned in Parliament, when in February 1897 Sir Edward Gourley questioned Sanderson about the legation's behavior and the personal responsibility of Sir Halliday Macartney.[104] Sun then learned that Salisbury had reprimanded the Chinese government for infringing its diplomatic privilege. At this time too he may have become acquainted with or at least attracted the interest of Michael Davitt, the Irish patriot, land reform agitator, and M. P., who in 1898 openly declared his sympathy with the revolutionary cause in China.[105]

Most important of all, the kidnapping episode strengthened Sun's self-confidence and sense of dedication. It convinced him that the Supreme Power had forestalled his enemies to preserve him for some high purpose. These personal religious overtones

100 *The Globe*, October 26, 1896.
101 Richard, *Forty-five Years* [96], p. 350.
102 *The Globe*, October 26, 1896.
103 Lo Chia-lun, *Biography* [192], I, 95, gives this name as "Morgan," but most Chinese sources refer to "Mulkern." See Lo Hsiang-lin, *Sun's University Days* [195], p. 119, note 79; Chin P'ing-ou (ed.), *Concordance of the San-min Chu-i* [155], p. 524, under "Mo-ken." Using the Hong Kong newspapers and Foreign Office and Colonial Office files, I have been able to identify him as Rowland J. Mulkern. In his letter to the London *Standard* in January 1898, protesting Sun's banishment from Hong Kong, Mulkern identifies himself as the secretary of the Friends of China Society. See FO 17/1718 [46], p. 163, clipping from *London Evening News* of January 11, 1898.
104 FO 17/1718 [46], p. 154.
105 CO 129/286, no. 7377 and no. 15766, April 2 and July 15, 1898 [46].

were sounded in a private letter to his friend and teacher in Hong Kong, the Christian minister Ch'ü Feng-ch'ih: "I am like the prodigal son and the lost sheep: I owe everything to the great favor of God. Through the Way of God I hope to enter into the Political Way. I hope you will not cease to write to me about the Way of God. . . ."[106]

The twelve-day imprisonment thus transformed Sun from a comparatively insignificant Cantonese rebel into a well publicized and extremely confident enemy of the Manchu regime. The actions of the Chinese government spoke for themselves. In the eyes of the world, the Manchu regime represented evil, duplicity, and as Sun liked to call it, "Tartar" cruelty, while Sun Yat-sen carried the twin banners of enlightenment and Christianity. Sun's victory at Portland Place helped erase the memory of the mis-managed defeat at Canton a year earlier. As a spur to his determination and optimism, it left a permanent mark upon his personality.

The Plea for "Benevolent Neutrality"

But just how decisive was this victory? Sun Yat-sen was not content with claiming a tremendous personal and propaganda triumph. He wanted it translated into official endorsement of the revolution. In that sense, the "kidnapping" episode fell short of his expectations. One of the basic premises of the Canton plot had been that the West, and especially Britain, would recognize its common interest in the anti-dynastic cause. Sun's clash with the legation not only reinforced this conviction but inflated it to unrealistic proportions. His detention, he reported further to Ch'ü Feng-ch'ih, "shook the entire country, agitated Europe and every country in the world." He boasted of the wave of indignation which threatened to "tear down the Legation" and which finally forced Salisbury to press for his release.[107] It was this kind of force, sweeping along with it the highest echelons

---

106 This letter appears in Sun, *Collected Works* [205], V, 15–16; the excerpt has been taken from Sharman's translation, *Sun Yat-sen* [107], pp. 47–48.

107 Sun, *Collected Works* [205], V, 16.

of government, which Sun hoped to unleash against the Manchus.

But public concern over a kidnapping by Oriental agents in the middle of London was one thing, political support of the revolution another. The British government already had ample proof of Chinese crudeness in administering justice. This further demonstration could hardly be expected to shake the foundations of its China policy. Yet Sun thought that it had made all the difference in the world. Five months after his sensational splash in the British press, he requested British approval of the "Reform Party's" struggle against the Manchus and mandarins. With the assistance of one Edwin Collins, he wrote an article, "China's Present and Future: The Reform Party's Plea for British Benevolent Neutrality," which appeared in the *Fortnightly Review* of March 1, 1897. It is interesting to note how in offering credentials as a serious and sober influence in Chinese politics, Sun distorted his earlier relationship with the literati bureaucrats; it was not that they rejected him but that he had disdained to join their corrupt ranks:

Of myself it may be sufficient to say that before I adopted the study of medicine, my early years were spent in intimate association with members of the Chinese official class, and that my friends were anxious for me to purchase an entry into public life, as very many of my acquaintances have done within the last ten years. Thus I have had every opportunity and incentive to study the subject on which I am now writing.[108]

In analyzing China's ills, Sun distinguished between the people and their rulers. In the ruling category he placed both the Manchus and the Chinese bureaucrats. Though the Manchus, he charged, benefited from the bureaucratic system and were incapable of reforming it, it was the system itself which was the source of Chinese backwardness. It was not the Chinese people but the Manchu-Chinese ruling complex which was corrupt, cowardly, and anti-foreign. A government which recruited its personnel through bribery and favoritism could neither modern-

---

[108] *Fortnightly Review* [116], p. 425. This article does not appear in any edition of Sun's collected works which I have seen.

ize the country nor defend its borders. He asserted that Li Hung-chang's technological innovations could be expected to remake China as much as one could expect "the conversion of cannibals to vegetarianism by the introduction of silver forks and Sheffield cutlery."[109] As for his own solution, Sun stated categorically that:

Nothing short of the entire overthrow of the present utterly corrupt regime, and the establishment of good government and a pure administration by native Chinese with, at first, European advice, and, for some years, European administrative assistance, can effect any improvement whatever. The mere introduction of railways, or any such appliances of the material civilization of Europe, would (even were it as feasible as those who put their faith in Li Hung Chang seem to think) rather make matters worse, by opening up new channels for extortion, fraud, and peculation. . . . Here it may be enough to say that the benevolent neutrality of Great Britain, and the other Powers, is all the aid needed to enable us to make the present system give place to one that is not corrupt. . . .[110]

The substance of his appeal was essentially the same as Ho Kai's. Ho in 1887 had attributed China's troubles to her "loose morality," and Sun now claimed that even her "physical evils are of moral origin." Echoing Ho's arguments of 1895, Sun promised that China under a new government would provide Britain with the commercial and investment opportunities which the Manchus had not granted, and that she would be strong enough to alleviate British worries over Russian encroachment. The promise that foreign advisers would be liberally employed was designed to assure his readers that reform would be undertaken seriously and that British influence would help to shape the new administration. That his own movement was capable of rallying the popular support and talent necessary for reform, Sun left no room for doubt. He boasted of wide support in the army, and by using the term "Reform Party" gave the impression that he spoke for the wide spectrum of progressive elements including the literati reformers who were already active. In addi-

[109] *Ibid.*, p. 438.
[110] *Ibid.*, pp. 424–425; 440.

tion, by concluding that the Manchus, against whom he asserted that "the whole people" were ranged, were the major obstacle to change, and ignoring his own evidence to the contrary, he posed the problem of Chinese modernization in highly simple terms.[111] The dynasty was about to topple; the reformers were prepared to take over, and all that was needed was the foreigners' "benevolent neutrality."

British policymakers could subscribe to the ultimate aims which Sun professed, but they had no more reason to encourage his political activities after the kidnapping than they had had in 1895. During this period, as Lord Curzon put it, Britain's aim in China was "to preserve in an age of competition what we had gained in an age of monopoly."[112] With other powers, and in particular Russia, competing for privileges and influence in China, the British were hardly likely to offend Peking by encouraging a subversive movement, even one that professed to be pro-British. As long as the Manchu dynasty was in a position to disburse favors to foreigners or deny them, Britain was not likely to gamble on a dark horse. Having a much larger stake in China than any other country, she could least afford involvement in Sun's political adventures. While Britain favored reform in China—in the hope of opening further channels for trade and investment—the immediate end of her policy was not the modernization of China, but the protection of her present advantages.

Actually, the one tangible gesture of approval which Sun Yat-sen sought during this time was only a small favor—the right to return to Hong Kong, the birthplace of his revolutionary ideas. For Sun, admission to Hong Kong would remain the test of Britain's policy, and aside from a brief interval in 1901–1902, he had to wait fifteen years before his expected election to the provisional presidency of the republic made him eligible for landing but not residing in the British colony. This banishment policy was established in the beginning of 1896 and reinforced

111 *Ibid.*, p. 440.
112 Quoted by 'Diplomaticus' in "Lord Salisbury's New China Policy" [32], *Fortnightly Review*, 65:524, April 1, 1899.

in the fall, just a few days after Sun's release from the legation.

Though the initial Chinese request for extradition had been turned down by Hong Kong after the Canton plot, neither Governor Robinson nor his superiors in London wanted the colony to be further involved in anti-dynastic plotting. On March 4, 1896, therefore, having been convinced of Sun's guilt and having learned—probably by way of the Canton yamen—that Sun was raising money in Hawaii for a new plot, Robinson felt that Sun's return to Hong Kong would be "very undesirable." With the approval of the Executive Council, he issued a five-year Order of Banishment against Sun, to take effect one month after the date of issue.[113]

Relations between Canton and Hong Kong were nevertheless strained by the refusal to extradite Sun, though he had already left the colony when the request came through. What rankled Governor-General T'an was the British attitude that "no one to be beheaded could be given up."[114] Other plots were anticipated, and British diplomats feared that relations with China would suffer as long as sedition remained an unextraditable offense.[115] So great was the desire to mollify the Chinese that in the summer of 1896, Robinson and Sir Claude Macdonald, the Minister in Peking, actually suggested surrendering this well-established principle of English law. Their only concern was that Peking might interpret the concession as a sign of weakness, and they therefore proposed that a quid pro quo be required in the form of a Chinese cession of territory to Hong Kong on the Kowloon side. Though the scheme was firmly rejected by London—Salisbury anticipated a parliamentary row and foreign complications, while Colonial Secretary Chamberlain was mor-

[113] CO 129/271, Robinson to Chamberlain, no. 62, March 11, 1896 [46]; a copy of the banishment order is enclosed in CO 129/283, Black to Chamberlain, no. 144, May 18, 1898 [46]. A fresh banishment order was issued in 1902, after Sun made a brief visit, and was "apparently" renewed in June 1907. See FO 371/1095, No. 46374, November 21, 1911 [46].

[114] CO 129/272, enclosed in Robinson's confidential letter to Chamberlain, July 7, 1896 [46]. T'an's memorial is dated March 11, 1896.

[115] *Ibid.*, Fraser to Beauclerk, April 9, enclosed in Robinson to Chamberlain, July 7, 1896 [46].

ally repelled at the thought of trading Chinese political refugees for territory—its very consideration reveals the realistic bases of British policy.[116]

The kidnapping of Sun Yat-sen aroused a certain degree of moral outrage in Britain, but British officials were quick to assure the Chinese that they had no sympathy for anti-dynastic plots. Though the Tsungli Yamen was rebuked for the undiplomatic behavior of its Minister in London,[117] Salisbury readily accepted the Chinese demand that Hong Kong should not be turned into a "base for movements directed against the tranquility of the Empire."[118] The Colonial Office then ordered Robinson to "anticipate and frustrate any revolutionary attempts against the constituted authority in China."[119] Thus, long before he wrote his article, the British had already posted their reply to Sun Yat-sen's request for "benevolent neutrality."

Sun waited until his return to the East before protesting this decision. In the meantime, as if aspiring to fit himself for the leadership role which he had assumed upon his release, he made a concentrated effort to broaden his knowledge. According to Slater's reports, which were still being sent to the legation, Sun spent most of his time during the first five months of 1897 in the reading room of the British Museum Library.[120] Cantlie, too, reports:

Sun wasted no moments in gaieties; he was forever at work, reading books on all subjects which appertained to political, diplomatic, legal, military, and naval matters; mines and mining, agriculture, cattle rearing, engineering, political economy, etc., occupied his

---

[116] *Ibid.*, see various enclosures in Robinson to Chamberlain, July 7, 1896 [46].

[117] FO 17/1718 [46], pp. 156–160.

[118] CO 129/274, no. 22701, October 26, 1896 [46].

[119] *Ibid.*, October 31, 1896. Robinson acknowledged these instructions in his dispatch to Chamberlain of January 5, 1897, in CO 129/275, no. 2542 [46].

[120] Lo Chia-lun, *Sun's Kidnapping* [191], appendix, p. 151. Had Slater's been more efficient, we might have a better idea as to whom Sun was meeting during this period besides Dr. Cantlie. His frequent and lengthy visits to 12 Albert Road from the end of October through December aroused the detectives' curiosity, but they were unable to satisfy it.

attention and were studied closely and persistently. The range of his opportunities for acquiring knowledge has been such as few men have ever had.[121]

Though it is questionable whether even as voracious a reader as Sun was reported to be could have digested so many books in less than half a year, there is no doubt that he became more politically sophisticated. He probably learned about Marx, Henry George (who was particularly in vogue in Britain at this time), Mill, Montesquieu, and others.[122] In addition, he made numerous personal contacts, including some among Russian political exiles.

One of these Russians was apparently Felix Volkhovsky (1846–1914), editor of *Free Russia*, the monthly organ of the English "Society of Friends of Russian Freedom." Convicted because of his liberal political views, Volkhovsky had endured seven years of solitary confinement in St. Petersburg's Schlusselburg fortress, and eleven years of exile in Siberia, before escaping to Canada in 1889 under the alias "F. Brant." He settled in London a year later.[123] Meeting a man of Volkhovsky's courage and determination must have been an enlightening and inspiring experience for Sun, just when he was being initiated into the hazards of a revolutionary career. These Russians, who continued to struggle against a much more efficient and ruthless tyranny than that of the Manchus, were the first foreign revolutionaries whom Sun met.[124]

[121] Cantlie and Jones, *Sun Yat-sen* [17], p. 242.
[122] For a discussion of George's influence in Britain, see H. Schiffrin and Pow-key Sohn, "Henry George" [102].
[123] Volkhovsky's copy of *Kidnapped in London* contains the inscription, "F. Volkhovsky Esq. with compliments of Sun Yat Sen.' Sun's letter of March 15, 1897 (see footnote 95) is a further indication of their acquaintanceship. On Volkhovsky, who later joined the Social Revolutionaries, see *Free Russia* [43], pp. 13, 15–16; and *Bolshaia Sovetskaia Entsiklopedia* [8], V. 12, pp. 822–823.
[124] Sun was probably referring to this period when in 1924 he mentioned meeting Russian exiles in a London library some time in the past. After an exchange of views, he recalled, they realized that they were all revolutionaries, and the Russians asked him how long it would take for the consummation of the Chinese revolution. Although he expected to organize

Contacts such as these, together with his intensive reading, infused Sun with a new understanding of European political trends. He became convinced that revolution, in some form or another, was a universal process. His first week in London had impressed him with the immensity of Europe's accomplishment, but when he left nine months later he realized that the industrial revolution had not been beneficial to all segments of Western society. The first visit to the West laid the basis for his future antagonism to laissez-faire capitalism. What he saw and read gave Sun reason to believe that nothing short of a violent upheaval could provide a remedy for the lack of social concern which had accompanied Western political and economic development. The signs of the coming turmoil and class strife were all around him: Socialists and Fabians in Britain, Populists and Single-taxers in America—all were protesting against the unjust distribution of wealth. Labor unions were coming into their own and resorting to strikes with ominous frequency. Even non-socialist governments were passing social legislation, and change in the direction of socialism, or further state intervention in the economic order, now appeared inevitable.[125] The only question was whether evolutionary methods would be sufficient, and Sun, according to his recollection, saw the future of Europe in terms of social revolution:

After escaping from danger in London, I stayed in Europe to carry out studies of its political practices and make the acquaintance of its leading politicians. During these two years [sic] what I saw and

---

another rising within the following few years and was optimistic over its chances of success, he decided to make a conservative estimate of thirty years. This astonished the Russians, who felt that in a country as large as China, a much longer period would be necessary. They themselves were satisfied with the hope that Russia would undergo a successful revolution within 100 years. (See Sun's speech of January 20, 1924, at the Kuomintang conference in Canton, in Sun, *Collected Works* [205], III, 350–351); for an earlier but briefer reference to this meeting with the Russians see his speech of October 11, 1923, in *ibid.*, 260–261.

[125] For a graphic description of the "fruits of industrialism" in the last decade of the 19th century, see Geoffrey Bruun, *European Civilization* [15]; Crane Brinton, *English Political Thought* [11], provides a lucid discussion of trends in British thinking during this period.

heard made a tremendous impression upon me. For the first time
I understood that though the European powers achieved national
wealth and power, they were not able to give their peoples full hap-
piness. For this reason, European men of determination were still
striving for a social revolution. I now wanted to create a single-
effort, eternal plan which would simultaneously solve the problems
of socialism, nationalism, and democracy. The Three Principles of
the People which I advocated were perfected from this [idea].[126]

Sun's memory failed him with respect to at least one statement
in this memoir; he was not in England for two years nor did
he visit any other European country, and I suspect that the
Three Principles were not so clearly formed at this time as
he recalled more than twenty years later.[127] When he became
famous, he found it much more attractive to attribute his political ideas to direct Western influence than to acknowledge his
intellectual debt to Japanese or, even worse, Chinese rivals like
Liang Ch'i-ch'ao. Yet the recollection of the impression rings
true. He saw the seamy side of the industrial revolution and
caught a glimpse of a possible advantage to his undeveloped
China; by taking preventive measures she could avoid the social
dislocation which had accompanied Western material progress.
Exactly how this was to be accomplished, however, was something that required further thought and stimulating inter-
change. Sun was not so much an original thinker as one who

[126] Sun, in *Collected Works* [205], II, 84. Sun later wrote that Lincoln's
"of the people, by the people, for the people" foreshadowed the spirit of
his three principles. See Sun's speech of June, 1921, in *ibid.*, III, 192; and
also *ibid.*, VI, 104.

[127] Some writers who have otherwise been careful in using Sun's auto-
biographical data, have in this instance perpetuated the notion of a two-
year stay in Europe after his detention. See, for example, Sharman, *Sun Yat-
sen* [107], pp. 58–59, and Jansen, *Sun Yat-sen* [69], p. 63, but the latter
corrects himself on p. 67 and note 23 on p. 241, when he cites authoritative
Japanese sources which show that Sun returned to the East no later than a
year after the kidnapping episode. In this as in other instances, I am indebted to the meticulous scholarship of Lo Chia-lun, who brought to light
Slater's reports which prove that Sun left England for Canada in July 1897
and did not make any stops on the continent. As described in the text, Sun
sailed for Japan from the west coast of Canada in the beginning of August.
See Lo Chia-lun, *Biography* [192], I, 75–76.

was highly sensitive to the people and currents of thought around him.

London had turned him into an international figure and broadened his knowledge. But when he left England on July 2, 1897, he still had no real organization behind him.[128] This was a deficiency for which he knew only one way to compensate: personal appeals for funds, conspiracy, and high-level intrigue.

Sun's return trip, by way of Canada this time, was uneventful, though it is worth noting that the legation still kept Slater's on his heels. From their reports we learn that Sun stayed in his cabin for practically the entire voyage and was only on deck for two or three hours. The ship's doctor, in fact, had to advise him several times to take more exercise, and it was noticed that he did not join the general conversation during mealtimes. This newly acquired reticence was probably the result of his increased respect for the Manchu intelligence service. In Canada his movements were extremely well-covered, since Slater's correspondents exhibited an ingenuity which was entirely lacking in the London office. From their reports, it appears that Sun acted very cautiously when he landed in Montreal on July 11 and joined some Chinese friends. He wrote his name "Y. S. Sims," and tried to hide his movements. Yet Slater's assiduous correspondents were even able to report the contents of two letters which he wrote to American *hua-ch'iao* supporters, a Walter N. Fong in San Francisco and an S. C. Chew of Boston. He tried to encourage his friends to raise money by painting a glowing picture of the movement's progress in China.[129]

In Montreal, Sun asked about the *Empress of India*, which was scheduled to sail for Yokohama from Vancouver on August 2, 1897. At first he was afraid that Chinese officials, returning to China from Queen Victoria's Diamond Jubilee celebration, would be among his fellow-passengers, but then he discovered that only the Japanese delegation would be on board. On his way west, he collected funds from the local *hua-ch'iao*, and in Vancouver and Victoria, where he devoted a few days to polit-

---

[128] Lo Chia-lun, *Biography* [192], I, 75.
[129] Lo Chia-lun, *Sun's Kidnapping* [191], appendix, pp. 156–170.

ical work, he enjoyed the hospitality of Chinese Methodists. He was apparently successful in his fund raising because he was able to pay one hundred dollars extra to change from intermediate class to a stateroom on the *Empress*, when he boarded it using his own name. At this point the detectives were called off the job by the new Minister in London, Lo Feng-lu, who undoubtedly remembered Sun from Li Hung-chang's yamen three years earlier.[130] In Japan there would be others to take up the watch. Yet Sun continued to expose himself. Courage was one leadership virtue he possessed in abundance.

[130] Lo Chia-lun, *Biography* [192], I, 76.

VI

Tokyo and the Re-infiltration of the Mainland

The years after 1896 were devoted to industrious exercise in the art of political sleight-of-hand, a more complex performance than even Sun had yet attempted. Reformist literati, secret society elders, old-fashioned gentry, Filipino independence fighters, imperialist agents, and anti-imperialist firebrands—all became the objects of Sun's untiring penchant for negotiating and plotting. Often various courses were pursued simultaneously, and the thread is not easily followed. From his arrival in Japan in 1897 until at least 1900, however, reliable traces of Sun's movements and schemes may be found in the activities of that romantic band of Japanese adventurers who were not only privy to all his plans, but were often their originators.

During Sun's absence, Ch'en Shao-pai had discovered that influential Japanese, motivated either by idealism or chauvinism or a mixture of both, were looking for a Chinese "hero" who, with their assistance, could save his country from Western imperialism.[1] Through Sugawara Den and other contacts, Ch'en met Miyazaki Yazō and then his brother Torazō, both ex-samurai pan-Asians dedicated to the idea of rallying the yellow race under Japanese leadership. Yazō died soon afterward, but his brother, commissioned by the prominent liberal statesman Inukai Ki to sound out Chinese reformers, became

---

[1] See Marius B. Jansen, *Sun Yat-sen* [69], Chapters I and II; this pioneer study gives the most complete account of the premises of Japan's China policy and of Sun's relations with both the Japanese government and the ex-samurai adventurers.

interested in the Hsing Chung Hui.[2] Ch'en, anxious to make an impression, showed him *Kidnapped in London* and tried to gloss over the real state of organizational affairs at home. Since Miyazaki was about to join other Japanese agents in China, Ch'en gave him the names of several sympathizers in Hong Kong, Macao, and Canton.[3] Once he had reached his comrade Hirayama Shū in China, Miyazaki tried to pursue Ch'en's leads. The first, a certain Ho Shu-ling, proved uncooperative, but Pastor Ch'ü Feng-ch'ih welcomed the offer of Japanese assistance and disclosed that Sun was due in Yokohama the next day. Eager to meet the revolutionary leader, the two Japanese departed for home immediately.[4]

Sun arrived in Yokohama about August 10, 1897.[5] After a warm reunion with Ch'en Shao-pai, it was decided that Sun would take over the Japanese contacts, while his friend would try his luck in Taiwan, whose recent annexation by the Japanese presumably offered fertile grounds for revolutionary agitation. A Japanese friend had invited Ch'en to the island and there he also found Yang Hsin-ju, recently established in business after fleeing from Canton. Yang was a cousin of Yang Ho-ling, whose Hong Kong store had been the center for political discussions in Sun's medical school days. Ch'en had been marking time in Japan for almost two years and was anxious for the feel of action.[6] Thus while one conspirator prepared to offer himself for Japanese tutelage, the other prepared to rally the discontented victims of Japanese aggression. This combination was no more paradoxical than Sun's attempted collaboration with the British, who were in the forefront of the imperialist assault upon China.

Sun moved into Ch'en's quarters in Yokohama, and there Miyazaki found him in the autumn of 1897. Already aware of

[2] *Ibid.*, pp. 64–65; Ch'en Shao-pai, *Hsing Chung Hui* [152], pp. 19–21.
[3] Ch'en Shao-pai, *Hsing Chung Hui* [152], p. 21.
[4] Lo Chia-lun, *Biography* [192], I, 76; Jansen, *Sun Yat-sen* [69], p. 65.
[5] Lo Chia-lun, *Biography* [192], I, 76.
[6] Ch'en Shao-pai, *Hsing Chung Hui* [152], pp. 22–23; Feng, in *Documents* [179], III, 348, under "Yang Hsin-ju."

Sun's reputation, Miyazaki Torazō wanted to probe deeper and assess his potentialities as a leader of the Chinese revolution and pan-Asianism. Despite the difficulty in communication—they had no language in common—Sun was usually at his best in face-to-face encounters and attuned his replies to the mood of his interlocutor. When Miyazaki asked for details of Sun's program and strategy, he replied that he held self-rule to be the highest principle of government, yet as long as China was under the sway of a "foreign race" (the Manchus), the revolution could not be confined to this single constitutional issue. For three hundred years the Manchus had deceived and degraded the Chinese people and had finally reduced the country to its current weakness.[7]

In support of his argument, Sun drew attention to the innately progressive qualities of the Chinese race. Contradicting those who claimed that China was too primitive for republicanism, Sun contended that the spirit and essence of republicanism had been foreshadowed by China's ancient sages and manifested in the Three Dynasties (Hsia, Shang and Chou). That the people still venerated the teachings of these sages was proof of their progressive spirit and idealism. Their local institutions attested to the people's ability to rule themselves and promote the general welfare. Were these not the attributes of what modern times is called a republic? The people's "patriotic determination" could be excited and their "progressive spirit" awakened, he claimed, "if only a hero would rise who would overthrow the Manchus . . . replace them with beneficent rule, agree upon laws . . . and satisfy their hunger and thirst."[8]

[7] Miyazaki Torazō, *Thirty-three Years' Dream* [200], pp. 144–145.
[8] *Ibid.*, pp. 145–146. The Chinese expression for the term "agree upon [a code of] laws" is *yüeh-fa*, which in the modern language means "provisional constitution." If Miyazaki's recollection of this conversation is correct, it means that at this time Sun was already thinking about his famous tutelary or second stage in the attainment of constitutional government. In 1905 the *yüeh-fa* proposal became part of the program of the T'ung Meng Hui, and in 1914 this second stage was renamed *hsün-cheng* or "tutelage." It is furthermore interesting to note that during the begining of the Former Han dynasty (206 B.C.), after Liu Pang cancelled the legal code of the Ch'in dynasty, he instituted a brief set of basic laws (*yüeh-fa*) "in three articles."

Sun then tried to show that the only missing element in previous dynastic overthrows was the concept of republicanism, especially a federated variety. Periods of turbulence had given rise to regional warlords, whose rivalry had prolonged disunity and finally allowed for a seizure of power by barbarian invaders or bandits. The way to avoid the catastrophes of the past, he declared, was to carry out revolution which is "as swift as a clap of thunder," and promulgate a republican constitution. Regional heroes would be appeased by granting them autonomy within a federation, while the central government would be strong enough to restrain any one of them.[9]

Evidently Sun had been thinking about past precedents in Chinese history and was groping for ways to break out of the old pattern of dynastic rise and fall. His confident assertion that a new formula, federated republicanism, would change this pattern, and that the Chinese could readily assimilate modern political institutions, reflected the optimism which became so characteristic of his later ideological phase.

To Miyazaki, this was sufficient proof that Sun was no run-of-the-mill anti-Manchuist, but someone with the education and intellectual capacity to provide modern political leadership. And when Sun added pan-Asian, anti-imperialist sentiments to his anti-Manchuism, Miyazaki was completely won over. "The vast territory of my China and her massive population," Sun lamented, "are like meat on a platter which ravenous tigers devour." Instead of using their wealth to support the "way of humanity" (*jen-tao*) and bring order into the world, the major powers terrorize the rest of the world. As one who believes in the "way of humanity," Sun declared, he could not remain indifferent, and especially since it was his own country that was victimized. He "must go forward and become the pioneer of revolution, responding to the demands of the situation." If

---

(See H. Dubs, *The History of the Former Han Dynasty* [34], I, 58.) As recorded by Miyazaki, Sun used the exact phrase, *yüeh-fa san-chang*, which appears in this dynastic history, indicating that his provisional constitution or tutelary proposal may have had its origin in his study of Han history.

[9] Miyazaki, *Thirty-three Years' Dream* [200], p. 146.

Heaven favored his cause and provided a more gifted leader, then he would readily "abdicate leadership and serve him like a dog or a horse." If not, then he could only undertake this monumental task himself. With the help of the Japanese, he concluded, his party would consummate the Chinese revolution and thereby "save China's four hundred million people, wipe away the humiliation of Asia's yellow race, and restore the universal way of humanity." Once the revolution is achieved, he said, "All other problems will be solved as easily as splitting bamboo."[10]

In this intimate conversation with Miyazaki, Sun revealed harsher and more bitter feelings toward the West than he had ever permitted himself. The protégé of the Anglican Bishop of Hawaii and the Hong Kong missionaries, who had only recently expressed his gratitude to British justice, disclosed to Miyazaki a personal grievance against Europeans and an identification with the yellow race. There was an obvious motive, to be sure, for striking this note in a plea for Japanese support, and Sun was endowed with radar-like sensitivity in adjusting to his targets. At heart, nevertheless, he was still a Chinese nationalist, and an anti-European outburst was not difficut to provoke, especially when his faith in the West was being severely tested. For while he was making contact with the Japanese, the British were discouraging the euphoria produced in London. Still fascinated by the thought of breaking British resistance with the power of public opinion, Sun had recently sent an indignant protest against his banishment to J. H. Stewart Lockhart, the Hong Kong Colonial Secretary:

I was told by some good authority that the Hong-Kong Government have outlawed me on account of my attempt to emancipate my miserable countrymen from the cruelty of the Tartar yoke. I had asked many of my English friends in London whether this is the case. They said that such is not an English law and usage. But my Chinese friends in Hong-Kong answered the question in the affirmative. Will you be kind enough to tell me whether it is true or not?

---

[10] *Ibid.*, pp. 146–147.

If it is the case, I will appeal it to the English public and the civilized world.[11]

This was the first occasion on which Sun publicly acknowledged his complicity in the anti-dynastic plot of 1895. His boldness, however, only strengthened the British distaste for his presence, and Lockhart's blunt reply of October 4, 1897, showed no concern over Sun's threats:

I am directed to inform you that this Government has no intention of allowing the British Colony of Hong-Kong to be used as an Asylum for persons engaged in plots and dangerous conspiracies against a friendly neighboring Empire, and that, in view of the part taken by you in such transactions, which you euphemistically term in your letter "emancipating your miserable countrymen from the Tartar yoke," you will be arrested if you land in this Colony under an order of Banishment issued against you in 1896.

It is uncertain, though probable, that this British rebuff preceded the conversation with Miyazaki, but this defeat after his success in London made the Japanese appeal to pan-Asian solidarity all the more enticing. This did not mean, however, that Sun was overlooking the possibility of changing Britain's attitude. In the gyrations of his strategy, a move in a new direction was rarely irreversible, and in this case, the new Japanese orientation was subject to his usual pragmatic considerations. Yet as Miyazaki's report indicates, Sun was ready to accept the Japanese as more than transient allies. In his appeal to them there was a unique warmth and fervor, and above all, a frankness which is missing in comparable claims on the British. Cantlie and Manson had known Sun for years, but it is doubtful whether they ever were as close to him as Miyazaki was after this first meeting. With Miyazaki there was no need for the petty deceit, the subterfuge, the conspicuous church attendance, and all the other devices necessary to prove Sun's Christian respectability.

[11] Sun's letter to the Hong Kong Colonial Secretary, J. H. S. Lockhart, is undated, but was probably sent in September 1897. Lockhart's reply was sent to Sun in care of Feng Ching-ju's address in Yokohama. Both letters are enclosed in Black (who was administering the government) to Chamberlain, May 18, 1898, in CO 129/283 [46].

Nor did he have to lean over backwards in endorsing the "opening of China" to the beneficent influences of trade and Christianity, as the *China Mail* expected. Miyazaki was an Asian, who shared his concern for China's distress and saw the need for applying radical solutions.

The contrast between his relations with Miyazaki and those with his European friends also illustrates the difference between Sun's attitudes toward Japan and Europe. His faith in Europe was based mainly upon his intellectual commitment to the higher values which he thought that Western civilization, including Christianity, stood for. Both Europe and Japan would repeatedly disappoint him. The West disappointed him by its seemingly irrational behavior, its failure to consider him in the light of its own values which he shared. His attachment to Japan was much more emotional; Japan would always receive his special consideration and tolerance, for despite her active participation in the imperialist attack upon China, Japan was for Sun a "natural ally," sharing a common East Asian cultural heritage and a common victimization by the West. If Japan joined Europe in outraging Chinese sovereignty, this was only a temporary aberration induced by the Western precedent. Europe, Sun thought, had to be persuaded to help him; Japan, he felt, should do so instinctively.

His relationship with Miyazaki was rapidly fortified by more than a coincidence of interests. The Japanese was captivated by Sun's personality, discerning in him a spirit of self-sacrifice worthy of a samurai hero. Though his government's policy was hardly as idealistic as his own, Miyazaki did not merely figure as an instrument of Tokyo's *realpolitik*, but became Sun's devoted comrade-in-arms. He thus epitomized Sun's expectations from Japan.[12]

The enthusiastic Miyazaki, joined by Hirayama Shū, quickly brought his discovery to Tokyo to be scrutinized by their chief,

---

[12] A modern Chinese historian, for example, compares Miyazaki to Byron and Lafayette. See Lo Kang, *Errors in Lo's Biography of Sun* [197], p. 64, and while he generally condemns Japanese motives for supporting the revolutionary movement during this period, the mainland writer, Ch'en Hsi-ch'i, includes Miyazaki among the few who were sincere friends of China. See Ch'en Hsi-ch'i, *Before the T'ung Meng Hui* [151], p. 49.

Inukai. Again Sun passed the test with flying colors.[13] With the influential Inukai as his patron, Sun made the rounds of Tokyo's important political cliques, his list of contacts amounting to a "Who's Who" of Japanese politics. He met the respected parliamentarian Ozaki Yukio, the oligarch Soejima Taneomi, and the ultranationalist leaders Tōyama Mitsuru and Hiraoka Kōtarō. Even the redoubtable Ōkuma, leader of the liberals and Foreign Minister, deigned to receive him.[14]

Ōkuma, however, was more prudent than Inukai, and instead of placing his hopes for China on the exiled revolutionary, he was more inclined to favor the rising reformist wing led by K'ang Yu-wei. Inukai nevertheless kept his eye on Sun while trying to win support for his own China policy. Sun had reached Tokyo near the end of 1897, and when the new year began, Ōkuma was out of office. With political affairs in a state of flux, Inukai was even more concerned to have his ultranationalist allies hold Sun in reserve.[15]

The key personality among the chauvinist expansionists was the renowned Tōyama, who remained in the background while guiding the strategy of his Fukuoka disciples. Among these was Hiraoka, a former soldier and now leader of the *Genyōsha*, an ultranationalist organization. With a large fortune at his disposal—he had inherited the family's holdings in Kyushu mines —Hiraoka had entered politics and had become allied with the Ōkuma-Inukai faction.[16] At Inukai's request, Hiraoka provided Sun with a house and all his wants. Since Sun was a stranger in Tokyo, Hirayama Shū, who understood some English, was appointed his companion, and various Japanese politicians were entertained in their home.[17] In order to account for his presence in Japan, Sun's friends had him designated as a Chinese language teacher for Miyazaki and Hirayama, while he himself was rapidly learning Japanese. On his first night in Tokyo, Sun

---

[13] Jansen, *Sun Yat-sen* [69], p. 67.

[14] *Ibid.*, p. 67; Lo Chia-lun, *Biography* [192], I, 78; Sun in *The 1911 Revolution* [167], I, 7.

[15] Jansen, *Sun Yat-sen* [69], p. 67.

[16] *Ibid.*, pp. 36–37.

[17] Ch'en Shao-pai, *Hsing Chung Hui* [152], p. 23.

had adopted the alias which stayed with him for the rest of his life: Sun Chung-shan. Chung-shan was the Chinese reading of characters meaning "Central Mountain" and read in Japanese as "Nakayama," which Hirayama had noticed on the name-plate of a house they passed.[18]

During the next three years, until June 1900, Sun never left Japan, and during that time there was no revolutionary project which did not enjoy the subsidization or personal assistance of his Japanese companions. The first of these joint undertakings, perhaps the most important in its potentialities, was the attempted merger of Sun's revolutionaries and K'ang Yu-wei's reformers.

Revolutionaries and Reformers: The First Contacts

When Sun Yat-sen had been practicing medicine in Canton from 1892 to 1894, he was said to have lived less than half a mile from K'ang Yu-wei (1858–1927) and Liang Ch'i-ch'ao (1873–1929).[19] But their proximity was only geographical. The difference in status precluded any real rapport. K'ang's school, the Wan-mu ts'ao-t'ang ("The grass hut amidst a myriad of trees") was close to Tso Tou-shan's bookstore, which K'ang frequently visited because of the translations it featured. This was the same store where Sun rented space for his medical clinic, and when he learned of K'ang's interest in Western literature, he tried to arrange a meeting. Using an intermediary, K'ang replied that if Sun wished to see him, he should first present a written application asking to become his student. Though offended at the time, Sun tried again in 1895 when he was preparing for the Canton coup. He and Ch'en Shao-pai visited K'ang's school but the master was absent. Later in the year, when he formed his Agricultural Study Society, Sun once more turned to K'ang and his students and even succeeded in interesting one of K'ang's favorite disciples, Ch'en Ch'ien-ch'iu, only to run up against the master's veto.[20]

18 Lo Chia-lun, *Biography* [192], I, 78.
19 Ch'en Hsi-ch'i, *Before the T'ung Meng Hui* [151], p. 50.
20 Feng, *Reminiscences* [160], I, 47; Hao, "Reformers and Revolutionaries" [52], pp. 93–94.

During this period the only revolutionary who made any contact with K'ang was Ch'en Shao-pai. On a mission for Sun in Shanghai in the early part of 1895, Ch'en stayed at a hotel that was largely occupied by Cantonese *chü-jen* on their way to Peking for the metropolitan examinations. Hearing the young scholars mention that the "sage, K'ang" (*K'ang sheng*) had arrived, Ch'en took a chance on finally cornering the elusive literatus. To the surprise of K'ang's awe-stricken admirers, who had warned that their idol was out of reach, Ch'en was granted the interview. According to Ch'en's account, K'ang agreed that while under Manchu rule, China could be neither reformed nor delivered from danger. Ch'en reports that K'ang took an interest in the revolutionaries' plans and wanted to know the extent of their strength. During the conversation they were joined by Liang Ch'i-ch'ao, who was also going to Peking for the examinations. The three of them continued the discussion for several hours.[21]

Whether K'ang Yu-wei was as favorably disposed toward an anti-Manchu coup as Ch'en relates is highly questionable, but before passing judgment, we might briefly sum up his role and accomplishments to this point. Actually, K'ang's response to China's precarious situation resembled Sun's. While Sun was enrolled at Iolani School in 1879, K'ang began taking an interest in Western institutions; a visit to Hong Kong had left him with the same feeling of admiration for Western accomplishments and of frustration regarding China's backwardness that Sun was to experience after living in the colony some years later.[22] Both came to the conclusion that drastic change was necessary if China were to avoid annihilation. But if they en-

---

[21] Ch'en Shao-pai, *Hsing Chung Hui* [152], pp. 24–26.

[22] K'ang's first visit to Hong Kong, which was his first trip outside of China, took place in 1879. According to his diary, he then first realized that Western political systems were not "barbaric." See Hu Pin, *Reforms of 1898* [173], p. 23. His remarks to Timothy Richard comparing Hong Kong to Chinese cities resemble Sun's impressions:

Coming down to Hong Kong . . . he was much struck with the houses, streets, and general order of the place, and soon became convinced that the

visioned the same broad goals, their efforts were confined to entirely separate compartments in Chinese society.

As a member of a renowned gentry family and as a degree-holder, K'ang had automatic entry to the main channel of opinion and decision making. If he had ideas, even radical ones, there was no problem of finding an audience. There were his students and colleagues at home; and in Peking, where on several occasions he joined thousands of other candidates for the highest literary degree, he could command the attention of the stars of the Confucian galaxy. While Sun had to follow a circuitous route to Li Hung-chang's yamen, K'ang could boldly address memorials to the emperor himself. This was the difference between a literatus working within the fold and a rank outsider trying to make himself heard.

The disparity in status and background was also reflected in their respective approaches to reform. Sun, as a Westernized Chinese, was concerned exclusively with elevating the political status of his country by casting its institutions in a modern, Western-inspired mold. But K'ang, though similarly aroused to the need of widespread reform, embarked upon an enterprise for which Sun was utterly unqualified and for which he had no inclination: the formulation of a new, radical interpretation of Confucianism which would enable him to invoke the name of the sage in order to justify institutional change. Sun ignored Confucianism; K'ang distorted it to the point of heresy. Sun was a political nationalist; K'ang was a cultural nationalist as well. To him, "the preservation of Confucianism was no less important than the preservation of the empire."[23] As Hsiao

---

so-called barbarians were not barbarians after all, but highly civilized and gentle folk, with whom it was a pleasure to have intercourse. Coming on to Shanghai he was confirmed more and more that there was a civilization outside of China higher than her own. When he got to Peking and saw the state of the capital, he became disgusted; for, instead of finding the Celestial Capital ahead of these ports, it was far behind them; and then he commenced to study Western literature.

This probably refers to his later visit to Hong Kong and Shanghai on the way to Peking in 1882. See Soothill, *Timothy Richard* [111], p. 218.

[23] Hsiao, "K'ang Yu-wei and Confucianism" [60], p. 175.

Kung-ch'üan has pointed out, K'ang's juxtaposition of Western institutions and Chinese learning differed in degree, but not in essence, from the formula first evolved by Feng Kuei-fen and later popularized by Chang Chih-tung.[24] But in order to encompass changes in the legal, administrative, and economic structure of China, K'ang was moved to expound a type of Chinese learning which had never been sanctioned by tradition. He posited a dynamic Confucianism which, though grounded in inflexible moral values, strove for a progressive change and refinement of human institutions.[25] Thus K'ang assumed a double burden; he not only wanted to change China, but also sought the transformation of Confucianism. Sun wanted to save the country by giving power to new men of talent, Western experts like himself, while K'ang aimed at converting traditional literati, all the way down from the emperor, to a new and revolutionary philosophy of change. The revisionist Confucian, in this case, had taken on a task of no less magnitude than the upstart revolutionary.

This leads to the interesting meeting which took place in Shanghai in the spring of 1895 between Ch'en Shao-pai, representing the revolutionaries, who were intent upon arming the Cantonese rabble, and K'ang Yu-wei and Liang Ch'i-ch'ao, who hoped to take over Peking with their petitions, memorials, and arguments harking back to Tung Chung-shu of the Han and the New Text school.[26] That Sun and his followers yearned for literati connections is understandable, but could it be possible that K'ang was entertaining anti-dynastic notions? While it is doubtful that he considered throwing in his lot with the revolutionaries, there is reason for accepting Ch'en's impression that K'ang evinced a certain curiosity and even sympathy concerning

[24] *Ibid.*, pp. 196–197.
[25] It was not only Western learning, but Mahayana Buddhism which helped K'ang "transcend traditional Confucianism." See *ibid.*, pp. 113–114; and Howard, "K'ang Yu-wei" [59], pp. 306–307.
[26] For K'ang's use of the doctrines of the New Text school of the Han dynasty, see Hsiao, "K'ang Yu-wei and Confucianism" [60], pp. 103–166; Levenson, *Liang Ch'i-ch'ao* [76], pp. 35–36; and Liang, *Intellectual Trends* [79], pp. 91–92.

the prospects of revolution. At this time he had good cause for feeling bitter and frustrated. Not only had the war with Japan turned into a disaster, but his own accomplishments during the past eight years had not kept pace with his ambitions. K'ang was no less impatient than Sun, and though he enjoyed unusual opportunities for articulate expression, these had thus far not brought him the national recognition and influence which he sought. He had attracted some bright young scholars in Canton, like Ch'en Ch'ien-ch'iu and Liang Ch'i-ch'ao,[27] but instead of being heralded as a new sage and savior of modern China, he had repelled the scholarly world and had aroused the suspicions of conservative literati by his iconoclastic interpretation of the classical tradition. In 1888, bureaucrats in Peking had refused to transmit his reformist memorial to the throne.[28] Though his first book, *Hsin-hsüeh wei-ching k'ao* (study of the classics forged during the Hsin period) created a "hurricane" in the intellectual world when it was published in 1891, three years later it was proscribed and its printing blocks burned.[29] That same year, 1894, saw him fail the *chin-shih* examination when he shocked the metropolitan examiners with his heresy.[30]

These disappointments, coupled with the new external crisis, may have provoked him to a brief and flirtatious glance at the revolutionaries when their paths crossed during the early part of 1895. In the following months, however, while Sun's conspirators were on the threshold of disaster in Canton, K'ang finally succeeded in gaining a foothold at the top of the official literati edifice. If a romance had been in the offing, K'ang's sudden success in Peking, which had national repercussions, widened the gap between him and the revolutionaries.

After leaving Ch'en Shao-pai in Shanghai, K'ang Yu-wei and his entourage arrived in Peking in March 1895, and a month later were exploiting the outcry at the peace terms which the

27 See Liang, *Intellectual Trends* [79], p. 93.
28 Hu Pin, *Reforms of 1898* [173], p. 26.
29 Lang, *Intellectual Trends* [79], p. 93.
30 Hu Pin, *Reforms of 1898* [173], p. 31.

Japanese had imposed upon Li Hung-chang in Shimonoseki on April 17. In May their protest movement reached its peak when K'ang drew up a 14,000-word memorial, signed by over 1200 examinees from various parts of the country. He demanded resistance to the Japanese and urged that the capital be moved from Peking so that a radical reformist era could be launched in relative safety. The measures he proposed covered practically every facet of political, economic, and social organization, including a suggestion that an advisory body, somewhat like a parliament, be chosen to advise the throne. In spirit and content, his proposals were similar to those advanced by Ho Kai on behalf of the Hsing Chung Hui. Though this memorial, too, was held up by the censorate, knowledge of its contents could not be suppressed, and K'ang was striding in the forefront of the patriotic, reformist movement. He finally passed his *chin-shih* examination and celebrated the occasion by addressing a third memorial to the throne. The peace treaty had been ratified so he eliminated his previous proposal to resist the Japanese and concentrated on his reformist (*pien-fa*) program. In June the document was passed on to the throne and it is said that the emperor's interest was finally aroused.[31]

Ignoring the lowly bureaucratic post to which he had been assigned, K'ang began to organize a reform movement. He founded a newspaper in Peking and formed the "Society for the Study of Self-Strengthening" in August 1895. Branches soon sprang up in Shanghai and other centers, and prominent officials, as well as influential foreigners like Timothy Richard and the British Minister, Sir Nicholas O'Conor, pledged their support. Governors-general, including Chang Chih-tung, Liu K'un-i, and Wang Wen-shao (Li Hung-chang's successor in Chihli), contributed five thousand taels toward the organization's expenses, and a rising junior official, Yüan Shih-k'ai, was among those who joined the reformist ranks. But Li Hung-chang's offer of assistance was refused, because in the eyes of the

[31] *Ibid.*, pp. 32–34; Teng and Fairbank, *China's Response* [121], p. 148; and Levenson, *Liang Ch'i-ch'ao* [76], p. 19.

patriotic reformers he had committed treason at Shimonoseki, and at all events, his power appeared to be waning.[32]

After this dazzling success, it is no wonder that K'ang made short shrift of Sun's overture in Canton in October; when the Canton plotters were scurrying for cover with prices on their heads, K'ang was hobnobbing with the cream of Chinese society. The following year, when a conservative intrigue forced the dissolution of K'ang's organization in Peking and Shanghai, its momentum was somewhat checked, but the movement did not stagnate. Flourishing journalistic enterprises like the Shanghai *Shih-wu pao*, edited by Liang Ch'i-ch'ao, and the Macao *Chih-hsin pao*, edited by K'ang's younger brother, K'ang Kuang-jen and another Cantonese disciple, Hsü Ch'in, faithfully transmitted the reformist message.[33]

A further attempt by the revolutionaries to seek links with respectable reformism was made early in 1896. The initiative came from Tse Tsan-tai, the early Hsing Chung Hui member, who met K'ang Kuang-jen in Hong Kong on February 21, 1896, and K'ang Yu-wei himself on October 4. According to Tse, who is not the most reliable chronicler, the elder K'ang "agreed to cooperate, after a confidential exchange of views." The brief talks proved inconclusive, but it was made clear that Sun Yat-sen would be excluded from any possible merger, a condition to which Tse, as a Yang Ch'ü-yün supporter, had no objection.[34] Especially after the London episode, it was much too risky for K'ang to have his name linked with Sun's, and his disciple, Mai Meng-hua, castigated Sun as "a bandit, a member of secret societies, and a man who had caused China great humiliation because he obtained his freedom from the Chinese legation through the interference of the Earl of Salisbury."[35] Although publicly repudiating Sun and secretly cultivating his rivals in the revolutionary camp, the reformers were quite willing to ex-

[32] Hu Pin, *Reforms of 1898* [173], pp. 36–37; Soothill, *Timothy Richard* [111], pp. 219–220.

[33] Hu Pin, *Reforms of 1898* [173], p. 38.

[34] Tse, *Chinese Republic* [122], pp. 11–12.

[35] Li Chien-nung, *Political History* [78], pp. 147–148.

ploit an invitation from the Sun-Ch'en faction for the purpose of extending their own influence among the *hua-ch'iao* in Japan.

Prior to Sun's arrival in Japan, Ch'en Shao-pai had decided to remedy the miserable state of Chinese education in Yokohama.[36] There was only one old-fashioned primary school and no secondary school at all. Those who wanted a better education had to choose foreign institutions, such as the French Catholic school attended by Feng Tzu-yu and T'an Yu-fa's younger brother. These two, the only Chinese among several hundred European and some Japanese youths, were natural victims of student pranks. The Europeans, Feng recalls, used to humiliate them by shouting, "Chinese people, too much dirty," and after four months of this "Western imperialist oppression," Feng decided to go home.[37]

His father, Sun's supporter Feng Ching-ju, and other influential *hua-ch'iao* readily agreed to Ch'en's proposal to establish a modern Chinese school in Yokohama. Sun also endorsed the plan when he returned from the West in 1897. But since Hsing Chung Hui members were neither qualified nor available for teaching, Ch'en proposed Liang Ch'i-ch'ao for the post. There could be no doubts concerning Liang's qualifications for administering a modern school, and Sun also welcomed another chance to get close to the reformers. Before he left for Taiwan, Ch'en addressed a letter to Liang. When their emissary, K'uang Ju-p'an, reached Shanghai, he found that Liang was not available, but K'ang recommended several other disciples. Though only a minor detail at the time, K'ang's insistence that the name Sun suggested, Chinese-Western School (Chung-hsi Hsüeh-hsiao), be scrapped in favor of Great Harmony School (Ta-t'ung Hsüeh-hsiao)—more in consonance with his own Confucian predilections—was indicative of his magisterial attitude toward what was ostensibly a joint venture.[38]

---

[36] Ch'en Shao-pai, *Hsing Chung Hui* [152], pp. 23–24.

[37] Feng, *Reminiscences* [160], I, 50–51.

[38] Ch'en Shao-pai, *Hsing Chung Hui* [152], pp. 24, 26; Hao, "Reformers and Revolutionaries" [52], p. 94; Feng, *Reminiscences* [160], I, 48; and Feng in *Documents* [179], III, 324.

The teachers recruited for the school, which was to be managed by Hsü Ch'in, arrived in 1897, and gave Sun's followers no
immediate cause for alarm. Though some of the Chinese Christians resented the kotow ceremony before a portrait of Confucius
every Sunday, and the few non-Cantonese objected to the teachers' provincial chauvinism, there was general approval of the
school's success in stimulating patriotism. The revolutionaries,
who were on good terms with Hsü Ch'in and his colleagues, were
not worried about ideological differences, such as the school's attitude toward the Manchu dynasty. They were happy to associate
with reformers and subscribe to the broad goal of "saving the
country," a slogan which evoked a fervent response as the German seizure of Kiaochow in the latter part of the year set off a
new wave of foreign aggression.[39]

But the crisis of 1897–1898 led to a startling change in K'ang's
status at home. The obstacles to reform appeared to have been
removed as more literati and the emperor himself reacted to the
unprecedented threat. After rushing off two more memorials and
forming his "Preserve the Country Association" (Pao Kuo Hui),
by June 1898 K'ang Yu-wei attained the ultimate honor—an audience with the emperor. The throne then issued edict after edict
bearing the impress of K'ang's radical reformist program, which
aimed to turn the country into a modernized constitutional monarchy.[40]

With their master standing at the side of the emperor and pre-
siding over what came to be known as the "Hundred Days of Reform," K'ang's Yokohama disciples found Sun's company highly
embarrassing. According to Ch'en Shao-pai, they received orders
from K'ang to break off contact with the revolutionaries. Thus
the institution which had become a focus of *hua-ch'iao* cultural
activity was shut tight against Sun and his influence. He and his
followers had initiated the scheme, raised the funds, and invited
the teachers. Now a sign, forbidding Sun's entry, hung from the
door, and the first joint project with the reformers had com-

[39] Feng, *Reminiscences* [160], I, 51, 122.
[40] For a chronology of K'ang's activities from 1888–1898, see Hu Pin,
Reforms of 1898 [173], pp. 108–110.

pletely backfired. As far as the Yokohama Hsing Chung Hui members were concerned, K'ang's meteoric rise had thrust Sun into the background, and even trusted followers like Feng Ching-ju, the head of the branch, were ready to switch allegiance.[41] During this period, Miyazaki, scouting prospects in Hong Kong, stopped off at Canton and made a fruitless attempt to mediate between Hsing Chung Hui supporters and K'ang's group.[42]

In September 1898, however, the "Hundred Days" abruptly ended when the reactionaries, led by the Empress Dowager and aided by some erstwhile reformers who felt that K'ang had gone too far, struck back with a vengeance. Six reformers, including K'ang's younger brother and the saintly T'an Ssu-t'ung (1865–1898), became martyrs of the cause, and K'ang, Liang, and a number of their followers fled for their lives.[43]

At this point, the Japanese attempted to steer the course of Chinese history toward their own goals, and the reformers forgot their previous strictures against accepting foreign assistance. With some of the most influential figures in Japanese politics—Ito, Ōkuma, and Inukai—masterminding the operation, Hirayama was sent to Tientsin to pick up Liang Ch'i-ch'ao, and Miyazaki was dispatched to Hong Kong, where K'ang had arrived under British protection. Both reformers were then accompanied to Japan, where their benefactors hoped to bring about a reconciliation between the two camps and thus have at their disposal a formidable instrument for the guided regeneration of China.[44] Sun, for his part, was ready to forget past insults, and welcomed the reformers as fellow refugees from Manchu tyranny. He assumed that the distance between them had been bridged and that a merger on an equal level was finally feasible. And in Taiwan, Ch'en Shao-pai gathered the Hsing Chung Hui members in a memorial service for the martyred reformers.[45]

K'ang Yu-wei, for all his imprecations against the "traitors"

[41] Ch'en Shao-pai, *Hsing Chung Hui* [152], pp. 33–34.
[42] Lo Chia-lun, *Biography* [192], I, 81.
[43] Li Chien-nung, *Political History* [78], p. 160.
[44] Jansen, *Sun Yat-sen* [69], pp. 76–77.
[45] Ch'en Shao-pai, *Hsing Chung Hui* [152], p. 36.

and "bandits" who led popular uprisings, had now been shunted off on to the low road himself. His beloved sovereign was virtually a prisoner; the only hope he had of restoring him to power, and ensuring his own political future as well, was to play Sun's game—collect funds among the *hua-ch'iao* and raise an army at home. But K'ang, as Ch'en Shao-pai put it, was not prepared to "play second fiddle" to any man,[46] and Sun had little to offer except his ambition, which K'ang could hardly satisfy except by giving up his own. In the negotiations which followed, therefore, K'ang found every excuse to avoid dealing with his opposite number, sending subordinates instead; he himself participated in discussions with the revolutionaries only when Sun was not present.

When K'ang arrived in Japan in November 1898, Sun attempted to meet him through Miyazaki but was rebuffed. The Japanese, who were subsidizing both exiled factions, still had hopes of bringing them together, and Inukai arranged a meeting between the two factions at his home. Again, K'ang begged off but had Liang represent him. For the revolutionaries there were Sun and Ch'en Shao-pai, who had just returned from his second visit to Taiwan. The meetings turned into an all-night session, and Inukai, who did not understand Chinese, did not remain to the end. Left to themselves, however, the three Chinese had an amiable discussion concerning future cooperation, and Liang declared that he would take up its implementation with K'ang.

Sun sent Ch'en Shao-pai and Hirayama on a visit to K'ang's quarters two days later, believing that an agreement could be reached. In addition to K'ang and Liang, three other reformists were present: Hsü Ch'in, Liang T'ieh-chün, and Wang Chao.[47] Wang was a former chief secretary of the Board of Rites (*Li-pu*) in Peking.[48] Ch'en launched the meeting by proclaiming the

---

[46] *Ibid.*, p. 38.

[47] *Ibid.*, p. 37.

[48] In August 1898, at the height of the reform campaign, Wang was instrumental in helping the young emperor thwart the designs of reactionaries, who sought to prevent the appointment of T'an Ssu-t'ung and three other reformers as probationary secretaries in the Grand Council. Wang was promoted at a result of his loyalty. See Li Chien-nung, *Political History*

bankruptcy of the Manchu dynasty, stating that without a revolution the nation could not be saved. Now that K'ang himself was the target of Peking's assassins, Ch'en voiced the hope that the reformist leader had come to share the conviction that there was no sense in trying to work through the Court. In his reply, K'ang indicated that his personal loyalty to the young emperor remained unshaken; he had been the recipient of the monarch's benevolence and he would not forget him during his time of troubles; his purpose was to raise an army and deliver the emperor from his enemies. Ch'en argued that the revolutionaries entertained no personal grudge against the emperor; their sole concern was to save the country. If the revolution succeeded and the emperor accepted it, they would do him no personal harm. After three hours of discussion, however, it was obvious that K'ang had not budged and that Liang's suggestion of cooperation had in no wise been sanctioned by his master.[49]

K'ang's personal relationship with the young emperor was his trump card; its value would be annulled should the legitimacy of the dynasty be denied. He insisted that he was still acting in the name of the emperor, that the latter had in fact instructed him to carry on the struggle against the usurpers who had sabotaged the reformist program and removed him from power.

In this context, the position of Wang Chao, the reformist mentioned above who had been the confidant of the emperor, assumed importance. His escape from Peking had also been engineered by the Japanese. But he was living in Tokyo less as K'ang's supporter than as his prisoner. Because of his former important position in the bureaucracy, Wang was the only one of the refugees who could verify or refute K'ang's claim that the emperor had handed him a secret edict, an *i tai chao*, constituting a mandate to raise troops and rescue him from the clutches

---

[78], p. 157; and Feng, *Reminiscences* [160], I, 49–50. Yet he returned to Peking in 1904, and after being arrested on March 27, was released three months later as a result of the amnesty proclaimed in celebration of the Empress Dowager's seventieth birthday. See Kuo, *Daily Record* [184], II, 1202; and Bland and Backhouse, *Empress Dowager* [7], p. 449.

[49] Ch'en Shao-pai, *Hsing Chung Hui* [152], pp. 37–38.

of the Empress Dowager. Wang apparently knew that the edict was a forgery, and K'ang took great pains to keep him from broadcasting this intelligence in Japan. Liang T'ieh-chün was the strong-arm man among K'ang's cohorts and had been assigned to keep guard over Wang and prevent him from talking.[50]

At the very outset of this meeting with the revolutionaries, however, Wang burst out with a strong protest against his treatment and complained that he was being denied the right to speak freely. K'ang became enraged and ordered Liang T'ieh-chün to take him out, explaining to the others that Wang was demented. This episode did not escape the notice of Ch'en Shao-pai, who instructed Hirayama to keep an eye on K'ang's unwilling guest and find out what his grievance was. Several days later, when K'ang and his friends left their prisoner unguarded, Hirayama spirited him away to Inukai's residence, where he disclosed the forgery of the *i tai chao*. A chagrined K'ang, aware that Ch'en had been instrumental in his exposure, now considered the revolutionaries his sworn enemies and the rift became even greater. He refused to show the purported imperial mandate to anyone in Tokyo, claiming that he had been forced to burn it when fleeing Peking.[51] The Japanese and Sun's crowd knew better, but this gambit was much more successful among the gullible and less educated *hua-ch'iao*, whose favor K'ang began to solicit.

K'ang's conflict with Wang Chao cooled his relations with the Japanese, who began to look upon him as a diplomatic embarrassment.[52] A new government, less enthusiastic over the reformers, had taken power in Tokyo late in 1898, and with the Manchu regime strongly protesting the help being given to K'ang, the Japanese decided that he should leave.[53] Provided with funds by his hosts (according to one source, these amounted to nine

[50] Feng, *Reminiscences* [160], I, 49–50.

[51] *Ibid.*, p. 49; and Ch'en Shao-pai, *Hsing Chung Hui* [152], p. 39.

[52] Feng, *Reminiscences* [160], I, 50.

[53] Jansen, *Sun Yat-sen* [69], pp. 77–78. On March 6, 1899, Chang Chih-tung wired the Tsungli Yamen advising that the Japanese Foreign Office be requested to expel K'ang, Liang, and Wang Chao. See Kuo, *Daily Record* [184], II, 1042. Japanese army leaders were apparently afraid of hurting Sino-Japanese relations by giving hospitality to K'ang. See Hao, "Reformers and Revolutionaries" [52], p. 112, note 36.

thousand yen[54]), K'ang went off to Canada in the summer of 1899 and in July formed there his Pao Huang Hui (Protect the Emperor Society), an organization destined to nearly ruin Sun's plans for the *hua ch'iao*.[55] But the Japanese were not writing the reformers off their books, nor did they give up hope of eventually reconciling them with the revolutionaries.

Clearly the reformist label had not been cut from one piece of cloth; in their writings and conversations, a number of K'ang's disciples showed an irreverence for monarchy and the Manchus which was no less extreme than that of the revolutionaries. The Hunanese reformer, Pi Yung-nien, a degree-holder and a comrade of T'an Ssu-t'ung, had already allied himself with Sun, and in the summer of 1899, none other than Liang Ch'i-ch'ao, K'ang's foremost disciple, became a fountainhead of heresy and a major exponent of revolutionary ideas.[56]

Liang Ch'i-ch'ao's principal medium was journalism, and in the *Ch'ing-i pao*, founded soon after his arrival in Japan, he carried on where he had left off with the Shanghai *Shih-wu pao*, introducing Western ideas and history to Chinese readers.[57] Even

---

[54] Feng, *Reminiscences* [160], I, 50.

[55] K'ang left Japan in the second moon (March 12–April 9) 1899. See Hao, "Reformers and Revolutionaries" [52], p. 98. Some sources state that the Pao Huang Hui was formed in Yokohama prior to K'ang's departure, but the authoritative Kuo, *Daily Record* [184], II, 1051, gives July 20, 1899 as the date for its establishment in Victoria, British Columbia, under the name "China Reform Association." Around this time Liang established the main branch in Yokohama.

[56] Pi, a native of Changsha and a *kung-sheng*, had been known for his anti-Manchu feelings and connections with the Ko Lao Hui even when he was associated with T'an Ssu-t'ung, T'ang Ts'ai-ch'ang, and other Hunanese reformers. T'an is said to have called upon him in September 1898, when he thought of using force against the Empress Dowager in order to save the reformist campaign. The plot, however, depended upon Yüan Shih-k'ai's collaboration, and Pi, deciding that Yüan was untrustworthy, did not comply with his friend's request. See Feng, *Reminiscences* [160], I, 73–74.

[57] *Ch'ing-i pao* (The China Discussion) was founded on December 23, 1898. It appeared every ten days and altogether ran to 100 issues until it ceased publication in 1901. The Yokohama *hua-ch'iao* contributed to its support, and Sun's former mainstay, Feng Ching-ju, was listed as publisher. On March 20, 1899, Chang Chih-tung telegraphed the Japanese Consul in Shanghai requesting that it be shut down. See Kuo, *Daily Record* [184], II, 1037, 1043; and Feng, *Reminiscences* [160], I, 63.

when K'ang was present, Liang veered dangerously close to anti-Manchuism, and on one occasion his master saw fit to destroy the plates of a particularly seditious article.[58] But with K'ang in Canada, Liang and another maverick reformer, Ou Ch'ü-chia, used the *Ch'ing-i pao* to disseminate republican ideas.

During the next year, Liang was also busy establishing in Tokyo an upper level continuation of the Yokohama school, Ta-t'ung Hsüeh-hsiao.[59] Besides a number of graduates of the junior academy, this new institution absorbed over ten former students of the Shih-wu Hsüeh-t'ang (Academy for the Study of Modern Affairs) in Changsha, where Liang himself had taught two years earlier during the height of the Hunan reform movement. The young Hunanese had previously shown a taste for radical ideas, and under Liang's renewed tutelage, they and the Cantonese from Yokohama studied foreign history and the Japanese and English languages. They learned about the Greek philosophers as well as Montesquieu, Voltaire, Rousseau, Darwin, and George Washington. Soon they began identifying with these foreign personalities, and the young Cantonese, Cheng Kuan-i, called himself "the Chinese Moses."[60]

Among these young intellectuals, forerunners of the great student migration to Japan after the turn of the century, Liang began to take on his seminal role in modern Chinese history. He ultimately became, through his prolific reading and interpretation of Japanese translations of European philosophy, history, and science, the mentor of a whole generation of Chinese intellectuals. Sun claimed to be practicing revolution; Liang actually taught revolution. Sun himself, for all his research in London's libraries, had much to learn about nationalism, democracy, and socialism from his reformist rival.[61]

[58] Feng, *Reminiscences* [160], I, 83.
[59] *Ibid.*, I, 72–73; Levenson, *Liang Ch'i-ch'ao* [76], pp. 62–63.
[60] Feng, *Reminiscences* [160], I, 83.
[61] Chang P'eng-yüan, *Liang Ch'i-ch'ao* [144] is the best study of Liang's ideological contribution to the 1911 Revolution. Levenson, *Liang Ch'i-ch'ao* analyzes the intellectual vicissitudes of Liang's entire career primarily in terms of the conflict between his particularistic attachment to Chinese history and his attraction to universalistic values.

With K'ang Yu-wei no longer an obstruction, it appeared that Sun and Liang could end their rivalry; the reformist-revolutionary constellation had been blessed with a propitious meeting of minds between conspirator and scholar. Liang did not confine his enmity to the Empress Dowager, Jung-lu, Yüan Shih-k'ai, and other villains of the September coup; rather, brought by his studies to an admiration of republicanism, he renounced the dynastic position entirely. In his negotiations with Sun, he is said to have agreed to become second in command under the revolutionary banner. Sun calmed his fears about K'ang's fate by saying, "if the disciple becomes a leader, will not the master be even more exalted?"[62] And according to the story, Liang himself asserted that K'ang could keep on writing books, and if he disagreed with the revolutionary program, they would pay no attention to him.[63] So close was the relationship of Liang and Sun that they began jointly publishing an anti-Manchu periodical, *Chung-kuo mi-shih* (Secret History of China). The two issues which appeared in the latter part of 1899 stressed racial themes from the Sung, Ming, and Taiping periods.[64]

For at least five years, Liang Ch'i-ch'ao had lived in the shadow of the man who privately considered himself the successor to Confucius, K'ang Yu-wei, and his defection at this time can, in part at least, be credited to a desire for self-assertion. Like other disciples of the "sage of Nan-hai," Liang had earlier adopted as the second character of his given name the ideograph *han* which resembles the ideograph for K'ang's surname. It had become a trademark for K'ang's disciples. Significantly, at the time he was extolling revolution in the *Ch'ing-i pao* and conspiring with Sun, he dropped this sign of deference and called himself "Jen-kung" instead of "Jen-han."[65] Many aspects of his behavior thus reflected an effort to throw off K'ang's spiritual domination.

[62] Lo Chia-lun, *Biography* [192], I, 86.
[63] Ch'en Shao-pai, *Hsing Chung Hui* [152], p. 38.
[64] Chang P'eng-yuan, *Liang Ch'i-ch'ao* [144], p. 126.
[65] Hao, "Reformers and Revolutionaries" [52], p. 99; Feng, *Reminiscences* [160], I, 63.

With twelve other disillusioned reformists, Liang sent a letter to K'ang affirming republican principles and suggesting that the master retire from politics.[66] He also asked Ch'en Shao-pai to sit down with the reformist Hsü Ch'in and work out a preliminary agreement.[67] But Hsü, who opposed the compact with the revolutionaries, informed K'ang of Liang's defection. K'ang was now back in Hong Kong and immediately dispatched a strong letter denouncing the thirteen "troublemakers" and ordering Liang and Ou, the major culprits, to leave Japan and thence proceed to Hawaii and San Francisco, respectively, to carry out assignments on behalf of the Pao Huang Hui. A messenger was sent with funds for the trips.[68]

It was now up to Liang either to confirm the breach or return to the fold repentantly. He chose the latter course, but qualified his submission by professing loyalty to the cause of cooperation and even sought Sun's support for his work abroad. As usual when dealing with scholar-reformers, Sun's response was a model of patience, and he ensured Liang's success by giving him a letter of introduction to his brother when Liang left for Hawaii at the end of 1899. Although Liang has often been accused of duplicity in accepting this commission from K'ang and concurrently soliciting Sun's help, it seems apparent that he was reluctant to decide between two causes, which were not really so far apart.[69] Perhaps, too, he had misgivings about entrusting leadership to men like Sun who, despite their patriotism and anti-Manchu militancy, must have impressed him as boors, with no respect for Chinese tradition and scholarship, and not especially brilliant expositors of Western learning either.

That Liang could not rid himself of such doubts about the Westernized, treaty port Chinese was readily discerned by Sun's colleague, Yang Ch'ü-yün, who, arriving in Japan in 1898, es-

---

[66] Hao, "Reformers and Revolutionaries" [52], p. 100.

[67] Ch'en Shao-pai, *Hsing Chung Hui* [152], p. 43.

[68] Hao, "Reformers and Revolutionaries" [52], p. 100; Feng, *Reminiscences* [160], I, 63; and *ibid.*, II, 31–32.

[69] Liang's letter to Sun from Hawaii, pleading for patience and understanding, appears in *Documents* [179], III, 291.

tablished less naive relations with the reformers. It will be recalled that Yang's admirer, Tse Tsan-tai, had been conducting independent negotiations with the reformers for a number of years in Hong Kong, and upon Yang's arrival in Japan, the parallel efforts merged. Yang was party to the negotiations carried on with Liang in the summer of 1899. In corresponding with Sun at this time, Liang in fact made a point of inviting Yang to their parleys.[70] But in June, Yang sent a pessimistic report of a meeting held with Liang at Feng Ching-ju's office in Yokohama:

He [Liang Ch'i-ch'ao] advised me to try my best to go on with the work of our party and he will try his best to go on with the work of his party. He does not like to cooperate with us yet. Hong's [K'ang's] party are too proud and jealous of our Chinese English scholars. They don't like to have the same rank as us; they always aspire to governing us or want us all to submit to them. They do not know what justice means, as Mr. U. Lai-un[71] remarked . . . and I have heard several wise Hunan men make similar remarks concerning them.[72]

By "Hunan men" Yang was undoubtedly referring to the former Changsha students, who, unlike Liang, had not been personal disciples of K'ang and did not feel constrained to join in his stubborn defense of the Manchu emperor. It is evident that the failure of 1898, combined with K'ang's imperious treatment of his associates, had opened up fissures in the reformist bloc. In Japan, Sun for the first time found himself in the company of non-Cantonese, traditionally educated Chinese who warmed to the subject of revolution.

In exploiting this opportunity, Sun did not stand on his pride. Once he went so far as to tell Pi Yung-nien and another Hunanese, T'ang Ts'ai-ch'ang, a disciple of T'an Ssu-t'ung, that if K'ang would dissolve his Pao Huang Hui and advocate revolution, not only could the two parties be united, but he would

[70] Lo Chia-lun, *Biography* [192], I, 88.

[71] This is Hu Li-yüan, mentioned in Chapter II as a prosperous Hong Kong businessman and friend of Ho Kai.

[72] Tse, *Chinese Republic* [122], p. 15.

have all his comrades accept K'ang's leadership.[73] While it is highly improbable that Sun was willing to pay so high a price for unity, this gesture reflected his conciliatory mood. Furthermore, his effort to win over Pi's militant friends, of whom T'ang Ts'ai-ch'ang and Lin Kuei were the leaders, drew him into reluctant cooperation in the planning of their Yangtze Valley rising of 1900.[74] Vacillating between "save the emperor" and anti-Manchu republican positions, these Hunanese activists, who had formerly been unquestioning admirers of K'ang Yu-wei, now constituted an uncertain factor as they prepared to take up arms under the banner of the Tzu-li Hui (Independence Association).[75]

The Manchu court itself did not regard the revolution advocated by Sun as more menacing than K'ang's brand of reformism. For the Empress Dowager and those who shared her power, K'ang, with his vow of personal vengeance upon them, was unquestionably the more disquieting of the two. Although they feared Sun, they considered K'ang, who camouflaged his "barbarian heart" with Confucian exegesis, a more immediate threat. Sun, at worst, appeared to be a Taiping-like rebel, feeding on the discontent of the lower classes, but K'ang, as a treacherous literatus, had succeeded in penetrating the palace, turning the emperor into an ally, and threatening the person of the Empress Dowager herself. The one was an intruder, who was known for what he was; the other, and his literati followers, were a cancer eating away at the traditional structure from within. Therefore the diplomatic resources of the dynasty were almost entirely occupied with the reformist rather than the revolutionary threat. Repeated denunciations of K'ang's seditious plans and reputedly vicious character showered the British Foreign Office, which was asked to prevent his use of the colonies as a springboard to China. The Chinese Minister in London even accused K'ang

---

[73] Feng, *Reminiscences* [160], I, 74.

[74] See Hao, "Reformers and Revolutionaries" [52], pp. 105–107, for a discussion of Sun's relations with T'ang's group.

[75] See Smythe, "The Tzu-li Hui" [109].

of attempting to rape the wife of one of his *hua-ch'iao* hosts in Canada.[76]

According to one report, the Chinese minister in Tokyo, Li Sheng-to, acknowledged K'ang's higher priority on Peking's blacklist by attempting to win over Sun's loyalties. At the close of 1899, Li is said to have offered Sun a generous emolument in return for renouncing revolution and accepting the authority of the Court. If true, this move would have been motivated by a desire to focus all anti-subversion activities upon one target, K'ang Yu-wei, and to gain the help of Sun's supporters in trying to check K'ang's agitation overseas. Sun, we are told, unequivocally rejected the bid, which was tendered via a Japanese intermediary.[77]

Yet, if the transformation of K'ang's reformist movement into an overseas-based subversive influence added to the Court's troubles, it also complicated Sun's situation. In order to increase his bargaining power with the reformers, or to survive independently, he had to invigorate and expand his movement, which had not yet fully recovered from the Canton disaster of 1895. Fortunately, his Japanese collaborators were prepared to offer ideas and money and even to risk their lives for this cause.

The Filipino Episode

Even before the reformers had been exiled from Peking in 1898, Sun and the Japanese had decided upon a spectacular project involving nothing less than an alliance with Filipino independence fighters. Their idea was to help liberate the islands from the Americans and then turn them into an auxiliary base against the Manchu dynasty.[78] If this seemed a circuitous way of

---

[76] Lo Feng-lu to Salisbury, February 7, 1900, in Fo 17/1718 [46], p. 254.

[77] Lo Chia-lun, *Biography* [192], I, 84. Li, it should be pointed out, was an old enemy of K'ang's, and had conspired with the Empress Dowager and Jung Lu against the emperor in 1898. See Li Chien-nung, *Political History* [78], p. 158. K'ang was particularly fearful when he heard that Li had been appointed Minister to Tokyo. See Lo Chia-lun, *Biography* [192], I, 82; and Miyazaki, *Thirty-three Years' Dream* [200], pp. 165–166.

[78] The following account of Sun's Filipino adventure is based largely

bringing about the Chinese revolution, it should be remembered that highly imaginative and romantic minds were at work here. At their very first meeting, Sun had warmed Miyazaki's heart with a heated protestation of pan-Asian loyalty, and the opportunity to live up to this ideal came sooner than he had expected.

The Filipino liberation movement, born under Spanish rule, was already active in 1895 when the Hsing Chung Hui was being formed in Hong Kong. Early attempts at securing Japanese assistance had failed. Later a new leader, Emilio Aguinaldo, succeeded in obtaining a foothold in Luzon, but by the end of 1897, when his mountain republic ran into difficulties, Aguinaldo had accepted a cash settlement from the Spaniards and retired to Hong Kong. He remained there until the Americans enlisted his assistance against Spain in the spring of 1898. Later, when the United States decided to retain its new conquest, the original movement was reactivated and soon was resisting the American take-over of the Philippines. Miyazaki, while on a mission to China, met the Filipino rebels in their Hong Kong headquarters. Aguinaldo called for outside assistance, and in June one of his emissaries, Mariano Ponce, reached Japan. Finding the Japanese sympathetic, but reluctant to become embroiled with the Americans, Ponce turned to Sun Yat-sen, who seized upon the venture as an outlet for Chinese revolutionary energies. When Miyazaki and Hirayama returned to Japan in the fall of 1898, Sun convinced them of the desirability of placing the Sino-Japanese revolutionary axis at the service of Aguinaldo's anti-American guerrillas. Inukai gave his approval, but to avoid offending the Americans, he had Sun designated the chief negotiator.

The Filipinos had funds but needed help in purchasing and transporting arms. This is the service which Sun and the Japanese were to perform. By means of a complicated use of figureheads and intermediaries, it was finally arranged that an antiquated Mitsui ship, stoked with coal donated by Hiraoka's mines, would carry a load of munitions to the Philippines. The arms

---

upon Jansen, *Sun Yat-sen* [69], pp. 68–73. See also Miyazaki, *Thirty-three Years' Dream* [200], pp. 183–194; and Lo Chia-lun, *Biography* [192], I, 83–84.

and ammunition were purchased from the Japanese army, which quietly blessed the venture. At best it might succeed in thwarting the white man's latest imperalist outrage. At the worst, it would leave a residue of good will for Japan as the protector of Asia.

Six Japanese adventurers, including Hirayama, went ahead as military advisers in the early summer of 1899, while several other Japanese fighters boarded the munitions ship, the *Nunobiki Maru*, which left on July 19. Sun, Yang Ch'ü-yün, and other Hong Kong revolutionaries were to join the independence fighters along with Miyazaki and Ponce as soon as possible. The plan came to naught, however, when the ship was sunk in a storm off the Chekiang coast. The munitions were lost and thirteen men, including three Japanese, were drowned. With 75,000 pesos still at his disposal, Sun outfitted another arms ship and tried to send it from Taiwan in January 1900. This time, however, the Americans had been alerted and the Japanese had no option but to terminate the voyage and have the arms unloaded.[79]

These unused munitions soon figured in Sun's plans as he pondered another uprising. But such a scheme would not be realistic until he had procured more fighting allies in China, and meanwhile, another matter still to be settled was the disputed leadership of the Hsing Chung Hui.

The question had been left in abeyance since the mass flight from Hong Kong in 1895. By virtue of his new notoriety and acceptance by the Japanese, Sun had in fact superseded Yang Ch'ü-yün, but he was not able to formally oust him until some time after Yang returned. During the two years after he left Hong Kong, Yang had made many stops before settling in Johannesburg early in 1897, where he had been hospitably received by the prosperous Cantonese community.[80] More in search of a haven than of political support, Yang nevertheless succeeded in forming a Hsing Chung Hui branch consisting of twelve members. In the autumn, after receiving encouraging reports

[79] Ch'en Hsi-ch'i, *Before the T'ung Meng Hui* [151], p. 62.
[80] Ch'en Shao-pai, *Hsing Chung Hui* [152], pp. 34–35.

from Tse Tsan-tai concerning negotiations with the reformers, he decided to return to Hong Kong. He had also been impressed with news of Sun's successes, both real and imagined. According to Ch'en Shao-pai, Yang had read in the foreign press that Sun had accumulated a war chest of several million dollars in Japan and was about to launch another revolt. As his own more modest contribution, Yang obtained several hundred pounds from the South African *hua-ch'iao*.[81] After a reunion with his family and Tse in Hong Kong harbor during March 1898, Yang went to Yokohama to meet Sun and Ch'en Shao-pai.[82]

The atmosphere was strained, and after a closed session with Sun, Yang left immediately. Ch'en Shao-pai hungered for details of the encounter, and Sun supplied what must have been a highly colored version of how he had put Yang in his place. Going back to the Canton episode, Sun related, he upbraided Yang for failing in his task: "You wanted to be the leader; I let you be leader. You said you wanted to come to Canton at the very end; I let you be the last to come. . . . But why didn't you come at the fixed time? Afterwards I wired you not to come, and the next day you sent six hundred men, and muddled up the whole situation. . . ." According to Sun, Yang was completely chastened. Then, having heard that Sun had raised funds for a new attempt, he asked for forgiveness and permission to rejoin the ranks. Pitying the abject Yang, Sun immediately forgave him.[83]

Though Sun supposedly had Yang on his knees, the leadership issue was still not resolved. This is one reason for doubting Sun's version of the conversation as recounted by Ch'en. It is also difficult to reconcile this account with our knowledge of Yang's fiery temperament. If after the confrontation, Yang was unable to wrest the initiative from Sun, there may have been another factor involved. While Sun and Ch'en enjoyed the largesse of their Japanese sponsors, Yang had to work for a living. He had a family to support and no rich brother to carry the burden. Realizing, as Ch'en says, that his return had been hasty (there was no fabulous party treasury to fall back on), he began teaching English

81 Feng, in *Documents* [179], III, 353.
82 Tse, *Chinese Republic* [122], p. 13.
83 Ch'en Shao-pai, *Hsing Chung Hui* [152], p. 35.

in Yokohama. While Yang still held nominal leadership, Sun continued to dominate the revived conspiracy by default.

Among the new activities was the Hsing Chung Hui's first newspaper. Ch'en Shao-pai grew impatient in Japan and returned to Hong Kong in the fall of 1899.[84] When he found that the British would not bother him, he asked Sun to send printing type from Japan. This was soon forthcoming, for Sun had made some profit from the Filipino arms deal, and at the end of the year, the first issue of the *Chung-kuo jih-pao* (Chinese daily) appeared.[85] Veteran supporters Ch'ü Feng-ch'ih and Ho Kai contributed their help, and six months later, when the Boxer disturbances made the British more tolerant of anti-dynasticism, the paper was able to take a belligerent stand in combatting Pao Huang Hui propaganda overseas.[86] This was Sun's first challenge to the reformers' domination of the field of journalism.

With Chen Shao-pai resuscitating the Hong Kong branch and Cheng Shih-liang continuing to cultivate his secret society connections there, Sun was getting closer to home. In Miyazaki and Hirayama, who in 1898 began scouting possibilities in South and North China respectively, he furthermore had two very effective agents.[87] Except for his brief trip north in 1894, Sun had never been outside the Kwangtung area of China and had little personal knowledge of the Ko Lao Hui. Hirayama was actually the first of the Hsing Chung Hui associates to establish contact with this important reservoir of fighters. But the Hunanese reformer, Pi Yung-nien, who had joined Sun, was quite friendly with the Ko Lao Hui elders. Sun hoped to extend his network through Pi's mediation to the Yangtze Valley, and for this purpose in 1899 he sent Pi back to China, where he spent about a month rounding up Ko Lao Hui leaders in Hunan and Hupeh.[88] Pi was joined by another new Hsing Chung Hui agitator, Shih

[84] *Ibid.*, p. 36; and Feng, in *Documents* [179], III, 325.

[85] Hirayama, in "Ma Pai-yüan's Conversations" [163], p. 604.

[86] Ch'en Shao-pai, *Hsing Chung Hui* [152], pp. 36, 40, 44; Lo Chia-lun, *Biography* [192], I, 86; and Feng, *Reminiscences* [160], I, 66.

[87] Jansen, *Sun Yat-sen* [69], pp. 84–85; and Lo Chia-lun, *Biography* [192], I, 81.

[88] Feng, Reminiscences [160], I, 74; Miyazaki, *Thirty-three Years' Dream* [200], pp. 195–196.

Chien-ju, a remarkable young man with an impeccable literati background who had decided that the future of China lay in the hands of Sun Yat-sen and the secret societies.

The story of Shih Chien-ju is illustrative of the revolutionary fever which began infecting young gentry in 1898.[89] Shih was a Cantonese, born in 1879, whose grandfather had been a wealthy Hanlin scholar. His father had died young, but his mother encouraged her sons to carry on the scholarly tradition. At an early age, however, Chien-ju came to hate the "eight-legged" essay and showed a fondness for history and modern studies. The war with Japan and the suppression of the 1898 reform movement turned him into a radical. He began studying fencing with a Japanese instructor and sought to toughen his body so that he might be of heroic service to his country. In 1898 he entered Canton Christian College, the same missionary institution Ch'en Shao-pai had attended. This fact is also significant; by the end of the century, not only peasant boys like Sun, but also products of the gentry tradition were beginning to show a preference for foreign learning. (One of Shih Chien-ju's sisters studied medicine in Canton.) Physics, chemistry, geography, and the rest of the sciences came to him quickly, and the head of the school, Reverend O. F. Wisner, considered him a prize student.

But Shih was not content with schoolwork, even modern studies, and craved action. In 1899 he heard that Takahashi Ken, representing the Canton branch of the Tōa Dōbun Kai, or East Asian Common Culture Society, was just the man to put him in touch with revolutionary sympathizers.[90] This organization had been formed in November 1898 for the ostensible purpose of promoting solidarity between China, Japan, and Korea. It was actually an arm of the same adventurous clique of Japanese that had been supporting Sun Yat-sen in his attempt to overthrow

[89] See Teng Mu-han's "Sketch of Shih Chien-ju" [213], pp. 245–248; Ch'en Shao-pai, *Hsing Chung Hui* [152], p. 58; and Feng, in *Documents* [160], III, 354–355, for further data on Shih and his family. Miyazaki's impressions of this young man appear in *Thirty-three Years' Dream* [200], pp. 200–202.

[90] Ch'en Shao-pai, *Hsing Chung Hui* [152], p. 57; and Teng Mu-han, "Sketch of Shih Chien-ju" [213], p. 245.

the Manchus. In addition to Takahashi, its promoters included Haraguchi Bunichi, and Sun's close friends, Miyazaki and Hirayama. On the Chinese side, a leading role was played by Sun's comrade from Hawaii, Teng Yin-nan.[91]

Under Takahashi's guidance, Shih learned of Sun Yat-sen and was put in touch with Ch'en Shao-pai, Yang Ch'ü-yün, and other Hsing Chung Hui members in Hong Kong.[92] Toward the end of 1899 he met Miyazaki, who was struck by the revolutionary ardor of this handsome youth. On this occasion, Shih told him that his elder brother might pay a call, and if so, would Miyazaki please tell him that he was taking Chien-ju to Japan with him. Without knowing the reason for this request, Miyazaki agreed. Ch'en Shao-pai then joined them and explained that Shih Chien-ju was anxious to work with the Ko Lao Hui in Hunan and Hupeh, but that his mother and brother would not give him permission. They knew of Miyazaki, however, through his connections with K'ang Yu-wei, and were willing to put Shih in his charge in the belief that the boy would associate with respectable reformers in Japan.

Miyazaki was impressed with Shih's ruse and asked about his political ideas. Shih replied that he admired the "lofty character" of Sun Yat-sen and would like to work for the realization of his principles. While he had not yet seen Sun, he had been fortunate in meeting Ch'en Shao-pai, who shared Sun's beliefs, and he had made up his mind to serve the revolutionary leader. He had heard that the Hsing Chung Hui had been joined by the Triads and Ko Lao Hui, and now he wished to learn how the Yangtze Valley societies operated. His brother, he went on, agreed with him in principle, but was "too timid" to act. While he realized that in lying to his mother and brother, he was guilty of disobedience, he felt that in this case he was actually showing filial piety

[91] See Kuomintang Archives, "The Tōa Dōbun Kai" [182]; and Jansen, *Sun Yat-sen* [69], p. 52, for a description of this organization.

[92] While Ch'en takes credit for inducting Shih into the Hsing Chung Hui, in his subsequent confession to the Cantonese authorities, Shih declared that Yang Ch'ü-yün enrolled him. See Tsou Lu, *The Kuomintang* [216], p. 674.

by putting their minds at ease. He then told Miyazaki the origin of his revolutionary ideal: "I am a Christian and believe in God. People throughout the world are the sons and daughters of God. Therefore I want to work for the realization of the principle that everyone is free and equal." Revolution was necessary in order to liberate Chinese minds from the stifling influence of the literati and the examination system:

> Anyone who kills a man must be hung. But what kind of punishment should be inflicted upon those who kill one's mind and intelligence? It should be worse than hanging! This is what officials of the present government are doing. . . . There is an examination system for the appointment of officials. Students study books in order to obtain better positions which will enable them to become wealthy by squeezing the people and none of them have any ideals about administering the country. If the water of a spring becomes muddy, it will never clear in the lower course of the stream. As long as it consists of these corrupt officials, the present government of China will remain decadent. . . . Only through revolution can the improvement of society be obtained. Otherwise it is merely theory without practice.[93]

When the solicitous elder brother showed up, Miyazaki played his part, and soon afterwards, when he set out for Japan with Ch'en Shao-pai, Shih Chien-ju accompanied them as far as Shanghai. There he met Pi Yung-nien, an old hand with the Yangtze Valley secret orders. The two went on together to Hankow and Shih made his long-sought acquaintanceship with the Ko Lao Hui lodges. Later they returned to the coast and went to Japan, where Shih met Sun Yat-sen. After lengthy discussions of revolutionary strategy, Sun sent his latest convert back to China, where he continued his work in the Yangtze Valley and then returned to Kwangtung to organize the Triads and provincial troops.[94]

Probably at this time Sun realized that the incorporation of the Yangtze Valley fighters could solve two problems at one and the same time. Besides extending his reach to the central provinces and giving his movement more of a national character, it could also give him a pretext for seizing the de jure leadership

---

[93] Miyazaki, *Thirty-three Years' Dream* [200], pp. 200–202.
[94] *Ibid.*, p. 203; and Lo Chia-lun, *Biography* [192], I, 87.

of the Hsing Chung Hui from Yang Ch'ü-yün. Pi Yung-nien had spoken to the Ko Lao Hui chieftains of a new alliance under Sun, and in the latter part of 1899, Sun confronted Yang with the fact that the Yangtze secret society leaders had "appointed him 'President'."[95] Yang was then faced with the choice of either giving way to Sun or splitting the movement. It was obvious that Sun had stronger connections, and Yang became reconciled to accepting a subordinate position in the new combination. Before formally resigning, however, he went to Hong Kong at the beginning of 1900 and sought the advice of Tse Tsan-tai. His friend agreed that in the interests of the movement Yang had made the correct decision. As for himself, Tse felt that he could be more effective working on his own.[96]

Although he surrendered the leadership to Sun, Yang was very anxious to be active in Hong Kong after being kept out of the picture in Japan. When he reported to Ch'en Shao-pai in Hong Kong, he brought a letter from Sun stating that "all were working together as before." Sun, however, was still wary of Yang and privately warned Ch'en not to trust him with "confidential matters."[97] Yet there is no indication that Yang entertained separatist ideas, and by Ch'en's own admission, Yang's presence greatly stimulated the Hong Kong office. Through Yang the wealthy Li Chi-t'ang came into the movement and became an important backer of the *Chung-kuo jih-pao*.[98] Li eventually dissipated a fortune in support of various revolutionary activities.

Collaboration with the Secret Societies

Meanwhile the reinforced Hong Kong office had been carefully cultivating the secret societies in the south. Here of course

---

[95] See Feng, *History of the Revolution* [159], I, 15; and Tse, *Chinese Republic* [122], p. 16. Yang's resignation may have preceded the actual formation of the new organization, although Pi had already obtained the agreement of the Ko Lao Hui leaders for whose benefit it was created. See also Lo Kang, *Errors in Lo's Biography of Sun* [197], pp. 68–69.

[96] Tse, *Chinese Republic* [122], p. 16.

[97] Ch'en Shao-pai, *Hsing Chung Hui* [152], p. 44.

[98] See Feng, in *Documents* [179], III, 355, for a brief sketch of Li's political career. He was sworn into the Hsing Chung Hui in the early part of 1900.

contact was made more easily than in the Yangtze Valley. Still, it was necessary to broaden the personal relations that provided the basis for agreement with the secret societies. Such individual arrangements, including perhaps cash bonuses, were more effective than ideological considerations in activating the esoteric orders.

Ch'en Shao-pai received valuable assistance in this area from Ch'en Nan, a Cantonese Hakka from Hawaii, who had joined the organization in 1894 and had participated in the Canton plot the following year. Ch'en Nan invited an aged Triad leader from Hakka territory to come to Hong Kong and induct Shao-pai into the society. Usually the induction ceremony called for the entire lodge to participate in an elaborate ritual, with symbolic blood-letting and the drinking of a few drops of the neophyte's blood mixed with wine. Ch'en Shao-pai apparently had little use for the hocus-pocus aspect of the secret orders (he was only interested in their reputed fighting qualities), and by special dispensation he was sworn in by the venerable Hakka in a simplified private ceremony. He was even designated a *pai-shan* (white fan), which was one of the higher offices in the lodge leadership. After the ceremony, Ch'en gave the old man a hundred dollars so that the other members could celebrate his induction with some refreshments.[99]

In the meantime word came that Pi Yung-nien had lined up the Yangtze Valley elders, and by the end of 1899 or the beginning of 1900, a delegation of several *Lung-t'ou* (dragon heads), including the chieftains of the important "Golden Dragon" and "Soaring Dragon" lodges, appeared in Hong Kong. With Sun's agents acting as the mediators, the Ko Lao Hui and Triad leaders were brought together for the first time. At Pi's suggestion, the representatives of the two secret societies agreed to form a grand alliance with the Hsing Chung Hui under the leadership of Sun Yat-sen. Sipping a mixture of pigeon's blood and wine, the delegates swore allegiance to their anti-Manchu alliance which was called the "Hsing Han Hui" (Revive Han Association), the word "Han" emphasizing their Chinese racial affiliation. Since Sun

[99] Ch'en Shao-pai, *Hsing Chung Hui* [152], pp. 39–41.

was to be the leader, a special seal was cut and brought to him in Japan by Miyazaki and Ch'en.[100]

It is interesting to note that there is no record that the Hsing Chung Hui had ever issued such a seal, the traditional symbol of an anti-dynastic movement which no longer recognized the authority of the emperor. Doing so at this time was perhaps a concession to the more traditionally-minded secret society elders who preferred to follow earlier patterns in challenging the authority of the dynasty. Yet this new combination was nothing more than a loose military alliance; none of the organizations surrendered its autonomy, nor were they closely bound by political ideas. The purpose of the agreement was to provide Sun with three geographic foci for an anti-dynastic uprising: Kwangtung-Kwangsi, Fukien-Chekiang, and the Yangtze Valley. But the loyalty of the secret society elders, especially those from the north, was highly questionable. Already Miyazaki suspected that one of the Ko Lao Hui representatives was secretly in league with K'ang Yu-wei.[101] In the meantime, several of the Ko Lao Hui chieftains, subsidized by Ch'en Shao-pai, went to Japan for a strategic conference with Sun; afterwards they were sent home to await further instructions.[102]

Nonetheless, Miyazaki was gratified by the turn of events. He considered the Hong Kong meeting with the secret society leaders a memorable occasion, and despite the bad news concerning the Filipino expedition, he felt that he and Ch'en had encouraged Sun with their report from Hong Kong. Miyazaki was elated, and when an old comrade asked what he had "on schedule," he replied that he was trying to "put Mill's doctrine of liberty into practice in China." (Was this perhaps because it was not so easy to realize the spirit of liberty in Japan?). He hoped to get a thousand rifles for the forthcoming action, and if not, he would join a group of Chinese bandits. But the promise of a five-thousand yen contribution from Nakano Tokujirō, an agent for Kyushu mining interests, strengthened his faith that

---

[100] Miyazaki, *Thirty-three Years' Dream* [200], p. 198.
[101] *Ibid.*, pp. 195–198.
[102] Ch'en Shao-pai, *Hsing Chung Hui* [152], p. 41.

the first Sino-Japanese revolutionary venture would be successful.[103] Tempering this impetuous Japanese mood, however, was
the more cautious attitude of Sun Yat-sen, who still had a few
non-military angles to pursue.

[103] Miyazaki, *Thirty-three Years' Dream* [200], pp. 204–205.

VII

Li Hung-chang, Sir Henry Blake, and Ho Kai

In the summer of 1900 it seemed that fate had finally favored Sun Yat-sen and his flexible tactics. The Boxer rising, which split Chinese officialdom and drew the wrath of the foreigners upon the dynasty, provided an ideal context for Sun's second attempt. The same embittered peasants whom Sun had earlier tried to enlist against the dynasty, joined the Boxer movement, (as will be explained in the next chapter) and their outburst manifested widespread hostility to the forced penetration of China by Western religion and commerce. Since 1899 reactionary officials, including a Peking Manchu faction led by Kang-i and Prince Tuan, had relied upon the Boxers, originally constituted as an ordinary secret society, as the ultimate weapon against the foreign threat. Other court officials and influential governors-general realized the folly of provoking the foreigners and attempted to suppress the movement.[1] However, with the aid of their patrons in the capital, the Boxers dominated Peking and its environs by June. The Empress Dowager, mistakenly convinced that the foreign powers were bent upon her replacement, gave the movement her blessing. As the Boxers massacred Chinese Christians, destroyed foreign property, and threatened the lives of foreign missionaries and diplomats, an international relief force attempted to fight its way to Peking from Tientsin. On June 18, this British-led column was attacked by Chinese troops.

---

[1] See Tan, *The Boxer Catastrophe* [120], pp. 76–92, for a discussion of the roles played by the anti-Boxer officials in the Yangtze Valley in the south.

On the 20th, the foreign legations in Peking were besieged by the Boxers, and on the next day, the Chinese government declared war against the foreign powers.

But anti-Boxer officials, led by Li Hung-chang and other provincial leaders, refused to acknowledge the declaration of war. Displaying shrewd diplomatic skill, this peace faction, which controlled China's overseas envoys, argued that the throne had not authorized the war. The Boxers and their patrons, they declared, were actually rebels. As long as these provincial officials suppressed Boxerism and other demonstrations of anti-foreignism, the foreigners were willing to accept the "rebellion" connotation and to restrict their belligerency to the north. Understandably, however, foreigners kept a wary watch on the behavior of these moderates who coupled their defiance of Peking's orders with protestations of loyalty to the dynasty.

As this extraordinary and highly delicate situation evolved, Sun Yat-sen discerned two lines of approach. He could seek collaboration with the powerful regional leaders, whose opposition to Boxerism threatened to sever their formal ties to Peking; or he could woo the invading foreigners, either on his own, or in alliance with a defecting official. There were various sub-plots to Sun's maneuvers, but all were linked to these two main considerations.

First there was renewed hope in Li Hung-chang, who had been appointed Governor-General of the Liang-Kwang provinces at the end of 1899. While Li and other southern leaders were recoiling from the xenophobic fever gripping Peking, Liu Hsüeh-hsün, the opportunistic lottery manager, opened negotiations with Sun.

Except for a mysterious visit to Japan in August 1899, when he sought Sun's help in meeting Inukai and Ōkuma,[2] nothing

[2] See Sun's letter of August 28, 1899 to Inukai, arranging for Liu's appointment two days later, in *Collected Works* [205], V, 16. The year is not given in the original copy of this letter, and Lo Chia-lun (ed.), *Sun's Calligraphy* [193], I, 124, suggests it was written the following year, that is, August 28, 1900. But since both Sun and Liu were in Shanghai on August 31, 1900, it does not seem possible that Sun would have arranged an August

had been heard from Liu Hsüeh-hsün since the Canton episode of 1895. At the end of May or the beginning of June 1900, as an official in Li Hung-chang's yamen, he wrote to Sun that his chief was thinking of declaring the independence of his two provinces and wanted Sun's participation. He invited Sun to Canton for a parley.[3]

Was Liu acting on behalf of Li, or as the agent of the Cantonese gentry, who wanted to be dissociated from the imminent Boxer war?[4] Or was the invitation actually a trap? With officials and gentry occupied by the Boxer crisis, it seemed unlikely that Sun's capture still rated high priority, but it was a possibility which could not be discounted. Sun nevertheless decided that the offer was worth exploring. On June 8, he sailed for Hong Kong on a French steamer, the S.S. *Indus*, with Ch'en Shao-pai, Cheng Shih-liang, Miyazaki, and two other Japanese, Kiyofuji Kōshichirō and Uchida Ryōhei. They arrived on June 17.[5] Although registered as "Dr. Nakayama" from Yokohama, Sun could not risk landing, and held an hour-long deliberation in a sampan with his two followers, and Hirayama, who had preceded them to Hong Kong, Yang Ch'ü-yün, and Tse Tsan-tai.

---

30 appointment for him in Tokyo. Bland, *Li Hung-chang* [6], p. 204, states that Liu was on a "secret mission" for the Empress Dowager; and Fan Wen-lan, *Modern Chinese History* [158], I, 356, claims that his object was to arrange for the assassination of K'ang and Liang.

[3] The contents of Liu's letter are summarized in Feng, *Reminiscences* [160], I, 77.

[4] When Li made preparations to leave a month later, Cantonese merchants threatened to lie in front of the wheels of his carriage in order to stop him; see the *Hongkong Telegraph*, July 17, 1900. See also Jansen, *Sun Yat-sen* [69], p. 89 and notes 18 and 19 on pages 245–246 for U. S. Consular reports on panic among the gentry in Canton.

[5] See the list of arrivals on the S.S. *Indus*, in the *Hongkong Telegraph*, June 18, 1900; list of departures in the *Japan Times*, June 10, 1900; and Sun's statement to Governor Swettenham of the Straits Settlements in FO 17/1718 [46], p. 351. Miyazaki's memory failed him in this instance, and his statement that they sailed from Japan on the *Nippon Maru* (Miyazaki, *Thirty-three Years' Dream* [200], p. 208) could not possibly be true since that ship left for San Francisco via Honolulu on June 12th; see the *Japan Times*, June 12, 1900.

Finally it was decided that Miyazaki, Kiyofuji, and Uchida, who under extraterritoriality were immune to Chinese arrest, should first meet Liu before Sun exposed himself. Liu had sent a gunboat which now conveyed the three Japanese to his spacious quarters.

What exactly ensued in the all-night discussion is not clear, but Liu apparently told Sun's emissaries that until Peking was occupied by the allied powers, the political situation would be in flux and that the governor-general could not commit himself.[6] On the following day, Li Hung-chang received instructions from the court to return to Peking.[7] This was the first intimation that his services were needed in the capital, and until he discerned the purpose for which he was wanted, to help wage the war which he opposed or parley for the peace which he sought, there was no need to commit himself to the drastic course of separatism.

Sun could not wait for his friends' return, but had to sail with the *Indus*, when it left for Saigon on the 18th. He was accompanied by Mulkern, who had kept his London promise and become the only Westerner actually to join the Hsing Chung Hui.[8] As the ship departed, it was sighted by Miyazaki's party on their way back, and a few days later Sun was telegraphed the results of the conference.[9] He himself sent a wire to Liu soon after his arrival in Saigon on June 21, an indication that Sun did not feel that the door to Canton was closed.[10] Peking's declaration of war against the foreign powers on the 21st may have led him to believe that Li Hung-chang would finally decide to declare independence.

[6] Miyazaki, *Thirty-three Years' Dream* [200], pp. 211–212; Tse, *Chinese Republic* [122], p. 19; and Feng, *Reminiscences* [160], I, 78.

[7] Tan, *Boxer Catastrophe* [120], p. 120.

[8] Mulkern's name also appears on the S.S. *Indus* passenger list; see *Hongkong Telegraph*, June 18, 1900, and Sun's statement in Singapore, in FO 17/1718 [46] p. 351. See also Feng, in *Documents* [179], III, 355, under "Mo-ken."

[9] Miyazaki, *Thirty-three Years' Dream* [200], p. 210; Lo Chia-lun, *Biography* [192], I, 94.

[10] See Sun's letter to Hirayama from Saigon on June 22 in *Collected Works* [205], V, 19–20.

Competition from the Pao Huang Hui

While Li's decision was pending, Sun and his lieutenants pursued yet another course—the well worn path to K'ang Yu-wei.[11] Since the end of January 1900, K'ang had been living in Singapore after a brief visit in Hong Kong on his way back from Canada.[12] Despite the disappointments of the past, there were compelling reasons for Sun and Miyazaki to decide upon a further attempt to negotiate with K'ang.

First, renewed negotiations with the reformers might be considered tangential to the effort directed toward Li Hung-chang and Liu Hsüeh-hsün. If the Cantonese gentry were bent upon breaking away from Peking, then Cantonese reformers could be just as helpful as revolutionaries. According to Japanese investigators, this was in fact the expressed desire of the gentry at the Liu-Miyazaki conference, and they are said to have supplied Miyazaki with a peace offering for K'ang and a promise that additional funds would be sent to Singapore.[13]

Second, and most important, the revolutionaries were losing to the Pao Huang Hui in the race for *hua-ch'iao* money. In addition to the Yokohama take-over, K'ang had done well in Canada, where he dazzled the *hua-ch'iao* merchants and peddlers with his imperial credentials. He raised $7,000 and formed Pao Huang Hui branches in Vancouver and Victoria.[14] He was also doing well in Singapore under the sponsorship of wealthy *hua-ch'iao* like Ch'iu Shu-yüan (Khoo Seck Wan), heir to one of the great fortunes in the Straits Settlements.[15] An even more alarming development, however, took place in Hawaii.

---

[11] Miyazaki, *Thirty-three Years' Dream* [200], p. 210.

[12] After returning from Canada in the end of October 1899, K'ang stayed in Japan for a few days and left for Hong Kong on the 28th, where he remained until his departure for Singapore on January 27, 1900. See Satow to Salisbury, October 31, 1899, in CO 129/295 [46]; and Blake to Chamberlain, January 27, 1900, in CO 129/297 [46].

[13] Jansen, *Sun Yat-sen* [69], p. 87.

[14] See Ch'en Shao-pai, *Hsing Chung Hui* [152], pp. 43–44, on K'ang's success in impressing the *hua-ch'iao*. See also Huang Fu-luan, *Overseas Chinese* [175], pp. 109–110; and Lo Feng-lu to Salisbury, February 7, 1900, in FO 17/1718 [46], p. 254.

[15] Png Poh Seng, "The Kuomintang in Malaya" [92], p. 1; Song Ong

After the first few months of 1900 came the news that Liang, instead of breaking with K'ang, had raised havoc with the Hsing Chung Hui. Soon after arriving in Honolulu, Liang had written Sun that circumstances dictated devious measures but that he still hoped they could cooperate. He was obsessed with the problem "day and night" and begged for time while he worked out a satisfactory solution.[16] But when he discovered the potency of the "protect the emperor" slogan, his desire for cooperation rapidly cooled. The Hawaiian *hua-ch'iao* responded with a wave of enthusiasm which almost drowned out the memory of Sun Yat-sen. The Pao Huang Hui branches which Liang established were not only more successful than the Hsing Chung Hui, but were even led mainly by Sun's former disciples.[17] Among those drawn away by Liang was Chung Kun Ai, one of Sun's closest friends, who provides a first-hand account of Liang's success:

Without previous announcement Liang Ch'i-ch'ao came to Honolulu as a political refugee. The news spread like wildfire. . . . Everyone wanted to meet this famous reformer. I too called and fell under the spell of the man. A group of us were so enthusiastic that we formed a branch of the "Protect Emperor Party". . . . We collected subscriptions to send to the main bodies in Macao and Hong Kong. In all, I must have sent $30,000 of our currency. Liang himself was in great demand as a speaker. His intimate, behind-the-scene sketches of political intrigue and corruption in Peking, his picture of the pitiful Emperor Kuang-hsü imprisoned in a small pavilion in the South Lake within the Forbidden City, and his outline of the reforms that would be necessary to make China a modern country;

Siang, *Chinese in Singapore* [110], pp. 101–102; Lo Chia-lun, *Biography* [192], I, 94.

[16] Liang arrived in Honolulu on December 31, 1899. His letter to Sun is dated January 11th. See Feng, *Reminiscences* [160], I, 15–16.

[17] In his letter to K'ang of April 29th, Liang admitted that the most influential Pao Huang Hui members formerly belonged to Sun's party, and whether they had been members or not, all had been in contact with Sun. Although these former supporters of Sun now felt that the Pao Huang Hui had more capable leadership, Liang explained, he was reluctant to send them to Hong Kong to participate in the contemplated Canton uprising because he was afraid they would discover that the Hsing Chung Hui was stronger in the British colony. For that reason he did not send any of Sun's former military cadets; see Ting, *Biography of Liang* [214], I, 124.

these and other talks kept our enthusiasm at white-heat. . . . Many persons gave Liang money for his personal use. . . .[18]

Even worse, Sun's brother, Sun Mei, assumed leadership of the Pao Huang Hui branch in Maui and contributed $1,000. Sun's letter of introduction, which Liang did not mention to his friends in Hong Kong and Macao,[19] facilitated this relationship, but even so it seems that Sun Mei, no less than the other *hua-ch'iao*, was overawed by the presence of a self-styled imperial emissary who carried prestige which Sun Mei's brother could never provide. Over Yat-sen's objections, Sun Mei later sent his son to Liang's Ta-t'ung school in Japan.[20]

Liang's great success was also due to the timing of his visit. His arrival practically coincided with the imperial decree which named Prince Tuan's son heir-apparent to the throne, a move interpreted as a death sentence for the imprisoned emperor.[21] Liang himself felt the urgency of his mission and imparted his concern to the *hua-ch'iao*, who thrilled to the idea of aiding in the emperor's rescue. Liang began organizing in January 1900, and six months later, he was still on hand to capitalize upon the latest excitement, the Boxer uprising.

Since Sun had last been in Hawaii, the annexation of the Islands by the United States, bringing with it the application to Hawaii of the notorious American exclusion law, had intensified *hua-ch'iao* nationalism. Only a few weeks after Liang's arrival, the American health authorities, while fighting an outbreak of bubonic plague, accidentally set fire to the entire Honolulu Chinatown. Chinese property-owners incurred damages esti-

[18] Chung Kun Ai, *My Seventy Nine Years* [26], pp. 301–302. Leong Yum-nam (Liang Yin-nan), Liang's relative, was elected head of the branch; see Ting, *Biography of Liang* [214], I, 106.

[19] Liang's letter to Hong Kong and Macao, June 17th, in Ting, *Biography of Liang* [214], I, 130.

[20] Feng, *Reminiscences* [160], I, 16; II, 4. A warm friendship seemed to have blossomed between Liang and Sun's brother, and *ibid.*, II, 4–5, has two letters sent by Liang to Sun Mei in July, thanking him for his contribution and pressing for more funds to support their pending uprising.

[21] Ting, *Biography of Liang* [214], I, 95–96. This decree, issued in the name of the Küang-hsü Emperor on January 24, 1900, is translated in Bland and Backhouse [7], pp. 303–304. It was rescinded in November, 1901.

mated at three million dollars, and compensation was not only slow in coming, but inadequate.[22] Exploiting the bitter anti-American reaction, Liang promised that once the emperor was restored, foreigners—in his letters he would sometimes call American "white bandits" (*pai-tsei*)—would no longer dare "insult" the Chinese, whether at home or overseas, with impunity.[23]

But there was more to Liang's success than a combination of fortuitous circumstances and high connections. He succeeded because he was convinced that the time had come for the use of force, and the pragmatic, activist mood which governed his behavior led him to not only emulate Sun Yat-sen's tactics, but to surpass them. Like Sun, he used projected military campaigns to attract *hua-ch'iao* support, and in addition to the Yangtze Valley plot already under way, he pressed for an attack on Kwangtung. He concluded from his study of strategy that one of the reasons for the Taiping defeat was the failure to secure their southern base.[24] Like Sun, he realized that action in their home province was more likely to attract *hua-ch'iao* money and fighters. He even joined the Triads, when he found that the secret society claimed the allegiance of most of the Hawaiian *hua-ch'iao*.[25] Despite his uncle's influence with the secret society, Sun had not yet taken this step.[26] That Liang did so, even when anticipating K'ang's disapproval, reflects his bold endorsement of unconventional methods. Though he admitted that activating the Ko Lao Hui was potentially dangerous, he warned K'ang that this was not the

[22] The fire took place on January 20, 1900. After deliberating two years the Hawaiian government reimbursed fifty per cent of the losses; see Chung Kun Ai, *My Seventy Nine Years* [26], pp. 191–192.

[23] Feng, *Reminiscences* [160], I, 16; Levenson, *Liang Ch'i-ch'ao* [76], p. 65. Liang was disturbed by the discrimination practiced by the American health authorities against Chinese. According to the anti-plague regulations, even Asians who were vaccinated could not go to the United States, but white men could. This interfered with his plan to raise money on the American continent; see his letter to K'ang, April 4, 1900, in Ting, *Biography of Liang* [214], I, 111.

[24] Letter to K'ang, April 12, in Ting, *Biography of Liang* [214], I, 113.

[25] Letter to K'ang, March 13, in *ibid.*, I, 102. At this time there were 25,767 Chinese in Hawaii; see Griswold, *Far Eastern Policy* [48], p. 344.

[26] Feng, in *Documents* [179], III, 333, under "Yang Wen-na."

time to stand on principle and rely only upon his purebred disciples.[27]

Again like his rival, Liang recognized the need for courting foreign support. Not all foreigners were enemies,[28] he lectured his colleagues, and he urged that they establish a foreign language newspaper to improve external relations.[29] Once the fighting started, he urged that they issue a proclamation promising the fulfillment of European claims and demands.[30] And in a move characteristic of Sun Yat-sen, Liang engaged an American businessman, reputedly connected with the Secretary of State and strongly recommended by the *hua-ch'iao*, to act as his agent in the United States. If the Americans invested money in the pro-emperor movement, Liang argued, they would eventually throw in men and arms to protect their investment.[31] He also advocated recruiting Filipino and Japanese fighters, again an idea originally conceived by Sun Yat-sen.[32]

But if Liang matched Sun's activist mood and his talent for imaginative scheming, he nevertheless adhered to the political aims of K'ang Yu-wei. On April 28, 1900, making his last conciliatory gesture to Sun, Liang wrote that the entire country was agi-

[27] Letters to K'ang, March 27 and April 29, in Ting, *Biography of Liang* [214], I, 107, 124.

[28] Letters to Ch'iu Shu-yüan, March 13, in *ibid.*, I, 104, and to K'ang, April 12, in *ibid.*, I, 113, 116.

[29] Letters to Ch'iu Shu-yüan, March 13; K'ang, March 20; *Chih-hsin pao* comrades (Macao), March 28; T'ang Fu-ch'eng and Ti Ch'u-ch'ing, April 20; in *ibid.*, I, 104, 106, 107, 119.

[30] Letter to K'ang, April 12, in *ibid.*, I, 116.

[31] This American is identified as "He-ch'in" (Hutchins?), who was in Peking in 1898 where Liang met him in Li Hung-chang's office and who later fought in Cuba. Liang at first was supposed to accompany him to New York and was prepared to invest $10,000 for six months' expenses. When he found that he could not use his Japanese passport to visit the United States, he gave "He-ch'in" $20,000 to act on his behalf, but I have not found any reference as to the outcome of this enterprise. See letters to K'ang, March 20, April 4, April 12, and April 29, in *ibid.*, I, 105, 111, 115, 123.

[32] Letters to K'ang, March 20 and April 12, in *ibid.*, I, 104–105; 116; letter to Yeh Hsiang-nan and others, April 8, in *ibid.*, I, 117. Liang advised that they also ask Inukai and Ōkuma whether the Japanese government would help them after they captured Wuchang or Nanking.

tated by the rumored threat to the emperor's life, and that those who wanted to save the emperor were "as plentiful as tall grass looking for rain." The pro-emperor slogan, he wrote, was too valuable to be sacrificed, and though he too admired republicanism, he felt it could best be realized by first restoring the emperor to power, and then making him president of the republic. Thus the aims of both groups would be satisfied, and together they could raise an irresistible force of "ten million" men.[33]

There is no record of Sun's reply, if any, to this proposal. It was clear to Sun, however, that Liang would never repudiate K'ang Yu-wei. Sun had always favored cooperation, but Liang had repeated the Yokohama school take-over on a grand scale. It was especially bitter that, by convincing the *hua-ch'iao* that an armed struggle to save the Kuang-hsü Emperor was the same as conducting a revolution, Liang had robbed Sun of his most exclusive claim.[34] In fact, the thin line separating "reform" and "revolution" had become blurred during this first half of 1900, when Liang and his Hunan-Hupeh friends were acting just as militantly as Sun Yat-sen. There was a real danger that Sun would be pushed out of the picture while the scholar reformers became activists. Even his own camp was not free from dissension; one maverick was Tse Tsan-tai, who in April suggested to Yang Ch'ü-yün that the senior returned-student, Yung Wing, be elected "President of the United Reform Parties."[35]

In these circumstances, Sun favored a further appeal to K'ang. The monarchical-republican issue may not have been of paramount importance then, since there was a strong possibility that the emperor would not live long enough to be rescued. The main effort was to coordinate his own bid for power with the

---

[33] *Ibid.*, I, 140–141. This letter is dated 29th day of third month, but I am assuming that this and other letters quoted by Ting are dated according to the lunar calendar. For example in his letter to K'ang, dated 13th of second month, he states that he has been in Hawaii for over seventy days, and since he arrived on December 31, 1899, the letter must have been written on March 13. See *ibid.*, I, 102. I have adjusted all dates to the Gregorian calendar.

[34] Feng, *Reminiscences* [160], II, 4.

[35] Tse, *Chinese Republic* [122], p. 18.

planned reformist risings in the south and along the Yangtze. Though dismayed by Liang's inconstancy, Sun felt that the situation might be saved by direct negotiations with K'ang.

But how would Sun reconcile the results of these negotiations with those still pending with Li Hung-chang? Possibly the Cantonese gentry desired K'ang's inclusion. Surprisingly enough, there is also evidence that Li himself was surreptitiously maintaining contact with the reformers after they had fled from China, and even as late as the spring of 1900, Liang replied politely to a friendly gesture from Li via Japanese intermediaries.[36] Yet despite these hesitant efforts at fence-mending dictated by the uncertain course of Chinese politics, there was overwhelming evidence of an unrelenting animosity between Li and the reformers. Li had been assigned to Kwangtung for the express purpose of stamping out the subversive activities of both K'ang and Sun. And he appeared to be performing this task with ruthless efficiency as far as the Pao Huang Hui was concerned. Relatives of overseas members had been arrested,[37] and an attempt on K'ang's life in Hong Kong earlier in the year was suspected to have been inspired by the Canton yamen.[38] Although he had assured Governor Blake of Hong Kong that he had rejected an offer to have K'ang assassinated, Li added 40,000 taels to the 100,000 taels which Peking had placed on K'ang's head.[39] Li and

[36] Ting, *Biography of Liang* [214], I, 100. See also Liang's letter to K'ang, April 4, 1900, in *ibid.*, I, 112, for evidence of Li's attempt to contact K'ang in Singapore.

[37] *Ibid.*, I, 100. Chung Kun Ai, *My Seventy Nine Years* [26], p. 305, describes the indignation felt by the *hua-ch'iao* when they learned that Leong Yum-nam's grandmother died of fear (?) in her native village when she learned that she and the rest of the family would be arrested because her grandson gave hospitality to his notorious cousin.

[38] Hao, "Reformers and Revolutionaries" [52], p. 108.

[39] The Shanghai magistrate offered an additional 5,000 taels award. The two imperial edicts announcing rewards for the apprehension of K'ang and Liang were issued on December 20, 1899 and February 14, 1900, and are translated in Blake to Chamberlain, January 3, 1900, in CO 129/297, and Macdonald to Salisbury, February 16, 1900, in CO 273/264 [46]. For Li's proclamation see the *Straits Times* report in Swettenham to Chamberlain, April 9, 1900, in FO 17/1718 [46], p. 318. See also Levenson, *Liang Ch'i-ch'ao* [76], p. 63.

even more his right-hand man, Liu Hsüeh-hsün, were considered the stumbling blocks to the pro-emperor forces in Kwangtung, and, writing from Hawaii, Liang pressed for their assassination.[40] The *hua-ch'iao*, incensed over the reprisals against their relatives, could have been expected to shower the Pao Huang Hui with contributions had it delivered the heads of Li and Liu.

While Sun could not resist a cautious nibble at the Canton bait, there was thus little chance that K'ang would touch it even from a distance. Liang may have on one occasion favored sparing Li Hung-chang and using him as a puppet to placate foreigners and local gentry, come the revolution,[41] but neither he nor K'ang felt Sun's compulsion to join forces with prominent officials. K'ang did not need the prestige of Li or any other governor-general, but on the contrary, jealously guarded his claim to the emperor's confidence and sought to disqualify the southern officials from participation in a projected reformist government.[42] He was in fact already acting like the premier of a government in exile, while Sun was seeking high and low for a toehold in the gentry-dominated political structure. In this political setting, Miyazaki set out for Singapore to negotiate with K'ang on Sun's behalf. In the end, K'ang's haughty intransigence, as well as his fears, turned Miyazaki's mission into a fiasco.

Accompanied by Kiyofuji and Uchida, Miyazaki arrived at the colony on June 29, 1900.[43] When he wrote to K'ang asking for an interview, he was politely but firmly put off, the excuse being that

[40] Letters to *Chih-hsin pao* comrades, March 28; Ch'eng, Chung and Ya, March 28; K'ang, April 8; headquarters in Macao, April 9; Hsü Chün-mien, April 29; in Ting, *Biography of Liang* [214], I, 106, 108, 117, 128.

[41] Liang's letter to K'ang, March 13, in Ting, *ibid.*, I, 116.

[42] In his letter of November 14, 1900, to the Marquis of Lansdowne, British Foreign Secretary, K'ang requested that in addition to restoring the Kuang-hsü Emperor and arresting reactionary officials, the foreigners should keep "careful watch . . . over the so-called friendly Viceroys of the south . . . take full account of their doings before you treat them as real friends of progress and of foreigners. Do they not send men, money, and armaments to the Empress Dowager, while they have signed an agreement of peace with the consuls? They are in reality obedient servants of the Empress Dowager, and it is important that Your Lordship should beware of them." FO 17/1718 [46], p. 383.

[43] Swettenham to Chamberlain, July 26, 1900, CO 273/257 [46].

K'ang was so well-guarded by the British that he could not receive visitors.[44] Actually, K'ang had already been warned by letter and telegram from Hong Kong that a party of Japanese were on their way to assassinate him, and it can be assumed that the fears of his associates were based upon knowledge of the earlier meeting with Liu Hsüeh-hsün.[45] As Miyazaki renewed his pleas for a meeting, K'ang's suspicions grew and on July 5 the British police went into action.[46]

Here we should point out that the British, despite the antiforeign tenor of some of K'ang's Chinese articles and the ridicule with which the Foreign Office generally greeted his pompous pronouncements,[47] were much more solicitous of his welfare than they were of Sun's. The fact that K'ang supported the emperor, still the legitimate ruler of China, made it difficult to treat him

[44] Miyazaki, *Thirty-three Years' Dream* [200], p. 214; Jansen, *Sun Yat-sen* [69], p. 87.

[45] Feng, *History of the Revolution* [159], pp. 51, 307. According to Miyazaki's acquaintance Kitamura, who worked for the newspaper published by K'ang's party in Singapore, the "assassins" were said to have come from Yokohama. See Miyazaki, *Thirty-three Years' Dream* [200], pp. 213, 216.

[46] On July 5th the British police entrusted with guarding K'ang first heard about the warning he had received, and subsequent investigation revealed the suspicious behavior of Miyazaki's party. It can be assumed that K'ang instigated the police action. See Swettenham's memorandum of July 12, 1900, in FO 17/1718 [46], p. 341.

[47] Acting Consul Bourne, for example, who interviewed K'ang as he fled on the S.S. *Balaarat* on September 25, 1898, described the reformist leader as being "stuffed up with nonsense by Timothy Richard." See Brenan to Foreign Office, September 26, 1898, in FO 17/1718 [46], p. 191. K'ang's lengthy communication to the British in Hong Kong, including a copy of his purportedly secret memorial from the Emperor and a denunciation of the Empress Dowager, was considered by the Colonial Office to be no more than a "quaint effusion"; see enclosure in Black (acting administrator of the Hong Kong government) to Chamberlain, November 15, 1898, in CO 129/286 [46]. Black, it should be pointed out, did not share the "too contemptuous" estimate of K'ang's reformist projects held by an official of the Peking Legation who accompanied K'ang from Shanghai; see Black to Chamberlain, October 8, 1898, in CO 129/285 [46]. A year later, when Lo Feng-lu wrote to Salisbury, protesting against K'ang's being granted asylum by the British, his reference to K'ang's "crude notions of reform" was considered "An excellent phrase" by an unidentified Foreign Office official; see Lo to Salisbury, December 6, 1899, in CO 129/295 [46].

as an ordinary rebel, even though they feared that friendliness toward him would enable other powers to persuade the Chinese that they were "encouraging . . . the overthrow of the existing order . . . in China."[48] Governor Blake of Hong Kong had provided K'ang with armed guards against Manchu assassins,[49] and in Singapore, where K'ang had arrived on January 31, 1900, Sir James Alexander Swettenham, Governor of the Straits Settlements, had followed London's instructions[50] and sent a detachment of Sikhs to protect him.[51]

While the police prepared affidavits to support an order of banishment against Miyazaki and party, a Japanese interpreter whom they employed warned his compatriots of what was brewing.[52] This may have been the reason for Uchida's sudden de-

[48] FO to CO, December 29, 1899, in CO 129/295 [46].

[49] Blake reported that K'ang was living a quiet life in Hong Kong and was not engaging in any political activities, his only visitors being members of his clan. Blake had eighteen constables protecting K'ang, and he suggested to London that the Peking government be forced to reimburse them for this expense; see Blake to Chamberlain, January 3, 1900, in CO 129/297 [46]. The Chinese at this time were exerting tremendous pressure upon the British to keep K'ang out of their colonies. Lo Feng-lu again reminded them that Hong Kong had served as a base for the Taiping rebels and he also contended that both the Japanese and U.S. governments had refused refuge to K'ang; see Lo's letter to Salisbury, December 6, 1899, in CO 129/295 [46]. Satow, British Minister to Japan, was informed by Foreign Minister Aoki that his government had resolved to prohibit K'ang's residence there; see Satow to Salisbury, October 31, 1899, in CO 129/295 [46]. The American position was not ascertained but it was assumed that the exclusion law would be sufficient to keep K'ang out.

[50] Though the Colonial Office would have been happier had K'ang found a more distant haven—like Ceylon—and Swettenham had actually wanted to persuade him to leave Singapore, London was determined to protect him if he decided to stay. See Swettenham to Chamberlain, January 30, 1900, in CO 273/264 [46]; Chamberlain to Swettenham, February 17, 1900, in CO 273/264 [46]; Swettenham to Lucas (Colonial Under Secretary), February 24, 1900 (private), in FO 17/1718 [46], pp. 301–306; Lo Feng-lu to Salisbury, February 7, 1900, in FO 17/1718 [46], pp. 253–254.

[51] *London Times*, February 10, 1900; London even considered protesting against the reward for K'ang's assassination, but Macdonald dissuaded them, though he did warn Li Hung-chang that the British would consider it an "insult" were K'ang murdered in their territory. See FO 17/1718 [46], pp. 264–271, February 16, 1900.

[52] Swettenham's memorandum of July 12, in FO 17/1718 [46], p. 342.

parture on July 6,[53] but Miyazaki, who had escorted K'ang to his haven in Japan just a year and a half previously, was disturbed by the assassination plot rumor and sent another letter to the reformer deploring police intervention and claiming the support of Ōkuma and Itagaki.[54] On July 6, however, the warrants were ready and Miyazaki and Kiyofuji were taken into custody.[55]

When the Japanese were searched, K'ang's alarm appeared to be well-grounded. Two "sharp and clean" samurai swords, one claimed by each, a dagger, claimed for Uchida, and more than $27,000 in Hong Kong and Shanghai currency were found by the police. It was also discovered that they had been sending and receiving telegrams in cipher. The impression they made under interrogation only confirmed police suspicions. Although K'ang had put a wrong construction on their business with him, they did not wish to disclose its nature to the British and instead took refuge in a flimsy tale which made them even more suspect. Their story had apparently been agreed upon ahead of time since they told practically the same thing, though examined separately. They had left Japan, they maintained, in the company of Uchida, who was on a mission to China on behalf of his uncle, the Kyushu mine-owner Hiraoka. Uchida and Kiyofuji were to go to Kweichow or Szechwan in order to buy mining concessions with $20,000 of the money in their possession, and Kiyofuji was to remain there as a school teacher. Miyazaki introduced himself as a newspaper correspondent carrying money subscribed by his

---

This Japanese may have been Miyazaki's acquaintance from Hong Kong, Kitamura. According to Miyazaki, Kitamura kept him informed of K'ang's suspicions and of the debate in K'ang's camp concerning the advisability of seeing him. K'ang offered to placate Miyazaki with some of Ch'iu's money but this infuriated him even more; Miyazaki, *Thirty-three Years' Dream* [200], pp. 215–216.

[53] Miyazaki, *Thirty-three Years' Dream* [200], p. 217; Swettenham's memorandum, July 12, FO 17/1718 [46], p. 342.

[54] Miyazaki's version of this letter, *ibid.*, pp. 216–217, does not include the remarks attributed to him by Swettenham.

[55] Swettenham's memorandum, FO 17/1718 [46], p. 342, gives July 7 as the date of the arrests. But in his report to Chamberlain of July 26, he stated that the arrests were carried out on July 6; see Swettenham to Chamberlain, in CO 273/257 [46]. This earlier date appears to be correct.

friends before he left Japan. The three had decided to come to
Singapore to "see a new place," and once they were there, Miyazaki felt it his duty to renew his acquaintance with K'ang Yu-wei.
In addition to being a journalist, Miyazaki described himself as
an election agent and "prodigal," who in the last five years had
spent $200,000 which friends had given him. As for the swords,
they both contended that no Japanese gentleman ever traveled
without one.[56]

On the same day, July 6, Sun Yat-sen left for Singapore accompanied by Mulkern and two Japanese, Fukumoto Nichinan
and Ozaki Yukimasa, who had followed him to Saigon.[57] After
all these years, he still looked forward to his first meeting with
K'ang Yu-wei. But when they arrived three days later, Sun's immediate request for an interview met with an even colder rebuff
than in the past.[58] And of course Sun tried to look up his Japanese friends. When he and his party discovered that Miyazaki
and Kiyofuji were under arrest, their first reaction was to seek
the fastest transportation out of Singapore. But when the Japanese consulate informed them of the reason for the arrests, Sun
was confident he could clarify the matter.[59] He approached the
British through the Japanese consulate and on July 10 made a
statement in the presence of Swettenham and two other members
of the Committee of the Executive Council.[60] Since the Manchus
were at war with Britain, Sun decided that at least a partial disclosure of his plans would be the best way to secure his friends'
release.

Miyazaki and Kiyofuji, he stated, had come with him to Hong
Kong from Japan in order to protect him as they had previously

[56] Swettenham's memorandum, FO 17/1718 [46], pp. 342–345; Jansen,
Sun Yat-sen [69], p. 88. See also Wang Gung-wu, "Sun Yat-sen and Singapore" [126], pp. 51–58.
[57] Fukumoto and Ozaki left for Saigon from Hong Kong on July 2 on
the S.S. *Laos;* see the *Hongkong Telegraph,* July 2, 1900. Ozaki was the
brother of Ozaki Yukio, the famous parliamentarian; see Jansen, *Sun
Yat-sen* [69], p. 246, note 26.
[58] Miyazaki reports that Sun and his party arrived three days after his
arrest; see Miyazaki, *Thirty-three Years' Dream* [200], p. 232; Swettenham
fixes this date as July 9th; see his memorandum in FO 17/1718 [46], p. 345.
[59] Miyazaki, *Thirty-three Years' Dream* [200], pp. 241–242.
[60] A summary of Sun's statement appears in FO 17/1718 [46], pp. 351–352.

protected K'ang. He too was wanted by the Manchus, though the reward was only a third of that offered for K'ang. Miyazaki, he said, was his "great companion" and a "gentleman" whose acquaintance he had made through Inukai and who was being supported by a rich Japanese and some mine owners. "He is useful in Chinese political matters I cannot explain," Sun went on, and "he is afraid of injuring my cause; that is why he tells lies." As for the money in the prisoners' possession, Sun was quite sure that some of it was his and some subscribed, but none of it was Hiraoka's.

In addition to vouching for his Japanese friends, Sun used the occasion to let the British know he was trying to exert a sobering influence upon the Chinese masses. He came to Singapore, he explained, to see K'ang Yu-wei and to recruit followers. Though K'ang did not share his anti-Manchu policy, he wanted to talk things over and arrange for joint action. The Chinese people, he asserted, were bound to rise sooner or later, but he was trying to pacify them and provide leadership. Although ultimately he hoped to crush the Peking regime, his immediate object was to form an independent southern government. He promised that his movement would not create much of a disturbance but "without this, China cannot be reformed." He claimed a well-organized following in several of the southern provinces and boasted that the present quiet was largely due to their not moving. Sun believed that all the insurgents, "except for K'ang's party, perhaps," could be united into one body. They shared the fear that China would be partitioned and some of his men were pressing for action. If nothing were done, he was afraid they would go over "to the other side" (i.e., the Boxers).

Swettenham, however, still felt that the presence of the Japanese was undesirable, fearing that if they were not able to convince K'ang to join Sun, they would use violence to prevent him from interfering with their plans. In addition, he suspected them of planning to purchase arms in Singapore and to use the colony as a base for Sun's uprising. On July 11, therefore, Miyazaki and Kiyofuji were informed they were to be banished from Singapore for five years, and, on the basis of information supplied by K'ang, similar orders were issued against Uchida, who had already left, and Hirayama, who had never appeared. According to Swettenham, the prisoners were anxious to leave immediately and were allowed to board the *Sado Maru*, which departed for Hong Kong on its way to Japan the next day. Although he took no official action against Sun, the governor made it clear that he would not permit revolutionary agitation in his territory, and even tried to convince Sun that "it was inexpedient for a patriotic Chinese to raise fresh disturbances in China just at the moment it was about to be invaded by foreigners."[61] Since K'ang's attitude had foiled the primary object of his visit, and the British were frowning upon his activities in general, Sun took his other companions and joined the banished Japanese on the *Sado Maru*.

On July 17, just a month after he had first arrived there with such high hopes, Sun was back in Hong Kong waters. Though the path to K'ang Yu-wei had led to a dead end, the possibility of aligning with Li Hung-chang was still alive. Sun was still awaiting the results of the approach via Liu Hsüeh-hsün, and, as their ship reached Hong Kong, he confided to Miyazaki that his friends in the colony had thought of yet another way to reach Li.

Even more than the Canton gentry, the British in Hong Kong were unnerved by the prospect of a power vacuum in the two Kwang provinces, where secret societies of the same breed as the Boxers might be expected to enjoy free rein. It was only a year since the uneasy take-over of the New Territories acquired in 1898, and the Triads had apparently played a part in Chinese resistance. Also, during the last days of T'an Chung-lin's administration, free-wheeling piracy on the West River and uninhibited banditry in the entire area had not allowed the British the fullest enjoyment of their new acquisition.[62] With Li Hung-

[61] Swettenham to Chamberlain, July 26, 1900, in CO 273/257; FO 17/1718 [46], p. 347; the banishment orders against Miyazaki and Kiyofuji appear in the *Straits Settlements Government Gazette*, July 20, 1900, pp. 1620–1621. There is no record of Sun's being arrested in Singapore. Though London approved of Swettenham's action, one official felt that the deportation of the Japanese was "rather high-handed."

[62] Endacott, *Hong Kong* [36], pp. 263–265; Sercombe-Smith to Canton Consul, October 20, 1898, in FO 17/1436 [46]; Blake to Chamberlain, August 18, 1899, in CO 129/293 [46].

chang's arrival at the beginning of 1900, the situation had improved. Until now, Li, like the other non-belligerent officials, had kept his domain comparatively quiet and peaceful, and the news of his impending departure in response to an imperial summons caused consternation in the colony. In addition to being worried over the security of Western lives and property in the area, including Hong Kong itself, the British suspected Li's motives. Why was he willing to obey an imperial edict though the extremists were still in control in Peking? The legations, besieged from June 20 to August 14, were at this time still cut off, and it was known that the German minister had been killed. There was no assurance that the other foreigners had not met with a similar fate. (Such was the panic and suspicion that gripped the treaty port communities that credence was placed in a particularly blood-curdling story, later attributed to someone called "The Shanghai Liar," according to which the legations had been overrun, and every foreign man, woman, and child boiled alive in oil. Memorial services were even held in St. Paul's and other churches abroad.)[63] Uncertain as to what was happening in the north, indignant, and perhaps a little hysterical over what they had heard, the British in Hong Kong were reluctant to let the Manchu regime dictate a change in the administration of the southern provinces. And considering the possibility that the whole country was about to be partitioned, they were anxious to protect their own interests in the two Kwang provinces. Knowledge of strong Japanese influence among the Chinese dissidents undoubtedly contributed to their fear of being left out. Thus they were receptive to the idea of underwriting an entente between Li Hung-chang and Sun, should the two get together along the lines suggested by Liu Hsüeh-hsün.[64]

According to Ch'en Shao-pai, Ho Kai was actively involved with Sun once more and tried to use the good offices of Governor Blake to persuade Li Hung-chang to declare the independence of

---

[63] Arnold Wright, *Treaty Ports* [132], p. 358.
[64] Swettenham's memorandum of July 12, in FO 17/1718 [46], p. 349, and Blake's telegram of July 13, in CO 129/300 [46], reflect concern over Japanese activities in China at this time.

the two Kwangs. This new southern government, headed by Li, would then invite the cooperation of Sun's forces and the protection of the British. The first step was for the revolutionaries to win Blake over and then have him, or the British representatives in Canton, act as intermediaries to Li. Sun is said to have agreed to the scheme, and to have signed along with other Hsing Chung Hui members a proclamation, drafted in English by Ho, which outlined the reasons for the establishment of the new regime and described its political program. The proclamation was sent to Blake, who gave it his approval and then requested the British Consul in Canton to sound out Li's feelings. Without committing himself, Li is said to have reacted favorably.[65]

While British sources do not confirm the details of Ch'en Shao-pai's account, they do offer proof of Blake's intention to act the honest broker between Li and Sun. There is no evidence, however, that he was involved to the extent claimed by the revolutionaries. It appears, for example, that Liu Hsüeh-hsün's original approach to Sun preceded Governor Blake's intervention, since the governor had been on a leave of absence from April through June and did not return to Hong Kong until July 2.[66] By that time, Sun had already received Liu's letter, which we are told came to him as a surprise, and had passed through Hong Kong on his way to Saigon.[67] This of course does not preclude the possibility of Ho Kai's having concocted the scheme prior to Blake's arrival. In that case he might have been in touch with Major General Gascoigne, who was temporarily administering the government of Hong Kong. But that official made no mention of the revolutionaries when on June 20 he first reported Li's having received orders to go north. He did suggest that Li should be restrained from leaving Canton, but the Colonial Office did not think such a course would be feasible.[68] The fol-

[65] Ch'en Shao-pai, *Hsing Chung Hui* [152], p. 45; Lo Chia-lun, *Biography* [179], I, 93.

[66] See *Overland China Mail*, July 7, 1900, reporting Blake's return from Japan on the S.S. *Laos,* the same ship which Fukumoto and Ozaki boarded in Hong Kong. The *Laos* had left Kobe on June 22.

[67] Feng, *Reminiscences* [160], I, 77.

[68] Gascoigne to Chamberlain, telegram, June 20, 1900, in CO 129/299 [46].

lowing day, Gascoigne reported that Li Hung-chang intended to come to Hong Kong on a China Merchants Company steamer with a personal guard of one hundred men and then to transfer to a Canadian Pacific ship bound for Shanghai and Tientsin. While Gascoigne still thought it advisable that Li be detained, he also realized that such a move would risk making an enemy of a man whom he still considered to be friendly to Britain.[69] Yet the fact that Li had requested permission to pass through the colony raised the possibility that he was fishing for an honorable way of disobeying the court. Or he may have wanted some sign of British approval to lend more prestige to his peace-maker role. Thus his protégé in London, Lo Feng-lu, sounded out Britain's attitude, and on June 22, Salisbury replied that Britain had no objections to Li's departure.[70]

Thus far, Hong Kong had not mentioned the revolutionaries in connection with Li. However Blake, upon returning to the colony, was immediately approached by one of Sun's representatives, probably Ho Kai, and he then commenced his telegraphic appeals to London on behalf of the conspirators. His first message informed the Colonial Office that anti-Manchu uprisings were scheduled to break out in Hunan and in the south within "a fortnight's time." "The Chinese gentlemen," who had taken him into confidence, assured him that the rebels were not antiforeign and hoped for British protection once they achieved some success. Li Hung-chang, Blake continued, "is coquetting with this movement and there are rumours that he wishes to establish himself either as king or as president." After mentioning the Liu-Sun negotiations, Blake concluded that the report of the projected uprisings seemed reliable and that Britain should be prepared to look after her interests on both the Yangtze and the West River.[71]

On the 13th, after being warned by Swettenham that Sun and his entourage were on their way back from Singapore, Blake wired London that British interests would best be served if Sun

[69] Gascoigne to Chamberlain, telegram, June 21, 1900, in CO 129/299 [46].

[70] *China No. 3* [47], June 22, p. 70.

[71] Blake to Chamberlain, July 2, 1900, in CO 129/300 [46].

were allowed to conclude a pact with Governor-General Li. According to Blake's sources, Li offered to arm the "reformers" and the British governor considered the proposed entente a guarantee for peace in the south. He feared that "any great disturbance may resolve itself into an anti-foreign movement."[72]

With Blake briefed by his friends, and both Hong Kong and London upset by the Boxer crisis, Sun Yat-sen came closer at this point to receiving official British approval than perhaps at any other time in his life. While Chamberlain and Salisbury concurred with the Hong Kong view, they nevertheless emphasized the qualifying clause in Blake's proposal; only if Sun returned to the colony with the approval of Li Hung-chang were they prepared to lift the banishment order.[73] But on July 8, Peking had already renewed its pressure on Li and appointed him to his former post as Governor-General of Chihli and Minister of Trade for the Northern Ports.[74] Conciliated by the court and urged by anti-war officials to go north and save the situation, Li was now prepared to abort the negotiations with Sun and go at least part of the way to Peking.

Blake received this news from Consul Scott in Canton on July 13 and sent instructions the next day that Li should be urged to reconsider his decision.[75] Salisbury also wired Scott that the cause of peace would best be served if Li remained in Canton.[76] Politely refusing this advice, Li inquired whether he could be granted an interview when he passed through Hong Kong. The governor in the meantime implored London for permission to detain Li by force. Sharing Gascoigne's opinion, Blake felt that Li would not object. He also cited a telegram from an official of the Hongkong and Shanghai Banking Corporation in Shanghai, who feared that Li's arrival there would harm the good relations which the British consul was enjoying with the

[72] Blake to Chamberlain, July 13, 1900, in CO 129/300 [46].

[73] CO to FO (secret and pressing), July 14, 1900, in CO 129/300 [46]; and FO to CO, July 16, 1900, in FO 17/1718 [46], pp. 336–337.

[74] Tan, *Boxer Catastrophe* [120], p. 121.

[75] Scott to Blake, telegram, July 13, 1900, and Blake to Scott, July 14, enclosed in Blake to Chamberlain, July 19, in CO 129/300 [46].

[76] *China No. 1* [47], July 14, 1900, Salisbury to Scott, p. 13.

Yangtze officials.[77] While London deliberated, Blake sent another telegram on the 17th announcing that he was expecting Li the following morning and that he and his military advisers believed that Li's new appointment must have been made by the notorious Prince Tuan and should not be recognized by the British government. He intended to detain Li pending receipt of instructions from Chamberlain, which he hoped to receive before nine in the morning.[78] He did not have to wait long, for on that same day a telegram arrived from Chamberlain forbidding the detention of Li Hung-chang or any forcible interference with his movements.[79] Thus the initiative was taken out of Blake's hands and passed over to Li.

By a coincidence, the *Sado Maru*, carrying Sun, Miyazaki, *et al.* arrived on the 17th, the day Li was due from Canton. When their ship pulled into the harbor, Sun and his friends realized that things were not going well. Sun was still barred from the colony, and Miyazaki and Kiyofuji, thanks to the Singapore episode, were also on the banished list.[80] Sun's local associates told him that in the scheduled meeting the following morning, Blake would make a last stand to keep Li in Canton. If Li agreed to remain, or if he were detained after the conference, Sun would be allowed to land and negotiate with him. Although Sun told Miyazaki that he did not have too much confidence in the aged statesman's ability to take a broad view of the political situation (Li was 77 years old at this time), he thought it worth a try. His friend agreed that this was a unique opportunity to establish a base in the Kwangtung-Kwangsi provinces.[81] Neither of course

[77] Scott to Blake, July 14, 1900, enclosed in Blake to Chamberlain, July 19, 1900, in CO 129/300 [46]; Blake to Chamberlain, telegram, July 14, in CO 129/300 [46].

[78] If Li were able to assure him that the legations were safe, Blake stated, "the position would be different"; Blake to Chamberlain, telegram, July 17, 1900, in CO 129/300 [46]. The Hong Kong papers, the *Daily Press*, the *Telegraph*, and the *China Mail*, were all urging Blake to exert pressure on Li to remain in Canton.

[79] Lucas to Blake, telegram, July 17, 1900, in CO 129/300 [46].

[80] Miyazaki, *Thirty-three Years' Dream* [200], pp. 244–245.

[81] *Ibid.*, pp. 251–252. Li's ship, the C.M.S.N. Company's *An-ping*, arrived in Hong Kong harbor on the evening of the 17th.

knew that Blake had already been immobilized by Chamberlain.

On the 17th, Ho Kai's friend and fellow-member of the Legislative Council, Wei Yuk,[82] called upon Blake, and speaking for the Chinese residents of Hong Kong who had families in Canton, begged the governor to use his influence to keep Li from leaving. He told Blake that a "well-known Chinese official, closely connected with the Yamen," had come to Hong Kong and informed him that, while Li did not dare to disregard the imperial edict, he would welcome an excuse for refusing.[83]

This official may have been Liu Hsüeh-hsün, and if so, he was apparently acting on his own, or on behalf of the Canton gentry, for when Li Hung-chang met Blake on the following day, he showed no sign of wanting to be restrained. And far from suggesting a rendezvous with Sun Yat-sen, he urged the governor to prevent subversive elements from using Hong Kong as a base. On the other hand, in his conversation with Blake, which he specifically requested be reported to Salisbury, Li hinted at his own availability should the foreign powers decide to replace the Manchus with a Chinese ruler.

Blake expressed regret at Li's decision to leave. Li replied that he could not disobey an imperial edict and insisted that this order had been signed by the Empress Dowager and the emperor,

---

82 Wei, sharing Sun's Hsiang-shan antecedents, was born in Hong Kong in 1849. In 1879, he succeeded his father as comprador to the Chartered Mercantile Bank of India, London, and China. After graduating from Government Central School (which Sun also attended) he studied in England and Scotland for five years and so was one of the first Chinese to study abroad. He was married to the sister of Huang Yung-shang, who had been active in founding the Hong Kong branch of the Hsing Chung Hui in 1895. Like Ho Kai, he was a Justice of the Peace as well as a representative of the Chinese community on the Legislative Council and a recipient of the C.M.G. See Arnold Wright, *Treaty Ports* [132], p. 109.

83 Blake to Chamberlain, July 19, 1900, in CO 129/300 [46]. The *China Mail* also remarked, "We have a shrewd notion that the veteran Viceroy would not make any rigorous objection if he were informed his presence were specially required in his own provincial capital." See *Overland China Mail*, July 21, 1900. Yet once he arrived in Shanghai, Li is reported to have said that he would not have stopped in Hong Kong had he not seen a couple of British destroyers prowling around the mouth of the Canton River; *Hongkong Telegraph*, July 27.

and not, as Blake suggested, by Prince Tuan. The governor
kept pressing him to change his mind and ensure the preservation of peace in the south, pointing out that if even so strong
an official as Chang Chih-tung could not keep order in Hupeh,
"how could the Cantonese province be controlled without its
viceroy?" Li replied that the Cantonese were more "sensible"
than the people of Hunan and Hupeh, and then, as Blake phrased
it, proceeded to "turn the tables upon" him by declaring that
the principal danger to peace in Kwangtung lay in Hong Kong.
He claimed the colony was filled with Triads and other "dangerous characters," who had been driven there and to Singapore by
his own effective measures of repression. Some thirty thousand
men, he asserted, were assembled in the two colonies in preparation for an attack upon Kwangtung in the near future. The governor then assured him that he would keep the peace in Hong
Kong and that known members of the Triad society were being
dealt with sternly.

But Li was not so interested in talking about Kwangtung as
he was in determining Britain's preference regarding the future
rule of his country. Specifically he asked, "whom would England
like to see Emperor?" Blake replied that as far as he knew, and
providing the legations were safe, Britain's main concern was
the restoration of order and the resumption of trade and business. She did not want to see China partitioned, nor did she
entertain any territorial ambitions of her own. If she were satisfied that the Kuang-hsü Emperor had not been responsible for
the actions taken in his name, he assumed there would be no
objection to his continued reign "under certain conditions,"
but this was only his own private opinion.

Li obviously had been giving the matter a great deal of
thought and propounded the following question. If it is true,
he said, that only the German minister had been killed by the
Boxers, then the foreign powers would not have the right to
decide who would be emperor. But if all the ministers were
killed (and at this time no news had been received from Peking
since July 8), the powers, he felt, could legitimately interfere
and declare, "We will set up an Emperor." If that happened,

he asked, "whom would the Powers elect?" He assumed, he
went on, that their choice would be "a person of Chinese nationality." All that Blake could say in reply was that the foreign
powers "would probably ask the advice of the strongest man in
China that they could find as to what was best to be done."
After being satisfied that his bid had been entered, Li asserted
that despite all her mistakes, the Empress Dowager was "undoubtedly the most capable ruler in China." In London, however, the Colonial Office made note of Li's "not being averse to
becoming Emperor himself."[84]

Li also took the opportunity to plead for magnanimity when
the allied powers should occupy Peking, and warned that a
vengeful spirit would cause universal hatred of foreigners. From
his attitude, it was clear that he was preparing for his future role
in the north, as China's ambassador of peace or possibly her new
ruler. If a chastened Peking gave him a free hand and the foreigners had no objections, there was no need to involve himself
in a separatist adventure in the south, such as had been broached
by Liu Hsüeh-hsün. But until he was certain these conditions
were satisfied, Li did not rush straight on to Peking, and Blake's
report of the rumor that Li planned to stay in Shanghai "until
the tide turns" proved to be well-founded.[85] The canny statesman spent three months in Shanghai before finally deciding that
the court had had enough of the Boxers and that he would be
free to sue for peace.[86] Once he left Hong Kong, however, the
revolutionaries' plan to enlist his cooperation fell through, and
when he visited Li's ship, Ch'en Shao-pai was told the bad news
by Liu Hsüeh-hsün and Tseng Kuang-ch'üan, another of the
governor-general's intimates.[87] The Hong Kong government, of
course, now had no reason for relaxing the banishment order,
and Sun Yat-sen stayed on board the *Sado Maru*, which departed for Japan on July 20.[88]

84 Blake to Chamberlain, July 19, 1900, in CO 129/300 [46].
85 *Ibid.*
86 Tan, *Boxer Catastrophe* [120], p. 125.
87 Ch'en Shao-pai, *Hsing Chung Hui* [152], p. 46.
88 *Hongkong Telegraph*, July 20, 1900.

Although the two-pronged approach to Li Hung-chang, through Liu and the Hong Kong Governor,[89] had failed, Sun did not yet despair of obtaining the direct assistance of these intermediaries, who were powers in their own right. Liu had money and Blake's position spoke for itself. Both could be of tremendous importance now that plans for the negotiated seizure of the southern provinces had given way to Sun's alternative scheme of a military assault on the eastern Kwangtung coast. While proceeding from Japan in June, the plotters had already mapped out a preliminary division of labor in which the Japanese were conspicuously prominent, and after the failures of July their sessions were increasingly devoted to practical war strategy.[90] At this stage, Blake became the object of Sun's attentions. Before the *Sado Maru* departed, there were a few days left for charting an approach to the governor in the hope of ensuring a friendly base at Hong Kong, and perhaps even more positive British support when the attack succeeded. Ho Kai presumably served as spokesman again, and on the 21st, according to Tse Tsan-tai, Ho reported that the governor was "in favor of a Southern Republic for China."[91]

While Blake seemed to be a sympathetic recipient of the conspirators' confidences, it is questionable whether his support was as unqualified as Tse related. Only four months earlier he had declared that a republic was impossible in China.[92] According to his dispatches to London during this period, his chief concern was the danger of violence in the south. Any kind of violence, even that directed against the Manchu regime, which

---

[89] In an interview with an Osaka *Mainichi* reporter, Sun asserted that his proposed alliance with Li was initiated entirely by Blake and did not admit his willingness to accept had Li agreed. (Reprinted in the *China Mail*, August 13, 1900.) The *Mail's* own story of July 24 (reprinted in the *Straits Free Press* of August 2 and in FO 17/1718 [46], p. 338) describes the Li-Sun negotiations and leaves Blake out of the picture. See the denial of Sun's story by Blake's private secretary in the *Overland China Mail*, August 18, 1900.

[90] Miyazaki, *Thirty-three Years' Dream* [200], p. 210; Jansen, *Sun Yat-sen* [69], p. 91.

[91] Tse, *Chinese Republic* [122], p. 19.

[92] Blake to Chamberlain, March 31, 1900, in CO 129/298 [46].

he and the treaty port spokesman held responsible for triggering the anti-foreign explosion in the north, was considered to be a threat to Western lives and property. Securing peace in the south had been the object of his unsuccessful dealings with Li Hung-chang, and now that Li had left, he still had to consider the prospect of uprisings by both Sun's and K'ang's forces. Blake's memorandum to the Colonial Office on August 3 reveals that Sun's agents approached him after Li's departure and that Blake replied by offering them an alternative to armed uprising.

First of all, Blake related that "some Chinese gentlemen who are deeply interested in the reform movement" (Ho Kai and Wei Yuk?) had told him of an imminent rebellion in the Canton area. Blake, giving the British position stated above, had warned the "reformist" spokesmen that, whatever sympathies he might feel for their aspirations, the attacks on foreigners which would probably result from such an uprising might provoke Western intervention and destruction of the insurgents, even without the participation of Chinese imperial forces. As an alternative, he suggested that they draw up:

a numerously signed petition to the Powers showing clearly the reforms that they demand, and stating that they took this course impelled by the desire to avoid any action that would embarrass the Powers in the present crisis, in the hope that, when ultimate arrangements are being made, their demands will be insisted upon and conceded without the loss of life and property and the general derangement that must follow an armed rebellion.[93]

Blake informed London that his suggestion had been conveyed to both Sun's "reformers" and K'ang Yu-wei's group. The latter, he disclosed, included the American adventurer, Homer Lea, who had been sent to China by K'ang's followers in San Francisco.[94] According to Blake's information, Lea was promot-

[93] Blake to Chamberlain, August 3, 1900, in FO 17/1718 [46], pp. 364-367.
[94] Homer Lea (1876-1912) was a former Stanford student whose book, *The Valor of Ignorance* (1909) was acclaimed in military circles. A frustrated military strategist, Lea began working with K'ang's San Francisco supporters, the "China Reform Association," in 1900 and assumed the title "General." In his article, "My Reminiscences" [118], p. 304, Sun describes

ing a fantastic scheme to attack Canton from Macao with a coolie army of 25,000 under American officers. The Portuguese authorities in Macao were to be bribed, and the Governor of Macao was to be placated with a promise of territorial compensation. Lea endorsed a merger with Sun's forces but was overruled by K'ang's supporters in Macao, who also turned down Blake's proposition. Probably because they were already committed to action on the Yangtze and were also afraid that further delay would jeopardize the emperor's life, they were not willing to forego a responsive uprising in Kwangtung.

Though K'ang had recently sent Blake a pro-European declaration and a request that the invading foreigners reinstate the emperor, the governor was more impressed by Sun's spokesmen.[95] Not only were they more consistently pro-Western, but on this occasion they agreed to "adopt the memorial to the Powers." This was Blake's understanding of their response. But the question arises as to whether they ever sent a petition to the foreign governments such as he had proposed.

It will be recalled that, according to Ch'en Shao-pai, who is followed by other revolutionary historians, a political program had been drawn up in English by Ho Kai, and after being signed by the Hsing Chung Hui leaders, was submitted for the consideration of Blake and Li Hung-chang. Blake could not have

---

his first meeting with Lea without giving the date, but their collaboration probably began in 1909. In 1911 they returned to China together, with Lea acting as Sun's military adviser. The best account of Lea's career is Chapin, "Homer Lea" [20]. According to Chapin, Lea was in China in 1900, as reported by Blake, but this is not confirmed by Chinese accounts. See Jansen, *Sun Yat-sen* [69], p. 247, note 38. According to Sharman, *Sun Yat-sen* [107], p. 90, Lea went to either Hong Kong or Macao as a "foreign agent" for the reformers. See Levenson, *Liang Ch'i-ch'ao* [76], pp. 74–75, note 75, for reference to further conflicting accounts of Lea's association with the reformers and revolutionaries. Given Blake's evidence, it appears that Chapin is correct with regard to Lea's presence in the Far East in 1900. See also Malone (ed.), *Dictionary of American Biography* [84], pp. 69–70, for a short summary of Lea's life. According to this source, Lea crossed the Pacific in 1899 and "arrived in time to join the relief of Peking during the Boxer uprising."

[95] Appended to Blake to Chamberlain, August 3, 1900, in FO 17/1718 [46], pp. 368–370.

entered the picture until the beginning of July. Nor did he mention such a statement when he was explaining the logic of a Li-Sun agreement to London. And finally, if he had already received Ho's document, there would have been no need to make a further request at his meeting with the "reformist" sympathizers, which probably took place in the latter part of July or the beginning of August 1900. This leads us to the tentative conclusion that Ho's statement, called the "Regulations for Peaceful Rule" (*P'ing-chih chang-ch'eng*) was not a product of the Li-Sun negotiations, but resulted from Sun's later overture to Blake, via Ho Kai, and was in response to the governor's above-mentioned proposition. In other words, Sun's group may have contemplated deferring the Waichow uprising it was then planning in the hope of riding to power on the coat-tails of the invading armies in the north.

This of course does not preclude the likelihood that similar proposals were advanced earlier for the benefit of Li. In that case, they would have been framed expressly for an independent Kwangtung-Kwangsi; but as Marius Jansen has noted, the fact that Ho's document outlined a future national government separates it from the proposition made to Li. That Ho's plan was inspired by Blake's suggestion, however, cannot be fully verified because the governor never forwarded it to London or acknowledged its receipt. Only the revolutionary sources claim that it was sent, and the only version available is the Chinese translation.[96]

There is no question that Ho was the author. The program contained proposals which he had consistently advanced and seemed expressly designed to win the approval of Europeans, who considered foreign tutelage the most effective means of reforming China. Boxers and Manchus were condemned for anti-foreignism while leading officials were charged with vacillation. The signatories were prepared to act but required foreign assistance in order to reconstruct China for the mutual benefit of Chinese and foreigners. They therefore submitted a six-point

[96] This appears in Sun, *Collected Works* [205], V, 16–19. It should be noted that this is a longer version than that in Tsou Lu, *The Kuomintang* [216], note 7, pp. 30–31.

program which they hoped Britain and her "comrade" nations would help to implement.

The plan did not explicitly declare for republicanism but merely defined the future head of government as one who would be responsive to the people's wishes and subject to constitutional restraints. Foreign diplomats would constitute a temporary advisory body to the central government while the various consuls-general performed a similar function in the provinces. The remaining proposals included: an emphasis upon federalism and local autonomy, the gradual introduction of suffrage, modernization of the bureaucratic, legal, and examination systems, the promise of an unrestricted and non-discriminatory opening of China to foreign commercial and industrial interests, continued surrender of Chinese Maritime Customs' autonomy, and protection of missionaries and churches. All were carried over from Ho's previous works. There was also an attempt to appease the traditional elite by suggesting that degree-holders, *kung-shih,* be sent to the provincial and national legislatures.[97]

An even more blatantly pro-European program, in which, for example, the proposed foreign advisers were simply called "dictators," was advanced by the *China Mail* at the beginning of August 1900.[98] Although the paper suggested that the Kuang-hsü Emperor be retained if alive, it outlined a reconstituted Chinese government, which was generally compatible with Ho's program, and at the end of the month, Ho in fact endorsed the *Mail's* plan as the recommended course for the allied powers.[99] Tse Tsan-tai even referred to the paper's editorial as "Dr. Ho Kai's article based on the terms of our political program."[100] This editorial, it might be mentioned, warned that 'from all

[97] A *kung-shih* was a successful competitor at the Metropolitan Examination who needed only to pass the Palace Examination in order to receive the *chin-shih* or highest literary degree. See Brunnert and Hagelstrom, *Present Day Political Organization* [14], p. 270.

[98] *China Mail,* August 1, August 4, 1900.

[99] See "Sinensis," open letter to "John Bull," in the *China Mail,* August 22, 1900.

[100] Tse, *Chinese Republic* [122], p. 19. According to an entry for the following day, August 2, Tse and Ho Kai discussed "terms of our Programme and Appeal to the Foreign Powers."

corners of the earth the avengers are speeding, and Peking will be reached though the road should be paved with dead. Peking will be swept off the face of the land. . . ."[101]

On August 18, Blake again asked London for permission to negotiate. He telegraphed Chamberlain that the K'ang and Sun factions were "enlisting foreigners of a doubtful character, and preparing for active operations in Canton and neighborhood." Since this would hurt British interests, he asked if it would "be prudent to have an assurance conveyed to K'ang and Sun that, if they abstain from action, Her Majesty's Government will, in the settlement of the present difficulties, consider and press for any fair and reasonable reforms that the people may demand."[102] Two days later Chamberlain replied that the British government could not "sanction any such promises," and Blake was further instructed to clamp down on Chinese agitators like K'ang and Sun.[103] Blake's second effort on behalf of Sun was therefore no more successful than his first in connection with Li Hung-chang.

Though it would seem logical to assume that Governor Blake would have at this time presented Chamberlain with a list of the "fair and reasonable reforms" drawn up by Ho, his failure to do so may have meant that the conspirators were hesitating to make the commitment he demanded. Or alternatively, he may have sought some sign of approval from Chamberlain before disclosing the details of his negotiations with Sun's representatives. But there was yet another unexplained development.

On September 24, a month after his exchange with Chamberlain, Blake sent the Colonial Secretary a copy of a document which he had received in Chinese from anonymous reformers. This turned out to be still another request that the allied powers forcibly carry out the reformation of China. They asked that the Kuang-hsü Emperor be restored, but if he did not agree to

101 *China Mail*, August 1, 1900.
102 Blake to Chamberlain, telegram, August 18, 1900, in FO 17/1718 [46], p. 354.
103 Chamberlain to Blake, telegram, August 20, 1900, in FO 17/1718 [46], p. 354. See Blake's acknowledgment in Blake to Chamberlain, telegram, August 21, 1900, in FO 17/1718 [46].

set up a new government, one of the governors-general should be chosen to "manage the affairs of the country." Foreign advisers were to be deputized to assist in carrying out reforms, including modernization of the penal code, but were to be withdrawn after affairs were settled. The new government was to be a constitutional monarchy like that of Britain and Japan, and the distinction between Manchu and Chinese was to be erased. The signatories had chosen anonymity because of the fear of reprisals, not only upon their relatives and friends, but upon the graves of their ancestors. They were convinced, however, that there was widespread support for their position, and requested that the treaty port consuls guarantee the safety of "officials, gentry, literati, and business men" so that they might sign an appeal of this nature.[104]

The signatories apparently did not belong to K'ang Yu-wei's party because they criticized the reformers of 1898 as being more interested in wreaking vengeance on the conservatives than in carrying out reforms. To what group, then, can this petition be attributed? Could this have been an attempt by Sun's party to comply with Blake's suggestion of the previous month that they present the powers with a "numerously signed petition" demanding intervention? The contents of the document are not incompatible with such a possibility.

At any rate, Blake, having previously been repudiated by London, was noncommittal in transmitting it. His only comment was that he had heard from "an apparently reliable source" that the reform party was preparing to rise should the question of reform be untouched in the pending Boxer settlement.[105] But when this intelligence reached London on October 26, Sun's uprising had already taken place and failed.

In retrospect, the Hong Kong-based intrigues appear to have been a watershed in Sun's career. This was the last occasion when Ho Kai would act as his spokesman. Sun had outgrown him. Ho, for all his patriotism and interest in constitutional

[104] Blake to Chamberlain, September 24, 1900, in CO 129/301 [46]. Both the Chinese text and an English translation are included.
[105] *Ibid.*

government, still bore the burden of a dual allegiance.[106] Though many of his specific proposals soon found their way into Sun's political vocabulary, his active participation was limited to presenting the revolutionary case to foreigners whenever the occasion arose.[107] He was essentially a conditional revolutionary, who could not conceive of activism except when supported by British gunboats.

Sun, on the other hand, was obsessed with the idea of revolution and the restoration of Chinese greatness. His total absorption in revolution had pushed him beyond the confines of Hong Kong and the treaty ports. His exposure to European political movements, to the influence of Miyazaki's radical pan-Asianism, to Liang Ch'i-ch'ao and other literati refugees—all pointed the way to a tougher nationalism which aimed at the unequivocal assertion of Chinese independence and equality. But most important of all was Sun's unswerving faith in himself as the agent of China's regeneration. The overtures to Li Hung-chang and

106 This dual allegiance is reflected in the letter which Ho and Wei Yuk sent to Lord Charles Beresford in 1899. See Beresford, *The Break-up of China* [4], pp. 211–230. Ho Kai, as well as some of the Anglicized Chinese like Dr. Lim Boon Keng (Lin Wen-ch'ing) of Singapore, are worthy of individual study. By background and training these men were eminently fitted for leadership roles in this difficult transitional period in Chinese history, yet their influence was limited by their conflicting loyalties. A Western-educated, non-literatus like Sun could respect Ho Kai, but modern intellectuals of literati antecedents demanded a more definite enunciation of nationalist aims. Nor could Ho find it easy to work for the mandarins in China. One report, worthy of investigation, is that in March 1897, when his brother-in-law, Wu T'ing-fang (Ng Choy) left Hong Kong to assume his post as minister in Washington, Ho accompanied him supposedly with the "intention of taking up an important appointment at Shanghai under the Shanghai government." However, he soon returned to the colony. See Norton-Kyshe, *Laws and Courts* [90], II, 491.

107 That all candidates for office be subjected to examinations; that the capacity for self-rule was inherent in the Chinese people and could be awakened by stimulating local self-government; that Yao, Shun, and the rulers of the Three Dynasties were harbingers of democracy (*min-ch'üan*) in China; that the *ch'üan* (sovereignty) of the people should not be confused with the *neng* (ability) of the officials—these were some of Sun's arguments on behalf of democracy which were foreshadowed in Ho's essays between 1895 and 1900. (See Chapter II, notes 61–62, for references to Ho's writings).

the British had not exhausted his capacity for intrigue. And nothing could dampen his commitment to action.

After the negotiations of July and August 1900 fell through, Ho Kai resumed his role as Justice of the Peace in Hong Kong while Sun Yat-sen held a council-of-war. This was the real difference between them.

VIII

The Waichow Uprising

Five years after the attempted Canton coup, China was even riper for revolution. The consequences of the war with Japan had been disastrous. Since 1894, the government had mortgaged a part of its income—customs, *likin*, and salt revenues—to foreign bankers, first to meet war expenses and then to indemnify the Japanese. By 1898, seven successive loans had brought China's total foreign indebtedness to almost 55 million pounds, or nearly three times the amount of the central government's annual revenue.[1] Meanwhile, the German seizure of Kiaochow in 1897 started the race for concessions and leaseholds which seemed to prefigure the country's partition.

A dynasty that became the caretaker of foreign interests could not retain the respect of its subjects. Yet if bandits, smugglers, and dislocated peasants took advantage of dynastic weakness, the specific occasions for disorder were often due to outside interference and the tightening foreign grip upon Chinese finances. It was ironic that the intruders, who continually proclaimed the need for peace and stability, were creating some of the conditions which made peace and stability impossible in China.

The presence of thousands of missionaries, whose right to preach the gospel had been secured by force, became especially provocative. Anti-Christian rioting, however, was motivated not so much by religious intolerance as by resentment of foreigners,

---

[1] Weale, *The Fight for the Republic* [130], p. 117; Hu Sheng, *Imperialism and Chinese Politics* [67], p. 113.

whose special rights violated traditional gentry prerogatives. And the lower classes, the particular victims of the economic burden imposed by imperialism—the higher tax rate to cover foreign loans, the influx of cheap manufactured goods, the replacement of junks by steamship—needed little encouragement to attack missionaries and converts, who symbolized the intruders' growing domination of the country.[2]

The disruptive role of missionaries is illustrated by the saga of Yü Man-tzu (Yü Tung-ch'en) of Szechwan. Yü became a bandit as a result of a land dispute with Chinese Catholics, who were supported by a French priest. In 1890, he launched a ten-year campaign of terrorism and robbery aimed mainly at Catholics.[3] While officials looked the other way, Yü collaborated with the Ko Lao Hui and raised a force of about ten thousand men in what a Communist historian has called the secret societies' first large-scale uprising against imperialism.[4]

In the summer of 1895, rioters struck at Protestant missions in Chengtu and Chungking. According to Dr. Griffith John, a leading missionary, hostility had not been religiously inspired but derived from officially encouraged anti-foreignism. Among the immediate causes were the opening of the Upper Yangtze to steam navigation, the rumor that Chengtu was to be opened as a treaty port, and the enforcement of the missionaries' right to purchase land or lease property without prior consultation with local officials.[5]

British observers likewise claimed that officially inspired anti-foreignism led to armed resistance in Kwangtung's Hsin-an district when they extended their Hong Kong holdings in April 1899.[6] The British also had been warned that the Triads, under

[2] Hsiao, *Rural China* [61], pp. 487–488; Tan, *Boxer Catastrophe* [120], pp. 33–34.

[3] Beresford, *Break-up* [4], pp. 140–141; for reports of Yü's various raids see Kuo, *Daily Record* [184], II, 837, 839, 1002, 1023, 1037, 1039; see also *North China Herald*, February 27, 1900, p. 337, and March 6, 1900, pp. 378–379.

[4] Li Wen-hai, "The 1911 Revolution and the Secret Societies" [186], I, p. 170.

[5] *The Anti-foreign Riots in Szchuan* [1], p. 5.

[6] Endacott, *Hong Kong* [36], pp. 264–265; Blake to Chamberlain, November 11, 1899, in FO 17/1436 [46].

a supposed follower of Sun Yat-sen named Chung Shui-yung, planned to revolt in Hsin-an and plunder Hong Kong.[7] The rebels' slogan was said to have been: "Since Our Emperor has leased to the British our territory, it is the duty of our brethren to hold the land ourselves, collect troops, gather taxes, and govern it ourselves. Those who can must be masters of the country."[8] Although Chung was absolved of responsibility for the anti-British resistance, which led to a heavy loss of Chinese lives,[9] the remaining portion of Hsin-an and the neighboring district of Kuei-shan provided fertile ground for Sun's followers when they clashed with Manchu troops the following year.

In Hankow in 1898, popular protests against the diversion of tax receipts for the payment of foreign loans had led to incendiarism and the destruction of millions of dollars worth of property. British merchants complained that local authorities lacked funds for law-enforcement because *likin* receipts were allocated to pay interest on the Anglo-German loan of 1898.[10] This was exactly the impression which the Governor-General, Chang Chih-tung, attempted to convey, and he warned Lord Beresford that the loss of revenue left him with insufficient troops to quell disturbances. When asked why he feared disturbances, he replied, "the people had got it into their heads that they were taxed in order to pay the foreigners. This had kindled the latent hostile feeling, always existing among the Chinese toward the foreigners."[11] Though British merchants had an answer to this dilemma, namely, that her Majesty's Government should protect them, it is significant that eighteen months later, when faced with the possibility of British gunboats entering his domain, Chang Chih-tung found enough troops to maintain order.[12]

[7] Sercombe-Smith to Canton Consul, October 20, 1898, in FO 17/1436 [46]. I have not been able to identify Chung Shui-yung. Could this possibly be Cheng Shih-liang? But the latter was a native of Kuei-shan and not Hsin-an as Chung was reputed to be.

[8] Enclosed in *ibid.*

[9] Kuo, *Daily Record* [184], II, 1044.

[10] Beresford, *Break-up* [4], p. 142.

[11] *Ibid.*, p. 157.

[12] Resolution passed by British Mercantile Community of the Hankow concession, in *ibid.*, p. 478.

This incident points up the delicate balance which Chinese officials were trying to maintain. They allowed, or perhaps even encouraged, popular rioting in order to demonstrate the anarchic consequences of foreign interference, but when such disorders got out of hand, threatened their own yamens, and invited further intervention, they spared no efforts to quell the disturbances.

In the summer of 1900, "controlled rioting" in North China turned into an anti-foreign crusade when reactionary Manchu leaders and some of the local gentry gambled on the Boxer movement against the foreign establishment.[13] Had they seen any chance of success, Chang Chih-tung, Li Hung-chang, and other moderates might have supported the Boxers. Instead, they sat on the sidelines and tried to keep their provinces quiet.[14] Yet popular unrest could not always be kept amenable to gentry manipulation. The Boxer movement itself had originally been anti-dynastic as well as anti-foreign,[15] and when the invading allied armies in North China revealed the weakness of Manchu leadership, anti-dynastic slogans were quickly revived.[16]

Even before the Boxer catastrophe, the peasant secret society bands had often been inclined to rise against the government. Kwangsi was not a wealthy province, but it carried an inordinately large share of the tax burden resulting from foreign loans. Bureaucratic corruption and natural disasters were contributory causes when, in 1897 and 1898, Li Li-t'ing led thousands of Triads in revolt there.[17] According to Hirayama, the

[13] Tan, *Boxer Catastrophe* [120], pp. 33–54; Hsiao, *Rural China* [61], p. 498.

[14] According to Bland, "Had China been strong enough to drive the foreigner into the sea, as Prince Tuan declared he was going to do, it can hardly be doubted that Li Hung-chang would have been among the first to bless the enterprise; but he knew the folly of that dream." *Li Hung-chang* [6], pp. 257–258.

[15] Purcell, *The Boxer Uprising* [93], pp. 194–222 and Wang I-sun, "The Bourgeoise and the Peasants" [220], I, 117.

[16] Chang Ping-lin, quoted by Lai Hsin-hsia, "Inquiry into the Great Popular Uprisings" [185], II: 75; see also Fan Wen-lan, *Modern Chinese History* [158], I, 350; and Purcell, *The Boxer Uprising* [93], p. 215.

[17] Lai Hsin-hsia, "Inquiry into the Great Popular Uprisings" [185], pp. 57–65, 68–72. In the following years after Li fled to the Nan Yang, the

magnitude of this Kwangsi rebellion had been exceeded only by the Taiping rising.[18] Three of Sun's followers attempted to join Li Li-t'ing but arrived too late.[19]

Thus far the revolutionaries' capacity for leadership and organization had not matched the peasant bent for violence. However, by July 1900, Sun and his lieutenants finally took on the assignments required for their contemplated uprising. On behalf of the revolutionists, Cheng Shih-liang had undertaken to establish a base on the Kwangtung coast. Yang Ch'ü-yün, Ch'en Shao-pai, Li Chi-t'ang, Fukumoto, and Hirayama concentrated upon fund-raising and logistics in Hong Kong, and Sun Yat-sen, assisted by Miyazaki and Kiyofuji, dealt with high-level strategy in Japan.[20] Although Li Chi-t'ang, who had met Sun for the first time in Hong Kong, had given him $20,000,[21] Sun was desperately short of funds.[22]

This chronic ailment had already caused a major disappointment in Shanghai, where the Yangtze Valley secret society leaders had been cultivated by Pi Yung-nien, waiting for Sun's orders and funds. These Ko Lao Hui *lung-t'ou*, who were fast spenders, got word of the vast sums reputedly being made available to the Hunanese leader T'ang Ts'ai-ch'ang by K'ang Yu-wei, and to Pi's dismay, they left him to join the Hunan activ-

---

Kwangsi Triads continued to rise annually until the disturbances reached a climax in 1904, when 100,000 troops were needed to put them down.

[18] Cited by Comber, *Secret Societies in Malaya* [27], p. 29.

[19] These three were Teng Yin-nan and Sung Chü-jen, both originally from Hawaii, and Yu Lieh; see Feng, *Reminiscences* [160], I, 43.

[20] Ch'en Ch'un-sheng, "The Waichow Uprising" [150], p. 235.

[21] Ch'en Ch'un-sheng, "The Waichow Uprising" [150], p. 241; Feng, *Reminiscences* [160], I, 92. Ch'en Shao-pai, however, reports that Li contributed $30,000 for this campaign; see *Hsing Chung Hui* [152], p. 46. In his own summary of his financial situation at this time, Sun records Li's contribution as $20,000. In this letter, sent to Wu Ching-heng (Wu Chih-hui) in 1909, Sun refuted charges that he had grown wealthy through his political career. The Waichow attempt, he claimed, cost about $100,000, and except for Li's contribution and a Japanese contribution of $5,000 (this was presumably Nakano's donation, mentioned in Chapter VI), he and his brother raised all of the money on their own. His brother, Sun added, went bankrupt in 1907, and he himself used up all his personal wealth which had accrued from his medical practice; see Sun, *Collected Works* [205], V, 83–84.

[22] See Sun's letters to Hirayama in the summer of 1900 in Sun, *Collected Works* [205], V, 20–21.

ists.[23] Pi himself had kept trying to win over his Hunan friends to Sun's cause, but T'ang, not really concerned over programmatic differences between reformers and revolutionaries, had decided that K'ang and the Pao Huang Hui had more money to offer. Dejected, Pi left politics and sought the anonymity of the Buddhist priesthood.[24] In a farewell message to Hirayama, who had been his companion during an encouraging tour of the Ko Lao Hui lodges, he wrote of his fears that China was doomed to enslavement and that all the people who could save her were motivated by selfish desires.[25] When this news reached Sun in Yokohama, he felt as if he had "lost his arms."[26] Without Pi he was cut off from the Yangtze provinces, and it was five years before his contact with this region could be resumed.[27]

Yet, ironically, lack of access to the highly touted Pao Huang Hui war chest proved to be one of the reasons for the eventual failure of T'ang's plot at Hankow. The interference of the Chinese consul in Honolulu, and the *hua-ch'iao* financial difficulties resulting from the Chinatown fire there, had prevented Liang from transferring pledged funds immediately,[28] while K'ang, who had in his hold the largest single donor, Ch'iu Shu-yüan, seemed reluctant to give full support to his mainland followers.[29] Perhaps he did not fully trust the Hunan firebrands, who contradictorily included a denunciation of the Manchu regime with a pledge to restore the Kuang-hsü Emperor. And

[23] Feng, *Reminiscences* [160], I, 75. In conjunction with the Ko Lao Hui T'ang formed a new lodge called the Fu-yu Shan-t'ang. K'ang was designated a "Chief dragon-head" and Liang, an "Assistant dragon-head"; see Fan Wen-lan, *Modern Chinese History* [158], I, 325.

[24] Feng, *Reminiscences* [160], I, 75.

[25] *Ibid.*, I, 76.

[26] *Ibid.*

[27] Hsüeh, *Huang Hsing* [66], p. 34.

[28] See Liang's letters to Hunan comrades and to K'ang, in Ting, *Biography of Liang* [214], I, 112, 117.

[29] There are conflicting reports concerning Pao Huang Hui collections and expenditures. It has been estimated that three hundred thousand dollars were subscribed at this time, of which one third came from Ch'iu Shu-yüan, the Singapore millionaire, another third from Liang in Hawaii, and the rest from other overseas supporters. (See Ting, *Biography of Liang* [214], I, 134; and Feng, *Reminiscences* [160], I, 16.) According to the Hupeh student, Chu Ho-chung, K'ang kept most of his money and thereby made himself wealthy

Liang, as we have noted, had attached more importance to a Kwangtung uprising.[30] Whatever the reasons, their failure to send large remittances on time caused T'ang's repeated postponements, which eventually led to his plot's exposure and suppression; on August 11, the Anhwei group led by Ch'in Li-shan was put out of action, and two weeks later Chang Chih-tung crushed the main body at Hankow.[31]

The relationship between Chang and the Tzu-li Hui offers an interesting parallel to Li Hung-chang's tentative dalliance with the Hsing Chung Hui. Sun had hoped to use Li in separating his two provinces from Manchu rule; T'ang had placed a similar hope in Chang Chih-tung. Approached by one of T'ang's Japanese sympathizers, the Hunan-Hupeh governor-general, like his southern counterpart, did not commit himself at first but preferred to await the outcome of overall political developments.[32] Had both imperial personages, or at least the Empress Dowager, failed to survive the fighting in Peking, independent action in conjunction with the reformers might have appealed to Chang.[33]

---

for the rest of his life. Only $20,000 was sent to T'ang Ts'ai-ch'ang, and the latter, according to Chu, spent most of it in the brothels and gambling dens of Shanghai. (See Chu Ho-chung, "The European T'ung Meng Hui" [157], II, 252.) Fan Wen-lan, *Modern Chinese History* [158], I, 325, claims that K'ang raised $600,000 and kept it all for himself. Chung Kun Ai, who had been one of the generous Pao Huang Hui contributors in Hawaii in 1900, reports his subsequent disillusionment with the organization as a result of his suspicions concerning its financial dealings. (See Chung, *My Seventy Nine Years* [26], p. 302.) A more sympathetic account, however, states that Ch'iu Shu-yüan contributed only $20,000 and that all of it went to the Hankow plotters. The Manchu government exacted revenge by arresting the entire Ch'iu clan in China. (See Jung-pang Lo, "The Overseas Chinese" [82], p. 3.)

[30] See Liang's letter to K'ang, April 12, 1900, in Ting, *Biography of Liang* [214], I, 113.

[31] The Anhwei uprising took place at Ta-t'ung on August 9th. The Hankow plot, also scheduled for the 9th, then postponed to the 19th and finally to the 23rd, was prematurely exposed on August 21. See Kuo, *Daily Record* [184], II, 1094, 1096.

[32] Fan Wen-lan, *Modern Chinese History* [158], I, 327.

[33] Chang and the other anti-Boxer officials may have felt that if the Empress Dowager survived, Russian intervention would still prevent the fall of the dynasty; see Fan Wen-lan, *Modern Chinese History* [158], I, 326.

By the end of August, however, when their majesties were safely evacuated and when Li Hung-chang had been empowered to sue for peace, Chang was not the one to upset the applecart.

Another factor, which weighed more heavily, was the attitude of Britain, the foreign power with the greatest interest in the Yangtze area. Again the parallel with the south holds true, only in this case the anti-governmental plotters found British representatives much less sympathetic than Sir Henry Blake had been at Hong Kong. As early as January, reformers in Shanghai had notified Britain's acting consul-general that unless the emperor were restored to the throne, they were prepared to stir up the secret societies throughout the country and compel foreign intervention. They also warned that popular risings would be likely to disrupt trade and injure missionary installations. Consul Warren, who refused them an interview, informed them that their proposed course would alienate the foreign powers.[34] The reformers, however, persisted in their representations, and at the end of March 1900, Yung Wing, who had been a leading figure in their Shanghai meetings, asked a Singapore police official if the British government would support an uprising. Yung, who had come for discussions with K'ang Yu-wei, contended that the reformers could not be considered rebels since they were supporting the emperor. Either through Yung or through other sources the British learned that the uprising was scheduled to take place in about three months and that the plotters claimed to have enlisted five hundred Americans.[35] (Either Liang or Homer Lea may have been responsible for arousing this expectation.)

At the end of three months, however, the Boxer trouble erupted, and the British were even more sensitive to any disturbance along the Yangtze. Though the Tzu-li Hui strategists had assumed a most proper posture on foreign affairs and hoped to capitalize on Peking's quarrel with the powers, the British were not prepared to sit by idly while the Ko Lao Hui and the

[34] Warren to Salisbury, August 30, 1900, in FO 17/1718 [46], p. 378.
[35] Swettenham to Salisbury, March 29, 1900, in CO 273/264 [46].

Big Sword Society went into action. Liang Ch'i-ch'ao and his friends may have erased the secret societies' anti-foreign slogans, but the British preferred more substantial measures of repression, and Chang Chih-tung, who was concerned lest the foreigners themselves should take the initiative, pledged his cooperation. On June 17, he informed Britain's acting consul-general in Hankow that he would maintain order and protect foreigners, and requested that British warships stay out of the Yangtze.[36] Further assurances, including his disavowal of Peking's declaration of war and a promise to honor foreign loans, were soon forthcoming from Chang, who acted in concert with Li and the other anti-Boxer officials.[37]

In keeping with his pledge, Chang took swift action against the Hankow plotters on the evening of August 21 and in the early hours of the 22nd, one day before they were finally scheduled to rise. One of their hideouts was located in the British concession, but Acting Consul-General Fraser instructed the municipal police to cooperate with Chang's forces and the leaders were easily apprehended. Amid the conspiratorial paraphernalia discovered by the police were what Consul Fraser called "two curious English documents" which he appended to his report.[38] These were copies of the Tzu-li Hui's program, featuring its statement unequivocally friendly to foreigners. And possibly in deference to foreign sensibilities, the reformist leaders —twenty of whom, including T'ang and Lin Kuei, were beheaded the same day they were seized—had also pledged that "captives shall be dealt with according to the belligerent laws of civilized nations, and shall by no means be murdered in a barbarous manner."[39]

[36] Kuo, *Daily Record* [214], I, 1076.

[37] Tan, *Boxer Catastrophe* [120], pp. 80–81.

[38] Fraser to Warren, August 23, 1900, enclosed in Warren to Salisbury, August 30, 1900, in FO 17/1718 [46], p. 372. Among the prisoners was a Japanese who fought the police with a bayonet and was later handed over to the Japanese consul.

[39] In a third document, apparently meant for foreigners, they declare that it is their "firm conviction to agree with the allied Powers to put down the fanatical and insane movement, and to bring the anti-foreign and wicked

Chang was grateful for British help, which as Fraser explained:

was given because, even supposing that the movement was really a "reform" movement, and that no action was to be taken against foreigners, the overthrow of the constituted authorities would let loose upon us all the disorderly rabble of the three cities, and because the present authorities, who have hitherto striven to maintain order here, are to be preferred to a self-constituted Government of high-sounding aims, but of doubtful experience and ability.[40]

This was the some reasoning which had remained impervious to the zealously pro-Western declarations of the revolutionaries, and which would in the future epitomize the foreign preference for "stable" and "legitimate" rule in China.

Those of T'ang's colleagues who escaped, including Ch'in Li-shan, who had been in Anhwei and eventually fled to Japan blamed the Pao Huang Hui leaders for the disaster. Ch'in went on to Singapore and demanded an account of K'ang's funds, and as a result of his accusations, their benefactor, Ch'iu Shu-yüan, broke off relations with the reformers.[41] This had been the first attempt of K'ang and Liang to emulate Sun's tactics. Their ineffectual support of the Tzu-li Hui turned the Hunan-Hupeh intellectuals against them, while the Ko Lao Hui chieftains, who ended up with no prize after changing horses in midstream, even tried to assassinate K'ang a few years later.[42] The

---

usurpers of the Government to punishment." While they repeat their intention to reinstate the Kuang-hsü Emperor and to establish a "Constitutional Empire," they also declare they "will no longer recognize the Manchu government as a political organization fit to rule over China." The full text of these documents, translated into English, is appended to Fraser to Warren, in Warren to Salisbury, August 30, 1900 in FO 17/1718 [46], pp. 372–373. The Chinese text of the objects and rules can be found in Feng, *Reminiscences* [160], I, 86–87. See also Feng, *History of the Revolution* [159], I, 67–77. In his confession, T'ang declared he had been inspired by the example of the anti-Bakufu movement in Japan, which led to the restoration of imperial rule.

[40] Fraser to Warren, enclosed in Warren to Salisbury, August 30, 1900, in FO 17/1718 [46], p. 372.
[41] Feng, *Reminiscences* [160], III, 183.
[42] The two most important Ko Lao Hui leaders, Yang Hung-chün, a Hu-

failure of the plot and the criticism he received particularly discouraged Liang, who threatened to retire from politics and become a monk.[43] Although he had advocated armed uprising for the past six months, the sequel of acrimonious internal squabbling and the martyrdom of the students, many of them his former protégés in Hunan and Tokyo, dampened his militancy. Liang had argued from the beginning that only extraordinary circumstances—the threat to the emperor and then the hope of international support—justified a resort to violence. Armed uprising, he felt, was no trifling matter and could not be repeated at will.[44] In the summer of 1900 he saw an opportunity which would occur "once in a thousand years," and when this proved illusory, he gradually returned to his natural role, that of pundit and editor, teacher, and critical expositor of ideas.[45]

Failure on the Yangtze caused the reformers to shelve their plans for Kwangtung and left Sun with a free hand. Until he had money and munitions, however, there was little sense in launching the attack. Yet the initial stage of the operation, the build-up on Chinese territory, was now proceeding as planned.

In their previous plot, the conspirators had attempted to subdue Canton by means of an immediate assault assisted by diversionary atacks. Now they decided to build up a base in the eastern part of the province, in Waichow (Hui-chou) prefecture, and approach Canton from the southeast. As their ren-

nanese, and Li Yün-piao of Hupeh, turned up in Hong Kong several years later and demanded money from K'ang, who promptly reported them to the police. Enraged, one of their friends borrowed a pistol from Ch'en Shao-pai in order to kill the Pao Huang Hui leader. It was Ch'en's intervention, the story goes, that saved K'ang from the vengeance of the Ko Lao Hui; see Lo Kang, *Errors in Lo's Biography of Sun* [197], p. 83.

[43] Hao, "Reformers and Revolutionaries" [52], p. 107.

[44] See his letter to K'ang, April 12, 1900, in Ting, *Biography of Liang* [214], I, 115.

[45] See his letter to Hong Kong and Macao comrades, June 17, 1900, *ibid.*, I, 130. Earlier Liang had urged T'ang to defer his rising until they should be fully prepared, but the outbreak of the Boxer troubles seemed too good an opportunity to pass up. It has been suggested that the Hankow plotters should have waited for local bandits to rise separately and then make their own appearance in the guise of a militia. Chang Chih-tung's forces, the argument runs, would not have been able to cope with both groups; see *ibid.*, I, 133.

dezvous and jumping-off point they chose San-chou-t'ien (Sam-chautin), a village in Kuei-shan (now Hui-yang) district only five miles north of Mirs Bay and less than ten miles east of the border of the British-held New Territories. As described by Acting Governor-General Te-shou, Waichow was inhabited by "ferocious" people—habitual bandits, salt smugglers, pirates, and members of secret societies.[46]

Even allowing for official distortion, there is no doubt that the prefecture was unusually difficult to handle. The mountainous coastal districts of Kuei-shan and Hai-feng in the southeast were made to order for piracy and smuggling. Only some ten years earlier, government troops had had their hands full with a plundering Triad band in eastern Kuei-shan and never succeeded in wiping it out completely.[47] A heavy concentration of Hakkas, the same people who bred the Taiping rebellion, formed another explosive factor in the Waichow situation. Moreover, Britain's recent penetration of Hsin-an district had created a new source of resentment.[48]

Strategically the area was well situated. With access to the sea, from which Sun expected to land with reinforcements, and to the British-held New Territories, it afforded two possible lines of communication to the outside. San-chou-t'ien, the main revolutionary base, was protected by forests and mountains, and its mountain passes offered numerous offensive possibilities. To the southwest there was Hsin-an (now Pao-an) district; to the northwest was Tung-kuan district through which Canton, only some 70 miles away, could be reached; directly north was the East River, and the prefectural capital, Waichow city, which was also the Kuei-shan district capital; and to the east was Hai-feng, a notorious center of sedition, bristling with Triads and robber bands, who "appeared and disappeared" whenever convenient.[49]

[46] See Te-shou's memorial in Tsou Lu, *The Kuomintang* [216], p. 668.
[47] *Ibid.*
[48] As an indication of the East River area's potentialities as a regional stronghold, there are the examples of Ch'en Chiung-ming and P'eng P'ai during the republican period. See Hsieh, "Ch'en Chiung-ming" [62]; and Shinkichi Eto, "Hai-lu-feng" [37].
[49] Te-shou, in Tsou Lu, *The Kuomintang* [216], p. 669.

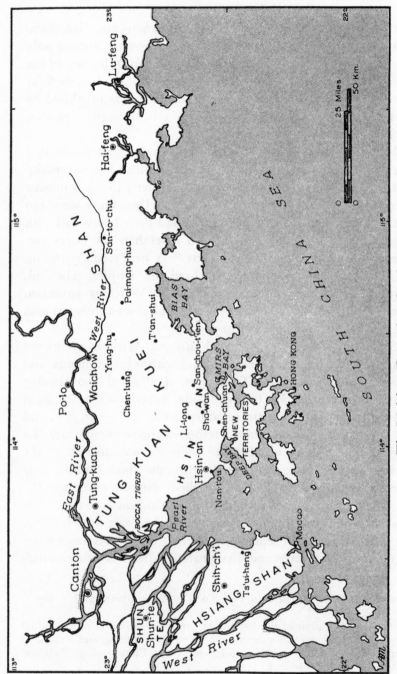

The Waichow Campaign, October 1900

The choice of Waichow as the site for the second revolutionary campaign was probably a result of the influence of Cheng Shih-liang, who was the ideal field commander for that area. He was a Hakka, a native of Kuei-shan, and a long-standing Triad member. Although fighters were recruited from all over Kwangtung including Hsiang-shan, most came from Waichow and were Hakkas as well as Triads.⁵⁰ In order to coordinate the scattered Triad bands, Cheng summoned a Triad notable by the name of Huang Fu from Sandakan in North Borneo.⁵¹ Huang, also a Kuei-shan native, acted as commander until Cheng arrived from Hong Kong. In fact, most of the field officers of the rebel army, except for Cheng Shih-liang, did not originally belong to the Hsing Chung Hui, but were local bandit or Triad leaders who commanded the personal allegiance of the various fighting groups. (One of these leaders is said to have broken out of a Waichow jail the previous year.)⁵² The Triad bands would move only when their own emissaries, called *ts'ao-hsieh* (straw sandals), received the word from Huang, who in turn took his orders from Cheng.⁵³ Thus the technique of indirect enlistment was carried over from 1895.

⁵⁰ See the testimony of Chiang Ya-erh, a reputed Manchu spy who joined the rebels from North Borneo, participated in the entire campaign, and was interrogated by the British upon his return to Hong Kong in November. His statement is appended to Blake to Chamberlain, November 21, 1900, CO 129/301 [46]. Chen Shao-pai, *Hsing Chung Hui* [152], pp. 46–47, says that the fighters were bandits (*lü-lin*) from Hsin-an district in southwestern Waichow and Triads from Chia-ying in northeastern Kwangtung.

⁵¹ Chiang Ya-erh, in Blake to Chamberlain, November 21, 1900, in CO 129/301 [46]; Ch'en Shao-pai, *Hsing Chung Hui* [152], p. 47.

⁵² Chiang Ya-erh, in Blake to Chamberlain, November 21, 1900, in CO 129/301 [46].

⁵³ Ch'en Shao-pai, *Hsing Chung Hui* [152], p. 47. The membership oath of the Triads indicates that the *ts'ao-hsieh* functioned as emissaries or agents who activated and imposed discipline upon the rank and file members, and that they were sometimes called "iron planks" or "night brothers." The Triad oath stipulates that "these men are destined to go about everywhere. . . . If there are public affairs, they are sent to transmit the reports. The brethren shall not turn them off; they have free nourishment and travelling expenses; but, for private affairs for the brethren, they must be paid, besides, according to the tariff. If a brother refuses to pay him—may he die of sword-wounds, or perish by the mouth of the tiger!" See Article 33 of the Triad oath in Schlegel, *The Hung League* [103], p. 143.

In Canton, Teng Yin-nan, the veteran Hsing Chung Hui member from Hawaii and, like Cheng, a personal follower of Sun Yat-sen, was the unofficial commander, while Shih Chien-ju inspired the group with his eager anticipation of personal sacrifice.[54] Together with a number of new recruits, they planned a surprise attack upon the capital in support of Cheng's drive from the east. Shih enlisted bandit leaders from the North, West, and East Rivers, and he hoped to have several thousand men converge upon Canton as soon as Cheng's main force opened its campaign in Waichow. With only about twenty thousand troops, and most of them tied down in Waichow, the Canton government was not expected to withstand a sudden attack upon the capital.[55]

Rebel leadership in Canton was dominated by Christians. In Canton Christian College, the party's members and sympathizers included Shih and a contingent of fellow students, as well as a Chinese faculty member. Its sister institution, the P'ei-ying Shu-yüan, was also a revolutionary hotbed. Two Chinese Catholic priests, the Hu brothers, a Chinese Presbyterian minister, and a gentry Christian convert were among the leading conspirators. Tso Tou-shan, the Presbyterian whose bookstore had been a revolutionary hideout in 1895, was again active; this time he was joined by Su Fu-sheng, another convert and the manager of Tso's new bookstore, the Ta-kuang Kuanshu-lou. Lien Ta-ch'eng, of lowly boatman origin, was another mission graduate and devout Christian who assumed a major role. Among the new Hsing Chung Hui members in Po-lo, a district capital north of Waichow city, was Li Chih-sheng, a chemistry teacher and convert of the Basel mission, which was especially active among the Hakkas of Eastern Kwangtung. Li

---

[54] While Shih was more prominent in the Canton phase, Teng remained the active agent behind the scenes and the main contact with Sun Yat-sen. See Liao P'ing-tzu, "Notes on the Shih Case" [188], p. 249; Ts'ui T'ung-yüeh, "My Revolutionary Past" [217], p. 633.

[55] Ch'en Ch'un-sheng, "The Waichow Uprising" [150], pp. 235–236; Kuomintang Committee, "Biography of Shih Chien-ju" [183], 624–625; Teng Mu-han, "Sketch of Shih Chien-ju" [213], pp. 245–246.

participated in the Waichow fighting and later contributed his professional knowledge of explosives to the revolutionary plots of overseas students in Japan.[56]

According to one estimate, thirty per cent of the participants in the Waichow campaign, including the Canton phase, were Christians and seventy per cent were Triads.[57] (These figures presumably refer to original participants and not to the thousands of peasants who joined the fighting later.) While the two groups were not mutually exclusive—some like Cheng Shih-liang and Li Chih-sheng were both Christians and Triads as well as Hakkas—it might seem paradoxical to find them linked, especially during the year of the Boxer rising, when converts were the chief victims. This cooperation under Sun's leadership, which repeated the 1895 experience, shows that the secret societies were not unalterably anti-Christian. The crucial factor was apparently that of leadership; when goaded by the gentry, the brotherhoods went on an anti-Christian rampage, but when organized by mission graduates, they played their historic anti-Manchu role.[58]

Rowland Mulkern also took an active part in the conspiracy. Living in Shameen, Canton's foreign quarter, and subsidized by Teng, he spied on Manchu defences in the Canton delta and located gun emplacements in Bocca Tigris and elsewhere. Herein lay the great value of foreign confederates: they could cross

[56] See the list of Hsing Chung Hui members for 1900 in Feng, *Documents* [179], III, 355–362, and Ts'ui T'ung-yüeh, "My Revolutionary Past" [217], pp. 631, 633, 636.

[57] *Ibid.*, p. 636.

[58] It should be pointed out that both secret society members and converts to Christianity exhibited a common defiance of orthodoxy by belonging to illegal or unpopular cults. And Timothy Richard notes that when members of the illegal cults become Christians, "they are generally of far greater value than Christians from the so-called non-religious or orthodox classes, as if made of higher stuff altogether." See Richard, "The Secret Sects of China" [95], p. 41. One of the first American students of Chinese secret societies found that most of the Triad members in the cities of the east coast professed to be Christians; see Culin, "Secret Societies in the U.S." [29], p. 42. Undoubtedly most of the converts and members of the secret cults belonged to non-gentry social strata.

borders and visit strategic sites without being challenged by the Chinese constabulary.[59]

Meanwhile, at the hinterland base of San-chou-t'ien, Cheng Shih-liang's lieutenants had assembled six hundred men during the course of several months. Though they purchased some arms from a Cantonese army officer, they had only three hundred rifles altogether and thirty cartridges each.[60] By the end of the summer, the mountain passes were occupied and the shock troops were ready. They waited for the final signal from Sun Yat-sen.

But the lack of funds and munitions caused repeated delays, which weakened morale. Among the first victims were Shih's Triads, whose appetites had been whetted by the thought of sacking the capital. Now they faded back into the countryside.[61] Alarmed, Shih offered to sell his family inheritance in order to raise money, but wealthy Cantonese preferred to transfer their funds to Hong Kong and Macao during this shaky period.[62]

Nor could Sun deliver effective help. The financial problem remained unsolved, and the barriers to Hong Kong complicated communications. Miyazaki and Kiyofuji were also denied access to this all-important base. And as an additional frustration, other Japanese who had been assigned crucial roles in the plot now proved unmanageable. Dismayed over the failure at Hankow, which reduced the chances of a nationwide uprising, Fukumoto and Uchida balked at what appeared to be Sun's dilatory tactics in the south. Uchida even wanted to clear the path for action by assassinating Li Hung-chang and Liu K'un-i, the two prominent governors-general who stood for peace and moderation. But Sun was more concerned with Western opinion, and during his visit to Shanghai at the end of August (he probably stayed in the harbor rather than risk landing), he succeeded in suppressing the assassination plot. Uchida, who commanded

[59] Feng, *Reminiscences* [160], I, 44; Liao P'ing-tzu, "Notes on the Shih Case" [188], p. 250.

[60] Miyazaki, *Thirty-three Years' Dream* [200], p. 278; Ch'en Ch'un-sheng, "The Waichow Uprising" [150], p. 236.

[61] Ts'ui T'ung-yüeh, "My Revolutionary Past" [217], p. 634.

[62] Kuomintang Committee, "Biography of Shih Chien-ju" [183], p. 625.

forty fighters, became disgruntled and turned his attention to Korea. Fukumoto also withdrew and concentrated upon the central provinces.[63]

But Sun had additional business in Shanghai. As previously indicated, he had not yet given up on Liu Hsüeh-hsün. Liu was part of Li Hung-chang's entourage, and the aged statesman was indeed taking his time about reaching Peking, having been settled in Shanghai since July 21.[64] Although there had been rumors of Li's return to Canton, it is doubtful that he still figured in Sun's plans.[65] It was Liu's money that Sun was after. Sun sent Hirayama with a letter for Liu, inviting him to a shipboard conference.[66] Like their previous exchanges, this meeting was shrouded in secrecy, but we can presume that Liu offered some encouragement without committing himself, probably waiting to see the results of Sun's plans. Chang Chih-tung's ruthless suppression of the Hankow plot during the previous week undoubtedly worried Liu.

A new prospect, however, emerged from this trip. While in Shanghai, Sun had an important meeting with Hirayama and Yamada Yoshimasa, another of the China-oriented adventurers who had been with Uchida's group. Unlike Uchida, Yamada still had faith in Sun's scheme, and suggested the possibility of enlisting the help of Kodama Gentarō, Governor-General of Formosa. They arranged that Yamada, who had messages from Japanese expansionists for Kodama, would proceed to the island by way of Amoy, while Sun would return to Nagasaki and join him later. Sun's return to Japan may have been for the purpose of contacting his old benefactor, Hiraoka Kōtarō, who had influence with Kodama.[67]

[63] Miyazaki, *Thirty-three Years' Dream* [200], p. 225; Jansen, *Sun Yat-sen* [69], pp. 93–94.

[64] Tan, *Boxer Catastrophe* [120], p. 121. Li was staying at Liu's home in Shanghai; see Bland, *Li Hung-chang* [6], p. 204.

[65] *Hongkong Telegraph*, July 27, 1900.

[66] See Sun's letter to Hirayama, dated August 31st, stating the Liu had agreed to see him and asking that Hirayama collect Liu's reply the following morning; Sun, *Collected Works* [205], V, 21. See also Lo Kang, *Errors in Lo's Biography of Sun* [197], pp. 83–84, for a reconstruction of this episode.

[67] Sung Yüeh-lun, *Sun in Japan* [211], p. 4; Lo Kang, *Errors in Lo's Biography of Sun* [197], p. 86; Jansen, *Sun Yat-sen* [69], p. 94.

During all this time Cheng Shih-liang, acting under Sun's orders, had tried to keep his men together, but with rations running low and the prospects of a fight disappearing, it had become difficult. By early October, his original band of six hundred is said to have been reduced to as few as eighty.[68] But while Sun negotiated in Taiwan, the Manchu government itself precipitated the astounding Waichow campaign.

The rebels' movement across the frontier and their preparations finally came to the notice of the Canton authorities. Rumor had it that a rebel force of "several tens of thousands" had imported arms and entrenched itself in the San-chou-t'ien region.[69] The Yangtze Valley plot had only recently been uncovered, and this new threat in Kwangtung was believed to be part of a grand design in which Sun and K'ang had joined forces. Faced with what appeared to be a large-scale rising and no ordinary bandit disturbance, the Acting Governor-General, Te-shou, cautiously deployed his forces. Since the rebels had the advantages of a difficult terrain and a friendly countryside, Te-shou decided upon a slow encirclement rather than an immediate frontal assault. As the rebel camp was only a few miles from the New Territories, he assumed that they planned to create a border incident involving British troops.[70]

From his headquarters at Bocca Tigris, the provincial Naval Commander-in-Chief, Ho Ch'ang-ch'ing, took several thousand men and occupied Sham Chun (Shen-ch'üan) on October 3. This town, across the river from the New Territories, is in Hsin-an

---

[68] Miyazaki, *Thirty-three Years' Dream* [200], p. 278. Miyazaki's account, written only two years after the event, has been followed by most revolutionary historians although it is not always corroborated by imperial and other sources. It should be noted that the government informer, Chiang Ya-erh, claims that the rebels started off with about two thousand men from a place called Ma-lung-t'ou-shan, near San-chou-t'ien. This larger figure may be due to a lack of distinction between imported fighters and local supporters. It seems clear, however, that despite the reduction of their original fighting column, the rebels had more than eighty men, since they were able to retain this base at San-chou-t'ien even after they moved out eighty men to attack a government patrol. Like all Chinese armies, the rebels probably had a coolie corps equal to the number of fighters or even greater.

[69] Miyazaki, *Thirty-three Years' Dream* [200], p. 279.

[70] Te-shou's memorial, in Tsou Lu, *The Kuomintang* [216], pp. 668–669.

district, only twelve miles southwest of San-chou-t'ien. The move not only brought the government forces within striking distance of the rebels but guarded the border against the expected provocation. In the northwest, an army battalion took up a position on the border between Kuei-shan and Tung-kuan, while another battalion was moved from Ch'ao-chou to the Hai-feng region east of the rebel bastion. Teng Wan-lin, commander of the provincial land forces with headquarters in Waichow, sent forces to block the rebels at Chen-lung, southwest of the prefectural capital, and Tan-shui, only sixteen miles northeast of Cheng's headquarters. Meanwhile patrol boats guarded the sea-approach to the troubled area.[71]

As the Manchu forces closed in, Cheng telegraphed an urgent plea for munitions to Sun Yat-sen in Taiwan. Taken by surprise, Sun replied that his arrangements had not yet been completed and ordered the revolutionary force to temporarily disperse and avoid contact with the enemy. Cheng was persistent, however, and wired that if Sun could send munitions to the Kwangtung coast, they could hold out. In the meantime, Admiral Ho's advance party of two hundred men had occupied the market town of Sha-wan, less than eight miles from San-chou-t'ien, and a mounted patrol drew even closer to the rebel camp. Cheng was still waiting for Sun's reply when his second-in-command, Huang Fu, not yet informed of Sun's orders to retreat, decided to lead eighty daredevils in an attack on Sha-wan, while he left the camp at San-chou-t'ien in friendly hands.[72]

With this battle, which took place on October 6, the active phase of the Waichow campaign began, and a more exhilarating start could not have been anticipated.[73] Huang's impetuous fight-

[71] *Ibid.*, p. 669; Miyazaki, *Thirty-three Years' Dream* [200], p. 279. According to Te-shou, Admiral Ho had 1,500 men under his command while Miyazaki estimates his force at four thousand. This larger figure is corroborated by the British, who were well placed for observing Sham Chun. Ch'en Ch'un-sheng, "The Waichow Uprising" [150], p. 247, reports that Teng Wan-lin's force numbered one thousand men.

[72] Miyazaki, *Thirty-three Years' Dream* [200], pp. 279–280; Ch'en Ch'un-sheng, "The Waichow Uprising" [150], p. 236.

[73] Tsou Lu, *The Kuomintang* [216], p. 666, gives the October 6th date which conforms to Te-shou's report in *ibid.*, p. 669, and the testimony of Chiang Ya-erh, although I have not always found this latter source reliable.

ers completely routed the government troops, killed forty, and eagerly seized the same number of rifles and several cases of ammunition. They also took thirty prisoners, whose queues they snipped off.[74] During the course of the campaign, they emulated the Taiping tactic of pressing prisoners into service as porters, though according to one report only the Cantonese troops received this reprieve. The Hunanese who fell into their hands were quickly executed.[75] The government commanders, having found substance to the reports of rebel strength, if not in numbers at least in ferocity, did not advance for further contact, but held on to their fortified positions and awaited the enemy's next move. The residents of Sha-wan took a neutral stand during the battle, thus confirming rebel expectations that the Manchus would gain no support from the countryside.

According to their original plan, Cheng's army should have continued to advance westward to subdue the rest of Hsin-an, including Nan-t'ou and the district capital. In Hsin-an and Bocca Tigris in the north, several thousand supporters, including perhaps some of Shih's recruits, were expecting them, and together they could have threatened Canton from the mouth of the Pearl River, while their saboteurs went to work within the city.[76] The immediate obstacle here would have been Admiral Ho's substantial force at Sham Chun, which guarded the approach to the southwestern part of the prefecture; however, the results of their first encounter with Ho's men did not invite respect for that particular adversary.

But the next day Cheng Shih-liang arrived with Sun's latest message and this strategy was abruptly scrapped. Although Sun finally authorized them to move, it was not in the direction they had anticipated. Instead of pressing toward Canton, he wired

---

Most other Chinese sources as well as Jansen say the attack began on October 8th, while the Hong Kong papers and Governor Blake report that the rising began on October 5th.

[74] Miyazaki, *Thirty-three Years' Dream* [200], p. 280; Ch'en Ch'un-sheng, "The Waichow Uprising" [150], p. 236.

[75] See the testimony of Chiang Ya-erh and the Hong Kong *Daily Press*, October 26, 1900.

[76] Miyazaki, *Thirty-three Years' Dream* [200], p. 280.

them to head northeastward in the direction of Amoy on the southern Fukien coast.[77]

The plan to secure a foothold at Amoy for the reception of a Taiwan-based expedition had already been broached during the debate among the conspirators in Hong Kong in July. At that time, Miyazaki and his Japanese colleagues, who did not share Sun's faith in their government, preferred to attack immediately and not wait for Japanese assistance from Taiwan. Sun, according to Miyazaki, felt that if half of Cheng's Waichow fighters reached Amoy, he could make the landing from Taiwan and then join the rest of the army for a concerted attack on Canton.[78] Sun's argument for waiting until Japanese help was guaranteed apparently won the day when the British refused admittance to Hong Kong, but all subsequent military preparations of the conspirators indicate that they had not chosen Amoy as an immediate objective. The reasons seem obvious. Amoy was about 250 miles from their base in San-chou-t'ien, and in order to reach it they would have to cross difficult, mountainous terrain. They would then face a long march back to Kwangtung and an alerted Manchu army. Furthermore, all of their efforts had been concentrated on recruiting support in Kwangtung, and there is no record that the Hsing Chung Hui had made any headway in Fukien. The movement was overwhelmingly Cantonese, and Kwangtung was the only province with which they were familiar and where they could expect a friendly reception. It does seem logical, however, that they expected to seize part of the eastern Kwangtung coast in order to receive reinforcements from abroad. Sun at this time was still planning to use the arms purchased for the Filipinos, and Taiwan was the most suitable port of embarkation. But it was not necessary to go all the way to Amoy for this purpose. San-chou-t'ien was only a few miles from the coast, and they could reasonably have expected to send a party further east and receive the Taiwan expedition at Hai-feng or Lu-feng, while deploying their main force closer to Canton. Sun's order

[77] *Ibid.*, p. 280.
[78] *Ibid.*, p. 247.

to send the whole column in the direction of Amoy, therefore, came as a complete surprise, and in his own words, was a "change of their original plan."[79]

The exact events of Sun's Taiwan stay in the early days of October are unclear, but it is certain that the sudden switch in strategy resulted from negotiations carried on by Sun and Gotō Shimpei, the island's Civil Governor, acting under orders of Governor-General Kodama. Hirayama and Yamada Yoshimasa were with Sun at this time, and Yamada's younger brother, Junsaburō, offers a colorful account of the proceedings. According to him, Kodama himself advised Sun to forego the initial subjection of Kwangtung, and since they were planning to capture the entire country anyway, to proceed directly northeast from Waichow and capture Amoy and Fukien on the way. He for his part would see that they would be supplied with arms at Hai-feng and Lu-feng. Sun then asked about a loan and promised to pay it back with interest once the revolution succeeded. Gotō replied that a loan on this basis was risky and repayment too complicated. He had a better idea. Once the revolutionaries were well-armed at Hai-feng and Lu-feng, they could take Amoy, where the local branch of the Bank of Taiwan, he disclosed, had several millions of yen on hand. Why not rob this bank and then afterwards, when the revolution was victorious, the Chinese could make a "moral" restitution? He Gotō, would take it upon himself to ensure that the Japanese would not investigate the robbery too thoroughly.[80] (Gotō had close connections with the bank, which loomed large in Japanese expansionist plans in Fukien. He was in a position to speak with authority concerning the bank's resources and its attitude toward the projected robbery.)[81]

Not all the details of this account are plausible. Kodama, in

[79] Sun, in *Collected Works* [205], II, pp. 85–86.

[80] Yamada Junsaburō, "Sun's Sino-Japanese Alliance" [228], pp. 262–263. This is apparently the source for a Chinese version recorded by Sung Yüeh-lun, *Sun in Japan* [211], p. 4, although they are not exactly alike; see also Lo Kang, *Errors in Lo's Biography of Sun* [197], pp. 86–87.

[81] According to Jansen, *Sun Yat-sen* [69], p. 99, the Amoy branch of the Bank of Taiwan was Gotō's "favorite project" for furthering Japanese interests in China.

the first place, was probably in Tokyo at this time and left the negotiations in Gotō's hands.[82] Furthermore, it seems unlikely that Sun would accept a plan to march north from Amoy without first consolidating in Kwangtung. But it *is* very likely that the Japanese were more interested in trouble in Amoy than in Kwangtung. In August and September they were all set to take over the port of Amoy themselves, and if Sun took it instead, they would be in a favored position, especially if he helped himself to their bank vault.[83] For Sun, the several million yen would have been a strong inducement to attack the city, after which he could have attempted to return to Kwangtung.

In his own account, Sun makes no mention of these details, only stating that Kodama promised to help after the revolutionary army rose, and instructed Gotō to act accordingly. Included in this projected assistance were Japanese army officers, whom Sun hoped to bring with him when he made the crossing to the mainland.[84] Whatever strings were attached, the Japanese offer was attractive enough to make Sun countermand his orders to Cheng, reverse the direction of the revolutionary drive, and postpone the juncture with their supporters in western Waichow and the environs of Canton. Although the new plan was nebulous, it was conceived under virtually hopeless circumstances. Pressed by his stranded fighters on the mainland, Sun needed help badly, and as usual, he was prepared to share the spoils with anyone who offered deliverance.

While he was in Taipei, and prior to the understanding with Kodama and Gotō, Sun made one final effort to win over Liu Hsüeh-hsün and obtain his lottery revenues. Learning that Liu had not accompanied Li Hung-chang when Li finally left Shang-

---

[82] This is the impression received from Chinese sources as well as from Jansen, *ibid.*, p. 103.

[83] See *ibid.*, pp. 96–100, for a discussion of the Japanese plot to seize Amoy at the end of August and the subsequent abandonment of the plan due to fears of the European reaction. See also the British report of Japanese provocation at Amoy on August 24th, in Satow to Salisbury, in FO 17/1414, October 27, 1900 [46].

[84] Sun, in *Collected Works* [205], II, 85.

hai for Tientsin on September 16,[85] Sun sent Hirayama to Shanghai with a letter for him.[86] Although Sun put up a brave front
and exulted over the chances of capturing Canton—he had not
yet discarded his original strategy—the proposition he outlined
to Liu could only have been born of sheer desperation. This
letter was apparently a continuation of his discussions with Liu
on August 31. At that time, Sun now reminded Liu, he had suggested two possible courses of action: one in case the Imperial
Court returned to Peking, and the other in case it moved westward. Without disclosing what these alternatives were, Sun wrote
that only the latter plan had become feasible. (The court had
left for T'ai-yüan from Ta-t'ung a few days after Sun's meeting
with Liu in Shanghai.)[87] What he then outlined was presumably
this second plan, the capture of Canton by simultaneous flanking
maneuvers and internal uprising. (He dismissed the idea of blowing up the city with dynamite as being too destructive and rendering it useless as a base.) The Waichow army had already risen,
he confided, referring apparently to the establishment of Cheng's
base rather than to the start of the fighting, and supporting columns from the North River and other places would soon join in.
The Manchus would have to send troops out of the city, which
would leave it easy prey to an internal rising. Elaborating on his
arrangements in a most confident vein, he disclosed that secret
arrangements for a landing had been made with the authorities
at Macao and that he was about to sail for the Netherlands In-
dies, presumably to recruit fighters.[88]

Before asking for money, Sun offered Liu a fabulous induce-

85 Tan, *Boxer Catastrophe* [120], p. 218; Feng, *Reminiscences* [160], I, 78.
86 This letter is dated the ninth month of the thirty-third year of the Meiji
period, which I assume refers to the Gregorian calendar. Otherwise it would
have been written between October 23 and November 21, which does not
seem possible from the context. The letter appears in Feng, *Reminiscences*
[160], pp. 78–80 and has been reproduced in *Development of the Revolution* [178], IX, 596–598, but I have not seen it in any edition of Sun's collected works. Hsüeh, in "Sun Yat-sen, Yang Ch'ü-yün" [65], p. 316, is the
first Western scholar to call attention to the letter and translate part of it.
87 The movements of the Court, which first left Peking on August 15th,
are traced by Tan, *Boxer Catastrophe* [120], pp. 116–120.
88 Feng, *Reminiscences* [160], I, 78–79.

ment. For the time being, he wrote, a five-man government would be sufficient. Whether its chief would be called "Emperor" or "President" would be left up to Liu, since Sun had decided that Liu should have the post. Sun himself would handle military affairs, and the other three cabinet members, in charge of home affairs, finances, and foreign affairs, would be chosen by Liu. Sun suggested, however, that these positions be given to Sheng Hsuan-huai, Yang Ch'ü-yün, and Li Chi-t'ang respectively, while men like Ho Kai and Yung Wing could be used as overseas envoys.[89] The country, he went on, faced the immediate danger of dismemberment because of the clash with the allied armies. Not a moment could be lost if China was to remain intact, and he hoped that Liu, together with Yang and Li (who were in charge of finances in Hong Kong), would quickly send him one million dollars. The money could be forwarded to him through Hirayama.

In closing he repeated his offer: Liu would definitely be head of the new government, since his original candidate, Li Hung-chang, had decided to accept the post of peace negotiator. Liu's appointment had already been announced to the revolutionary army, he declared, and would later be made public. He also raised the possibility of cooperating with Liu K'un-i and Chang Chih-tung, who, if allied with the revolutionaries, could prevent the foreigners from invading. If they would not, then Sun proposed going to Kiangsu and Hupeh to see the two governors-general after the seizure of Kwangtung.[90] As the ultimate temptation offered to a man who had been nursing imperial ambitions for many years, this was an able effort and shows the measure of Sun's capacity for improvisation. But Liu was too shrewd to depend upon Sun as a king-maker and preferred to hold on to his million dollars.[91] Soon afterward, Kodama came along with his offer and Sun forgot about Liu.

[89] *Ibid.*, I, 79.
[90] *Ibid.*, I, 80.
[91] In his later years Liu boasted that Sun Yat-sen had offered to "name him emperor," and he also claimed to have invested a great deal of money in Sun's movement (interview with Dr. Tseng Yu-hao, Hong Kong, October

In the meantime there was yet another, more tangible hope of assisting Cheng: by sending him the munitions left over from the aborted Filipino expedition. Sun had presumably kept these arms in mind when he first planned the expedition, and Miyazaki had been assigned to handle this matter when he returned to Japan from Hong Kong in July. In October, his forces in desperate need of these munitions, Sun ordered Miyazaki to dispatch them promptly. In reply, however, his friend informed him that their Japanese agent had embezzled the funds earmarked for the Filipino arms; all they had was a heap of worthless scrap iron.[92]

During the past two or three months Sun had tried almost everything. He had offered Li Hung-chang an independent Kwangtung-Kwangsi; the British, a share in tutelary rule over the entire country; and Liu Hsüeh-hsün, a kingdom. Now only the Japanese were left; we are not sure exactly what he had promised them.

While their ultimate fate was being decided by Kodama and his associates, Cheng Shih-liang and his improvised army met with unexpected success. After the occupation of Sha-wan on October 6, 1900, they were joined by over a thousand fighters from neighboring towns and proceeded north in the direction of Chen-lung, less than fifteen miles from Waichow city. Though many were armed only with spears, the fighters charged down the mountains, routed a government force near the approaches to the town, and achieved their first major victory. Dozens of prisoners were taken, including the assistant-magistrate (*hsien-ch'eng*) of Kuei-shan district. They also picked up seven hundred rifles and twelve horses. This battle took place on October 15 and in the evening they occupied Chen-lung.[93]

8, 1963), although I have not been able to find any record of his financial contributions. Another possible source on Liu is the series of articles written by Sun Ch'iu-sheng, "Liu Hsüeh-hsün" [203], which appeared in the Hong Kong *Hsin wan pao* (date unknown). I have only seen the twelfth and last installment of this biographical sketch.

[92] The story of this swindle, perpetrated by a Japanese named Nakamura, appears in Jansen, *Sun Yat-sen* [69], pp. 71–74. See also Lo Chia-lun, *Biography* [192], I, 95.

[93] Miyazaki, *Thirty-three Years' Dream* [200], p. 281; Ch'en Ch'un-sheng,

Meanwhile, their supporters in Po-lo and Waichow city went into action. As Manchu reinforcements headed south, a revolutionary band ambushed them from the sugar cane fields, and both cities were besieged by insurgent forces. The threatened capture of Waichow, a fortified city which had resisted the onslaught of the Taipings, threw panic into official quarters, for if the city fell, the East River approach to Canton would be opened. But the provincial commanders now committed all their resources to the defense of Waichow and Po-lo, and the poorly armed revolutionaries were forced to retreat and scatter. With twenty thousand soldiers at its disposal, the government concentrated on eliminating Cheng's main force.[94]

This revolutionary army had not thrown its weight into the battle for the prefectural capital; in accordance with Sun's new orders it proceeded east toward its next objective, Yung-hu. Defeating the imperial troops in minor skirmishes, the rebels advanced without much trouble and recruited several thousand peasants, while friendly villagers supplied them with food and drink. On October 17, they left Yung-hu and advanced on Pai-mang-hua. On the way, armed with only a thousand rifles, they clashed with another government force, five or six thousand strong, and again won an astonishing victory. Teng Wan-lin, the provincial commander, was put out of action during this battle and the rebels took several hundred prisoners, five or six

---

"The Waichow Uprising" [150], p. 237. It has not always been possible to correlate all the sources on the course of the Waichow campaign but since both Ch'en, who worked for the *Chung-kuo jih-pao,* and Miyazaki wrote from personal experience and with an understanding of the revolutionaries' strategy, I have generally preferred them to Te-shou and Chiang Ya-erh. British sources and the Hong Kong press are not always reliable concerning the movements of the revolutionary army.

[94] Miyazaki, *Thirty-three Years' Dream* [200], p. 281; Feng, in *Development of the Revolution* [178], IX, 553, estimates the government force to be only ten thousand at this time, but he may not have included Admiral Ho's column, which was on the revolutionaries' southwest flank. As for Ho, a dispatch from Hong Kong dated October 16, reports that he "continued to display a masterly inactivity and has not moved in pursuit of the rebels .... We fear that the gallant Admiral, if he delays his advance much longer, will find that the enemy has moved beyond his reach. Perhaps this is what he anticipates!" (*Hongkong Telegraph,* October 22, 1900).

hundred rifles, and a large quantity of ammunition. Pai-mang-hua, now left undefended, was occupied in the evening. The rebels, now ten thousand strong thanks to the enthusiastic response of the Kuei-shan villagers, advanced easterly along the valley of the West River, here a tributary of the East River.[95]

Within ten days of the first battle, government troops had effectively blocked the rebels' threat to Waichow and Po-lo, but as long as Cheng's main army not only remained intact but grew in a remarkable fashion, the uprising appeared to be a serious rebellion, which had a good chance of capturing the entire province. Foreigners were particularly impressed with the discipline of the rebels and their ability to win the sympathy of the local population. A report from the East River area, printed in the *Hongkong Telegraph*, said that the rebels "have everywhere refrained from pillage and outrage, having contented themselves with taking just sufficient food for their wants and gathering together as many arms as possible. Hence the people are everywhere friendly toward them and do not look upon their advent as a calamity, as is the case when Imperial troops pass through a district."[96] Foreigners were also happy to learn that rebel banners, in addition to proclaiming the names of Cheng and Sun, bore a slogan, "Pao-yang, mieh-Man" (Protect the foreigners, exterminate the Manchus), which was the reverse of the Boxers'.[97] At the beginning of the campaign, when they occupied Sha-wan, they left untouched the village of Li-long, only a few miles to the west, where the Basel Mission had a station.[98] Anti-Christian disturbances were then easing off in Kwangtung—missions and chapels had previously been looted and converts robbed—and foreigners were understandably concerned over new peasant outbreaks, but Cheng's force gave them no cause for concern and even earned their approval.[99]

[95] Miyazaki, *Thirty-three Years' Dream* [200], p. 282; Ch'en Ch'un-sheng, "The Waichow Uprising" [150], p. 238.

[96] Dispatch dated October 17th in the *Hongkong Telegraph* of October 22.

[97] Ch'en Ch'un-sheng, "The Waichow Uprising" [150], p. 239.

[98] This was happily noted by Blake in his dispatch to Chamberlain, October 26, 1900, in CO 129/301 [46].

[99] See the *Hongkong Telegraph* of October 9, 1900 for reports of anti-

There is little evidence of a calculated propaganda campaign aimed at the Waichow populace, but this apparently was not necessary. Local grievances and the feeling of national shame as the allied armies ran loose in the north were enough to fan flames of resentment against the provincial authorities and the dynasty as a whole. The revolutionists' program of constitutional proposals, educational reforms, the remodeling of the civil service, made good reading for foreign sympathizers, but the rebel troops sweeping through the towns and villages of eastern Kwangtung appealed to the people's hatred for the officials, who exploited them on the one hand and appeased the foreigners on the other. This broad patriotic appeal, reminiscent of the Hsing Chung Hui manifesto, characterized the rebel proclamation that was posted in every town and village they captured.[100]

There was nothing in their statement to distinguish Cheng's campaign from a typical anti-dynastic peasant rebellion. Although in their overseas propaganda the revolutionaries are said to have called themselves the "Chinese Republican Association" (Chung-kuo Ho-chung Cheng-fu She-hui), there is no record of their having advertised any republican aims at home.[101] In fact it is doubtful whether the name Hsing Chung Hui was publicized during the campaign. It was never mentioned by Governor

Christian disturbances in Kwangtung. But Consul Brenan in Canton reported on November 15 that attacks on missions and converts' property had ceased for over six weeks, and these had not generally been accompanied by attacks on their persons. See Brenan to Satow, November 15, 1900, in FO 17/1422 [46].

[100] The proclamation is translated in the *Hongkong Telegraph*, October 22, 1900. This first appeared in the Hong Kong Chinese paper *Wah Tsz Yat Pao* (*Hua-tzu jih-pao*).

[101] Tse, *Chinese Republic* [122], p. 15, records that in August 1899, Yang Ch'ü-yün informed him that "exhortations" were sent to the *hua-ch'iao* of America, Honolulu, Canada, Australia, and Southeast Asia in the name of this party. There is no evidence, however, that the appeals elicited any response. And as far as the republican slogan was concerned, Tse himself was coming to the conclusion that this form of government was too advanced for the Chinese people, and in the beginning of 1903, when he made his own attempt at capturing Canton, assisted by Li Chi-t'ang, his plan was to establish a "Commonwealth" government under a "Protector" (Tse, *Chinese Republic* [122], p. 16).

Blake, and the day the fighting broke out, it was as Triads that
the revolutionaries made a public appeal for foreign sympathy
in a letter to the *Hongkong Telegraph*:

Sir: We are not "Boxers." We are members of that Great Political
Society of Masons, commonly known as Triads. . . . We number
countless millions, and our able brethren in America, The Sandwich
Islands, Australia . . . are only waiting for the "Grand Signal." We
are reformers. After we have accomplished our work, we will institute beneficial reforms and throw the Country open to the Trade
of the World. . . . History will repeat itself, and in working to accomplish what our patriotic and illustrious predecessors swore to
accomplish nearly Three Hundred years ago, we trust Great Britain,
The United States, and Japan will observe strict neutrality, and if
necessary afford us their friendly advice and suport. . . .[102]

The anonymous writer, who gave his address as Kuei-shan district in Waichow prefecture closed by recalling that the British
had frustrated the Triads' aims in 1862 by lending the Manchus
the services of General Gordon. Gordon, he went on, regretted
his assistance to the Manchus, and the writer hoped the mistake
would not be repeated.

In other words, the rebels appeared as armed reformers, Ming
restorationists, Triads, and patriots, not as members of an anti-
monarchical political party. But Sun's strategy had not called for
reliance upon an indigenous, ideologically oriented, political
movement. He had always depended upon extraneous factors:
defecting officials, foreign intervention, or both. Cheng Shih-
liang's army might even have had a slim chance of succeeding
had it concentrated on Canton from the beginning, where con-
solidated forces could have panicked the capital and caused defection among the provincial troops. As it was, Sun's gamble on
Japanese assistance forced the rebel troops into a hinterland campaign for which they were ill-prepared, and which was beyond
their capacity.

[102] *Hongkong Telegraph*, October 10, 1900. This letter may have originally been sent in English, but a Chinese translation can be found in Ch'en
Ch'un-sheng, "The Waichow Uprising" [150], pp. 241–242.

Trekking toward the Fukien border, Cheng's peasant-augmented force reached Peng-kang-hsü by October 18 or 19 and emerged victorious in a night battle with a government army of some seven thousand men. Lack of ammunition, however, prevented them from pursuing the enemy, who could afford to play a waiting game while the rebels dissipated their energies traversing the sparsely settled mountains of eastern Kwangtung. By October 20 they had reached San-to-chu, on the eastern border of Kuei-shan and over 150 miles from Amoy, but this was about as far as they got. Their next station should have been Mei-lin, a four- or five-day march, but there were fewer villages now and food was running low, with little chance of replenishment.[103] One sign of their plight was the report that they looted a village in this area, the only such report during the entire campaign.[104] A government force was also closing in, and according to their sources, defeated the rebels in the vicinity of San-to-chu in a day-long battle on the twentieth. Several hundred rebels were said to have been killed in this engagement, and the imperial army was able to rescue a large number of prisoners including the assistant district magistrate, who had been captured the previous week.[105] Although Cheng's army was far from routed and may even have numbered as many as twenty thousand men, its initial impetus had been checked, and the cause for panic was over.[106] At the same time, the Triads of neighboring Hai-feng district rallied several thousand fighters, but were dispersed by loyalist troops. According to one report, these Triads did not render effective help to Cheng when he was in trouble, another sign that the secret societies did not take undue risks but carefully calculated their chances of success before plunging into battle.[107]

At this juncture, October 23 or about two weeks after the fighting had started, a courier from Sun Yat-sen brought the dismal news that even if Cheng succeeded in reaching Amoy, no

---

103 Miyazaki, *Thirty-three Years' Dream* [200], p. 283.
104 See Chiang Ya-erh's testimony.
105 Te-shou, in Tsou Lu, *The Kuomintang* [216], p. 670.
106 Miyazaki, *Thirty-three Years' Dream* [200], p. 283.
107 See Chiang Ya-erh's testimony.

help would be forthcoming.[108] The Japanese had also decided that their China interests would best be served by withdrawing from the plot. Two weeks earlier, Kodama had perhaps toyed with the idea of putting the revolutionaries to work and salvaging the Amoy project, which had been so dear to him. But fear of Russian opposition, an important factor in determining British policy as well, dictated moderation, and by now it was clear that the revolutionaries would not make it to Amoy.[109] Here was one of the fallacies of Sun's externally oriented strategy. No single foreign power felt strong enough to handle China alone, fending off all other imperialist powers, and the Boxer violence had demonstrated the high price of "breaking up China." Although Cheng was doing well and still had his main force intact, this was not enough for the Japanese. Not only was the relief expedition called off, but Sun and Hirayama were expelled from Taiwan, and Sun had neither funds to offer the beleaguered Cheng Shih-liang, nor even enough to get back to Japan himself. He had to borrow a hundred yen from his hosts.[110]

Sun's emissary to the Waichow army, Yamada Yoshimasa, reached Cheng by way of Hong Kong and Hai-feng, bringing with him the revolutionary flag, Lu Hao-tung's white sun on a blue sky, which had been secrétly sewed in Japan under the pretext of being used for a school athletic meet.[111] For the first time, the flag was flown on Chinese soil, but without more substantial assistance, Cheng could not keep it flying long. Some of the fighters wanted to revert to their original strategy: return to the base at San-chou-t'ien, almost sixty miles to the southwest, and try to join forces with the Triads of Hsin-an and Bocca Tigris, whence

108 Miyazaki, Thirty-three Years' Dream [200], p. 284.

109 Jansen, Sun Yat-sen [69], p. 97. While most Chinese sources, including Sun, attribute the change in Japanese policy to the fall of the Yamagata cabinet at the end of September, Jansen shows that this was not the decisive factor, but that Kodama and other expansionists in the new government "had been forced to moderate their enthusiasm because cooler heads feared the opposition of Russia to the North." See ibid., pp. 103–104.

110 Hirayama, in "Ma Pai-yüan's Conversations" [163], p. 606.

111 Yamada Junsaburō, "Sun's Sino-Japanese Alliance" [228], p. 263; Ch'en Ch'un-sheng, "The Waichow Uprising" [150], p. 241.

an attack on Canton could be launched.[112] According to Manchu sources, Admiral Ho's dilatory troops had finally moved and had captured San-chou-t'ien by October 20.[113] Cheng now faced a fully mobilized provincial army, which had never in the least deprecated the rebel threat and which was prepared for an all-out campaign. Among the government commanders called into action was Liu Yung-fu, the Black Flag leader of Taiwan renown.[114] However poorly equipped the Cantonese army may have been by international standards, it enjoyed overwhelming superiority over Cheng's men, who had fewer than two thousand rifles and a dwindling supply of ammunition. Further organized resistance would have been senseless, and since Sun had left the future of the campaign to the discretion of his field commanders, Cheng gave the order to disperse. Most of the fighters returned to the countryside, while the leaders and paid recruits made their way to the coast and reached Hong Kong by junk.[115]

The Hong Kong authorities gave the retreating army no trouble.[116] During the fighting Governor Blake had written pro-revolutionary dispatches to Chamberlain and had opposed the Kwangtung government's request to purchase arms in the colony.[117] At the same time, despite Blake's personal sympathy, the fact that the rebels had been unable to use the colony as a base undoubtedly contributed to their defeat.[118]

From their lightning skirmishes and several major battles, the rebels emerged with remarkably few losses. The Manchus claimed to have killed hundreds, but revolutionary sources report only four leaders killed.[119] One victim was Yamada, the

[112] Miyazaki, *Thirty-three Years' Dream* [200], p. 284.
[113] Te-shou, in Tsou Lu, *The Kuomintang* [216], p. 670.
[114] *Ibid.*, p. 671.
[115] Ch'en Ch'un-sheng, "The Waichow Uprising" [150], p. 241; testimony of Chiang Ya-erh.
[116] Ch'en Shao-pai, *Hsing Chung Hui* [152], p. 50, describes the favorable reception the rebels received upon their return to the colony.
[117] See his dispatch to Chamberlain of October 26, 1900 in CO 129/301 [46].
[118] See the *Hongkong Daily Press*, October 31, 1900.
[119] Ch'en Ch'un-sheng, "The Waichow Uprising" [150], p. 241.

faithful messenger, who was caught by imperial troops near San-to-chu after completing his mission, and, as Sun later recorded, became "the first foreigner to lay down his life for the Chinese Republic."[120]

In Canton, there was a loud but futile echo of the hinterland campaign, which sounded the death knell for one rising star of the revolutionary movement. Although he had been taken un-awares by the surprise attack at Sha-wan, Shih Chien-ju was not one to sit patiently by while reports of the campaign reached Canton. He decided that a sudden dramatic move in the capital might relieve the pressure on the Waichow fighters and save the situation. If leading officials were assassinated, Canton would be thrown into confusion and become an easy prey to the North and West River Triads. A blow at the capital, while the bulk of the provincial army was bogged down in the East River area, could make the difference between defeat and victory. Although he lacked enough money to arm his bandit fighters as originally planned, he and his brother were able to sell enough of their inheritance, some three thousand dollars worth, to purchase sev-eral hundred pounds of German dynamite, which Teng Yin-nan and several other comrades smuggled in from Macao or Hong Kong.[121]

They chose Te-shou, Acting Governor-General and the most powerful figure in the Cantonese hierarchy, as their first victim. Shih's reconnaissance revealed that since the Waichow outbreak, the governor-general had taken extra precautions. His yamen was strongly guarded, and he rarely ventured outside. Adjoining his back garden, however, were a number of private dwellings, and using the name of a friend, a Chinese bannerman and Presby-terian, Shih rented one of these apartments. By October 23, after his friend's wife had lived there briefly to allay suspicion, Shih and several fellow conspirators moved in. The dynamite, fuse, and other paraphernalia were secretly transported through the

120 Sun, in *Collected Works* [205], II, 86.
121 Teng Mu-han, "Sketch of Shih Chien-ju" [213], pp. 245–246; Kuomin-tang Committee, "Biography of Shih Chien-ju" [183], p. 625; Ts'ui T'ung-yüeh, "My Revolutionary Past" [217], p. 634.

city by sedan-chair. Though the Waichow campaign was already over, the news was probably late in reaching the capital, from which soldiers were still streaming toward the east. And even if he had known, Shih would have felt morally obligated to match the courage of Cheng's fighters. Working all through the night of October 26, the conspirators dug a tunnel and planted the explosives in a bucket about fifty to one hundred yards from the yamen. At dawn the next day the fuse was set and they headed for Macao, expecting any minute to hear the blast that should blow Te-shou to the "Western Heaven." By the time they reached the dock, however, nothing had happened. After putting his brother and another accomplice on the boat, Shih returned to investigate. A dampened fuse was the cause of the trouble, and Shih, who had not closed his eyes during the several days since the dynamite had been brought, worked alone through the entire night, until by dawn on October 28 the charge was again made ready. According to plan, he should have left immediately for Macao or Hong Kong, but remembering his previous experience, Shih decided to stay in the city until the explosion came off. While resting in a Presbyterian chapel, he finally heard the blast which shook the city out of its morning slumber. Although the first rumors stated that Te-shou had been killed, it soon turned out that the explosion had missed its target. Six people were killed and five injured in nearby dwellings, but Te-shou was merely jolted out of bed and the only damage in the yamen was some broken crockery.[122]

It seemed incredible that Te-shou had escaped unharmed, and Shih could not resist returning to verify the bad news. In fact, in his ignorance of explosives, he had used too small a detonator and only part of the dynamite had gone off. Already thinking of a new attempt, Shih then visited his friends, the Hu brothers. These two Catholic priests urged him to get out of the city, but this was Sunday and the ferries had already stopped running. Forced to wait until the next day, Shih was picked up by the

[122] Teng Mu-han, "Sketch of Shih Chien-ju" [213], p. 247; Kuomintang Committee, "Biography of Shih Chien-ju" [183], pp. 625–626; *Hongkong Telegraph*, October 29, 1900.

police, who were watching the docks. A witness had seen him leave the apartment and a traitor guided the government investigation. The case against Shih was completed when a search of his clothing produced a sheet of instructions, written in German, explaining how to assemble the explosive charge.[123]

Te-shou ordered the prisoner taken to the Nan-hai magistrate for questioning. In view of his youth and gentry background, the officials considered Shih a mere pawn and tried to win his cooperation by mild treatment. Plying him with opium, they urged him to divulge the names of the rebel ringleaders. When he insisted that he alone had been responsible for the plot, the magistrate turned to more conventional methods of interrogation. He was beaten, branded, and had his fingernails and toenails extracted, but refused to satisfy his inquisitors, who asked him to identify his accomplices from a list of forty suspects.[124]

While Shih was being tortured, Reverend Wisner, his teacher at Canton Christian College, Dr. Kerr of the Canton Hospital, and a Chinese Christian friend pleaded with the American consul at Shameen to intervene. The consul, upon learning that Shih was not actually a convert but only a student in a Christian institution, informed the delegation that he could do nothing. Thus far, he said, his power of intervention extended only to converts and not to students.[125]

This power was of course highly respected by the Chinese authorities. In 1895, several of Sun's accomplices had been extricated from the hands of the police because of their religious affiliation, and now, just after the Boxer trouble, Chinese Christians received even stronger protection. Among those arrested at this time was Liu Chin-chou, another Christian said to be a minister, who was guarantor for the flat rented by Shih Chien-ju. Chinese officials considered him idiotic when he recited verses from the

123 Kuomintang Committee, "Biography of Shih Chien-ju" [183], pp. 626–627; Liao P'ing-tzu, "Notes on the Shih Case" [188], p. 249.

124 Teng Mu-han, "Sketch of Shih Chien-ju" [213], p. 248; Kuomintang Committee, "Biography of Shih Chien-ju" [183], pp. 626–627. Ts'ui T'ung-yüeh, "My Revolutionary Past" [217], p. 636.

125 Ts'ui T'ung-yüeh, "My Revolutionary Past" [217], p. 637.

New Testament, and Dr. Kerr obtained his release.[126] Tso Tou-shan, for the second time implicated in a revolutionary scheme, was also released after arrest.[127] Yang Hsiang-fu, trained in modern medicine, was arrested and sentenced to death for writing an anti-dynastic slogan. Because he was a Christian, the sentence was commuted to imprisonment, from which he was released after the revolution.[128]

Shih, however, in addition to being without a baptismal certificate, was by his own admission more involved than any of these suspects, and could not escape the fate of Lu Hao-tung, for whom even foreign intervention had been unavailing. Only twenty-one years old, Shih was beheaded on November 9.[129] Although he did not betray any of his Canton friends, according to Manchu sources, he did name Yang Ch'ü-yün as the man who had brought him into the Hsing Chung Hui and appointed him head of the plot in the capital.[130]

By this time Sun was back in his Japanese sanctuary. Most of the prominent fighters in the Waichow campaign, with the exception of Cheng Shih-liang, who remained in Hong Kong, had fled to Southeast Asia where they helped arouse the *hua-ch'iao* political consciousness.[131] Again, as in 1895, the frustration of the current plot brought to a halt Hsing Chung Hui activities in Canton, while in Hong Kong its organizational life was restricted mainly to the publication of the *Chung-kuo jih-pao*.[132]

The Canton government, however, was not prepared to let the rebel leaders live in peace. With the capture of only Shih

[126] Teng Mu-han, "Sketch of Shih Chien-ju" [213], p. 248; Liao P'ing-tzu, "Notes on the Shih Case" [188], p. 250; Ts'ui T'ung-yüeh, "My Revolutionary Past" [217], p. 636.
[127] Ts'ui T'ung-yüeh, "My Revolutionary Past" [217], p. 636.
[128] Liao P'ing-tzu, "Notes on the Shih Case" [188], p. 250.
[129] Teng Mu-han, "Sketch of Shih Chien-ju" [213], p. 248.
[130] Te-shou, in Tsou Lu, *The Kuomintang* [216], p. 674.
[131] Feng, *Reminiscences* [160], I, 25. Cheng may have temporarily taken refuge in Southeast Asia (see Jansen, *Sun Yat-sen* [69], p. 96), but he was soon back in Hong Kong. Huang Fu and Huang Yao-t'ing, two of the secret society leaders, went to Southeast Asia. See Feng, in *Documents* [179], III, 356–357, under "Huang Fu" and "Huang Yao-t'ing."
[132] Feng, in *Documents* [179], III, 322.

and a few of the Waichow leaders to their credit, they looked for additional culprits and fastened their attention on Yang Ch'ü-yün. Not only was he already implicated in Shih's confession, but in addition he boasted of having been the brains behind the Waichow rising.[133] There is in fact evidence that he had been the key figure in the Hong Kong base.[134] When the Kwangtung authorities raised the price on his head to thirty thousand taels, friends warned him to flee to Southeast Asia, but he insisted upon remaining in Hong Kong and supporting his family by teaching English.[135] On January 10, 1901, a gunman entered Yang's classroom, which was part of his living quarters on Gage Street, and shot him down in front of his students, while his wife and daughter sat in the adjoining room. Before he died in the hospital the next morning, Yang made a statement accusing the Chinese government and mentioning the reward it had issued for his assassination. Indignant Hong Kong officials launched an intensive investigation and two years later, one of the culprits—there were four altogether—was arrested, tried, and executed after he returned to the colony. At the trial the prosecution charged that the assassination had been organized by Li Chia-ch'ao, the same Cantonese official who had zealously pursued the Hsing Chung Hui plotters in 1895, and that it had been authorized by Te-shou himself. Testimony revealed that, in addition to sharing the cash reward, three of the criminals had been honored with the mandarin button of the fifth rank. The Cantonese authorities themselves, however, had beheaded the chief assassin in September 1901, probably to keep him quiet. He had been discovered with a letter from the Hong Kong superintendent of police in his possession.[136]

In the latter part of August 1901, Cheng Shih-liang, the real hero of the Waichow uprising and one of Sun's oldest friends,

133 Ch'en Shao-pai, *Hsing Chung Hui* [152], p. 52.

134 See Chiang Ya-erh's testimony in Blake to Chamberlain, November 21, 1900, in CO 129/301 [46].

135 Feng, *Reminiscences* [160], I, 5.

136 See the *Hongkong Weekly Press and China Overland Trade Report*, May 23, 1903, for the proceedings of the trial. See also Ch'en Shao-pai, *Hsing Chung Hui* [152], pp. 52–53; Feng, *Reminiscences* [160], 5–6.

also met with an untimely death. After taking refuge in Hong Kong, Cheng had gone to Japan to receive further instructions from Sun. Upon his return, he suddenly fell ill while dining with friends and soon died. A police investigation concluded that he had suffered a stroke, but there was also talk of his having been poisoned by a Manchu agent.[137] With the loss of these three stalwarts—Shih, Yang, and Cheng—whatever hope Sun may have had of reviving his Hong Kong-Canton field of activity was shattered.

Thus in the course of the last six months of 1900, Sun Yat-sen had plumbed the depths of frustration. K'ang Yu-wei had ignored him, and Liang had betrayed him. Li Hung-chang still wanted no part of him, and Liu Hsüeh-hsün continued to tease him. The Tzu-li Hui had rejected his espousals and the Ko Lao Hui had sold him out. Sir Henry Blake had offered to open the door at Hong Kong, but Chamberlain had kept it shut. A Japanese swindler had deprived him of arms, and just when its help was most needed, the Tokyo government had left him in the lurch.

Yet Sun's single-minded dedication to anti-dynastic conspiracy was not without compensation. At Canton in 1895, his move had been choked off while it was still a back room plot, but at Waichow his people broke out into the field and kept shooting long enough to reveal popular support for revolution. For the first time his movement tapped the grass-roots of peasant unrest and found them sturdier than its treaty port tendrils. Sun and his lieutenants proved that even during the Boxer period, armed peasants would not turn into bandits or anti-foreign fanatics if they were given proper direction.

Yet Waichow also revealed that his strategy and technique were hopelessly inadequate for fully capitalizing upon this widespread sentiment. Though Sun was now established as the foremost exponent of revolution, he had extended the old formula to its limits. Subversion could not be carried out effectively

137 Feng, *Reminiscences* [160], I, 25; Lo Chia-lun, *Biography* [192], I, 108. Suspicion was directed at a friend of Cheng Kuan-i, Ch'en Shao-pai's rival at the *Chung-kuo jih-pao*.

through sporadic infiltration from Hong Kong and overseas. Nor could revolution be carried on the backs of foreign armies. Revolution required a program and organization. It required organizers, propagandists, and subversive agents at home.

The intellectuals who could assume these roles and provide Sun with a more durable political instrument had thus far ignored him.[138] But while Sun was resting on his laurels in Yokohama, a few miles away a new breed of nationalist intellectuals was gathering strength in Tokyo. These Chinese students found their own path to political action, and until a mutual adjustment enabled Sun to move into their midst, they would be the chief standard-bearers of nationalistic revolutionary sentiment.

[138] According to Feng Tzu-yu, Sun's propaganda organ, the *Chung-kuo jih-pao* was weak in Western ideas and made little impression upon the scholarly world. See Feng, *Reminiscences* [160], I, 11.

IX

Students and Emigré Intellectuals

By sending young men to Japan, Chang Chih-tung and other governors-general strengthened the outlawed reformist and revolutionary movements. But the government had finally become convinced of the need to acquire foreign learning and had little choice.[1] It was less expensive to send students to Japan than to Europe or America, and the "barbarous procedure of the American Customs House people"[2] could be avoided. Furthermore, since Japan continued to venerate traditional values while modernizing her arms and industry, she appeared a safe model to people like Chang, who saw no conflict between Confucianism and specialized foreign knowledge. If China must have a taste of foreign ideas, it seemed wiser to imbibe the Japanese product, from which the more noxious strains had presumably been filtered out. Yet even in 1900, over twenty of Chang's Hunan-Hupeh students returned to join T'ang Ts'ai-ch'ang's Hankow plot.[3]

---

[1] In his *Exhortation to Learning* (1898) Chang proposed sending students to Japan. See Wang, "Intellectuals and Society" [127], pp. 396–397; and Sanetō Keishū, *Chinese Students* [202], p. 413. For an excellent treatment of the new education see Wang, *Chinese Intellectuals* [129], pp. 51–73.

[2] Quoted by Hackett, "Chinese Students" [49], p. 139.

[3] Feng, *Reminiscences* [160], I, 80–81; and Chu Ho-chung, "European T'ung Meng Hui" [157], p. 252. Ten returned students were among those executed by Chang for complicity in the plot. See Wang, *Chinese Intellectuals* [129], pp. 230–231. According to a report in the *Japan Mail*, quoted in the *Hongkong Telegraph* of July 7, 1900, twenty-four Chinese military students left for Shanghai on June 7. These were probably volunteers for

From only about one hundred in 1900, the number of students in Japan rose to about one thousand in 1902, to 8,000 or so in 1905 and to 15,000 or more in the peak year of 1906.[4] Many received an abbreviated and superficial education, and most were interested chiefly in getting jobs at home. However, a significant minority became politically conscious. The little they learned was sufficient to weaken their loyalty to the Manchu regime and Confucian culture. They had been sent abroad to acquire non-Chinese modes of thinking. But it proved impossible to restrict the new learning to professional expertise. Furthermore, how could Chang Chih-tung and other literati leaders command the students' respect if they were ignorant of the foreign learning, which by their own admission was the key to China's survival? As Y. C. Wang has written: "In a tradition which had always justified power by moral excellence and executive competency, the admission of failure, and the continued inability to make corrections, deprived the regime of any moral claim to power."[5]

Student Organizations and Activities

In 1900 two veterans of the Tzu-li Hui, Shen Hsiang-yün and Chi I-hui, both officially sponsored students from Hupeh, formed the first Chinese student organization in Japan, the Li Chih Hui (Determination Society). Vaguely nationalist in objective, but lacking a specific political orientation, the group disbanded a year later, when its more moderate members were attracted by new government regulations which offered official posts to returning students.[6] Though this was the fate of most of these early attempts at organization, nationalist feeling continued to

T'ang's Tzu-li Chün, the military arm of the Tzu-li Hui. But the *Japan Times* of June 21 reports that twenty-four cadets studying at Ichigaya and Ushigome were on June 19 ordered home by the Chinese government.

[4] Feng, *Reminiscences* [160], I, 98; and Hackett, "Chinese Students" [49], p. 142. See also Wang, *Chinese Intellectuals* [129], p. 54.

[5] Wang, "Intellectuals and Society" [127], p. 400.

[6] Feng, *Reminiscences* [160], I, 99. Shen, originally from Chekiang, had been a student at the Wuchang "Self-strengthening" Academy. See Feng, *Reminiscences* [160], I, 80–81. His reply to Chang Chih-tung's reprimand of the revolutionary students, printed in *Huang Ti Hun*, appears in Chang Nan and Wang Jen-chih, *Selected Articles* [143], I, ts'e 2, 764–775.

be roused by new instances of Manchu vulnerability to foreign demands.

In the spring of 1901, when the French included Kwangtung in their sphere of influence, newspapers carried the rumor that the Manchus were about to cede the province. Cantonese students in Japan, joined by several hundred *hua-ch'iao*, formed a Kwangtung Independence Association to protest and declare for provincial independence. Among the leaders were Cheng Kuan-i, Feng Tzu-yu, and Wang Ch'ung-hui (1881–1958). Wang, a Hong Kong-born Cantonese, was the son of Wang Yü-ch'u, the Christian preacher who had befriended Sun Yat-sen.[7] Through Feng and Wang, Sun was able to make his first close contact with the Cantonese student movement and was consulted by the Independence Association.[8]

In April 1902, Chang Ping-lin (Chang T'ai-yen), Ch'in Li-shan, and other firebrands called a memorial meeting in Tokyo to mourn the 242nd anniversary of the death of the last Ming emperor. Alerted by the Chinese Minister, the Tokyo police ordered it canceled, but it was too late to notify the students and several hundred turned up. Sun had met Chang in 1899 and was invited to participate. A similar meeting was held in Yokohama, where there were now signs that the *hua-ch'iao* were being stirred by the student nationalists.[9]

Chang Ping-lin (1868–1936), a Chekiang native and a formidable classical scholar, had previously been associated with K'ang and Liang. Never sympathetic to the Manchus, Chang had nevertheless supported reform as long as he felt that the dynasty could defend China against the foreigners. After 1900 he joined those demanding restoration of Chinese rule.[10]

Most of the students' extracurricular activity was confined to provincial groupings. However, confronted by the growing in-

[7] Feng, *Reminiscences* [160], I, 98, 100; and Boorman (ed.), *Men and Politics* [7], pp. 136–137.

[8] Feng, *Reminiscences* [160], I, 98.

[9] *Ibid.*, I, 57–60.

[10] A short biography of Chang appears in *ibid.*, I, 53–56. On his political thought, see Hu Sheng-wu and Chin Ch'ung-chi, "Chang Ping-lin's Political Thought" [174].

terest in political activity, barriers began to fall. Students speaking different dialects communicated in the written language.[11] In 1902 the Chinese Student Association took shape as a multi-provincial social and service organization. But political overtones were not lacking. Wu Lu-chen, a military student from Hupeh, told the inaugural meeting that the association's Tokyo center was like Philadelphia's Independence Hall.[12] At the end of July, student solidarity and audacity led to a clash with the Chinese envoy, Ts'ai Chün. The students staged a disturbance at the legation and had to be ejected by force.[13] Among the leaders was Wu Chih-hui (1865–1953), a degree-holder from Kiangsu and formerly a teacher at the Nan-yang Kung-hsüeh (Southern Public School), a modern school in Shanghai.[14] Wu had been sent to Japan that year to supervise a group of Cantonese students which included Hu Han-min (1879–1936), a brilliant classical scholar and another future star in the revolutionary galaxy.[15]

At the insistence of the Chinese minister, Wu and another of the demonstrators were expelled from Japan. As he was leaving, Wu attempted suicide by jumping into the moat surrounding the Imperial Palace. His Japanese police escort hauled him out, but the incident redounded to his fame and the Student Association wired the Chinese Foreign Office demanding Minister Ts'ai's recall.[16] Although the Japanese, through the intervention

---

[11] Nozawa Yutaka, *Sun Yat-sen* [201], p. 82.

[12] Hsueh, *Huang Hsing* [66], p. 7; and Hackett, "Chinese Students" [49], pp. 144–146.

[13] Lo Chia-lun, *Biography* [192], I, 110–111; and Hu Han-min, *Autobiography* [171], pp. 380–381. Hu erroneously dates this incident a year later. The exact date was July 28, 1902. See Kuo, *Daily Record* [184], II, 1165. According to Wang, "Intellectuals and Society" [127], p. 401, note 28, Ts'ai had refused to recommend students to Japanese military academies because there were too many applicants, and the following year a new regulation limited entry to government students. For this reason Chiang Kai-shek could not enroll in a military academy when he first went to Japan in 1905. See S. I. Hsiung, *The Life of Chiang Kai-shek* [63], pp. 49–50.

[14] On the Nan-yang Kung-hsüeh, founded by Sheng Hsuan-huai in 1897, see Biggerstaff, *Earliest Modern Schools* [5], pp. 76–77.

[15] Feng, *Reminiscences* [160], III, 76, under "Wu Ching-heng"; and Wu Ching-heng, "Sun's Righteous Behavior" [223], IX, 3.

[16] Lo Chia-lun, *Biography* [192], I, 111; and Chiang Wei-ch'iao, "Chinese

of the Tōa Dōbun Kai, worked out a compromise, not all the students were satisfied; the leader of the Cantonese, Hu Han-min, withdrew from his studies and returned to China in protest.[17]

Before the year ended, the militants had formed the first definitely anti-dynastic organization. Some of the members of the Li Chih Hui, like Feng Tzu-yu, were inspired by Mazzini's Young Italy and proposed calling their group The Young China Association. Finally deciding to be more discreet, they chose Ch'ing-nien Hui (Youth Association), a name already being used by the YMCA in China. Over twenty students joined, many of them from Ōkuma's Waseda University, a pioneer institution for the spreading of modern, liberal ideas. The temperament of the members may be discerned from the objectives named in their charter: nationalism and "destructionism."[18]

Among the leaders was Chang Chi (1882–1947), later one of the important figures of republican China. The son of a Chihli literatus and the recipient of an excellent classical education, in 1899 Chang came to Waseda, where he studied politics and economics.[19] Another Waseda student prominent in Ch'ing-nien Hui was Ch'in Yü-liu, a Kiangsu youth who had studied in the Shanghai Southern Public School and the Kiangnan Naval Academy.[20]

Emboldened by their successes and enjoying reinforcements sent at government expense, the activists created a scandal at the student New Year celebration in Tokyo on January 29, 1903.

Educational Society" [153], p. 486. Neither Lu Hsün, the great novelist, nor his master, Chang Ping-lin, were impressed by Wu's heroic gesture: "Chang T'ai-yen referred to this later when he and Wu were battling with their pens: 'He leaped not into the sea but into a ditch—exposing his face.' Actually the canal outside the Japanese imperial palace is not too small, but, since he was escorted by police, whether his face was exposed or not, he would have been fished out anyway." Lu Hsün, "A Few Matters Connected with Chang T'ai-yen," in *Selected Works* [83], IV, 274.

[17] Hackett, "Chinese Students" [49], p. 152; Hu Han-min, *Autobiography* [171], p. 381.

[18] Feng, *Reminiscences* [160], I, 102–1104.

[19] Biography of Chang Chi in Boorman (ed.), *Men and Politics* [9], p. 1.

[20] See his biography in Feng, *Reminiscences* [160], I, 123–124.

Despite the presence of the government student supervisor and Minister Ts'ai Chün, a Kwangsi student and former K'ang Yuwei disciple, Ma Chün-wu, took the floor and delivered a revolutionary speech. He was followed by Liu Ch'eng-yü, a Hupeh student, who declared that China could be saved only by overthrowing the Manchus. Both Ma and Liu were said to have been briefed by Sun Yat-sen, and Liu, deported as a punishment, later entered Sun's service in the United States.[21]

During 1903, actual or suspected imperialist inroads in China gave the students a number of opportunities to demonstrate their patriotism. It was difficult to tackle the foreigners directly, but the students threw off all restraints in accusing their own government of appeasement and collaboration. In the spring, for example, a report was circulated that the Governor of Kwangsi, Wang Chih-ch'un, had suggested borrowing French soldiers and money to quell the Triad outbreak in his province. The Tokyo students protested, and in a letter to Peking, demanded the governor's removal.[22] Then came a more serious crisis involving the Russians, who had not yet evacuated the Chinese territory in southern Manchuria which they had occupied during the Boxer crisis. At the end of April, they moved into new areas and presented the Chinese with a seven-point program demanding monopolistic concessions as the price for evacuation. Though Peking's diplomacy in defense of the northeast provinces had not been entirely ineffectual in the past, the court now faced the choice of either submitting to the Russians or opening Manchuria to all the powers.[23] The issue created a sensation in Japan. Bolstered by their recent alliance with Britain (February 1902), Japanese nationalists began beating the drums for war with Rus-

[21] Lo Chia-lun, *Biography* [192], I, 117, quotes Liu's account, in "Sketches of Sun's Character" [189].

[22] Chiang Wei-ch'iao, "Chinese Educational Society" [153], p. 489; Hackett, "Chinese Students" [49], p. 156. Hackett erroneously names Wang as the "Kwangtung Viceroy."

[23] For a discussion of this episode and its background, and of the eventual Chinese decision to open Manchuria to the powers, see Kosaka, "Ch'ing Policy Over Manchuria" [71].

sia.[24] Infected by the excitement, the Chinese students went into action to urge resistance.

Taking the lead was Niu Yung-chien, a graduate of a Kiangsu officers' school and a former supervisor of a Kwangtung military academy, now in Japan for further army training. Niu turned to the Chinese Student Association with the proposal that a Resist Russia Military Corps be formed. When the student officers, anticipating the government's disapproval, refused to cooperate, Niu turned to the Ch'ing-nien Hui and it welcomed the idea. With the help of two Ch'ing-nien Hui members—Ch'in Yü-liu and Yeh Lan, another Kiangsu student—Niu organized a mass meeting attended by over five hundred students in the beginning of May. The Student Army, as it was now called, was formally established under the command of Lan T'ien-wei, a Hupeh student attending a Japanese military academy. Over 130 students volunteered for action, another fifty signed up for duties in Tokyo, and twelve women students joined as nurses, thus forming the largest militant student organization yet created.[25] Among its active organizers was yet another future leader of the revolutionary movement, Huang Hsing (1874–1916), a traditional degree-holder from Hunan and a graduate of Chang Chih-tung's modern academy at Wuchang. Sent to Japan by the Hupeh government for normal school training in 1902, Huang devoted his spare time to studying military science.[26] He became the outstanding fighting man of the revolution.

Although the student army volunteered to return to China and lead a drive to expel the Russians, its ranks were riddled with potential anti-Manchuists and its leadership took pains to exclude dynastic loyalty from its patriotic objectives. When orator Yeh Lan shouted the question, "For whom will our army fight,

[24] See Nozawa, *Sun Yat-sen* [201], pp. 81–82.

[25] Feng, *Reminiscences* [160], I, 104; Hsüeh, *Huang Hsing* [66], p. 10. For biographies of Niu, later an important revolutionary general, and Lan, see Feng, *Reminiscences* [160], III, 78, and for Yeh, *ibid.*, III, 68.

[26] Hsüeh, *Huang Hsing* [66], is the best biography of this revolutionary leader and one of the few English-language accounts of the 1911 revolution.

for the people [*kuo-min*] or for the Manchus?" Niu answered,
"For the people!"[27] They presumptuously telegraphed Yüan
Shih-k'ai, the most powerful official in north China, if not in
the entire country, and asked that he resist the Russians. If not,
they would "break off with him." Niu and another member were
then deputized to approach Yüan and offer the services of the
student corps.[28] In the meantime a Hupeh student informed the
Chinese minister in Tokyo that the Student Army was actually
a revolutionary instrument.[29] Minister Ts'ai then telegraphed
Tuan-fang, acting Hunan-Hupeh governor-general, and mainland authorities were alerted against the expected infiltration of
student subversives. Peking officials saw a parallel between this
group and T'ang Ts'ai-ch'ang's Hankow plotters of 1900. Above
all they feared student contact with the secret societies, and Peking warned all provincial officials to keep a sharp eye on returning students.[30] At the same time, Minister Ts'ai prevailed upon
the Japanese to force the student army's dissolution and forbid
Chinese students from engaging in military drill.[31]

After the disbanding of their formal organization, it took the
students only a few days to go underground. Relying on a smaller
group of diehard militants, including Huang Hsing, Ch'in Yü-
liu, and Niu, who had not yet left for Tientsin, they formed a
new association, the Chün Kuo-min Chiao-yü Hui (Militant People's Educational Association). From the date of its inception,
May 11, 1903, until the summer of 1905, when it entered into
the T'ung Meng Hui, the first all-inclusive revolutionary party,
this group was surprisingly adept at concealing its revolutionary

27 Feng, *Reminiscences* [160], I, 110.
28 *Ibid.*, I, 105. Niu's companion was T'ang Erh-ho; see *ibid.*, I, 106. I believe this is the same T'ang Erh-ho who later became president of the National Medical College of Peking; see Chow Tse-tsung, *The May Fourth
Movement* [25], p. 52.
29 Feng, *Reminiscences* [160], I, 106, 109.
30 See Ts'ai's telegram to Tuan-fang in Feng, *Reminiscences* [160], I, 106,
in which he is mistakenly identified as the Nanking governor-general, and
the court's instructions to all governors-general and governors in *ibid.*, I,
106–107.
31 *Ibid.*, I, 107.

purpose.³² Ostensibly dedicated to the "cultivation of the military spirit and patriotism," its secret declaration, drawn up by Ch'in Yü-liu, challenged both the Manchus—China's "barbarian" conquerors—and the aggressive "civilized powers," who could potentially inflict even greater harm upon the nation.³³ In the meantime Niu's mission to Yüan Shih-k'ai, as could have been expected, ended in failure. He and his fellow emissary, T'ang Erh-ho, were fortunate to escape arrest by fleeing to Shanghai.³⁴ However, before they got away, nationalist circles were excited by the rumor that Yüan had executed Niu in Tientsin.³⁵ The Tokyo group was aroused and took a pledge to agitate, rebel, and assassinate when they returned to their respective provinces.³⁶ Two such agents active in Hunan the same year were Huang Hsing, who had completed his studies at the Kōbun Institute, and Ch'en T'ien-hua (1875–1905), a degree-holder turned revolutionary, soon to become one of the greatest of the revolutionary pamphleteers.³⁷

Consideration of this "Resist Russia" movement also draws attention to Shanghai, another source of nationalist ferment. Its modern schools, its growing business class, and above all, the sanctuary it provided in the International Settlement made it no less subversive than Tokyo.

Undoubtedly the most impressive of the radical Shanghai intellectuals was a former Hanlin Compiler from Chekiang, who taught at Southern Public School. Ts'ai Yüan-p'ei (1867–1940) was another of those traditional scholars who turned to foreign learning as a result of the catastrophic events of the 1890's. Sym-

---

³² *Ibid.*, I, 107, 112. Kuo, *Daily Record* [184], II, 1179.

³³ Hsüeh, *Huang Hsing* [66], pp. 10–11. The Chinese text of Ch'in's declaration, partially translated by Hsüeh, appears in Feng, *Reminiscences* [160], I, 109–112.

³⁴ Lo Chia-lun, *Biography* [192], I, 117. Yüan, though he opposed acceding to Russian demands, refused to see the student representatives; see Li Chien-nung, *Political History* [78], p. 193, and Chiang Wei-ch'iao, "Chinese Educational Society" [153], p. 490.

³⁵ Kuo, *Daily Record* [184], II, 1181. Kuo dates this at June 7.

³⁶ Feng, *Reminiscences* [160], I, 112.

³⁷ *Ibid.* See E. Young, "Ch'en T'ien-hua" [138], for an illuminating account of Ch'en's revolutionary activities and his ideological contribution.

pathizing with the reformers of 1898, he finally came to despair of gradualist reform programs. The post-Boxer period found him in the company of political extremists.[38]

In the spring of 1902 Ts'ai joined Chang Ping-lin, recently returned from Japan, and other radical scholars to organize the Chinese Educational Association, for the ostensible purpose of publishing original modern texts.[39] This was the period when recently formed modern schools relied mostly upon Japanese books, sometimes translated so hastily that the Japanese flags remained printed on the covers.[40] The leaders also hoped to serve revolution through the Association. Without funds or a concrete plan of action, they were nevertheless able to encourage radical intellectuals throughout the southeastern provinces.[41]

In August, Wu Chih-hui denounced the Manchus at a large meeting in Shanghai called by the Educational Association in support of the Tokyo demonstrators. Since the government was interfering with overseas students, it was suggested that they establish their own independent modern school.[42] At this time the Nan-yang students went on strike when discussions of current politics and the reading of modern books were prohibited. Ts'ai Yüan-p'ei left with his students, who then turned to the Educational Association.[43] In November the Association formed the Patriotic School (Ai-kuo Hsüeh-she) and absorbed over a hundred ex-Nan-yang students.[44] Ts'ai was the principal and Wu became educational supervisor. Chang Ping-lin taught Chinese literature. Like Ts'ai, who directed the translation department of the Commercial Press, most of the teachers had other jobs and volunteered their services. The school was on a high school level and offered English language courses.[45]

[38] For a brief biography of Ts'ai and a discussion of his syncretic philosophy, see Sakai, "Ts'ai Yuan-p'ei" [99].

[39] Feng, *Reminiscences* [160], I, 115.

[40] Wang, "Intellectuals and Society" [127], p. 399.

[41] Chiang Wei-ch'iao, "Chinese Educational Society" [153], p. 485; Feng, *Reminiscences* [160], I, 116.

[42] Chiang Wei-ch'iao, "Chinese Educational Society" [153], pp. 486–487.

[43] Kuo, *Daily Record* [184], II, 1170; Feng, *Reminiscences* [160], I, 116.

[44] Feng, *Reminiscences* [160], II, 80, says that 132 students left for the new school, but Kuo, *Daily Record* [184], II, 1170 gives a figure as high as 200.

[45] Chiang Wei-ch'iao, "Chinese Educational Society" [153], pp. 487–488.

Huang Chung-yang, one of the founding members of the Association, was its chief fund-raiser. A protégé and fellow townsman of Weng T'ung-ho, the emperor's tutor, Huang was an accomplished writer and poet as well as a Buddhist monk. Through him, two women from wealthy Shanghai merchant families contributed funds for the establishment of this school and another institution that the Association founded, the Patriotic Girls' School (Ai-kuo Nü-hsüeh).[46]

In April 1903 the Shanghai nationalists received a telegram from their Tokyo friends reporting the proposal to use French troops in Kwangsi. At a large meeting Kwangsi merchants resident in Shanghai joined in a vigorous protest to Peking.[47] Another meeting responded to the alarm over Manchuria. The gathering not only protested to Peking but telegraphed various foreign governments for help against the Russians. There was talk of closing shops and stopping work, and an abortive attempt was made to create a pro-constitutional political body. Following the lead of the Tokyo actionists, they organized a volunteer army corps.[48]

A notable feature of this nationalist awakening in Shanghai was scholar-merchant collaboration. The leaders of course were the gentry-born scholars, young masters of the old tradition. As teachers they infused revolutionary ideas into their own gentry stratum. As propagandists they clashed head on with their government and aroused nationalist sentiment among all groups of Chinese society, including the most distant *hua-ch'iao* communities.

Seeking a vehicle to combat the conservative papers, *Shun-pao* and *Hsin-wen pao*, which dominated the metropolis, Chang Ping-lin and his friends fastened upon the *Su-pao* (Kiangsu Journal) and its publisher, Ch'en Fan.[49] Ch'en was a Hunan degree-holder and a former district magistrate in Kiangsu who had

[46] Lo Chia-lun, *Biography* [192], I, 111–112.

[47] Chiang Wei-ch'iao, "Chinese Educational Society" [153], p. 487. This meeting took place on April 25. See Kuo, *Daily Record* [184], II, 1177–1178.

[48] Lo Chia-lun, *Biography* [192], I, 118. This second meeting took place on April 27. Kosaka, "Ch'ing Policy Over Manchuria" [71], p. 142; Chiang Wei-ch'iao, "Chinese Educational Society" [153], p. 490.

[49] Chiang Wei-ch'iao, "Chinese Educational Society" [153], p. 489.

retired to Shanghai because of a missionary incident. His elder brother, Ch'en Ting, had been imprisoned for involvement with the 1898 reformers. In 1898, Ch'en Fan took over *Su-pao*, a daily founded two years earlier by a Chinese named Hu Chang. The paper was registered with the Japanese consulate in the International Settlement under the name of Hu's Japanese wife. For four years Ch'en gave the paper a pro-K'ang Yu-wei slant. However, the incidents of 1903 convinced him that China was being betrayed by her Manchu rulers and he welcomed cooperation with the Educational Association.[50] Chang Ping-lin and Wu Chih-hui became regular contributors and on May 27, Chang Shih-chao was appointed editor. Chang (b. 1881), a former military cadet in Nanking who had defected to the Patriotic School, began at this point the brilliant journalistic career which for the next half century reflected his inconstant ideological loyalties.[51]

But the outstanding contributor was Chang Ping-lin. Even the International Settlement could not provide immunity once Chang started wielding his vitriolic brush for *Su-pao*. A master polemicist, whose essays were so filled with literary allusions that they were often unfathomable except to skilled classicists, Chang at this time was all too successful in making his seditious ideas understood.[52] On May 27 he began a series of articles in which he insulted the emperor, once referring to him as *hsiao-ch'ou*, "low wretch," and advocated revolution.[53] Moreover, several of these articles were in praise of an even more inflammatory work

50 Chang Huang-ch'i, "Record of the *Su-pao* Case" [142], p. 367; Lo Chia-lun, *Biography* [192], I, 119; Feng, *Reminiscences* [160], I, 120.

51 Chang Huang-ch'i, "Record of the *Su-pao* Case" [142], pp. 367–368. After his youthful radicalism, which saw him through the 1911 revolution, Chang (who studied in Japan and England) came to share Walter Bagehot's preference for "animated moderation." By 1916 he was in opposition to the anti-traditionalism which came to a head with the May Fourth Movement, but after 1949 he became a supporter of the Communist regime. During the early period under discussion he was a friend and editorial colleague of Ch'en Tu-hsiu; see Chow, *The May Fourth Movement* [25], pp. 42–43.

52 Of his *Ch'iu shu*, published in 1899, Lu Hsün wrote: "I could not even punctuate the sentences let alone understand them; and the same was true of many young people in those days." Lu Hsün, "Some Recollections of Chang T'ai-yen," in *Selected Works* [83], IV, 266.

53 Hsüeh, *Huang Hsing* [66], pp. 14–15. Hummel (ed.), *Eminent Chinese*

which had recently been printed in Shanghai, Tsou Jung's *The Revolutionary Army* (*Ko-ming chün*). This pamphlet was a truly great propaganda piece that compares with Tom Paine's revolutionary tracts, and a review of the author's life presents an arresting profile of a Chinese youth drawn into the revolutionary vortex by the national crisis and the impact of foreign ideas.

Tsou Jung (1885–1905) was born into a middle-class, Szechwan merchant family. He became a child prodigy, and by the age of twelve was well on his way to mastering the classical studies required for traditional examinations. Yet, as we have noted in the case of Shih Chien-ju, it was easy to get off the track in those days. With China buffeted by foreign intruders, the "eight-legged" essay seemed a poor weapon, and the 1898 reform movement inspired Tsou to seek more dramatic means of defense. As in the case of so many others, the teachings and example of T'an Ssu-t'ung first gave him the audacity to "break out of the net" and seek the new learning.[54]

Whereas Shih Chien-ju, on a similar quest for enlightenment, had turned to American missionaries, Tsou's first modern teachers were Japanese. His home town, Chungking, had been opened to foreign trade as a result of the Sino-Japanese War, and in 1898 he studied English with a newly arrived Japanese by the name of Narita Yasuteru. This same year a Japanese army officer, Idogawa Tatsuzō, taught him Japanese. Under the influence of these two visitors, Tsou also began studying foreign science and history and became an admirer of the Japanese reform movement. In 1901 he was ready for more systematic study and went to Shanghai in preparation for a trip to Japan.[55]

---

[68], II, 769. There is a great deal of inconsistency in dating the appearance of Chang's various articles. See Lo Chia-lun, *Biography* [192], I, 119–120; Kuo, *Daily Record* [184], II, 1180–1181; Chang Huang-ch'i, "Record of the *Su-pao* Case" [142], pp. 368–370; Tu Ch'eng-hsiang, "Development of Tsou Jung's Thought" [218], pp. 196–197.

[54] Tu Ch'eng-hsiang, "Development of Tsou Jung's Thought" [218], pp. 190–192. Feng, *Reminiscences* [160], II, 52. "Break out of the net" is T'an's phrase. See Hummel, *Eminent Chinese* [68], II, 705.

[55] Tu Ch'eng-hsiang, "Development of Tsou Jung's Thought" [218], p. 192.

He studied at the Kuang Fang-yen Kuan (a modern government school attached to the Kiangnan Arsenal)[56] for several months, and in the spring of 1902 he went to Tokyo as a private student supported by a monthly stipend from his family.[57] His stay in Shanghai had already set him on a radical course and his arrival in Japan, soon after the Ming memorial meeting, threw him into the thick of student agitation with radicals like Chang Chi and Feng Tzu-yu.[58] He studied at an institution established by the ubiquitous Tōa Dōbun Kai.[59]

Now his political ideas began to jell and he definitely broke with K'ang's constitutional monarchism. Revolutionary history and in particular the American Revolution fascinated him and he became convinced that only a similar upheaval could save China.[60] Drawing upon his readings, which included Carlyle's *French Revolution*, Mill's *On Liberty*, Rousseau, Montesquieu, and "some Herbert Spencer," he began composing a panegyric to revolution.[61] "The Revolutionary Army" as he called it, contained both an emotional cry for destruction, steaming with anti-Manchu racism, and a positive demand for a new political order based on Western constitutionalism and an enlightened and educated citizenry.

Before completing the draft, however, he and Chang Chi had to leave Japan in a hurry. During the "Resist Russia" campaign of the spring of 1903, they tangled with a Chinese supervisor of military students, snipped off his queue, and hung it from the rafters of the student union.[62] Fleeing to avoid arrest, they ar-

---

[56] On the Kuang Fang-yen Kuan, whose establishment was originally proposed by Feng Kuei-fen, see Biggerstaff, *Earliest Modern Schools* [5], chapter III.

[57] According to this testimony at his trial in December, Tsou received twenty dollars per month from his family. See *The Shanghai Sedition Trial* [106], p. 20.

[58] Tu Ch'eng-hsiang, "Development of Tsou Jung's Thought" [218], pp. 194.

[59] Feng, *Reminiscences* [160], II, 52.

[60] Tu Ch'eng-hsiang, "Development of Tsou Jung's Thought" [218], pp. 194–195.

[61] *The Shanghai Sedition Trial* [106], p. 20.

[62] Feng, *Reminiscences* [160], II, 53. Three other students were involved in this incident.

rived in Shanghai in time for the excitement over Manchuria and Kwangsi, and became fast friends with Chang Ping-lin and Chang Shih-chao, the four of them forming a "compact of brothers with different names." Chang Ping-lin, the eldest of the quartet, acted as mentor to the fledgling Tsou Jung and shared his lodgings with him. He also took an interest in the manuscript which Tsou had brought from Japan. After Chang made some revisions and wrote a preface to it, *The Revolutionary Army* was published as a pamphlet in May 1903.[63]

Chang's laudatory articles in *Su-pao* stimulated immediate interest in *The Revolutionary Army*. But the author and his work received even greater publicity as a result of the government's stubborn effort to overcome the jurisdictional boundaries of the International Settlement and punish him, as well as the ringleaders of the anti-Manchu movement there. On June 21 the Chinese authorities requested the arrest of four agitators, Ts'ai Yüan-p'ei, Wu Chih-hui, Niu Yung-chien, and T'ang Erh-ho. The list was later increased to include Chang Ping-lin, Ch'en Fan, and Tsou Jung. The foreign consuls were inclined to agree with the request but the Municipal Council resisted, backed by Shanghai's foreign language press. On June 29, 1903, an agreement was negotiated and the Settlement police attempted to carry out the arrests at the *Su-pao* office and the Patriotic School. By this time, however, most of the accused were not available. Ts'ai had gone to Tsingtao about ten days earlier and the others, with the exception of Wu Chih-hui, who headed for London, were on their way to Japan. Only Chang Ping-lin and his protégé made no effort to escape the net. Chang was arrested on the 29th, and two days later Tsou Jung walked into a police station and gave himself up.[64] One reason for his surrender was the desire to attend to Chang, whose nearsightedness rendered him practically helpless.[65]

---

[63] Tu Ch'eng-hsiang, "Development of Tsou Jung's Thought" [218], p. 195; *The Shanghai Sedition Trial* [106], p. 21. According to Chinese sources, the Shanghai *Ta-t'ung* publishing firm printed *The Revolutionary Army*, but its name did not appear on the pamphlet.

[64] Lo Chia-lun, *Biography* [192], I, 120–121.

[65] Tu Ch'eng-hsiang, "Development of Tsou Jung's Thought" [218], p. 197.

Su-pao and the Patriotic School were shut down on July 7, and while Chang, Tsou, and four other prisoners were held in the International Settlement, the Chinese waged a six-month diplomatic struggle for their extradition.[66] Arguing quite correctly that the Settlement was not a foreign colony, the Peking government claimed that treaty regulations gave them jurisdiction over their own criminals.[67] Their case was well-stated by Chang Chih-tung, who recalled his experience in dealing with the Hankow plotters of 1900. At that time the British consul had not hesitated to hand over prisoners taken in the foreign concession, and Chang interpreted this as a precedent. The foreigners, he remarked bitterly, were not above "twisting principle" to suit their interests. Their intention, he charged, was to extend their sovereignty over the Settlement and turn it into foreign territory.[68] This in fact was exactly what the Municipal Council had been striving for, and this particular case was just another round in the long tug-of-war with the Chinese authorities for jurisdiction over Chinese in the International Settlement.

While the other foreign consuls, including the American, French, and Russian, were willing to accede to Chinese demands, the British, having a predominant interest in the International Settlement, refused to hand over the prisoners.[69] Unfortunately for the Chinese, a recent example of their brutality in treating political criminals had hardened British resistance or at least

[66] Among the other prisoners was Lung Tse-hou (Lung Chi-chih) a Kwangsi literatus wanted for his involvement with the Hankow Plot. See Feng, *Reminiscences* [160], III, 55; and *The Shanghai Sedition Trial* [106], p. 1, where the names of all six accused, including the absent Ch'en Fan, are given.

[67] The background to this jurisdictional struggle is ably traced by Elvin, "The Mixed Court" [35].

[68] See Chang's telegram to Tuan-fang of July 21, 1903 in *The 1911 Revolution* [167], I, 427–428. Other official Chinese correspondence in connection with the *Su-pao* case and dating from June 21, 1903 to December 10, 1903 can be found in *ibid.*, I, 408–480. These are all taken from Tuan-fang's archives.

[69] See Tuan-fang's two telegrams of August 25, 1903 to Chang Chih-tung in *ibid.*, I, 474.

provided it with an excuse. In the same year, Shen Chin, a Kwangsi student and journalist who had supported T'ang Ts'ai-ch'ang, had been apprehended and beaten to death in Peking.[70] But the main issue was still that of jurisdiction, and it is one of the anomalies of this period that Chinese nationalists like Chang and Tsou, and before them, Sun and K'ang, were protected by the same imperialist infringements upon Chinese sovereignty which they denounced.

The case then finally went before the Mixed Court in December[71] 1903. This institution, according to earlier agreements, had jurisdiction over Chinese who had committed offenses in the Settlement or who were defendants in actions brought by foreigners. In the first instance a Chinese magistrate alone was supposed to try the case, but it had become the practice for a foreign assessor, usually a consular official, to sit in.[72] This particular case, according to treaty regulations, should have been tried before the Chinese magistrate alone, but a British assessor assumed supreme judicial powers, while his two Chinese colleagues, the native city district magistrate and the Mixed Court magistrate, served mainly in advisory capacities.[73] Furthermore,

[70] See Hummel, *Eminent Chinese* [68], II, 769; and various communications between Tuan-fang and other Ch'ing officials concerning the effect of Shen's execution in *The 1911 Revolution* [167], I, 432, 435, 476. Shen Chin and his friend Lung Tse-hou had been on Chang Chih-tung's wanted list for collaborating with T'ang Ts'ai-ch'ang. See Feng, *Reminiscences* [160], III, 55, under "Shen K'e-ch'eng." In 1903, the year of his execution, Chang Shih-chao (under the pen name Huang Chung-huang) eulogized him in a pamphlet, *Shen Chin*, and Chang Ping-lin dedicated a poem to him: see *ibid.*, III, 153; and Lu Hsün, "Some Recollections of Chang T'ai-yen," in *Selected Works* [83], IV, 267.

[71] The trial took place on December 3, 4, 5, 7, and 16. See *The Shanghai Sedition Trial* [106].

[72] See Elvin, "The Mixed Court" [35], pp. 141–142. During the trial, lawyers for the Chinese government argued that in the U.S. Treaty of 1869 it was explicity stated that, subject to existing conventions, the Chinese authorities did not surrender their right of jurisdiction over Chinese subjects in the settlement; see *The Shanghai Sedition Trial* [106], pp. 5–6.

[73] A key issue was the role of the assessor. Lawyers for the plaintiff, i.e. the Chinese government, insisted that the assessor, in a case of this nature, should not sit as a judge. The British assessor, however, ruled that the term "assessor" had two different meanings. The assessor of the Chefoo Conven-

though the case was tried under Chinese law, both the plaintiff (the Chinese government) and the defendants were represented by British lawyers. The charge was that of seditious libel.[74]

Although both Chang Ping-lin and Tsou Jung were said to have desired arrest as a means to glorify the revolutionary cause, the half-year already spent in jail apparently left them uninterested in further martyrdom, and they did not flaunt their revolutionary sympathies. Chang's seditious statements were contained in an open letter of rebuttal to K'ang Yu-wei, which had been sold as a ten-cent pamphlet, but he claimed that he had meant it as a private communication, and that it had been published without his knowledge. He also denied having written for *Su-pao*.[75] Flippant and even insolent, Chang's attitude evoked one of the rare comments of the Chinese district magistrate: "He ought to be flogged."[76]

Though his pamphlet was more obviously seditious than Chang's, Tsou assumed a less aggressive stance. Like Chang he claimed that his essay had not been meant for publication, and that it had been written as a classroom exercise in Japan. In addition, he asserted that he no longer held the revolutionary views expressed in the pamphlet. Instead of advocating the extermination of the Manchus, he now favored socialism, which was to be the subject of his future writings.[77]

While *The Revolutionary Army* did contain a unique protest

---

tion (1876) might have only power of protest, but in the Mixed Court, he "has a part in the judgment given, which cannot be rendered without his consent." The Chinese officials were present, he declared, only to determine questions of Chinese law, and he ruled unequivocally that "no sentence can be passed and no decision given on any point that may arise in the course of the hearing without my concurrence." This arbitrary ruling does not appear to be in consonance with the original purpose of the Mixed Court.

[74] "Seditious libel" would have been an equivalent charge in a British court. The full charge here was that of "having written, printed and published seditious articles . . . in order to excite treason and discontent and create disturbance in His Imperial Majesty's Empire." See *The Shanghai Sedition Trial* [106], pp. 25–26. Chang was accused on the basis of his pamphlet refuting K'ang Yu-wei, and Tsou for *The Revolutionary Army*.

[75] *Ibid.*, pp. 15–16.

[76] *Ibid.*, p. 29.

[77] *Ibid.*, pp. 21–22.

against agrarian injustice—unique, that is, for the political literature of this period—there is little reason to believe that Tsou's
new preference for socialism was at odds with his recently declared revolutionary faith. In spite of his obvious attempt to
escape the consequences of his incendiary essay, under cross-
examination some of his true intentions seeped through:

"Is it your idea to dethrone the dynasty?"
"I don't want to dethrone the dynasty, but I want to be a second
Rousseau."
"Do you want to bring about another French Revolution?"
"If Rousseau was a revolutionary, why was a monument erected
to him?"
"Were not the writings of Rousseau one of the primary causes of
the French Revolution?"
"I only wished to learn what Rousseau had done and did not care
what happened to my writing when it was written."
"Then you didn't want to produce a revolution in China?"
"No, my idea is that there should be no rich and no poor, but
that everyone should be on the same footing."[78]

Since both defendants had admitted writing seditious material, the court's verdict was never in doubt. Yet the sentences,
passed on May 22, 1904, were much more lenient than those
sought by the Chinese authorities. Chang was given three years
and Tsou, two. Though Chang was released in June 1906, and
resumed revolutionary activities in Japan, his young friend died
in prison in April 1905, just a few weeks before he was to be
released.[79] Only twenty years old at the time of his death, Tsou
was already the most famous anti-Manchu author of his time.
In July, during the diplomatic controversy over his detention,
parts of *The Revolutionary Army* were published in the British
and European press.[80] That year new editions came out in Hong
Kong, Singapore, Yokohama, and Shanghai, and in 1904 Sun
Yat-sen had it printed in the United States for distribution there

[78] *Ibid.*, p. 22.
[79] Tu Ch'eng-hsiang, "Development of Tsou Jung's Thought" [218], p.
198.
[80] *The Shanghai Sedition Trial* [106], p. 29.

and in other *hua-ch'iao* communities. Huang Hsing secretly handed out copies to students and military cadets in Hupeh. Altogether the book ran into twenty editions and over a million copies. Among its enthusiastic and impressionable young readers were such contrasting personalities as Hu Shih and Chiang Kai-shek.[81]

Nationalist Journals and Tracts

While *The Revolutionary Army* was the first popular revolutionary tract, it was still part of the immense propaganda output of the students and intellectuals in Tokyo and Shanghai. It should be stressed, however, that in style and content many of these literary enterprises derived from the pace-setting journals of Liang Ch'i-ch'ao. More than one fiery article was plucked out of *Ch'ing-i pao* and its fortnightly successor, *Hsin-min ts'ung-pao* (A New People, 1902–1907). Until 1903 Liang was in his radical phase, and the first flurry of student political journalism bore his imprint, thereby justifying the claim that the 1911 Revolution "was largely the result of his pen."[82] Without trying to draw up a comprehensive list, I should mention some of these student publications and their significant themes.[83]

---

[81] Tu Ch'eng-hsiang, "Development of Tsou Jung's Thought" [218], pp. 200–201; and Hsüeh, *Huang Hsing* [66], p. 16.

[82] Lin Yu-tang, *History of the Press* [80], p. 97. Only Yen Fu wielded a comparable influence with his translations of Western political thought. See Schwartz, *Yen Fu and the West* [105].

[83] There are various lists of Chinese publications and periodicals of this period including those of the overseas students. Britton, *Chinese Periodical Press* [13], is the best English-language survey of the subject but is not strong on student publications. Lin Yu-tang's *History of the Press* [80], is helpful but incomplete and not free of errors. Sanetō, *Chinese Students* [202], pp. 418–420, has a list of publications appearing in Japan from 1898 to 1911 though his dates are not always consistent with those of Chinese sources. Feng, *Reminiscences* [160], III, 139, 158 gives an extensive list of reformist and revolutionary literature and periodicals but is not always trustworthy. Chang Ching-lu (ed.), *Source Materials* [141], is a collection of articles and documents dealing with the Chinese press from 1862 when the *T'ung-wen kuan* started with its translations until the eve of the May Fourth movement. Volume one, pp. 77–97, has a list of periodicals for the late Ch'ing period, including some revolutionary items; Chang Yü-ying's two articles, "List of Periodicals of the 1911 Revolution" [148] and "List of Books of the 1911

In late 1899 or 1900 Cantonese students, led by two products of Liang's Ta-t'ung school—Feng Tzu-yu and the self-styled "Chinese Moses," Cheng Kuan-i—founded a semi-monthly journal in Yokohama, the *K'ai-chih lu* (Journal of New Learning).[84] Featuring translations like that of Rousseau's *Social Contract*, the journal supported the "natural rights" of liberty and equality and attempted to counteract the influence of the Pao Huang Hui, even though Cheng Kuan-i was at this time working for *Ch'ing-i pao*. The new magazine used the press and distribution facilities of the pro-emperor journal, which enabled it to reach the overseas communities. In 1901 Cheng was forced out of his position with *Ch'ing-i pao*, and the *K'ai-chih lu*, which had received a 200 yen contribution from Sun Yat-sen, then ceased publication.[85]

In December 1900 a number of Kiangsu students started publishing the first student monthly, *I-shu hui-pien* (Translation Magazine), in Tokyo. This periodical also featured translations of political works, including those of Montesquieu, Rousseau, Mill, and Spencer. The journal lasted for only about a year, but set a precedent for future publications by provincial groups.[86]

The first out-and-out revolutionary journal was *Kuo-min pao* (The Chinese National), launched in the spring of 1901. Among its founders and editors were K'ang's former partisan, the em-

---

Revolution" [149], provide short descriptions of most of the important items. Also helpful and usually reliable but not so extensive is the description of the twenty-five periodicals and books in Chang and Wang, *Selected Articles* [143], I, *ts'e* 2, pp. 966–970. The editors list only those publications from which selections were made in their collection. Dates of publication can sometimes be checked by using Ichiko Chūzō (ed.), *Chinese Newspapers and Magazines* [176]. This publication of the Tōyō Bunko lists the Chinese periodical holdings of all Japanese libraries, which, outside of Mainland China, are probably the most extensive in the world. The Kuomintang archives in Taichung are also strong on student periodicals of this period.

[84] Chang and Wang, *Selected Articles* [143], I, *ts'e* 2, p. 966, gives the earlier date, but most other sources give 1900.

[85] Feng, *Reminiscences* [160], I, 82–84, 95; Chang and Wang, *Selected Articles* [143], I, *ts'e* 2, p. 966; Feng in *Development of the Revolution* [178], X, 665. Cheng then went to work for the *Chung-kuo jih-pao* in Hong Kong.

[86] Sanetō, *Chinese Students* [202], pp. 261, 418; and Feng, *Reminiscences* [160], I, 98–99.

bittered Ch'in Li-shan, Chang Chi, Wang Ch'ung-hui, Shen Hsiang-yün, and Chi I-hui. In addition to the usual translations, including the American Declaration of Independence, it carried news items, essays, and an English section written by Wang. But despite Sun Yat-sen's contribution of one thousand yen, it ran into financial difficulties and closed down after four issues.[87]

Ch'in and Chi moved to Shanghai in December 1902, where they founded another monthly, *Ta-lu* (The Continent). Though less blatantly revolutionary, it continued the campaign against K'ang and Liang and lasted for 34 issues. Printing such articles as "The Theories of the Two Masters of Materialism (Diderot and Lamettrie)," it was influential in spreading new ideas.[88]

At this time various student provincial organizations came out with a spate of nationalist monthlies. In November 1902, Hunan students led by Yang Shou-jen, Ch'en T'ien-hua, and Huang Hsing, founded *Yu-hsüeh i-pien* (Translations by Students Abroad), which ran to twelve issues and printed articles such as "Krueger, Hero of South African Independence," "The Railroad Policies of the Powers in China," "A Record of the Disorders in France during the Close of the Eighteenth Century," and "Nationalist Education."[89]

In January 1903 Hupeh students under Liu Ch'eng-yü founded *Hu-pei hsüeh-sheng chieh* (Hupeh Students' Circle), which lasted until 1904. Besides dealing with a variety of subjects—science, education, history, economics—it stressed the ethnic issue and identified the Manchus with earlier barbarian enemies. Yo Fei, the anti-Mongol general of the Sung period, was designated "the first Chinese nationalist."[90] In February,

87 Feng, *Reminiscences* [160], I, 82, 96–98, 100; and Feng in *Development of the Revolution* [178], X, 666. The English title, *The Chinese National*, appears on the cover of the magazine, reproduced in Chang and Wang, *Selected Articles* [143], I, *ts'e* 1, opposite page 26. See also *ts'e* 2, p. 966.

88 Chang and Wang, *Selected Articles* [143], I, *ts'e* 2, p. 967. The article on materialism appears in *ts'e* 1, pp. 411–412.

89 Hsüeh, *Huang Hsing* [66], p. 9; and Chang and Wang, *Selected Articles* [143], I, *ts'e* 2, p. 967.

90 Chang and Wang, *Selected Articles* [143], I, *ts'e* 2, 967. After the fourth issue, the name was changed to *Han-sheng*.

Chihli students founded a similar journal, *Chih-shuo* (Chihli Speaks),[91] and Chekiang students, assisted by Ma Chün-wu, a prolific translator from Kwangsi, launched *Che-chiang ch'ao* (Tides from Chekiang).[92] Lasting for about a year, it emphasized anti-Manchuism and glorified the seventeenth century rebel, Cheng Ch'eng-kung (Koxinga) as "a Chinese patriot."[93]

Chiang-su, established in April by Kiangsu students, including Ch'in Yü-liu, was the most ardently republican periodical. Huang Chung-yang, of *Su-pao* notoriety, joined its staff. Running to twelve issues, it featured biographies of early anti-Manchu rebels like Koxinga and Shih K'o-fa, and of "China's First Revolutionary, Ch'en She," the anti-Ch'in rebel of the third century, B.C. Its political interests were reflected in such articles as "On the Evolution of Political Systems," "The Establishment of a New Government," "Can Revolution be Avoided?," and "The Question of China's Constitution."[94] And an article appearing in November 1903, "The Arguments for Preserving or Dismembering China," by "Yat-sen," marked Sun's modest debut as a pundit for the student world.[95]

Like *Ch'ing-i pao* and *Hsin-min ts'ung-pao,* student magazines were circulated at home as well as in Japan.[96] Each issue was printed in large quantities and copies were sent to Shanghai and smuggled into the interior by returning students. Some issues of *Che-chiang ch'ao,* for example, were reprinted several times, each printing running to five thousand copies.[97] This was at a time when there were only several thousand students

[91] *Ibid.*

[92] See Chang Yü-ying, "Books of the 1911 Revolution" [149], p. 173, for a list of Ma's translations of Spencer, Darwin, and Mill in 1902 and 1903.

[93] Chang Yü-ying, "Periodicals of the 1911 Revolution" [148], pp. 100–101.

[94] *Ibid.,* pp. 534–596, 968.

[95] *Ibid.,* pp. 597–602.

[96] Although all publications of K'ang and Liang were banned from China by imperial edict in the hope that, "if nobody will buy their papers, then the rebels can do no harm," *Hsin-min ts'ung-pao* was so popular at home and abroad that some issues were reprinted a dozen times; see Lin Yu-tang, *History of the Press* [80], pp. 97–98; and Saneto, *Chinese Students* [202], p. 415.

[97] Saneto, *Chinese Students* [202], p. 420n.

in Japan. Though these five provincial organs ceased publication by the end of 1904, the following year new, and even more radical journals began replacing them. By 1907 there were 27 such magazines, and not only in number but perhaps also in quality they excelled their counterparts in China. It was of course much easier to take a strong anti-Manchu line in Japan; sometimes Japanese were listed as editors and publishers to allow for even greater license.[98]

Even after the *Su-pao* affair, nationalists in Shanghai managed to put out several lively periodicals. In August 1903, a month after *Su-pao* shut down, Chang Shih-chao, Chang Chi, and others founded a new daily, the *Kuo-min jih-jih pao* (National Daily). Specializing in attacking bureaucratic corruption, it soon became known as "the second *Su-pao*." A foreigner, A. Somoll, was listed as publisher, and later the paper obtained British registry under the name of a Hong Kong Cantonese who had graduated from a British naval academy. After several months, however, the pressure of Chinese protests became too great and the paper went the way of its predecessor.[99] In December Ts'ai Yüan-p'ei, back on the scene after studying German in Tsingtao, formed a group called the "Tui-O T'ung-chih Hui" (Society of Comrades for Resisting Russia), which published a new daily, *O-shih ching-wen* (Important News from Russia), later changed to *Ching-chung jih-pao* (The Alarm Bell).[100] Although its ostensible purpose was to attack Russian designs in Manchuria, the paper carried on in the *Su-pao* tradition. It also gave currency to the Russian anarchist ideas and tactics, to which Ts'ai had recently become attracted and which he was expounding at the Patriotic Girls' School. He taught the girls how to make bombs,[101] and in *Ching-chung jih-pao* he

[98] *Ibid.*, pp. 418, 420–421.

[99] Feng, *Reminiscences* [160], I, 135–136. Chang Ching-lu (ed.), *Source Materials* [141], I, 97. *Kuo-min jih-jih pao* has been reprinted and can be purchased in Taiwan. Britton, *Chinese Periodical Press* [13], p. 113, gives the name of the publisher as A. Gemell.

[100] Feng, *Reminiscences* [160], II, 85–86. The paper was launched on December 15, 1903; see Kuo, *Daily Record* [184], II, 1192.

[101] Chiang Wei-ch'iao, "Chinese Educational Society" [153], p. 494.

advanced such proposals as the abolition of private property and the marriage institution.[102] But in the beginning of 1905, when the paper became openly seditious, the authorities of the International Settlement responded to Chinese pressure and shut it down. Its editors and publisher barely escaped arrest.[103]

Another significant revolutionary periodical in Shanghai was *Chung-kuo pai-hua pao*, founded in December 1903 by Lin Hsieh, a Fukienese associate of Ts'ai Yüan-p'ei. Its use and promotion of *pai-hua*, the vernacular language, foreshadowed one of the epochal achievements of the May Fourth Movement fifteen years later.[104]

As for pamphlets, according to Hu Han-min, the most effective in combating the constitutional monarchists were *The Revolutionary Army*, Chang Ping-lin's *Po K'ang Yu-wei cheng-chien shu* (Refutation of K'ang Yu-wei's political views) and the works of Ch'en T'ien-hua.[105] Like the other two pamphlets, Ch'en's *Meng hui-t'ou* (Sudden Realization) was published in Shanghai in 1903. All three condemned the Manchus for surrendering Chinese sovereignty to foreigners, and Ch'en also pioneered in the use of the vernacular style.[106]

The previous year Ou Ch'ü-chia's *Hsin Kwang-tung* (New Kwangtung), a stimulating pamphlet advocating the autonomy of Kwangtung as a prelude to a national revolution, was printed in Yokohama by the *Hsin-min ts'ung-pao* press. An unorthodox Cantonese reformer implicated in Liang's temporary defection to the revolutionaries in 1899, Ou had been sent by K'ang to cool off in San Francisco. Instead, as editor of the Triad or Hung-men journal, *Ta-t'ung pao*, he remembered his youthful

[102] Sakai, "Ts'ai Yuan-p'ei" [99], pp. 174–175.

[103] Feng, *Reminiscences* [160], II, 86. Lin, *History of the Press* [80], p. 111.

[104] Chang and Wang, *Selected Articles* [143], I, ts'e 2, 968. On Lin, see Feng, *Reminiscences* [160], III, 116.

[105] Hu Han-min, *Autobiography* [171], III, 384–385. Feng Tzu-yu also published a joint edition of *The Revolutionary Army* and Chang's refutation of K'ang Yu-wei in Yokohama in 1903; see Feng, *Reminiscences* [160], III, 154.

[106] E. Young, "Ch'en T'ien-hua" [138], pp. 116–117. In 1904 Ch'en published an equally influential pamphlet, *Ching-shih-chung* (Alarm to arouse the age).

admiration of the secret societies in his home district of Kuei-shan (Hui-chou prefecture) and urged their mobilization as a revolutionary force.[107]

Another work in this same genre, *Hsin Hu-nan* (New Hunan) by Yang Shou-jen (Yang Tu-sheng 1871–1911) was published in Tokyo in 1903. Yang was a Waseda student from Changsha and according to a Communist source, "China's first populist."[108] He was impressed by Japanese accounts of the Russian Narodniks and had gone through the familiar reformist-revolutionary metamorphosis in Tokyo after giving up a promising literati-bureaucratic career. As already mentioned, Yang was one of the key personnel in the Hunan student journal and specialized in the articles dealing with political and racial (*chung-tsu*) revolution.[109]

Among the various translations of this period, one was particularly significant for its contribution to the rise of Sun Yat-sen. After the failure at Waichow in 1900, a "sick and dispirited" Miyazaki Torazō wrote his autobiography, *Sanjū-sannen no yume* (The Thirty-three Years' dream), which was published in Tokyo in 1902.[110] The title reflects Miyazaki's despondency, the feeling that his quest for a regenerated China had turned into an elusive dream. Yet his personal account of Sun's revolutionary activities and above all, his verdict on Sun as the outstanding candidate for the leadership of the Chinese revolution, constituted a recommendation which could not go unnoticed. The recommendation came from a chivalrous Japanese adventurer for whom the young Chinese had the highest admiration.[111] Until then nothing had been writen about the Hsing Chung Hui leader except his own *Kidnapped in London*. And now, only a year after Miyazaki's book appeared, the influential

---

107 Feng, *Reminiscences* [160], II, 33.

108 T'an Pi-an, "Russian Populism" [212], I, 38. This author erroneously dates the publication of *Hsin Hu-nan* in 1902, and I have found no corroboration of his assertion that Yang was a member of the Hsing Chung Hui.

109 For a short biography of Yang Shou-jen, see Feng, *Reminiscences* [160], II, 125–128.

110 Jansen, *Sun Yat-sen* [69], p. 112.

111 Lo Kang, *Errors in Lo's Biography of Sun* [197], p. 64, makes this point concerning the influence of Miyazaki's book.

Shanghai activist, Chang Shih-chao, published an abridged translation of it entitled *Sun Yat-sen*. It stirred up so much interest that a Kiangsu student, Chin Sung-ts'en, who knew more Japanese than Chang, did a complete translation which was also published in Shanghai in 1903.[112]

Part of Chang's translation—Miyazaki's conversation with Sun in 1897 and his exalted appraisal—also appeared in another popular, nationalist publication, Chang Chi's *Huang Ti Hun* (The Spirit of Huang Ti). This volume, published in Shanghai in 1903, contained twenty-nine articles taken from *Kuo-min pao, K'ai-chih lu, Su-pao,* and other nationalist journals and books.[113]

In addition to these, dozens of revolutionary pamphlets and books, including many translations, were published in both Japan and Shanghai. The birth of the publishing industry in Shanghai, the flourishing of the "Golden Period"[114] of the Chinese press, and the proliferation of bookstores were all symptoms of the tumultuous change in the Chinese intellectual world after 1895. Purely revolutionary propaganda was only one product of this general upheaval. Even without being overtly revolutionary, a translation of almost any foreign historical work, political or sociological treatise, or even a novel could inspire dangerous thoughts and audacious action. Thus *Uncle Tom's Cabin*, translated by Lin Shu in 1901,[115] provoked a re-

---

[112] Chang Shih-chao, "Commentary on Huang Ti Hun" [146], I, 243–244. Chang Yü-ying, "Books of the 1911 Revolution" [149], p. 152. Chin Sung-ts'en also helped finance the publication of Tsou Jung's *The Revolutionary Army*; see Feng, *Reminiscences* [160], III, 87. Chang's abridgement, with a preface by Chang Ping-lin, is reprinted in *The 1911 Revolution* [167], I, 90–132.

[113] Chang Shih-chao, "Commentary on *Huang Ti Hun*" [146], pp. 217–304, describes each of the forty-five items included in the enlarged edition of this work which appeared in 1911. See also Chang and Wang, *Selected Articles* [143], I, *ts'e* 2, 970. Both this source and Chang Yü-ying, "Books of the 1911 Revolution" [149], p. 159, say that the later edition had only forty-four items.

[114] This is Lin Yu-tang's designation of the period 1895–1911; see his *History of the Press* [80], p. 94.

[115] Lin's translation was entitled *Hei-nu yo-t'ien lu* (A Negro Slave's Cry to Heaven); see Chang Yü-ying, "Books of the 1911 Revolution" [149], p. 181.

viewer to warn his countrymen that unless their nationalist consciousness were awakened, the yellow race would share the fate of the American Negro.[116] Indeed, of all the concepts the young Chinese learned from the West, none made a greater impression than that of race. In publications such as those mentioned above, they responded with their own militant formulas for surviving the racial struggle which Europe appeared to be conducting against them.

[116] The review, appearing in the June 1904 issue of *Chüeh-min*, a monthly published in Sung-chiang (near Shanghai), is reprinted in Chang and Wang, *Selected Articles* [143], I, *ts'e* 2, 869–871.

X

The Language of Nationalism and Revolution

In the years following the Boxer disaster, student journals and pamphlets gave expression to the main current of Chinese nationalism. Their chief concern was with foreign aggression and the dynasty's failure to defend China against it. They attributed this aggression to a motive force deeply embedded in modern industrial societies. In a word, they discovered the phenomenon of imperialism. Every aspect of the association between China and the West—missionaries, schools, hospitals, trade, industrial development, financing—was interpreted as a part of Europe's urge to seduce China and exploit her resources. In attempting to understand the mood of these young Chinese, to question the validity of their analysis, i.e. whether imperialism was really a necessary and inevitable stage of capitalism, is irrelevant. What is relevant is G. M. Young's dictum: "The real, central theme of History is not what happened, but what people felt about it when it was happening."[1]

Both Liang Ch'i-ch'ao and the young intellectuals whom he first inspired were probably influenced by Japanese literature on imperialism. This was a period when Japan had entered her expansionist stage and imperialism had both its apologists and its accusers. Among the former was Ukita Kazuomi, whose *Imperialism (Teikoku shugi)* was translated into Chinese as early as 1895.[2] In 1902, just a year after its publication, Kōtoku

[1] G. M. Young, *Victorian England* [139], p. 6.
[2] The translation is listed in Chang Yü-ying, "Books of the 1911 Revolu-

Shūsui's (Kōtoku Denjirō) *Imperialism: The Specter of the 20th Century (Niju seiki no Kaibutsu teikoku shugi)* was also translated.[3] Ukita's book, which attempted to differentiate between the aggressive expansionism led by militarists and the "natural" expansion ostensibly dictated by economic interests, justified a benign sort of imperialism that would follow Britain's example in developing colonies and providing them with good government.[4] While the Chinese could hardly have matched Ukita's enthusiasm for benevolent colonial rule, they must have been impressed by his case for the inevitability of imperialism as an outlet for surplus capital. At any rate, his frank advocacy of an imperialist course for Japan on the Asian continent seemed to indicate that China held an irresistible attraction for modern industrial powers. Kōtoku, on the other hand, was a socialist who denounced capitalism as well as the imperialism which it spawned. He saw imperialism "spreading like a forest fire" and denounced it as nothing more than "armed robbery". It was the result, he claimed, of the inequitable distribution of wealth in capitalist societies and could be eliminated only by a world-wide, social revolutionary movement.[5]

Through Kōtoku's writings and those of other socialists, the Chinese may also have been indirectly influenced by American anti-imperialists, who had fought bitterly against the annexation of the Philippines. The break with traditional American continentalism had been one of the major issues in Bryan's campaign against McKinley in 1900, and the Anti-Imperialist League lambasted the militarism and expansionism preached by Roosevelt, Mahan, and others. William James, William Graham Sumner, John R. Commons, and other leading scholars entered the lists against imperialism, and Mark Twain called it "a pious fraud devised to conceal commercial greed and lust

tion" [149], p. 174; but I have not found any other reference to a book with this title by Ukita. It may have been taken from an article in the *Kokumin Shimbun* to which he contributed. I have seen his 1901 publication, listed below, and used it to learn his views.

[3] See Chang Yü-ying, "Books of the 1911 Revolution" [149], p. 174.
[4] Ukita Kazuomi, *Imperialism and Education* [219].
[5] Kōtoku Shūsui, *Imperialism* [180], pp. 1, 70–72, 80, 91–92.

for power".[6] Britain, rocked by a vicious struggle with the Boers, also contributed to the literature of anti-imperialism, and Hobson's famous *Imperialism* appeared in 1902, at the onset of the student awakening.[7]

Chinese intellectuals had already been taking a hard look at the world around them. It is not difficult to believe that they reached similar conclusions independently. Whether original or not, the thinking of young China paralleled that of contemporary Western social critics. Even before being treated to Lenin's classic analysis, itself a by-product of bourgeois exposés of expansionism, they took to an economic interpretation of imperialism.

One of the first articles on this subject, "On the Development of Imperialism and the Future of the 20th Century World", appeared in *K'ai-chih lu* in 1901.[8] Modern imperialism was defined as pure aggression caused by scientific advances, population growth, the disparity between strong and weak nations, and the respite which Europe had gained after consummating her internal revolutions. The surplus of goods and the need for markets were among its immediate causes. The author found imperialism holding sway in the three most advanced industrial countries—England, America, and Germany—and warned that their next colonial enterprise would be China. The recent examples of South Africa and the Philippines were cited as warnings. Imperialism, he predicted, would reach its height in the twentieth century. "The Aryan race dropped its mask and showed its true face" during the Boxer incident when "the northern part of our country incurred the tragedy of extreme savagery." While some would argue that this was an isolated,

---

[6] Kōtoku refers to the American anti-imperialist movement in *ibid.*, pp. 75–91. See Beard and Beard, *A Basic History* [2], pp. 348–349; and Hofstadter, *Social Darwinism* [57], pp. 193–195.

[7] As far as I know, there were no Chinese or Japanese translations of Hobson during this period.

[8] "Lun ti-kuo chu-i chih fa-ta chi erh-shih shih-chi shih-chieh chih ch'ient'u," from *Ch'ing-i pao ch'üan-pien, ts'e* 15. Author and exact date and issue of *K'ai-chih lu* are not given. Reprinted in Chang and Wang, *Selected Articles* [143], I, *ts'e* 1, pp. 53–58.

unpremeditated event, the author replied that after South Africa had been "ground to the dust," who would dare to assert that this era would not be marked by cruelty? Although people had hoped the twentieth century would be a period of freedom and justice, he predicted that the deterioration of these ideals would exceed that of the preceding century.

Liang's *Hsin-min ts'ung-pao* expounded further on imperialism in the summer of 1902. The conflicts of the twentieth century, wrote an anonymous author, would not be politically inspired like those of the preceding century, but would be economic in origin and global in scope. Western countries acted like "ravenous tigers" because, due to the advances of modern science, consumption had not kept pace with the increase in capital. It was not that politicians or military men had "evil hearts," but that businessmen and industrialists had "evil hearts." "In the past," he declared, "we were fearful of the savage ambitions of absolute monarchs, but now the desires of the mighty capitalists are even more to be feared." In the past, one company subdued India, but today the British Empire, the United States, Germany, and Japan are all "big companies." Their governments serve the companies. "Kings and ministers are their officials. McKinley and Chamberlain are their chief clerks. . . . Will today's expansionists be restricted to England and America? Will the Transvaal and the Philippines be the only victims?"[9]

He charged that although imperialists justify their activities in the name of either "Nietzsche's extreme individualism or Darwin's theory of evolution, . . . speaking truthfully, it is robbery. It has nothing to do with duty, heavenly-appointed tasks, so-called civilization, or so-called primitiveness." Europeans simply do not have enough to satisfy their greed and "covet other people's property." In tracing the history of Western commercial relations with China, the author tried to ex-

---

[9] *Ibid.*, pp. 196–199; from "Lun shih-chieh ching-chi ching-cheng chih ta shih" (On the general situation of world-wide economic competition), *Hsin-min ts'ung-pao*, nos. 11 and 14, July 5 and August 18, 1902. The author writes under the pseudonym, "Yü ch'en tzu" (son of rain and dust).

plain the change in tactics which characterized recent European policy. After their military victories over China in the nineteenth century, the foreigners began seizing spheres of influence in anticipation of the country's dismemberment. After the Boxer uprising, however, they suddenly began advocating the preservation of Chinese sovereignty and the Open Door. "Dismemberment and spheres of influence belonged to political aggression . . . while preservation and Open Door policies constitute economic aggression," and who could tell which would turn out to be the more destructive.[10]

The reason for the shift in tactics, he explained, was that since the Boxer disturbance, the powers had realized that dismemberment would not be profitable. The center of world trade had moved to the Pacific area, and the Europeans and Japanese had a concentrated market in China, which they controlled without assuming the extra burden of political administration. Since China's economic potential was still unexhausted and since the foreigners' profits were still on the rise—here he presented statistics showing foreign trade with China—"why should they not be in favor," he asked, "of preserving China's territorial integrity?"[11]

Survival in the modern world, the author concluded, depended upon the ability to wage economic warfare; in the coming economic struggle, the Chinese could not rely upon the assistance of their government, which had traditionally obstructed commerce and industry and inhibited the innate commercial abilities of the Chinese people. The only thing that could save China was nationalism. The Chinese people themselves had to repeat the nationalist awakening which had shaken Europe in the nineteenth century and created its economic power in the twentieth.[12]

Modern imperialism, a *Kuo-min pao* writer pointed out, could conquer a country without occupying it. It carries out "invisible conquest" by whittling away at the victim's sovereign-

[10] *Ibid.*, pp. 199–203.
[11] *Ibid.*, p. 204.
[12] *Ibid.*, pp. 205–206.

ty. Where is China's sovereignty? he asked. Foreign armies pursue bandits within her borders and foreigners try Chinese criminals. Foreigners control the Chinese coast, rivers, and their maritime customs and communications. Everywhere, he concluded, Chinese sovereignty had virtually disappeared.[13]

None of the Chinese intellectuals were more alarmed than the Hunanese, residents of a traditionally anti-foreign province, whose barriers were among the last to fall before the onslaught of foreign capital. Ch'en T'ien-hua, one of the most eloquent of these Hunanese nationalists, used the term, "racial imperialism" (*min-tsu ti-kuo chu-i*) to describe this foreign drive, which he too interpreted as the result of overpopulation and land hunger. He expounded upon the impetus of foreign rapacity and its cost to China in his *Sudden Realization* and other inflammatory tracts.[14]

The sinister implications of modern imperialism and its social Darwinist apologia were also explicated by Ch'en's fellow provincial, Yang Shou-jen in his *Hsin Hu-nan* (New Hunan), published in 1903. There were two forces, Yang found, that shaped Western policies. The first was a distant, historical impulse—the creation of nation-states—and more recently, there had been the change from nationalism to imperialism. Though nationalism, he claimed, already contained the seed of imperialism, at first it had been restricted to the "mad ambitions" of a few generals. But once nationalism became imperialism, the situation changed: "The motive force of this ideology does not stem from the mad ambitions of a few individuals in the government, but it comes from the increase of population." Industrial and commercial expansion led to an abundance of capital, and the imperialist creed held sway throughout entire nations. This gave modern imperialism its tremendous impetus. It was a violent force, "like a vast ocean flooding a great continent."[15]

---

[13] *Ibid.*, pp. 78–81; from "Chung-kuo mieh-wang lun" (On the destruction of China) *Kuo-min pao*, nos. 2, 3, 4; June 10, July 10, and August 10, 1901. No author given.

[14] E. Young, "Ch'en T'ien-hua" [138], pp. 117–122.

[15] Chang and Wang, *Selected Articles* [143], I, *ts'e* 2, pp. 622–623.

After demonstrating that world-wide imperialism was converging upon one target—East Asia, in fact, China—Yang declared that unless the Chinese awakened, they would meet with the same fate as the American Indians. There was also the example of the Hawaiian natives, who were being extinguished since the arrival of the white man. Who could imagine, he asked, how oppressive the white man would be when he became the new master of China?[16]

Yang then surveyed the whole pattern of the imperialist design, which he subsumed under the heading, "colonial political strategy." This strategy motivated their entire program—leasing territory, building railroads, mining, missionary endeavors, industrial and commercial policies. Beginning with modest demands in these fields, they eventually assumed sovereign rights over Chinese territory. Although their holdings were still called spheres of influence, they were actually political enclaves. Entire provinces had in this manner been annexed, with foreigners monopolizing communications and mineral production. "The signboards have not changed but the age-old shops have already passed into foreign hands."[17]

Yang believed that the entire Western world—journalists, politicians, soldiers, theologians, and industrialists—was involved in this colonial strategy. He too interpreted the current Open Door policy as a subtle twist to imperialist tactics. The powers had discovered that they could use the Manchu government to achieve their aims: "The Manchu government is the decoy and the various powers the net." As for his native Hunan, Yang warned that unless the white man were resisted, he would draft local residents to police the province for him, just as the British used Indian troops and as the Russians pitted Pole against Pole. When the Allied expeditionary force entered Peking, Chinese Christians led the way and were killed fighting their fellow Chinese. When the British took Weihaiwei, they trained Chinese troops and the Germans had done the same in Kiaochow. These troops, he asserted, would not be used in Europe nor in

16 *Ibid.*, pp. 623–624.
17 *Ibid.*, p. 625.

America: "They will be used in China, that is certain. When the foreigners enter Hunan they will train Hunanese braves. They will use Hunanese against Hunanese."[18]

According to Yang, there was a definite correlation between the anti-Christian disturbances in his native province and imperialist penetration. Hunanese miners were uneducated, he wrote, but "when they learn that they are sweating for foreigners and that their rights are being usurped by foreigners, they know of no way to save themselves except to kill a foreigner today and burn a church tomorrow." The Heng-chou missionary incident resulted in an indemnity of 370,000 pounds sterling and the Ch'en-chou case an indemnity of 80,000 pounds, all of which added up to an unbearable burden on the province. But this was part of the imperialist design: "Because of intervention in the mines, there are missionary incidents; and the repetition of missionary incidents creates intervention in the mines. Mines and missionaries are inseparable."[19]

The disparity between the avowed aims of missionaries and the practices of their governments was also attacked by a *Ta-lu* writer. "Jesus," he wrote, "preached equality and fraternity, principles which are basically in accord with the teachings of our ancient sages." But instead of reforming Chinese morals and customs, foreigners took advantage of China's weakness, and Kiaochow, Port Arthur, Dairen, and Weihaiwei, fell victim to their imperialist incursions. "When the allied armies entered Peking, they plundered recklessly, and brazenly did things to us which no civilized people would allow to be done to animals. . . . Is this what is meant by the doctrines of equality and fraternity?" At home, the Europeans had carried out bloody wars and massacres for religious purposes, "but there was never such a pursuit of selfish aims under the guise of public morality (*kung-i*) as in the case of their treatment of our China."[20]

This pervasive anti-imperialist theme furthermore led to a

[18] *Ibid.*, pp. 626–628.

[19] *Ibid.*, p. 621.

[20] *Ibid.*, I, *ts'e* 1, p. 420, from "Chung-kuo chih kai-tsao" (China's reconstruction), *Ta-lu*, nos. 3, 4, 8, February, March, July 1903.

rehabilitation of the Boxers. They were praised for their bravery and patriotism, and their ignorance was regretted.[21] After the Allied occupation of Peking, the atrocities committed by foreigners rather than Boxer outrages received the students' attention.[22] Again, a Liang Ch'i-ch'ao journal first struck a new positive note in evaluating the Boxers' contribution.[23]

Another aspect of the anti-imperialist motif was the defense of the *hua-ch'iao*, whose persecution and exploitation by the white man was decried by Liang, Tsou Jung, and a number of other writers.[24] In 1902 Liang's Hawaiian journal, the *Hsin Chung-kuo pao*, called for a militant response to the American exclusion policy and proposed a boycott of American goods, a suggestion that materialized a few years later. To those who doubted a boycott's legality, the author retorted with a quotation from Chu Hsi which would be heard from Mao Tse-tung forty-six years later: "Treat them according to their own behavior."[25]

On the other hand, scorn for the wealthy, assimilated *hua-*

[21] In the summer of 1900, one of the students, Ch'in Li-shan, tried to persuade a Boxer leader to give up the anti-foreign orientation and cooperate in an anti-dynastic uprising. However, he was rejected as an "erh mao-tzu" (Christian convert). See Feng, *Reminiscences* [160], I, 86.

[22] Western sources attest to these atrocities committed by the Allied armies. See a London *Times* dispatch in Hobson, *Imperialism* [56], p. 307; and the testimony of an American general in Stillman and Pfaff, *The Politics of Hysteria* [113], p. 93.

[23] See "I-ho-t'uan yu-kung yü Chung-kuo shuo" (Speaking about the Boxers' benefit to China), from *Ch'ing-i pao ch'üan-pien*, ts'e 16, reprinted in Chang and Wang, *Selected Articles* [143], I, ts'e 1, 58–62. See also another anonymous article, "Min-tsu ching-shen lun" (On the essence of the nation), from *Chiang-su*, nos. 7 and 8, January and February 1904, in *ibid.*, I, ts'e 2, 847.

[24] See Tsou Jung, *The Revolutionary Army* [215], I, 341. Jung-pang Lo, "The Overseas Chinese" [82], p. 2; and Chang and Wang, *Selected Articles* [143], I, ts'e 1, 65.

[25] "Ni ti-chih chin-li ts'e" (A proposal to boycott the exclusion regulations), reprinted in *Hsin-min ts'ung-pao*, nos. 38 and 39, combined issue, October 1903, Chang and Wang, *Selected Articles* [143], I, ts'e 1, 352–359. The quotation from Chu Hsi appears on p. 359, and is also cited by Mao in "On the People's Democratic Dictatorship" (June 30, 1949), in *Selected Works* [198], IV, 1483.

ch'iao, like the Anglicized Chinese of Hong Kong of whom Sun's mentor, Ho Kai, was an outstanding example, was evinced by Ou Ch'ü-chia. Ou lamented the fact that wealthy Chinese of Hong Kong contributed more to the Boer War memorial fund and the Queen Victoria Diamond Jubilee fund than did the colony's British residents.[26] The tendency of successful *hua-ch'iao* to identify themselves with the interests of their host countries rather than with the mainland-oriented subversive movement would incidentally prove to be one of the factors limiting Sun Yat-sen's subsequent drive for funds in the larger *hua-ch'iao* communities, as in Thailand, for example.[27]

Needless to say, such a militant posture toward the outside world as that assumed by Liang and the young intellectuals had never been openly exhibited by Sun Yat-sen, except perhaps in the limited scope of the Hsing Chung Hui preamble, and it was certainly not voiced by his spokesman, Ho Kai. At the same time, writers in the *Hsin-min ts'ung-pao* and pamphleteers like Yang Shou-jen and Tsou Jung were also far ahead of Sun in elaborating programs of popular rights, constitutionalism, and republicanism. Yang, for example, writing in 1903, listed *ko-jen ch'üan-li* (individual rights and privileges) and *min-tsu chien-kuo chu-i* (nationalism or "the principle of nations creating states") as the two great, universal principles discovered in the West and necessary for China's regeneration.[28] Here we have referents for two of Sun's Three Principles, which he first enunciated clearly in 1905. (It is significant that Yang linked the demand for popular sovereignty with anti-imperialism by charging that "conquest by the white man cannot be avoided" as long as China retained the perverted Confucianism which justified dynastic despotism, even under barbarian invaders.)[29] An even

[26] From *Hsin Kwang-tung* (1902), in Chang and Wang, *Selected Articles* [143], I, *ts'e* 1, 284.

[27] Given the opportunity in nineteenth century Thailand, Chinese proved capable of integrating into a host society, and only when the rise of the Thai nationalist movement challenged their advantageous economic position a few years before the revolution of 1911, did these *hua-ch'iao* respond to the mainland oriented nationalist movement. See Skinner, *Chinese Society in Thailand* [108].

[28] Chang and Wang, *Selected Articles* [143], I, *ts'e* 2, 631.

[29] *Ibid.*, p. 635.

closer parallel to Sun's Three Principles can be found in an article by an anonymous *Hsin-min ts'ung-pao* contributor, also writing in 1903, who found that modern Europeans have three great principles—rights and privileges for the majority of the people, benefits from taxation, and national states.[30] Furthermore, this same *Hsin-min ts'ung-pao* writer pointed out that although Europeans had generally achieved political equality, the socio-economic sphere was still characterized by inequality. As he put it: "Are not the countries' land and property rights held completely in the hands of a few wealthy people, and the rich getting richer and poor poorer?" This foreshadowed Sun's approach, but the writer did not go into details, remarking that further discussion "belongs to the realm of socialism," which was not his current concern.

A Focus on the Manchus

Though Sun Yat-sen's anti-Manchuism came to be shared by the students after 1900, their indictment of the dynasty derived from a different source and took a different form. When appealing to the secret societies, Sun had tried to exploit traditional ethnic antipathy toward a "barbarian" dynasty, but when speaking to foreigners, who were his primary concern, he blamed the Manchus for preventing a rapprochement with the West. The students, on the other hand, who spoke primarily to Chinese audiences, condemned the Manchus for appeasing the West. Intellectual anti-Manchuism, as reflected in the nationalist literature of this period, was definitely a by-product of anti-imperialism. Why were foreigners able to seize chunks of Chinese territory and violate her sovereignty? The most popular answer of the student nationalists was that the Manchus "preferred giving their property to friends (i.e. foreigners) than to household slaves (i.e. Chinese)."[31] In different versions, this quo-

[30] "Yü Ch'en tzu," (pseud.), "Chin-shih Ou-jen san ta chu-i' (Three great principles of modern Europeans), from *Hsin-min ts'ung-pao*, no. 28, March 1903; in Chang and Wang, *Selected Articles* [143], I, ts'e 1, 343–348.

[31] See Tsou Jung, *The Revolutionary Army* [215], p. 345, with reference to Jung-lu; and similar remarks in Chang and Wang, *Selected Articles* [143], I, ts'e 1, 91, 273.

tation, sometimes attributed to the hated Kang-i or Jung-lu, both high Manchu officials, appears in various articles and pamphlets. Ironically it may have originated with Liang Ch'i-ch'ao,[32] who not only knew better, but also later refuted the revolutionary argument that culturally the Manchus were not Chinese.[33] This juxtaposition of Manchu rule and imperialism, however, remained the prevalent attitude reflected in student journalism and pamphleteering. Yang Shou-jen charged that European oppressors used the Manchu government as the "keepers of their treasure,"[34] and Ch'en T'ien-hua saw the Manchus as puppets facilitating the imperialist conquest of China.[35] Tsou Jung warned that the Chinese would be delivered into foreign slavery by their present overseers, the Manchus. Shantung, the birthplace of Confucius, he cried, and as holy to Chinese as "Jerusalem is to Christians," had been handed over to the foreigners by the Manchus, whom he accused of dispensing with Chinese land as if it were "other people's property."[36]

There were a number of other accusations against the Manchus, including their disproportionate control of high government posts, and there was the popular argument, also advanced by the *Hsin-min ts'ung-pao*, that common history was an important factor in modern nationalism, and that the lack of common historical ties between Chinese and Manchus retarded the development of Chinese patriotism. Even a ruler with the power of Napoleon, it was asserted, could not unite people with different national traditions.[37]

Yet there was one anti-Manchu argument which significantly assigned an instrumental rather than terminal value to antidynastic revolution. In addition to warning that under the Man-

---

[32] Hu Sheng, *Imperialism and Chinese Politics* [67], p. 114, cites the following quotation from Liang's *Wu-hsü cheng-pien chi*: "Kang Yi, Grand Secretary and member of the Council of State, often said that he would rather give his property to friends than to slaves at home."

[33] See Levenson, *Liang Ch'i-ch'ao* [76], pp. 160–162, for Liang's position on this subject after 1905.

[34] Chang and Wang, *Selected Articles* [143], I, ts'e 2, 626.

[35] E. Young, "Ch'en T'ien-hua [138], pp. 122–123.

[36] Tsou Jung, *The Revolutionary Army* [215], I, 355, 344–345.

[37] Chang and Wang, *Selected Articles* [143], I, ts'e 1, 347–348.

chus the Chinese would be capable only of a "primitive rising" —presumably of the Boxer type—against the foreign aggressor, Yang Shou-jen developed an argument which prefigured Toynbee's "challenge and response" theory.[38] Overthrowing the Manchus, he claimed, would stimulate effective resistance to the European and Japanese intruders. The Manchus, he charged, were never able to consolidate the Tibetans, Mongols, and other "races" comprising the Chinese empire, but the Chinese, provoked by two stimuli, anti-Manchuism and anti-imperialism, would succeed. It is also significant that instead of pressing for the extermination of the Manchus, Yang proclaimed that once the Chinese proved themselves in their national struggle, they would assist Manchus, Mongols, Tibetans, and Moslems to effect their own "consolidation" and, under the banner of an "Asian Central Government, repel the white menace." Manchu domination of the Chinese, Yang felt, showed the white man that Chinese racial (national) power was "immature" and encouraged his aggression.[39]

The argument that anti-Manchuism was required both as a stimulus for the assertion of a Chinese national spirit and as a step toward effective resistance to the Europeans was also developed by Lin Hsieh. "If we do not have the ability to overthrow the Manchus, drive them out, and oppose them," he declared, "then we do not have the ability to accomplish other things. . . . If we have the ability to kill, then we have the ability to live. If Germany had not been able to defeat the other states which make up her federation, would they have been willing to join her? If our Han race does not have this type of ability, to oppose a single race, then let me ask how we will have the majestic power to rule the various races?" And he further demonstrates how the Chinese image of a predatory world influenced their own racial consciousness:

The contemporary world is characterized by extremely violent racial struggles. Our Han race must think about contending with the races of the world. This type of ability is not nurtured overnight. . . . It

---

[38] *Ibid.*, I, *ts'e* 2, 626.
[39] *Ibid.*, pp. 613–614.

first has to be tested on the local level. If we cannot attend to this minor matter of expelling the Manchus, then how can we consummate our imperial design, our rule of majestic power? . . . . In this present-day world of racial competition, we must take two attitudes: unite against the Manchu government and carry out the expulsion of the barbarians; and unite against the various continental countries and defend ourselves.[40]

And Tsou Jung declared: "If we wish to resist foreign aggression, we must first purge the internal evil."[41]

At this same time, Chang Ping-lin, one of the senior and most influential of the nationalist writers, also concluded that anti-Manchuism had immediate precedence over anti-imperialism. In his famous rebuttal to K'ang Yu-wei in 1903, Chang admitted that China was not yet strong enough to drive out the Europeans. But an anti-Manchu revolution, he argued, would equip the nation with the unity and self-confidence required for ultimately achieving the anti-imperialist goal. He also refuted K'ang's argument that an internal uprising would inevitably invite further foreign aggression. Though Europeans, he admitted, would love to exploit such an opportunity, he considered them too realistic to take on a united China. If revolution were carried out swiftly and if it avoided anti-foreign provocations, foreigners would have to accept it. The example of the Meiji Restoration in Japan, he felt, was pertinent to China's dilemma. Though the French favored the Shogunate, the demonstration of wide support for the imperial restorationists forced them to keep their hands off.[42]

An anti-Manchu revolution, which was meant as a repudiation of Chinese despotism as well as an overthrow of "barbarian" rulers, called for the use of violence and terror, incitement of the masses, including manipulation of the secret societies, and the heroic leadership of "men of determination." Strongly inspired by Russian terrorists, the student writers filled hundreds of pages glorifying revolution and promoting a cult of violence.[43]

[40] *Ibid.*, pp. 902–903, 911.
[41] Tsou Jung, *The Revolutionary Army* [215], I, 349.
[42] "Po K'ang Yu-wei shu" (Letter refuting K'ang Yu-wei) [145], pp. 760–761.
[43] See for example, "Lou-hsi-ya hsü-wu-tang" (The Russian Nihilist Party),

So intense, in fact, was the exulting affirmation of violence in the nationalist literature, especially among writers such as Tsou Jung, Ch'en T'ien-hua, Yang Shou-jen, Liu Shih-p'ei,[44] and Lin Hsieh,[45] as to suggest a tendency to accord a transcendent value to revolution. Though revolutionary anti-Manchuism, as I have indicated, originated as an intermediate or instrumental goal in relation to the larger task of confronting the foreigners, infatuation with revolution turned it into an end in itself. The conviction that revolution or any act of violence committed in the name of revolution was by itself a mark of achievement, a symbol of Chinese maturity, became especially noticeable as the student nationalists attempted to put their theories into practice.

By 1905, the young nationalists came to realize the immensity of the task they had hoped to undertake. How could they accomplish so much: overthrow the Manchus, establish constitutional government, and belligerently redress the wrongs committed by foreigners. Their mentor, Liang Ch'i-ch'ao, had decided to forego the hue and cry of anti-dynasticism, and instead focus upon institutional reform and build up the national capacity for resisting the major enemy, the foreign powers. While no less aware of the external threat, the students nevertheless shifted their focus to the easier hurdle, the floundering Manchu dynasty. In the same manner they recoiled from the social and cultural im-

---

Chiang-su No. 4, July 1903, in Chang and Wang, *Selected Articles* [143], I, *ts'e* 2, 565–571; "Hsü-wu-tang" (Nihilist Party), *Su-pao*, June 19, 1903, in Chang and Wang, *Selected Articles* [143], I, *ts'e* 2, 696–698; and Liang Ch'i-ch'ao, "Lun O-lo-ssu hsü-wu-tang" (On the Russian Nihilist Party), *Hsin-min ts'ung-pao*, nos. 40–41, combined issue, November 1903, abridged in Chang and Wang, *Selected Articles* [143], I, *ts'e* 1, 369–375. In 1902 Ma Chün-wu wrote a book, *O-lo-ssu ta feng-ch'ao* (Great ferment in Russia), and in 1903 Chang Chi translated a work on anarchism. See also T'an Pi-an, "Russian Populism" [212], I, 35–44. The French Revolution was likewise a prominent model. Several pamphleteers featured Bertrand Barère's dictum: "The tree of liberty only grows when watered by the blood of tyrants."

[44] See Liu's "Lun chi-lieh ti hao-ch'u" (On the advantages of violence), from *Chung-kuo pai-hua pao*, No. 6, March 1, 1904, in Chang and Wang, *Selected Articles* [143], I, *ts'e* 2, 887–890.

[45] See Lin's "Kuo-min i-chien shu" (The people's viewpoint) from *Chung-kuo pai-hua pao*, nos. 5–8, 16–18, 20, February-August 1904, abridged in Chang and Wang, *Selected Articles* [143], I, *ts'e* 2, 892–921.

plications of revolution, which they had touched upon tangentially in their polemics and upon which Liang continued to expound, and elevated anti-Manchuism to the highest priority.

The inclination to cut the obstacles down to size fed upon their underlying doubts of China's ability to react fast enough to meet the multifarious challenges. Their doubts, pessimism, and impatience were reflected in their propensity for individual acts of violence and heroism as substitutes for a popularly based nationalist and social movement. Lin Hsieh even warned them that whereas a popular revolution would invite foreign interference under the guise of protecting missionary and commercial interests, assassination of key Chinese officials would eliminate such pretexts.[46] Though the young intellectuals frequently advocated education and mass agitation, a number of them chose self-immolation as a faster means of inflaming the masses. They already had the example of T'an Ssu-t'ung's choice of martyrdom in 1898, and a similar attitude was evident in Shih Chien-ju's heroic behavior in 1900. The course eventually followed by Yang Shou-jen also offers an instructive insight into the young nationalist mood. Though in 1903 Yang advocated starting a popular revolution in Hunan, the following year he thought of bombing the imperial palace in Peking to thereby "rock the entire country" with one blow. Finally, in the spring of 1911 he committed suicide while despondent over the prospects for revolution.[47] But as early as 1905 his fellow Hunanese, Ch'en T'ien-hua, had also committed suicide for the same reason.[48] This common choice on the part of two of the most influential of the nationalist pamphleteers reflected the desperation which gripped young China.

This desperation contributed to the enshrinement of anti-Manchuism and temporarily deflected the nationalist thrust from its original collision course with the West. It was not that the young nationalists forgot their anti-imperialist grievances, but that they despaired of winning such a clash and became recon-

---

[46] Chang and Wang, *Selected Articles* [143], I, ts'e 2, 915.

[47] Feng, *Reminiscences* [160], II, 126–127.

[48] Ch'en committed suicide in Japan in December 1905. See E. Young, "Ch'en T'ien-hua" [138], pp. 146–149.

ciled to a holding action in foreign relations. An internal political revolution, they may have hoped, would provide China with the international stature and respect that would automatically remove her from the path of imperialist designs. At all events, they felt they had no choice but to allocate priorities, and when the choice fell upon anti-Manchuism, the acceptance of Sun Yat-sen became easier.

In the meantime Sun was getting ready to show them a more simplified revolutionary strategy. The main themes, nationalism, popular sovereignty, and the tutelary role of heroic leaders, had already been sounded, and Sun would offer the final assurance that foreign ideas, removed from their historical and cultural context, could be effectively transplanted to China. That Sun, the consort of imperialists and apprentice of the missionaries and compradors so hated by the student nationalists, could eventually become their leader was one of the surprise turnings of the Chinese revolution. It testified to the nationalist urge for an abbreviated means of salvation. It also demonstrated Sun's ability to leapfrog his achievements.

XI

Sun Yat-sen: A New Turning

When his young compatriots proclaimed their discovery of Rousseau, George Washington, and John Stuart Mill, the voice of Sun Yat-sen was barely heard. Conspiracy had long been a preemptive occupation and Sun required time to develop an approach to the student-intellectuals. He had to adjust his style to the bristling anti-imperialism of Tokyo and Shanghai. And to counteract innate gentry prejudice, he had to show polemical skill and greater political sophistication. Wu Chih-hui is an example: upon first hearing of Sun, he dismissed him as a "rustic ruffian" and voiced the suspicion that he was illiterate in Chinese.[1] After the Waichow rising, Wu realized that Sun was "no ordinary rebel," and he and other intellectuals were impressed with the martyrdom of Shih Chien-ju, grandson of a Hanlin scholar, but Chang Ping-lin testified to the prevailing opinion of Sun as an "uncultured outlaw." According to Chang, the students felt that Sun was "hard to get along with" and they generally avoided him.[2]

Suspicion was probably mutual. The traumatic result of his involvement with Liang Ch'i-ch'ao must have cautioned Sun against putting his trust in the revolutionary protestations of intellectuals, who appeared to be bewildered amid the hard realities of revolutionary intrigue. Most of them in fact had been mere teenage admirers of K'ang and Liang when Sun had already declared war on the dynasty.

---

[1] Wu Ching-heng, "Sun's Righteous Behavior" [223], pp. 2–3; and "Sun Yat-sen" [222], p. 13. See also Hu Han-min, *Autobiography* [171], p. 377.

[2] Hsüeh, *Huang Hsing* [66], p. 35.

He therefore remained in Yokohama, where he felt more at home among the *hua-ch'iao*. His first close friends among the students were young Cantonese *hua-ch'iao* like Feng Tzu-yu and Wang Ch'ung-hui, whose fathers had helped him in the past and who now steered Sun to their fellow provincials. As for non-Cantonese students, Shen Hsiang-yün, Wu Lu-chen, and Chi I-hui had begun to take notice of Sun toward the end of 1898.[3] Through Shen, Sun came to know Ch'in Li-shan and others from various provinces. Yet though he is said to have been on close terms with a score of students by 1900, none joined the Hsing Chung Hui or the Waichow uprising. At that time the militant students were absorbed in the Hankow plot, and even after the greater success at Waichow, there was only a trickle and not a stampede in Sun's direction.

Chang Ping-lin was apparently one of the first among the older, non-Cantonese émigrés to notice Sun. Even before meeting him, Chang ventured the opinion—which is indicative of the literati evaluation of Sun—that although Sun was only "slightly familiar with foreign subjects (*yang-wu*), he understood racial distinctions," i.e. anti-Manchuism. This formed their common bond after Liang introduced them in 1899.[4] Chang joined Liang in discussing politics with Sun and in giving him insights into Chinese history. In 1902 he invited Sun to his anti-Manchu demonstration and mentioned Sun in his writing. Another factor in lifting Sun's prestige at this time was the appearance of Miyazaki's book. Still, as reported by Chang Chi, Sun made no attempt to enlist students and intellectuals into the Hsing Chung Hui.[5] Though it may be true, as Chang suggests, that he had already decided to use them as the cornerstone of a new organization, there is stronger evidence that Sun was skeptical of his ability to harness the student movement and that he preferred to

[3] Feng, *Reminiscences* [160], I, 80–81. Niu Yung-chien and Ch'eng Chia-ch'eng, the first Anhwei student in Japan, were among these early admirers. See Wu Ching-heng, "Sun's Righteous Behavior" [223], p. 3.
[4] Feng, *Reminiscences* [160], I, 54. See also Y. C. Wang, "The *Su-Pao* Case" [129], p. 7.
[5] Wang Te-chao, "Sun's Thought During the T'ung Meng Hui Period" [221], p. 70. Ch'in Li-shan introduced Chang Chi to Sun.

recover and expand his *hua-ch'iao* base before venturing into new territory.

During this interval in Yokohama Sun evidently had just enough money to support himself[6] and, if rumor is true, a mistress who frequently accompanied him on his travels and did the laundry for him and his comrades.[7] Though he generously contributed to student journals, his funds, presumably coming from Hong Kong and the handful of loyal *hua-ch'iao* in Yokohama, were not enough to encourage serious plans. Little is known of Sun's activities during the two years after Waichow, but in addition to studying Boer guerrilla tactics, he must have given financial problems high priority. This may have been the purpose of his mysterious six-day visit to Hong Kong, where he landed on January 28, 1902, between banishment orders.[8] He also renewed his efforts to obtain foreign support.

The circumstances are obscure, but according to Sun, Paul Doumer, Governor-General of French Indo-China (1897–1902), used the facilities of the French minister in Tokyo to invite him to the Hanoi Exposition, which opened in November 1902.[9] Sun's visa was issued in Shanghai, but how the original contact was made and for what purpose is not clear.[10] Sun left Japan in

6 According to Inukai, Sun "spent money as soon as it came in, and he lived happily in borrowed clothes when out of money." See Jansen, *Sun Yat-sen* [69], p. 115. In his letter to Hirayama in 1903, Sun writes that he wanted to visit his old comrade in Kyushu but did not have enough money for the trip. See Sun, *Collected Works* [205], V, 23.

7 Cheng's "Bibliographical Note" [22], p. 27, is the source for information concerning this mistress, who is said to have associated with Sun since 1895. In the Sun Yat-sen residence in Macao, there is a picture of a later concubine by the name of Ch'en Ts'ui-fen, who is said to have lived in Singapore during the period of Sun's second marriage.

8 Tse, *Chinese Republic* [122], p. 21. Sun arrived on the *Yawata Maru* and stayed at 24 Stanley Street, Hong Kong. A new banishment order was issued this same year, when the old one expired. Feng, *Reminiscences* [160], I, 68, erroneously dates this brief visit in 1901.

9 Sun, in *The 1911 Revolution* [167], I, 10. On Doumer, a prominent French politician whom Sun finally met in Paris in 1905, see Chin P'ing-ou, *et al.* (eds.), *Concordance of the San-min chu-i* [155], p. 527.

10 Jansen, *Sun Yat-sen* [69], p. 115, uses Georges Soulié de Morant, *Soun Iat-senn*. De Morant, a French official in Shanghai, issued Sun's visa.

December 1902 and first stopped in Hong Kong, where he borrowed $1,000 for expenses from Li Chi-t'ang, who had provided
major financial support for the Waichow rising.[11] When he arrived in Hanoi, however, Doumer had already returned to
France. The head of his secretariat had been instructed to welcome Sun, but there is no record of what ensued. In the meantime Sun used the opportunity to agitate among the *hua-ch'iao*.[12]

After moving into a third-class French hotel, he sent for Ch'en
Shao-pai. Under assumed names at first, they sounded out *hua-
ch'iao* political sentiments, and Sun's initial recruit was an anti-
Manchuist Cantonese tailor, Huang Lung-sheng, to whom he
disclosed his true identity.[13] Huang led them to five other Cantonese, including a wealthy rice merchant who had good contacts with the French.[14] Two additional members were recruited
in Haiphong but it was difficult to overcome the prevailing political indifference. Sun's six-months' stay in Hanoi may have
stimulated some interest in home affairs, but no help was forthcoming from this area until after 1905.

Meanwhile Yu Lieh, one of the original "four bandits" of
Hong Kong, pioneered the movement's penetration of Malaya.
He actually began his work among the *hua-ch'iao* in Yokohama,
where in 1898 he became the leader of a social-educational club,
the Chung Ho T'ang, which attracted petty merchant and working class elements. Together with Ch'en Shao-pai, Yu tried to
give this group a political orientation and combat the influence
of K'ang Yu-wei.[15] Yokohama still remained under the Pao
Huang Hui's influence, but Yu met with better success in Malaya, where he used this formula for recruiting lower class *hua-*

---

[11] Lo Chia-lun, *Biography* [192], I, 113. Tse, *Chinese Republic* [122], p.
22, fixes Sun's arrival in Hong Kong for December 13, on the S.S. *Indus*. He
apparently left for Saigon on the same day.

[12] Lo Chia-lun, *Biography* [192], I, 113.

[13] Ch'en Shao-pai, *Hsing Chung Hui* [152], pp. 60–61.

[14] Feng, in *Documents* [179], III, 362–363, lists the names and occupations
of these recruits in Indo-China. See also *Development of the Revolution*
[178], X, 228–230.

[15] Feng, *History of the Overseas Chinese* [161], p. 44; and Lo, "The Overseas Chinese" [82], p. 10.

ch'iao. Arriving in Singapore in 1901, he set up a clinic and established himself as an expert on venereal diseases. His work enabled him to win the confidence of workers and farmers, who were members of the local Triads known as the I Hsing Hui. The wealthier *hua-ch'iao,* to the extent that they were politically active, still supported K'ang Yu-wei, but Yu was able to form branches of the Chung Ho T'ang with his lower class adherents in Singapore and Kuala Lumpur. These were social and recreational clubs, resembling the Triads in organizational structure and secrecy, and even retaining the cult of Kuan Yü, the traditional god of war. At the same time, Yu introduced anti-Manchu slogans and the Hsing Chung Hui flag—blue sky, white sun—although few of the members realized its significance. What was new about these clubs, which later spread throughout Malaya, was their educational function; they stimulated reading and political discussions on the part of Chinese who had never been articulate at home. Yu was assisted by several refugees from the Waichow campaign, and by 1903 he had interested two wealthy *hua-ch'iao* merchants, who, during the excitement over the *Su-pao* affair, had organized telegraphic protests to the British consul in Shanghai. These revolutionary patrons, the Hokkien timber merchant Ch'en Ch'u-nan and the Cantonese draper Chang Yung-fu, helped to subsidize the printing of five thousand copies of Tsou Jung's *The Revolutionary Army,* and in the spring of 1904, their capital launched the first revolutionary daily in Malaya, the Singapore *T'u-nan jih-pao.*[16]

The penetration of Malaya, though it did not bring tangible rewards until after 1905, revealed the patriotic potentialities of lower class *hua-ch'iao.* It also indicated the widespread effect of the *Su-pao* case, and with it, interest in Tsou's pamphlet. Yet it took Yu several years to establish the movement. Sun himself never undertook the long-term organization of a particular *hua-ch'iao* community. Impetuous and impatient, he tried to cover too much ground, and until he had organizers and agitators to

[16] Feng, *History of the Overseas Chinese* [161], pp. 73–76; Png Poh Seng, "Kuomintang in Malaya" [92], pp. 2–3; Wang, "Sun Yat-sen in Singapore" [126], p. 58.

act on his behalf, his overseas network remained extremely frag-
ile. Later, when he controlled enough activists to consolidate his
organization, even his brief presence in an overseas community
would be sufficient to stimulate generous support. At this stage,
however, the half year spent in Hanoi was insufficient, and at the
same time he missed out on the more dramatic events in Tokyo,
including reverberations of the *Su-pao* case.

Meanwhile in Hong Kong, his long-time party rival Tse Tsan-
tai had arranged for another stab at Canton without Sun's knowledge or that of the local Hsing Chung Hui. Tse and his father
had become acquainted with one Hung Ch'üan-fu, a putative
nephew of Hung Hsiu-ch'üan and a veteran of the Taiping campaign. Hung was living in Hong Kong as an apothecary and
agreed to raise a Triad army while Li Chi-t'ang, who had recently inherited a fortune, provided the capital. Though Sun
passed through Hong Kong on his way to Hanoi, he did not
learn of the plot until he was in Indo-China. This was strictly
Tse's show, but the script held no surprises for Sun Yat-sen.
The usual Triad roughnecks, missionaries, compradors, and converts, including some Waichow veterans, were brought into the
scheme. It called for an attack on Canton on the eve of the Chinese New Year, January 28, 1903. The Hong Kong journalists
again cooperated, and Alfred Cunningham of the *Daily Press*
helped Tse draft a "Proclamation and Appeal to the Powers."
The influential G. E. Morrison of the London *Times* is also said
to have promised his support. Tse's major achievement, though,
was his claim to have had Yung Wing on hand for the presidency
of a "Provisional Government" after the capture of Canton.[17]

On the 24th, however, the Hong Kong police raided the rebel
headquarters and informed the Canton yamen, which acted in
time to prevent the rising. In 1895 Sun's band had tried to smuggle guns in cement barrels; this time his former colleagues buried
their weapons in coffins near the Canton North Gate. Li Chi-
t'ang is said to have invested half a million dollars in the plot,

---

[17] Lo Chia-lun, *Biography* [192], I, 114–115; Tse, *Chinese Republic* [122],
pp. 16, 20–23; Feng, *Reminiscences* [160], III, 72, under "Hung Ch'üan-fu."

far more than was invested in the Waichow affair.[18] Though the figure may be exaggerated, Li did go bankrupt afterwards, and according to the Canton government, the plotters had at least $180,000 worth of weapons and munitions. The Chinese authorities believed this to be a Sun Yat-sen enterprise linked with the Kwangsi rebels. They also took note of the large Christian participation (Hung himself was connected with Hong Kong German Mission) and even accused the eminent Ho Tung—later Sir Robert Ho Tung—of being part of the conspiracy.[19] Ho, another Hsiang-shan native and graduate of Central School, had risen to become Jardine's comprador and ruled a powerful financial empire of his own, which included extensive interests in China.[20] Ho Kai was not mentioned but his literary collaborator, Hu Li-yüan, was on the Manchu suspect list.

With this failure, Tse stepped out of the picture to "allow Dr. Sun Yat-sen and his followers a free hand." Henceforth, he decided, he would promote "reform" and "independence" in the columns of the Hong Kong English-language press.[21]

On Sun's return, he found that only some ten *hua-ch'iao* had remained loyal in Yokohama. The Hsing Chung Hui had never been built for durability and Pao Huang Hui inroads had left it completely enervated. On the student and émigré front, however, the prospect had improved. Huang Chung-yang, formerly the head of the Shanghai Educational Association and a refugee from the *Su-pao* persecution, took a flat in Sun's house. Like other literati who were able to overcome their prejudice and establish close contact with Sun, Huang was impressed, and the two became fast friends. Ch'en Fan, the former *Su-pao* publisher, also found a haven in Yokohama and began exchanging political views with Sun. As for the students, there were said to be scores

[18] Feng, in *Documents* [179], III, 355, under "Li Chi-t'ang."

[19] See a copy of the secret inquiry conducted by an agent of the Chinese government and appended to Blake to Chamberlain, June 18, 1903, in FO 17/1718 [46], pp. 556–560. This was obtained through bribery by Hu Li-yüan and passed on to the British.

[20] See a short biography of Ho Tung in Arnold Wright (ed.), *Treaty Ports* [132], p. 176.

[21] Tse, *Chinese Republic* [122], p. 24.

of frequent visitors now, including Ma Chün-wu, Yang Shou-jen, and two eager Cantonese, Hu I-sheng (brother of Hu Han-min) and Liao Chung-k'ai (1878–1925).[22] Liao was born in San Francisco and came to Japan in 1902 to study at Waseda and Chūō Universities; later he became one of Sun's chief lieutenants and a major consultant on foreign ideology.[23]

According to Feng Tzu-yu, some of the students had begun pressing Sun to expand the Hsing Chung Hui, but he had been waiting for a suitable opportunity.[24] Now that self-supporting students found it difficult to enroll in military academies, Sun decided to train them himself. Among his Japanese friends was Major Hino Kumazō, with whom he had studied Boer war tactics. Hino, a confidant of the Japanese high command, enlisted the help of another Japanese officer, and took charge of a secret military school for Sun's protégés in Aoyama.[25] In August 1903 the first class began what was scheduled to have been an eight-month course; the venture apparently had the blessing of Inukai, who welcomed a visit by Sun and several of his young friends.[26] The curriculum included military science, with an emphasis on Boer tactics, which Sun had decided were most suitable for the Chinese revolution, and in a more practical vein, the manufacture of arms.

The enrollment of Li Tzu-chung pointed up a significant trend. Li, a brother-in-law of Feng Tzu-yu, was the son of Li Yü-t'ang, the "Insurance King" of Hong Kong and a pioneer in modern business enterprise. (Li Yü-t'ang's seven brothers were wealthy merchants in America.)[27] The younger Li's presence in

[22] Feng, *Reminiscences* [160], I, 132–133.
[23] See biography of Liao in H. Boorman, *Men and Politics* [9], pp. 80–85. The date of his arrival in Japan is given in Liao Chung-k'ai, *Collected Works* [187], p. 1, which gives 1877 and not 1878 as his date of birth. See also Ho Hsiang-ning (Liao's widow), "My Reminiscences" [165], I, 12–14.
[24] Feng, in *Development of the Revolution* [178], X, 81.
[25] Feng, *Reminiscences* [160], I, 133–134; and Jansen, *Sun Yat-sen* [69], pp. 115–116.
[26] Lo Chia-lun, *Biography* [192], I, 123. According to this source, p. 125, the course was scheduled for six months.
[27] Feng, *Reminiscences* [160], I, 193–194; Feng in *Documents* [179], III, 363, under "Li Tzu-chung."

Tokyo as a student, along with San Francisco-born Liao Chung-k'ai—and before either of them, Feng and Wang Ch'ung-hui—is one sign of the *hua-ch'iao* attraction to both modern education and nationalism, two forces which would bring them together with sons of gentry families.

This trend ultimately benefited Sun Yat-sen, but at this time only fourteen or fifteen students enrolled in the military course, and except for two Fukienese, all were Cantonese.[28] However, it seems clear that Sun was experimenting with a new organizational form to attract student support. Each cadet took an óath of loyalty, the contents of which indicated Sun's greater interest in program and ideology.

To the old Hsing Chung Hui oath which called for "the overthrow of the Manchus, the restoration of China to the Chinese, and the establishment of a republic" (now Sun used the more popular term, *min-kuo*), he added a fourth plank, "the equalization of land rights" (*p'ing-chün ti-ch'üan*).[29] The precise meaning of this new slogan was not clarified until a few years later. It is apparent, however, that the problem of land ownership had interested him for some time. The Henry George influence, first felt in London, was probably reinforced by Miyazaki's brother Tamizō, at this time one of the leading Japanese disciples of George.[30] In discussions with Liang Ch'i-ch'ao in 1899, Sun had also delved into traditional Chinese means of curbing agrarian inequality.[31] His conversation with Chang Ping-lin around 1899, which was not published until 1902, likewise reflects this concern.[32] When Sun explained what he meant by "equalization of

28 Feng, in *Development of the Revolution* [178], X, 71. Though Liao Chung-k'ai does not appear in Feng's list, according to Liao's widow he was registered in the course. See Ho Hsiang-ning, "My Reminiscences" [165], p. 14. I am indebted to Mr. Martin Bernal for calling my attention to this point.

29 Feng, in *Development of the Revolution* [178], X, 71. Feng, *Reminiscences* [160], I, 134.

30 See Schiffrin and Pow-key Sohn, "Henry George" [102], pp. 99–100, 103.

31 Feng, *Reminiscences* [160], II, 143–144.

32 From *Ch'iu-shu*, in Chang and Wang, *Selected Articles* [143], I, ts'e 1, 312–313.

land rights" (this was first during 1905 and 1906, and in greater detail in 1912), he revealed his debt to George and especially to John Stuart Mill by advocating governmental expropriation of the "unearned increment"—the increase in land values resulting from social progress and not from the improvements made by the owner.[33]

Liang Ch'i-ch'ao had already predicted that the West would be faced with social revolutions, and by 1902 students were reading translations on socialism from the Japanese. In Shanghai during the same year, the former Nan-yang students discussed the idea of establishing a Chinese socialist organization.[34] Nationalist and constitutional goals, however, usually had precedence in student circles. But Sun, perhaps because of his lower-class origins and impoverished childhood, and also because of his aspirations for ideological prominence, gave equal emphasis to social justice. Thus by 1903 Sun had ready the rough outline of the "Three Principles of the People," which, as set forth in 1905 and 1906, combined the goals of the nationalist, republican, and social revolutions.

The publication of Sun's article in the November 1903 issue of *Chiang-su* was another landmark in his progress toward adjustment to the intellectual milieu. He was more confident of his ability to compete with student political commentators, and they, in turn, were showing more respect for his opinions. In this short essay discussing the "preservation or dismemberment of China," Sun began using the nationalistic language and metaphors popularized by Liang and the young patriots of Tokyo and Shanghai. His tone is reminiscent of the Sun Yat-sen who had impressed Miyazaki in their first conversation in 1897, but never before had he exhibited his militancy in public. The essay spoke of the imperialist component in European and Japanese policies toward China and included a few kind words for the Boxers. It is noteworthy that Sun also inserted a bitter condemnation of the recently deceased Li Hung-chang. His attitude to-

[33] Schiffrin, "Sun Yat-sen's Early Land Policy" [101], pp. 449–464.
[34] Wang Te-chao, "Sun's Thought During the T'ung Meng Hui Period" [221], p. 182.

ward Li, in fact, could serve as a measure of the changes in Sun's definition of his role in Chinese politics. In 1894 he wanted to be Li's protégé; in 1900 he wanted Li as a partner; and in 1903 he joined the student nationalists in lamenting the late governor-general's failure to drive out the European invaders.

The main purpose of his article was to establish his expertise in foreign affairs. Sun wanted to demonstrate his understanding of foreign and especially Japanese thinking on China. He furthermore sought to prove that there existed a friendly segment of foreign opinion and suggested that if handled correctly, foreigners might not necessarily intervene in the wake of a revolution. In his opinion, Western advocates of partition were motivated by fear. Aware of China's potentialities—her size, her immense population, and her people's commercial skill—they were afraid that a modernized China "would put the white race to shame and rule Europe." Therefore, they preferred to dismember China while she was still weak rather than face the "specter of another Hannibal." In order to "ward off . . . the Yellow peril," they sought to "break up China into foreign colonies."[35]

On the other hand, Sun argued, there were Westerners who favored China's preservation because they admired her traditional civilization and her moral power. They believed that the Chinese "are the most peaceful race on the globe," who even at the height of power usually eschewed military conquest and instead exercised cultural hegemony over their tiny neighbors. According to Sun, these Sinophiles attributed China's present weakness to the "floundering of the Ch'ing Court," but they continued to believe in the "morality" of the Chinese people. In the interests of "world peace" and "humanity" these Western friends wanted to help China reform and develop her resources. By "opening the door" for China, they hoped to benefit the entire world.

But Japanese protectors of China, Sun continued, had an even deeper concern. They feared that if China were partitioned, Ja-

---

[35] "Preserving or Dismembering" [207], p. 597.

pan herself would be endangered. She would be barred from the China trade and she too would soon fall under European domination. Therefore they argued that "the preservation of China means self-preservation." They were moreover aware of their cultural and racial ties with the Chinese.

Sun then turned to those Japanese who favored partition. This group, he stated, had no faith in either the Chinese government or the people's capacity. They despaired of China's ability to reform or to defend her borders. Though they too preferred a sovereign and intact China, they believed that it was too late to prevent partition. The Manchu dynasty, they argued, was already giving away territory to the Russians and it was up to the Japanese to protect their own interest: "Let Russia take over Manchuria and Mongolia in the east, and Tibet and Turkestan in the west. We will take Korea in the north, Fukien and Chekiang in the south." These Japanese advocates of partition, Sun concluded, appeared to be hard-headed realists, while those who wanted to protect China were sincere idealists. Yet in his opinion, both policies were "untenable." The reasons, he argued, could be found by examining "the country's situation" and "the people's feelings."[36]

"The country's situation," Sun explained, was characterized by traditional political despotism, a legacy from the Ch'in dynasty (3rd century B.C.), and alien Manchu rule. Despotism plus alien rule, he asserted, increased popular suffering and thwarted Chinese patriotism. Chinese who served the Manchus were "traitors." High officials, like Liu K'un-i and Li Hung-chang, wielded unlimited power. The former controlled a population of 55 million, and the latter, 65 million. Either of them singly had been potentially stronger than Japan, the leading power in East Asia. If Liu or Li, Sun argued, had responded to popular opinion, they could have driven out the foreign powers on their own. Their failure proved that "Han traitors" could not defend China.[37] But the Manchus, Sun declared, were even less reliable in resisting

[36] *Ibid.*, pp. 597–598.
[37] *Ibid.*, pp. 598–599.

foreign invaders. He then repeated the accusation made by Liang, and others: "The Manchus say . . . that they 'prefer to give
presents to powerful neighbors than to lose out to thieves at
home,' which is the same as saying that they prefer to give Chinese territory to others than to return it to the Chinese." Sun
then ridiculed the Manchu reform program. By sending some
students abroad and by "hiring a few military instructors," he
charged, they were only applying superficial remedies, which
could not cure China's basic complaint. This analysis, Sun concluded, proved that the preservation of China's territorial integrity was impossible under her current rulers.[38]

But Sun's second consideration, "the people's feelings," argued
against the feasibility of partition. The only reason that foreigners found the Chinese docile and disorganized, he claimed, was
that they were oppressed by a "slave" dynasty. The Taiping Rebellion proved the people's courage and was fresh in their minds.
And if the British had not assisted the Manchus, Hung Hsiu-
ch'üan would have been victorious. While the whole modern
world clamored for freedom and popular rights, how could anyone expect the Chinese not to fight for independence as well? He
denied the charge that Chinese were divided and declared that
as a result of foreign aggression provincial loyalty had been replaced by a feeling of national unity which would make dismemberment difficult. He warned foreigners not to intervene if the
Chinese overthrew the monarchy:

Though the Chinese are meek and not martial, they will resist to
the death. . . . Even though the Chinese submit to a slave dynasty,
they will still defend their villages. . . . Look at the Boxers. Suspect-
ing dismemberment, they rose in violent resistance to the foreigners
and fought like madmen. . . . Only they were stupid . . . and did
not know the value of firearms and merely depended upon naked
blades. . . . If they had cast aside these crude weapons and changed
to modern ones, it is doubtful whether the allied expeditionary
force would have achieved such quick results. But the Boxers consisted only of Chihli people. If the entire country were aroused,
there would be no comparison.[39]

---

[38] *Ibid.*, pp. 599–600.
[39] *Ibid.*, pp. 600–601.

Would-be partitioners, Sun advised, should take heed of what happened in South Africa and the Philippines. They should remember too that China's 400 million people could not be compared to the 200,000 of the Transvaal. Like Mao Tse-tung at a later time, Sun found strength in his country's limitless multitude: "When they dismember [China], they will never be able to slaughter most of the Chinese people."[40]

Having argued that both preservation and dismemberment were unfeasible, Sun concluded that the only way to plan for peace in East Asia was "to listen to the Chinese people." As to the new policy of an independent China, "this is still a confidential matter," he wrote. "Our party does not value empty talk and we will wait for another occasion" to present it concretely. Thus we have an additional hint of Sun's intention to create a new party whose program had not yet been announced.

Why found a new party? Sun had given up on the Hsing Chung Hui and his experiment with the military school was discouraging. Only four months after its establishment, internal dissension led to the students' dispersal, and only four or five of the cadets were of any future benefit to the revolutionary movement. Even more important, Sun did not wait to observe the outcome of this endeavor. At the end of September 1903, only a month after his academy's inauspicious opening, he left Japan for his second round-the-world trip, and when his *Chiang-su* article was published, Sun was already in Hawaii.[41]

Again, the fact that Sun Yat-sen found no straight or easy path to the nationalist intellectuals comes to the foreground. His stock was definitely on the rise, but there was so far no hope of a successful claim to leadership. Sun must have sensed also that until he reknit his tattered overseas network, he could not impress the students with his organizational skill, nor could he supply the funds required to translate revolutionary theory into practice. He also had a score to settle with Liang Ch'i-ch'ao, who had not merely robbed him of his Hawaiian support but, in Sun's view, had also obscured the distinction between reform

[40] *Ibid.*, p. 602.
[41] Lo Chia-lun, *Biography* [192], I, 124.

and revolution and had usurped his role as the symbol of anti-Manchu militancy.

Money was his main object now, and sources in Japan were apparently depleted. This time it was his new friend, Huang Chung-yang, who lent him 200 yen for travel expenses, and he left Yokohama for Honolulu on September 26.[42]

Almost ten years had passed since Sun had formed the Hsing Chung Hui in Hawaii, and he found little to celebrate. He had last been in Hawaii in 1896 and since Liang's visit in the interval, Hsing Chung Hui membership had diminished to about ten.[43] A different Sun Yat-sen, however, undertook to reconquer the Islands. He was prepared to challenge Liang Ch'i-ch'ao's publicizing talent as well as his role as the peerless interpreter of Western political theory. In the course of his stay, Sun addressed thousands of *hua-ch'iao* at mass meetings and defined his revolutionary, republican goal. Also, for the first time in his life, he used the newspaper medium to attack his political rivals and to explain the distinguishing points of his own program. With the exception of a few Western-educated clerks and clergymen, this *hua-ch'iao* audience, of course, was not of the same intellectual caliber as the Tokyo students, but this campaign was good practice and it also gave him a chance to break the K'ang-Liang stranglehold on overseas funds.

Honolulu, the main seat of the *hua-ch'iao* community, was also the chief Pao Huang Hui stronghold, and aside from a few loyal stalwarts like Ho K'uan, the response was at first discouraging. So Sun started his campaign in Hilo, the Islands' second city. There the path had already been cleared by the arrival of Mao Wen-ming several months earlier from Canton. Mao was a Presbyterian minister who had joined the Hsing Chung Hui in 1900 and had been close to Shih Chien-ju, combining his pastoral duties with revolutionary agitation. At his invitation, Sun addressed a meeting of over a thousand *hua-ch'iao* in a Japanese theater. This was his first public speech on nationalism for a

[42] *Ibid.*, p. 125.
[43] *Ibid.*

hua-ch'iao audience, and the results were encouraging, if not spectacular. He stayed in Hilo for two months and with Mao's help enrolled ten new members—farmers, laborers, and merchants, all natives of Hsiang-shan. Reassured, he returned to Honolulu in December prepared to carry the fight to his rival's main bastion.[44]

Again a member of the Chinese Christian clergy assisted him. This time it was Huang Hsü-sheng, a relative of Mao Wen-ming and a pastor in a Honolulu church, who joined the party and with a few of the old comrades rented the Hotel Street Theater for Sun's three-day speaking engagement.[45] Here several thousand *hua-ch'iao* were exposed to Sun's freshly discovered oratorical talents. He attracted the notice of a Western reporter, whose story on the first meeting appeared the following day, December 14. As Lyon Sharman describes the occasion: "The reporter for the English-language press was caught by the foreignized appearance of the speaker with his suit of linen and his short-cut hair; his listeners wore Chinese clothes and the long queues. To this newspaperman Sun Yat-sen did not seem a fanatic, but an impressive speaker, punctuating his words with forcible gestures."[46] He portrayed Sun as a "natural-born leader" who kept his audience entranced when he denounced the Manchus and spoke of emulating the American republican and presidential systems.[47]

The Pao Huang Hui people answered the challenge and Ch'en I-k'an, a former writer for K'ang's *Chih-hsin pao*, published a vicious attack on the "revolutionary party" and its leader. Though Sun's friends were outraged, they were not equipped to wage journalistic warfare. Sun suggested transforming an old-fashioned Chinese paper, *Lung-chi pao*, into a revolutionary mouthpiece, and asked Feng Tzu-yu and Ch'en Shao-pai, now working on the Hong Kong *Chung-kuo jih-pao*, to send one of

---

[44] Feng, *Reminiscences* [160], II, 103; and Lo Chia-lun, *Biography* [192], I, 126. On Mao, see Feng in *Documents* [179], III, 361.
[45] Lo Chia-lun, *Biography* [192], I, 126.
[46] Sharman, *Sun Yat-sen* [107], pp. 77–78.
[47] "Sun's Activities in Hawaii" [204], p. 283.

their writers to take charge. In this aspect of the revolutionary struggle, the "hired pen" was more important than the "hired gun." But Sun's agent could not get a visa from the American consul in Hong Kong; his Hawaiian friends never managed to import an editor, but eventually relied upon teachers in the local *hua-ch'iao* school. Later, when he was in the United States, Sun asked Ch'en and Feng to feed articles to the paper.[48] In the meantime, with no one else to do the job, Sun himself wrote a "Rebuttal to the Pao Huang Newspaper" (*Po Pao-huang pao shu*). Published in the *Lung-chi pao* in the beginning of 1904, this was a direct reply to Ch'en I-k'an's attack of December 29.

Sun based his rebuttal on what he called his opponent's misuse of Western concepts. Originally, he wrote, he had not intended to examine these arguments in detail, but because of their "only apparent rightness" and forced interpretations, he had to refute them "to choke off the poisonous flame and eradicate fallacious reasoning." His critic, he wrote, was ignorant of logic and was "extremely stupid" in his use of political science. (In referring to "logic," "political science," and other Western terms, Sun inserted the English words as well as the translation in order to make his meaning clear and perhaps to stress his foreign education.)[49]

He attacked Ch'en's use of the term "patriotism." "Does this mean patriotism toward the Ch'ing dynasty or patriotism toward China?" Sun asked. "If the dynasty is the object of their patriotism, expressions like 'getting rid of the foreign race' . . . should not be coming out of their mouths. And if their patriotism was directed toward China, they could not use "Protect the Emperor" as a patriotic policy."[50]

Sun then used the argument invoked by the Tokyo pamphleteers, who accused the Manchus of appeasing the foreigners:

He [Ch'en] also says, 'The partition of China is imminent. The foreigners are lurking like robbers, waiting to seize the opportunity

---

[48] Feng, *Reminiscences* [160], II, 102–103, 111.

[49] Sun Yat-sen, "Refuting the 'Protect the Emperor' Newspaper" [209], p. 226.

[50] *Ibid.*

to start. Each nation has marked out its sphere.' But do they [the Pao Huang Hui] understand the reason for 'partition'? It is because the people are not aroused. . . . In contemporary international relations, there is only the authority of force and not the expounding of morals and benevolence [*jen*] and righteousness [*i*] . . . . If the people . . . could rise and overthrow the worthless, rotten, and destined-to-die Manchu government, every country would respect and esteem us. . . . Would it then still be possible to 'partition'?

Sun cited the Kuan-tzu classic as proof of the intrinsic military ability of the Chinese, and blamed the Manchus for the nation's current weakness. The Manchus, he charged, had invited foreign encroachments: "The Manchu government not only signs treaties hacking and mortgaging us, but it pacifies the country for the foreigners and then presents them with Kwangtung's Hsin-an district and Kwang-chou-wan." Cowardice and subservience to the foreigners could only invite further violations of Chinese sovereignty, Sun warned, and he challenged Ch'en I-k'an to kotow to the foreigners every day and see whether that would stop them from demanding further concessions from the Manchu government.[51]

Seizing upon a Pao Huang Hui admission that China had never been able to avoid *ko-ming* throughout her history, Sun equated these dynastic changes with revolutions and offered them as proof of a Chinese political maturity which Liang's supporters had denied. When the Pao Huang Hui also contended that a deficiency of self-governing ability made a constitutional monarchy more suitable than a republic, Sun countered with the same evidence of local self-rule which he had given to Miyazaki seven years previously. While these village institutions, Sun admitted, "have not attained the perfection of Western governments," they attest to the "naturally endowed democratic ability" of the Chinese people. Though the opposition argued that village self-rule only reflected the non-interference of the central authority, and was therefore a "primitive" form of freedom, Sun replied that this "natural" capacity for self-rule was in fact the

---

[51] *Ibid.*, p. 227.

best guarantee that the Chinese would easily acquire "civilized freedom." "If you have genuine jade," he explained, "then you can perfect it by polishing."[52]

Trying to strengthen the case for gradualism, editor Ch'en I-k'an had argued that "a constitution is for the transitional period, a republic is the final result." Sun, in his rebuttal, spelled out the English words, "constitution" and "transition" to give the *hua-ch'iao* a lesson in Western terminology and then attacked the concept of gradualism itself:

Let us look at China, which until now has had no steam engines. Now we are starting to build them and everyone chooses the newest models. If we followed his [Ch'en's] idea, since China is in the stage of early growth, we should use old American and English models of several decades ago, gradually changing and substituting the newer models and adopting the modern ones only at the very end— in a completely progressive sequence. Does the world have such a pattern? Do the people in it have such stupidity? Now this constitutional monarchy is a transitional stage, with democratic constitutionalism as its end result. It has to pass through a second destruction before reaching the stage of democratic constitutionalism. How does the first stage change into the second? . . . Since we have the strength to destroy [absolute monarchy], the choice of monarchy or democracy is ours.

To prefer constitutional monarchy, he concluded, would be like setting out to cross a stream and then stopping in the middle.[53]

Ten years earlier, when trying to impress Li Hung-chang with his expertise in foreign studies, Sun had had to justify his inability to write an "eight-legged" essay and qualify for a literary degree. However, when the interpretation and adaptation of Western theories and experience were the central issues, he flaunted his non-literati status and proudly asserted the right to challenge gentry scholars: "Your humble servant is no literary scholar. Basically I have no desire to struggle with the 'eight-legged' essay the whole day long and raise pen and ink in battle.

[52] *Ibid.*, pp. 228–229.
[53] *Ibid.*, p. 230.

... But when false doctrine is propagated ... I must oppose what is erroneous."[54]

The main thrust of this article is Sun's clarification of the major distinction in values between himself and the reformers. This distinction was best expressed by the argument just quoted, which he would keep reiterating until the end of his days; namely, that if the newest Western model—whether a steam engine or a form of government—were available, why should China be content with anything less? This facile equation of the products of technology with political and social institutions lay at the very root of Sun's political philosophy. Reminiscent of the rationalist faith of the French Enlightenment,[55] Sun's conviction that knowledge itself was the key to progress allowed him to cater to the nationalist premium on speed and to calculate a crash program for overtaking the West. He would have his people believe that a prescient elite, men like himself and the student intellectuals, could rush China through a telescoped recapitulation of European experience, and by sidestepping Europe's pitfalls, attain new heights of civilization. This faith, reflected in his onslaught upon gradualism in 1904, justified the Three Principles, the blueprint for bypassing Europe's social revolution while incorporating her nationalist and republican achievements.

Although the mood of the Three Principles was already evi-

[54] *Ibid.*, pp. 231–232.

[55] That rationalist Asian innovators would quickly bridge the gap separating them from the West had been predicted over a century earlier by Condorcet who wrote: "The advancement of these peoples will be quicker and surer than ours, because they will receive from us what we have been obliged to discover for ourselves, and because, in order to acquire those simple truths and those infallible methods at which we have arrived only after long periods of error, it will suffice for them to be able to grasp the developments and the proofs offered in our discourses and in our books." (*Esquisse d'un tableau historique des progrès de L'esprit humain*, Paris, 1795); quoted in Hildebrand (ed.), *The Idea of Progress* [55], p. 340. My attention was called to Condorcet's remarks by Bennett and McKnight, "Japanese Innovator" [3], p. 103. Sun's interest in stage-skipping can also be compared with the conviction of nineteenth century Russian Populists that Russia could bypass capitalism and move directly to socialism faster than the industrialized West. See Franco Venturi, *Roots of Revolution* [124].

dent, the moment for a formal declaration had not yet arrived. It was sufficient, Sun apparently felt, if he merely convinced the *hua-ch'iao* that he alone stood for anti-Manchuism and republicanism, and that Liang, for all his militant protestations, was still the prisoner of K'ang's monarchist loyalties. Sun was gambling on a swing in the direction of anti-dynasticism. The failure of the Hankow plot of 1900 and the absence of any subsequent pro-emperor risings weakened *hua-ch'iao* faith in Liang. The more radical elements would rather have their money spent on bombs and guns than on the publication of learned essays. Sun's sensational attempt at Waichow and Shih Chien-ju's attack on the Canton yamen offered real evidence of revolutionary intentions. The plot attempted at Hankow did not have nearly so much meaning for the *hua-ch'iao*, who were mainly Cantonese, as the events which had taken place in their own province. Other factors must also be considered in measuring *hua-ch'iao* attitudes at this time: namely, the effects of the Boxer settlement in China, which still left the Empress Dowager in control, and the spread of American, republican influences in Hawaii itself.

In addition, the current contradictions between Liang and K'ang themselves served as grist to Sun's propaganda mill. The revolutionary threats of the one were nullified by the other's pronouncements of loyalty to the emperor. Taking advantage of this situation, Sun followed up his first article in *Lung-chi pao* with an "Open letter to his fellow countrymen" warning them of the "distinction between 'protect the emperor' and 'revolution'."

"It is a mistake," he wrote, "to say that 'pao-huang' is an assumed name for carrying out revolution. In everything there must be conformity between things and names. . . . How can men of learning like K'ang and Liang . . . fail to match substance and names?" Sun then reviewed the K'ang-Liang relationship with the Kuang-hsü Emperor, comparing it to the ancient bond between lord and subject. After the failure of the 100 days of reform, they went abroad and founded the Pao Huang Hui, which, according to Sun, was their way of repaying the emperor's kindness and his faith in them. But if they are really what the public thinks—that is, in name "protectors of the emperor" and in reality, revolutionaries—"then what kind of people are they?" By reading K'ang's recent publications they could discover that he has not betrayed the emperor's trust but advocates prolongation of Manchu rule under a constitution.[56]

But what about Liang Ch'i-ch'ao? "Liang," Sun wrote, "is among the leaders of the Pao Huang Hui, a man of deep experience who is intimately acquainted with the ways of the world." He has now discovered that he is "out of touch with the heart beat of the revolutionary temperament" and that his efforts have not matched the popular mood. So he suddenly "casts off his original aim . . . and unexpectedly espouses revolution in the *Hsin-min ts'ung-pao*. His sudden talk of destruction and his sudden love of his racial brothers overwhelm his affection for his benefactor, the Kuang-hsü Emperor. His sudden love of honesty is greater than his affection for his teacher, K'ang Yu-wei." But Sun dismissed this transformation as "the delirious utterings of a sick man, who is not really against the Ch'ing and for the Han." "But how can we know for certain?" he asked rhetorically. "K'ang, since he has engraved his subjection to Kuang-hsü in his heart, shows plainly that '*pao-huang*' is not counterfeit, while Liang, without definitely making a break, keeps on talking revolution. What is the truth? . . . Liang is a man with two ways of talking, like a rat looking both ways. If his revolutionary talk is sincere, then his '*pao-huang*' talk must be spurious. If his '*pao-huang*' talk is sincere, then his revolutionary utterances must be false."[57]

Advocates of constitutional monarchy, Sun charged,

defame the Chinese as being unqualified and undeserving of popular rights [*min-ch'üan*]. Now the Manchus are illegitimate offspring of northeast nomads but they can enjoy imperial prerogatives, while the Chinese, a race with a 4000-year old culture cannot enjoy popular rights. What kind of talk is this? . . . Thus it is manifestly clear that when they say, '*pao-huang*,' they really mean '*pao-huang*,' and

---

[56] Sun Yat-sen, "Warning Letter" [208], pp. 23–24.
[57] *Ibid.*, p. 24.

when they say 'revolution' they mean counterfeit revolution. From this standpoint 'revolution' and '*pao-huang*' are two distinct things. . . . The purpose of revolution is to overthrow the Manchus and restore the Chinese. The purpose of '*pao-huang*' is to support the Manchus and the Ch'ing administration. These are opposite roads and speeds, mutually opposed like fire and water.[58]

Since the advocates of constitutional monarchy were burdened with a Manchu and not a Chinese monarch, we can see how Sun, like the Tokyo students, could link the republican and ethnic themes. If Chinese were not qualified to be citizens of a republic, how were Manchus qualified to be emperors? This became one of the major issues in the three- or four-year-long ideological struggle with the K'ang-Liang forces which began the following year.

Yet even while Sun was exposing them, Liang himself was resolving the contradictions upon which his rival had seized. Two years earlier, Liang had announced that he considered it a mark of intellectual progress if his ideas of today negated those of yesterday,[59] and while in America at this time, he began to regret the advocacy of violence and incitement to anti-Manchuism which had characterized his articles in *Hsin-min ts'ung-pao*.[60] In analyzing a personality as complex as Liang's, changes of political attitude cannot be attributed to any single factor. Of course his disciple relationship with K'ang, which also included a financial dependence must be considered as well as his distaste for violence, resulting from the martyrdom of his former students at Hankow.[61] As we have seen, however, his abhorrence of sponsoring revolutionary action did not prevent him from

[58] *Ibid.*, p. 25.

[59] From Liang Ch'i-ch'ao, "Pao-chiao fei so-i tsun K'ung lun" ('Preserving the teachings' is not the way to honor Confucius), *Hsin-min ts'ung-pao*, No. 2, February 1902, in Chang and Wang, *Selected Articles* [143], I, *ts'e* 1, 163.

[60] Liang's doubts concerning revolution cropped up during his stay in America in 1903 whence he returned to Japan at the end of the year. For a detailed analysis of this transformation, see Chang P'eng-yüan, *Liang Ch'i-chao* [144], pp. 163–176; and Wang, *Chinese Intellectuals* [129], pp. 221–224.

[61] Chang P'eng-yüan, *Liang Ch'i-ch'ao* [144], pp. 167–168.

preaching what was tantamount to revolution in his journals. But by 1903, when he was touring America, he learned how his journalistic seeds had blossomed into a cult of violence among the students and young intellectuals of Tokyo and Shanghai. Apprised of the revolutionary, anti-Manchu fervor which had seized these circles and of the clashes with authority which characterized the events of the spring and summer of 1903, Liang was shocked and dismayed. Writing to a friend in August, he exclaimed, "China will not be destroyed by reaction, but by the new parties."[62]

Was it because he realized that the new parties would inevitably fall back on a man like Sun Yat-sen, whom he had already disqualified from leadership? His personal doubts concerning Sun undoubtedly helped move him back to K'ang's gradualist position, but there were other reasons for this change. Liang, as we have noted, feared imperialism as much as, if not more than, any Chinese of his generation. A violent clash with the established authority, whether he called it *ko-ming* or *pien-ko*, seemed likely to invite further foreign intervention.[63]

There was another factor as well. Although Liang retreated from his earlier advocacy of violence, he did not accept K'ang's renovated Confucianism or his slogan of *"pao-chiao"* (preservation of the teachings).[64] He was still a universalist and, because of his knowledge of world history, could not make out the special case for China which republicanism demanded. Acutely aware of the social, historical, and institutional antecedents which enabled the West to achieve popular sovereignty, he came to see republicanism as the culmination of a gradual, evolutionary process rather than as the result of sudden change.

[62] Letter to Chiang Kuan-yün of August 19, 1903, in Ting, *Biography of Liang* [214], I, 186.

[63] Chang P'eng-yüan, *Liang Ch'i-ch'ao* [144], pp. 170–171. On *"pien-ko,"* the term Liang coined to denote radical institutional change, see his article, "Shih-ko" (Explaining *ko*) in Chang and Wang, *Selected Articles* [143], I, *ts'e* 1, 242–246. This is taken from *Hsin-min ts'ung-pao*, no. 22, December 14, 1902.

[64] See Hsiao Kung-ch'üan, "K'ang Yu-wei" [60], p. 205; and Levenson, *Liang Ch'i-ch'ao* [76], pp. 121–122.

Sun, digging up republican precedents from China's remote past, was actually more of a traditionalist than Liang, and in his "locomotive" analogy, defied everything that Liang had learned of world history.

Inevitably Liang Ch'i-ch'ao's behavior affected the political fortunes of Sun Yat-sen. Although Sun did not realize it yet, he was attacking a position that Liang had already vacated.[65] In fact, it was Liang's voluntary abdication rather than Sun's attacks which cleared the way for Sun's rise as the spokesman for unconditional revolution.

Sun's exposition of the inconsistencies between K'ang and Liang gained for him vital experience in the art of journalistic controversy. Although he did not completely nullify his rival's spectacular Hawaiian raid, he did restore the faith of some of his old comrades and draw a few new ones to the revolutionary banner. The three-year-old monopoly of the Pao Huang Hui was finally broken. Showing his mettle as a public speaker as well, Sun was able to give himself and the revolutionary movement a more respectable image. If he did not subdue the Pao Huang Hui, he at least got himself back into the running.

Again there is evidence that Sun was not set on simply reviving the Hsing Chung Hui. According to a local account, while in Honolulu he organized a new body, "The Chinese Revolutionary Army" (Chung-hua ko-ming chün) and used the new four-plank oath he had tried out in Tokyo.[66]

---

[65] In a later explanation of his "revolutionary" period, Liang wrote as follows: "While Liang Ch'i-ch'ao daily espoused the revolutionary and republican cause against the Manchus, his teacher K'ang Yu-wei strongly disapproved of it, frequently reprimanding Liang and following this with tactful persuasion. In a period of two years, his letters (to Liang) ran to several tens of thousands of words. Liang, on his part, had also become somewhat displeased with the work of the revolutionaries, and in a mood of precaution (lit., 'once burned by hot soup, thereafter blowing upon even cold salad') he slightly altered his stand. Nevertheless, his conservative instincts and his progressive instincts frequently fought against each other within himself whenever his emotions were aroused, and his views of one day contradicted those of an earlier day." Liang Ch'i-ch'ao, *Intellectual Trends* [79], pp. 102–103.

[66] "Sun's Activities in Hawaii" [204], page 283.

The return to the Islands also enabled him to see his family once more after a seven years' absence. His mother, wife, and three children were still being taken care of by Sun Mei on Maui. The misunderstanding concerning Liang Ch'i-ch'ao had apparently been straightened out, but in the meantime the elder brother's fortunes had suffered as a result of new American land regulations. Sun Mei was no longer the wealthy "King of Maui" and could never again act as the movement's financial benefactor.[67] Sun Yat-sen, however, was able to pick up some money by selling his ten dollar patriotic bonds, redeemable at $100 after the revolution.[68] Had he wished to do so, he might have earned more through practicing medicine. The Islanders still remembered he was a physician and several difficult cases were brought to his attention. Although he treated them successfully, he refused to accept any fees. This demonstration of medical competence, however, enhanced his prestige among the *hua-ch'iao*.[69]

We also learn from Chung Kun Ai that, despite Sun's financial plight, never in their long association did he show a personal interest in money.[70] Sun preferred to conduct his financial transactions in a business-like way, and took his debts seriously; for example, he did not forget that he owed Huang Chung-yang 200 yen.[71] In contrast to his confident platform manner, however, Sun was often reduced to a peddler's role in trying to raise funds for the movement. Chung informs us that on one

[67] Feng, *Reminiscences* [160], II, 7.
[68] "Sun's Activities in Hawaii" [204], p. 282. According to Chung Kun Ai, *My Seventy Nine Years* [26], p. 109, these bonds were honored after the revolution. Sun raised the bonus in later years, and Chung reports that a $50 bond was redeemed for $1,000.
[69] Lo Chia-lun, *Biography* [192], I, 126. In his visit of 1894, however, Sun, as a physician could do little for Chung's ailing wife. "I asked Dr. Sun to examine her and he prescribed some medicine which did not help her much. Then I got some medicine from a Chinese herbalist. . . . I was ignorant and did not realize that she had tuberculosis, from which she died." *My Seventy Nine Years* [26], pp. 140–141.
[70] *My Seventy Nine Years* [26], pp. 109–110.
[71] See his letter to Huang from America in 1904, in Sun, *Collected Works* [205], V, 27.

occasion when Sun arrived from Japan, he brought $500 worth
of silk, which he asked his friend to sell. After disposing of the
goods among Sun's followers, Chung returned the cash to a
surprised Sun, who informed him that in most cases he never
received any money nor did he get the silk back.[72]

As a whole the visit to Hawaii was successful enough to give
Sun hope of penetrating another Pao Huang Hui stronghold,
the United States, which had recently been canvassed by Liang
Ch'i-ch'ao. It was suggested by Yang Wen-na, his maternal
uncle, that in order to ease his way into these larger Chinese
communities, he first ought to equip himself with Chih Kung
T'ang (i.e., Triad society) credentials in Hawaii, because the
Triads there belonged to the same lodge as did those in America.
Yang was a Triad notable and arranged for Sun's induction over
the objections of Pao Huang Hui elements, who had earlier
accepted Liang into the brotherhood.[73] That Sun was making a
special play for Triad support can also be discerned in his open
letter and article, where he identified himself with the old anti-
Manchu goal of the secret society. At this time Sun was given
the important title of *hung-kun* ("red staff"), which in Triad
parlance denotes a disciplinary officer of high military rank.[74]

Sun's new interest in the Triads deserves further attention.
In the past, we have noted, Sun often entered into ad hoc arrangements with Triad chieftains as part of his strategy in a
particular plot. The Triads were partners in a military engagement rather than an integral part of the revolutionary movement. The only apparent exception to this strategy took place
during 1899 and 1900, when Sun tried to form a new supra-
organization which included his own Hsing Chung Hui and
various Triad lodges from different localities. But this arrangement did not outlast the Waichow campaign and, in fact, there
is doubt whether the so-called Hsing Han Hui ever really functioned as an organization. In 1904, however, Sun accepted the
fact of Triad organizational autonomy and attempted to mold

[72] *My Seventy Nine Years* [26], p. 110.
[73] Feng, *Reminiscences* [160], II, 110–111.
[74] For a description of this Triad title, see Schlegel, *The Hung League*
[103], pp. 47, 49, and quatrains nos. 315–317, p. 108.

it to his own use by enlisting in its ranks and instilling his own ideological orientation. Liang had taken this step more than three years earlier. Sun was to use even more openly in America this tactic of leaving the traditional Triad hierarchy undisturbed but turning the society into a revolutionary front organization by infiltration. Meanwhile, a similar method of grass-roots organizing was already being successfully pursued by Yu Lieh in Malaya.

While his membership in the Triads provided an excellent introduction to the American *hua-ch'iao*, there was yet another problem, how to evade the American exclusion laws. Anticipating provocation from the Pao Huang Hui, Sun's brother and friends persuaded him to claim Hawaiian birth, which would allow him the privileges of American citizenship. It is difficult to believe that a hardened conspirator like Sun would have any compunctions about lying in order to get past the American immigration authorities. He had already used this deception in Yokohama in 1895. But according to revolutionary sources he first had to be assured that "acting according to the requirements of the situation" was an ancient and honorable Chinese practice.[75] On March 9, 1904, therefore, he presented the American officials in Maui with a deposition stating that he had been born in Oahu in 1870, and his brother produced several aged fellow countrymen to authenticate the deception.[76] Sun Mei had yet another service to perform. Although he could spare no cash, he could not let Sun Yat-sen go abroad without giving him anything, and he parted with some precious ambergris which his younger brother could sell when in difficult circumstances.[77] Whether Sun Yat-sen made use of it at once or had enough proceeds from his bond sales is not known, but when he sailed on the S. K. *Korea* on March 31, he is said to have traveled in "first class style."[78]

When Sun's ship arrived in San Francisco on April 6, 1904,

---

[75] Feng, *Reminiscences* [160], II, 110.
[76] Sharman, *Sun Yat-sen* [107], p. 79.
[77] Lo Chia-lun, *Biography* [192], I, 127–128.
[78] Sharman, *Sun Yat-sen* [107], p. 80. Sharman, using primary American sources, is most reliable in dating Sun's activities at this time.

the rival Pao Huang Hui, thanks to its Honolulu intelligence service, was better prepared to receive him than his new Triad comrades. Most of the customs interpreters were K'ang supporters, and according to revolutionary accounts, they informed the immigration authorities that Sun was a notorious bandit, and even enlisted the help of the Chinese consul in an attempt to have him deported. Acting on evidence supplied by these Pao Huang Hui loyalists, the consul informed the Americans that Sun's deposition was false and that he had been born in Hsiang-shan. Once their suspicions were aroused, the immigration authorities, already accustomed to dealing out arbitrary treatment to Chinese regardless of their claims to citizenship, prevented Sun from landing and kept him aboard the *Korea* overnight. Many of the sailors were Waichow Triads, who respected him and treated him royally. But the next day, when he was moved to a place of detention in the harbor and held incommunicado, he started getting worried.[79] There he was interrogated by the immigration officers and after a few days they announced that he would be deported to Hawaii as soon as the *Korea* made its return voyage.

By chance, Sun noticed a fellow-inmate reading the *Chung-hsi jih-pao* (Chinese-Western Daily) and the name of its publisher, Wu P'an-chao, reminded him of a letter he had been carrying in his luggage since his first flight from Canton in 1895. At that time his fellow conspirator, the Presbyterian convert Tso Tou-shan, and another Cantonese Christian had given him a letter of recommendation to two leaders of the Chinese Christian community of San Francisco. One was the clergyman, Ssu-t'u Nan-ta, and the other, the same Wu P'an-chao. Wu had an excellent command of English and had been a pioneer in the field of Chinese journalism in America.[80]

Again we find Sun making the most of his Christian connections during times of stress, and after what he had gone through

79 Feng, *Reminiscences* [160], II, 111–112.
80 *Ibid.*, pp. 112–113. On Wu and Ssu-t'u, see *ibid.*, III, 94–95. It is not clear whether Ssu-t'u Nan-ta was Chinese or whether his name was transliterated from English.

in London, his present escape plan must have been routine. Getting hold of an American newsboy, Sun scribbled an urgent message to Wu, and just as in London, appended a request in English that the messenger be rewarded. When Wu answered his summons and appeared at the detention shed, Sun told him what had happened and handed him the old letter of recommendation from their mutual friends in Canton. Yu and Ssu-t'u recognized the handwriting and their assistance was assured. The next step was to be a protest to the Department of Commerce and Labor in Washington, which had jurisdiction over immigration, but since most of his flock had families in China, Pastor Ssu-t'u advised moving with discretion. Sun also told them of his Triad affiliation, and the San Francisco Chih Kung T'ang, known to the Americans as the Chinese Masons, was brought into the picture; thus we have another instance of secret society-Christian cooperation. Although the Chih Kung T'ang was riddled with Pao Huang Hui supporters, the head of its San Francisco lodge and titular leader of all the American lodges, Huang San-te, was a revolutionary supporter. Sun's plight as an example of Pao Huang Hui cooperation with the Manchu authorities reinforced his anti-K'ang sympathies and he backed the appeal to Washington.

As it happened, Wu P'an-chao also served as the Chinese consul's paid adviser, and the consul usually deferred to his opinion on legal questions. Wu therefore persuaded him not to let the Chinese Legation in Washington know of their appeal to the Department of Commerce and Labor. The consul agreed but asked Wu to be careful not to get him involved. Wu and the Chih Kung T'ang's English-language secretary consulted the lodge's American lawyer—later to be an adviser on railroad affairs for the Chinese republic—who arranged for Sun's release on a $500 bond pending Washington's decision. In the meantime Sun was made welcome by the secret society dignitaries and Christian elders and ate his meals at Wu's newspaper office.[81]

---

[81] *Ibid.*, pp. 113–114. The Chinese consul was none other than Ho Yu, the "black sheep" brother of Ho Kai, Sun's patron in Hong Kong! Ho Yu

By the end of the month the decision came from Washington; Sun was considered a bona fide Hawaiian-born Chinese and therefore there was no reason to deport him. (Perhaps one of the reasons for his detention was the coincidental arrival of a Manchu Prince, whom the Americans wanted to see safely on his way to the east coast before letting Sun loose.)[82] This victory over Pao Huang Hui-Manchu intrigue, made possible by his own deception, encouraged Sun, and as it turned out, proved to be the brightest feature of this American trip.

Once he was free and had made his contacts, Sun went after his primary goal, tapping the financial resources of the American *hua-ch'iao*. He was learning the value of propaganda, and thanks to Tsou Jung, he had something pertinent to distribute. With the generous help of Wu, who donated his newspaper's printing facilities, and Huang's Chih Kung T'ang, which bore mailing expenses, he ordered 11,000 copies of *The Revolutionary Army* printed and had them distributed in America and Southeast Asia.[83]

As in Hawaii, the question of a propaganda newspaper arose. The San Francisco Chih Kung T'ang paper, *Ta-t'ung jih-pao*, was at this time edited by Ou Ch'ü-chia, who will be remembered as the author of the fiery *Hsin Kwang-tung*. Despite his anti-Manchu militancy, however, Ou was still Liang Ch'i-ch'ao's confederate and was hostile toward Sun. Backed by the leadership of the Chih Kung T'ang, Sun was able to remove Ou and invite as a replacement, Liu Ch'eng-yü, the Hupeh student whom he had met in Japan. When Liu arrived in the summer and became editor, Sun obtained another friendly newspaper.[84] While in America, he also received from Singapore some of the early copies of the recently established *T'u-nan jih-pao*.[85] Sun

apparently secured the appointment through the influence of their brother-in-law, Wu T'ing-fang, the Chinese Minister to Washington. (Interview with Mr. Fu Ping-ch'ang).

[82] Sharman, *Sun Yat-sen* [107], pp. 81–82.

[83] Feng, *Reminiscences* [160], II, 114.

[84] *Ibid.*, pp. 119–121.

[85] Wang Gung-wu, "Sun Yat-sen and Singapore" [126], p. 58.

and his friends now had four newspapers at their command. Though still outnumbered by Pao Huang Hui organs, this was significant progress and attests to the growing tendency of intellectuals to enter Sun's orbit.

Considering the Christian community his best bet, Sun addressed a meeting in a San Francisco Presbyterian church, and after explaining his revolutionary goal, tried to sell the ten-dollar bonds he had had printed in Hawaii. He also offered membership in the Hsing Chung Hui with each purchase. His audience, however, was still afraid of Manchu reprisals and refused to join the organization. Sun therefore withdrew the bonus and just put the bonds on sale. As long as they could remain anonymous, at least some of the *hua-ch'iao* were ready to invest in the revolution and Sun collected $2700. Among the more enthusiastic participants in the meeting was its chairman, Kuang Hua-t'ai, a teacher at the University of California whom Sun had met on an earlier trip to the United States. Kuang was the only person who formally joined the Hsing Chung Hui, and he alone sold $1300 worth of bonds in Berkeley.[86]

Seeing little prospect of establishing a flourishing organization of his own, Sun decided to rely upon the Chih Kung T'ang to divert the funds which were still flowing toward K'ang. He had the confidence of the top echelon in San Francisco, and now he undertook to revise the society's constitution so as to tighten the control of this central lodge over the scattered branches and to turn the entire organization into a fund-raising network for the revolution.

In writing the constitution or charter, Sun included the four new aims introduced in Tokyo and Hawaii, thus indicating his purpose of turning the secret society into a front organization. He had the society pledge to cooperate with all those who shared these aims and to treat as enemies all those who opposed them. This latter category included the Pao Huang Hui, referred to as "Han traitors," who "advocate reform and talk

[86] Feng, *Reminiscences* [160], II, 114–115. On Kuang, see Feng in *Documents* [179], III, 367–368. He was better known as Walter N. Fong. See Yu, *Party Politics* [140], p. 28.

about a constitution." There were strictures against imperialist aggression, too. Sun asserted that the world was governed by the "survival of the fittest" doctrine. The white race, he wrote, had already occupied the five continents, and in East Asia only Japan and China still endured. China's weakness has already been exposed, however, and the Manchus are incapable of protecting her. "Fortunately," he said in the preamble, "the patriot Sun Yat-sen has come to America . . . to lecture on the Hung-men (Triad) aims and elucidate revolutionary affairs. Since the American *hua-ch'iao* are living in a land of "equality and liberty" under a republican form of government, there should be no obstacle to their organizational activities."[87]

In June, 1904, Sun, accompanied by the Chih Kung T'ang leader, Huang San-te, and armed with this new charter, set out on a nation-wide registration drive. If each of the estimated seventy to eighty thousand Triad members paid a registration fee of two dollars (U.S.), there would be a tidy sum for both the secret society and Sun's revolutionary enterprises.[88] But in December, after visiting tens of cities, including Fresno, Bakersfield, Los Angeles, New Orleans, St. Louis, Chicago, Atlanta, Pittsburgh, Wilmington, Baltimore, and Philadelphia, they reached New York empty-handed. Instead of collecting a war-chest, Sun and Huang had dissipated on travel expenses the few thousand dollars he had raised on the west coast. The vaunted Triad network was revealed to be a loose collection of branches without any responsibility to the central lodge. They turned out to hear what Huang and Sun had to say, but insofar as their interests were political, they still preferred the more illustrious leadership of K'ang Yu-wei and Liang Ch'i-ch'ao.[89]

Actually, Sun Yat-sen had expected too much too soon. His fame and popularity could still not match that of his rivals, who could barnstorm America, draw thousands of listeners and willing contributors, and be received by the Secretary of State and

[87] Feng, *Reminiscences* [160], I, 148–151.

[88] *Ibid.*, p. 152; and Feng, *Overseas Chinese Revolutionary Organizations* [162], p. 24.

[89] Feng, *Reminiscences* [160], II, 123–124.

President Roosevelt. (Liang had been in Washington the previous year and K'ang made his triumphant entry the following year.)[90] Before Liu Ch'eng-yü's arrival, Sun had no newspaper support while the K'ang-Liang forces controlled papers in both San Francisco and New York. Ultimately, his rivals' overseas activity profited the revolutionary movement by stimulating homeland oriented political thinking among the *hua-ch'iao*. By sponsoring modern schools and journals, the reformers were sowing fields which would inevitably be reaped by the nationalist movement under Sun and his successors.

But Sun, aware of the tumult in Tokyo, in Shanghai, and in the interior of China as well, wanted to return to the East with proof of his overseas connections and fund raising ability. Considering his handicaps and his rivals' advantages, he had done remarkably well. He was not in control of *hua-ch'iao* funds, but he had made his presence felt from Hawaii to the west coast of America, while his agent Yu had created a strong base in Malaya. He had also gained a few enthusiastic recruits on the long journey across the continent.[91] These advances paid dividends shortly afterward, even though it was no consolation to the man who was still thinking of the immediate overthrow of the dynasty in a single blow.

The New York winter found him dejected and almost broken in spirit. He decided to let Huang continue on the registration drive alone, while he sought the solace of his Christian friends. A sympathetic Chinese pastor, in charge of a Chinatown mission, took him in, and it must have been salt to his wounds when the predominantly pro-K'ang *hua-ch'iao* threatened to boycott the mission for harboring him. Dr. Hager, who had known him for almost twenty years and who had recently seen him on the west coast, found him "careworn and oppressed with anxiety."[92]

Yet New York offered some relief from his bitter experience

[90] Levenson, *Liang Ch'i-ch'ao* [76], pp. 72–73; and Sharman, *Sun Yat-sen* [107], p. 93.

[91] See Feng, *Reminiscences* [160], III, 93–96, for list of Sun's supporters in America at this time.

[92] Sharman, *Sun Yat-sen* [107], pp. 91–92.

with the "closed minds" of the *hua-ch'iao*. Wang Ch'ung-hui,
now at Yale Law School, and a few other students in the area
came to see him and Sun had an opportunity to air the ideas
which he had kept to himself for the past year. As a result of
these discussions and the failure of his tour, Sun decided to try
another tack. If the uneducated *hua-ch'iao* did not respond to
the revolutionary slogan, perhaps the Americans themselves,
imbued with the republican spirit, would recognize the justice
of his cause. Sun had always believed that the interests of the
West could be served by a Chinese revolution, and now he made
a direct plea for American support similar to those made to
Britain by Ho Kai in Hong Kong and by himself in London in
1897. *The True Solution of the Chinese Question,* which he
called his little pamphlet, benefited from the editorial assistance
of Wang Ch'ung-hui, but the main arguments resemble Sun's
earlier statements, including his article in *Chiang-su* of the
previous year.[93]

As we would expect, Sun adopted a different tone in addressing foreigners. When he had discussed the conquest of the
Philippines with his compatriots, Sun shared the student concern with imperialism. In Tokyo he had spoken of Aguinaldo's
fighters—in whom, it will be recalled, he had more than an
academic interest—as heroes who should be emulated by the
Chinese and whose fierce resistance could deter further Western
expansion. In New York, however, he merely noted that the
conquest of the islands had made America "one of the nearest
neighbors of China." This geographical proximity plus American interest in Chinese markets were cited as reasons for the
importance of the Far East and especially China to the United
States. He also pointed out that whatever the outcome of the

[93] Feng, *Reminiscences* [160], I, 101; and Lo Chia-lun, *Biography* [192],
I, 134–135. The English text of the pamphlet appears in *Tang-shih shih-
liao ts'ung-k'an* (Serial publication of historical materials on party history).
(Chungking, n.d. 1944?), pp. 1–10. I am grateful to Professor Shelley H.
Cheng for lending me his copy. Sun's handwritten English version appears
in Hu Han-min (ed.), *Collected Works of Sun Yat-sen* [172], IV, 349–368.

Russo-Japanese War, it would not solve the Chinese question nor satisfy these American interests.[94]

He then argued, as he had in the past, that it was the corruption of the Manchu regime that lay at the root of the Chinese question. If the Manchu government had not been so helpless, he continued, the war over Manchuria might have been avoided. He made it a point to distinguish between Manchus and Chinese and described the Chinese as an oppressed people under an alien conqueror.

Having made his case for this ethnic distinction, he proceeded with his main intention: to relieve Americans of what he claimed to be two popularly held fallacies concerning China. The first was that the Chinese were naturally seclusive and that they could only be opened to foreign intercourse with the bayonet. Going back to pre-Ch'ing history, he cited instances of Chinese willingness to accept foreign religious teachings: Buddhism, the Nestorian Tablets, and Father Matteo Ricci's reception under the Ming. This tradition of tolerant interest was suppressed, he charged, with the advent of the Manchus, who were forced to cut off foreign intercourse lest it lead to the enlightenment of the Chinese and their own downfall. Thus Sun, who had recently blamed the Manchus for the feebleness of the Boxer response to imperialism, now blamed them for fostering the anti-foreignism which led to Boxerism.[95]

Using Western concepts such as "due process of law," "liberty of speech," and "inalienable rights of life, liberty, and property," Sun and his Yale editor built a case for a Chinese revolution in the tradition of the American. "We, the Chinese people," he declared, "in order to redress our wrongs, and to establish peace in the Far East and in the world generally, have therefore determined to adopt measures for the attainment of these objects, 'peaceably if we may, forcibly if we must.'" He asserted that "the whole nation is ripe for revolution," and pointed to his

[94] Sun, *True Solution* [117], pp. 1–2.
[95] *Ibid.*, pp. 2–5.

own Waichow uprising and the more recent Canton and Kwangsi movements with which he was not connected. And though he
knew better, he claimed that the Chih Kung T'ang, which he
called the Chinese Patriotic Society, was full of anti-Manchu
fervor.[96]

Sun then dealt with the second fallacy, that of the "Yellow
Peril." Repeating his analysis of the previous year, he described
the argument of some Western statesmen who feared that if
China modernized, she would become "a sort of Frankenstein;"
therefore, the argument went, "it is wiser to keep the Chinese
down." This policy, Sun stated, was not only immoral but untenable. Though normally a law-abiding people, he declared,
the Chinese would rise in self-defense. (But this was not the
place to speak of the Boxers as representatives of the Chinese
spirit). Then, hinting at a possible Russian or Japanese manipulation of China, he asserted that "the Chinese would be a
menace to the peace of the world only if they were properly
drilled by some foreign country and made use of as an instrument for the gratification of its own ambition." (Ironically,
during the course of his career Sun was constrained to invite
such assistance from both these powers.) A modernized China,
he claimed, would be a boon to international commerce and
industry. "Nations are to each other as individuals. Is it econom-
ically better for a man to have a poor, ignorant neighbor than
. . . a wealthy, intelligent one?"[97]

The only solution was to replace "this out-of-date Tartar
monarchy" with a "Republic of China." Since fewer than 20,000
foreign soldiers were able to bring the dynasty to its knees in
1900, he claimed that revolution would not be difficult, especially since, "we could easily raise a hundred or a thousand times
more men from our patriots." But to accomplish the revolution
even more easily, he closed with a plea for assistance:

To work out the salvation of China is exclusively a duty of our
own, but as the problem has recently involved a worldwide interest,

---

96 *Ibid.*, pp. 5–7.
97 *Ibid.*, pp. 7–8.

we, in order to make sure of our success, to facilitate our movement, to avoid unnecessary sacrifice, and to prevent misunderstanding and intervention of foreign powers, must appeal to the people of the civilized world in general and the people of the United States in particular for your sympathy and support, either moral or material, because you are the pioneers of Western civilization in Japan; because you are a Christian nation; because we intend to model our new government after yours; and above all, because you are the champion of liberty and democracy. We hope we may find many Lafayettes among you.[98]

This was good pamphleteering, expressly geared to the interests and sentiments of the American public. And despite his more militant approach to Chinese audiences at this time, this statement was also consistent with Sun's deep-rooted faith that the entire modern world would benefit by the rejuvenation of China. Only a few years earlier, J. A. Hobson had warned that, "nationalism that bristles with resentment and is all astrain with the passion of self-defense is only less perverted from its general genius than the nationalism which glows with the animus of greed and self-aggrandizement at the expense of others. From this aspect, aggressive Imperialism is an artificial stimulation of nationalism in peoples too foreign to be absorbed and too compact to be permanently crushed . . . and we joined with other nations in creating a resentful nationalism until then unknown in China."[99] For a long time, however, Sun Yat-sen, as an individual, could not be considered an exponent of this "resentful nationalism."

Sun had ten thousand copies of the *True Solution* printed and is said to have distributed them among foreigners of various countries. His Hong Kong journal, the *Chung-kuo jih-pao*, published a Chinese translation, and a Tokyo paper published one in Japanese.[100] But whom did it actually reach in America and Europe? More important, even if some Western statesmen might have agreed with his opinions, how could they credit him with

[98] *Ibid.*, pp. 9–10.
[99] Hobson, *Imperialism* [56], p. 9.
[100] Feng, *Reminiscences* [160], II, 124.

any influence in China? While he may have had the overseas students in mind for at least a year, the advance guard of revolutionary returnees were still getting along without him.

As we have seen, the Tokyo-Shanghai nationalist axis was characterized by a flourishing literary output as well as by a few sporadic attempts at clandestine organization. By the end of 1903 and during 1904, the most daring of these young intellectuals tried to put their writings into practice. During this period, when Sun was abroad and Liang's conscience had begun to bother him again, revolutionary conspiracy spread to the interior of China, to Hunan and Hupeh, and to Chekiang and Kiangsu on the coast. The first batch of revolutionary students began to come home, carrying bombs as well as books. While still in Tokyo, some of the members of the Militant People's Educational Society—itself a secret organization—formed an ultrasecret assassination corps. Among its members was Yang Shoujen, who had studied explosives with one of the former Waichow campaigners, Liang Mu-kuang, at that time a refugee in Yokohama after participating in the 1903 Canton plot. Yang lost an eye during his experiments, but this disciple of Russian terrorism nevertheless went on to Tientsin in 1904 with some bombs and a plan to demolish both the Emperor and the Empress Dowager in their palaces.[101]

Two other ex-students accompanied him, and Chang Chi, teaching in Hunan, arranged to join them. After staying in Tientsin for several months, however, they could not find a suitable opportunity to penetrate the Forbidden City in Peking, and the plot was scrapped.[102]

In the meantime, Yang's fellow Hunanese, led by Huang Hsing, were planning a more elaborate enterprise at home. Huang, after finishing his studies in Japan, had begun teaching in his native province in the fall of 1903. After his experiences in Tokyo, however, he concluded that revolution, not education would be his main career. He immediately began distributing inflammatory literature, pamphlets by Ch'en T'ien-hua and

101 *Ibid.*, p: 126. On Liang, see Feng in *Documents* [179], III, 357.
102 Feng, *Reminiscences* [160], II, 126.

Tsou Jung, and in December, formed a revolutionary organization, the Hua Hsing Hui (Society for the Revival of China). Most of the early members were also returned students, among them Ch'en T'ien-hua and Liu K'uei-i. Through Liu they were able to form an alliance with Ma Fu-i, the recently crowned leader of the Hunan Ko Lao Hui, and in an episode reminiscent of Ch'en Shao-pai's experience of 1899, Huang and Liu sealed a pact with Ma on a snowy mountain near Changsha and drank wine to their anti-Manchu alliance. Again it was found expedient not to enlist the secret society members in this association of ex-students and literati, but to form a special affiliated group for their Ko Lao Hui comrades. And in another repetition of the Hsing Chung Hui pattern, the young revolutionaries were aided by a Chinese clergyman, this time the rector of an Episcopalian Church in Changsha. Nor was the movement's political policy better defined than that of the early Hsing Chung Hui. Anti-Manchuism was the main common denominator between the intellectuals and the Ko Lao Hui.[103]

An innovation of the Yangtze Valley operation was the participation of a large number of cadets from the modern army academy in Wuchang as well as that of many soldiers from the local forces. Many of the overseas students had acquired military training in Japan and their influence was now being felt in the Chinese army. Huang Hsing actually modelled his organization along the lines of the Japanese army. In addition to the Ko Lao Hui, which boasted of tens of thousands of members, there were about five hundred former students in the Hua Hsing Hui making it the first revolutionary movement in China dominated by this group. Moreover, their network was more extensive than in any of Sun's Cantonese operations. There was also action in Hupeh, where an affiliated organization under the cover name, The Science Study Group (*K'o-hsüeh pu-hsi so*), joined students and soldiers. Contacts were also made in Szechwan, Kiangsi, and Shanghai, where Yang Shou-jen and Chang Shih-chao acted as agents. In contrast with Sun's plots, there was no intensive

[103] Hsüeh, *Huang Hsing* [66], pp. 15–19; Lo Chia-lun, *Biography* [192], I, 128.

search for foreign assistance. There were no Europeans involved in the plot nor were funds collected from the overseas Chinese, who were overwhelmingly Cantonese and Fukienese. Gentry connections were more extensive among these groups and may have led to some financial help. Huang and Liu are said to have borrowed $50,000 to meet expenses and subsequently went bankrupt.[104]

Yet these Yangtze plotters were just as precipitous as their Cantonese predecessors and concentrated their planning upon an immediate military coup. Huang Hsing planned to attack the Hunanese capital, Changsha, on November 16, 1904, when officials would be busy celebrating the Empress Dowager's seventieth birthday. This attack was to have been the signal for simultaneous risings by his Ko Lao Hui allies in five other parts of the province.[105] But on this occasion, too, the government was forewarned by spies, and on October 24 an order was issued for Huang's arrest. After a dramatic flight from Changsha in the Sun Yat-sen manner—a disguise, the helping hand of a Christian minister—Huang made his way to Shanghai.[106]

There he encountered difficulties in connection with an entirely different episode, yet one which was still part of the student nationalist furor. During 1903, it will be recalled, the Governor of Kwangsi, Wang Chih-ch'un, had been the object of nationalist wrath for his proposal to use French troops and his alleged pro-Russian sympathies. On November 19, 1904, Wan Fu-hua, an Anhwei student connected with Yang Shou-jen and Chang Shih-chao, made an unsuccessful attempt to assassinate Wang in the International Settlement. He was caught and a number of other suspects, including Huang Hsing, were also arrested. Since he was found not to be implicated in this case, Huang was released, but the Chinese soon requested his re-arrest in connection with the Changsha plot. After fleeing to Japan, Huang and Liu

---

[104] Hsüeh, *Huang Hsing* [66], pp. 19–20; Lo Chia-lun, *Biography* [192], I, 135–136.

[105] Hsüeh, *Huang Hsing* [66], p. 19.

[106] *Ibid.*, pp. 21–23.

K'uei-i returned to the mainland in order to help Ma Fu-i, who was planning another uprising in western Hunan. An encounter with customs inspectors on the Yangtze, however, led to a gun battle and a second flight to Japan. Ma Fu-i had in the meantime been arrested, and by 1905 the Hunan student front was temporarily stalemated, while its leader was in exile.[107]

During this time things had been moving in Shanghai as well. In 1904, Kung Pao-ch'üan, a member of the Tokyo assassination corps, returned and, together with Ts'ai Yüan-p'ei and T'ao Ch'eng-chang, organized the Kuang Fu Hui (Restoration Society) in order to consolidate revolutionary work on the lower Yangtze, encompassing the provinces of Chekiang, Anhwei, and Kiangsi.[108] T'ao, a former military student from Chekiang, was the group's expert on secret societies and worked with a lodge in his native province called the Lung Hua Hui. The regulations which he drew up for this traditional secret society offer an interesting example of the methods by which the students attempted to infuse new political concepts into these moribund associations.[109] He tried to make revolution and republicanism more palatable by invoking the prestige of Confucius, whose teachings, he charged, had been twisted by the "Confucianists" who followed him.[110] This, as we know, was a popular revolutionary technique, but in addition, T'ao injected an unusual land-reform plank striking out against landlords and calling for public ownership of land.[111]

The Kuang Fu Hui leaders in Shanghai, who were in touch with the imprisoned Chang Ping-lin, planned to support Huang Hsing's projected Changsha coup with a rising of their own.

---

[107] *Ibid.*, pp. 23–25; On Wan Fu-hua, see Feng, *Reminiscences* [160], III, 109.

[108] Lo Chia-lun, *Biography* [192], I, 136. On Kung Pao-ch'üan, see Feng, *Reminiscences* [160], III, 98.

[109] The Lung-hua Hui declaration appears in *The 1911 Revolution* [167], I, 534–544. It is taken from Hirayama's *History of Chinese Secret Societies.*

[110] *Ibid.*, pp. 534–536.

[111] *Ibid.*, p. 538.

When Huang's scheme failed, they shelved their plans until a future opportunity.[112]

By the end of 1904 therefore, neither of the parallel movements was in a position to assume sole responsibility for attaining its revolutionary goals. Though the nationalist fervor of the Tokyo-Shanghai pamphleteers had not been dulled, the transition from theory to action had come too swiftly. Instead of reducing their unwieldly discourses on nationalism and republicanism into practical political formulas and creating an organization for winning mass support for these slogans, they followed the more impulsive pattern of the early Hsing Chung Hui. Even before the ink had dried on their emotional declarations, they began assembling bombs. When their plots were foiled and their attempts at assassination miscarried, they ended up as refugees in Tokyo or in Shanghai's International Settlement, and in respect to organizational cohesion and group purpose, they were no better off than the exiled leader of the Hsing Chung Hui. Moreover, neither of these groups had any contacts with the Cantonese and Fukienese *hua-ch'iao*, whose wealth was the largest potential source of revolutionary finances.

It was in the context of these student frustrations, along with Liang's recent abdication of his quasi-revolutionary position, that the fortunes of Sun Yat-sen suddenly rose. The students' penetration of the mainland had created a new base for revolutionary agitation, and their initial failure had left an opening for an older and presumably wiser hand in the art of conspiracy. Sun's reputation as a revolutionary was undisputed. When in the summer of 1904 a general amnesty of rebels was proclaimed in honor of the Empress Dowager's forthcoming birthday, there were three exceptions. Sun's name appeared along with those of K'ang and Liang as the public enemies whose crimes could never be forgiven.[113]

Sun was still in New York when the door to the students suddenly opened. Liu Ch'eng-yü informed his Hupeh friends study-

112 Hsüeh, *Huang Hsing* [66], p. 46.
113 Kuo, *Daily Record* [184], II, 1205. The amnesty was granted on June 21.

ing in Europe that they would have a chance to meet Sun as he passed through on his way back to Japan.[114] "We were feeling like a bunch of dragons without a head," recalls Chu Ho-chung, a student in Berlin, and they welcomed the idea.[115] Sun, who was out of money once more, obtained travel expenses from either Huang San-te or the European students, and on December 14, 1904, embarked for London.[116]

[114] Lo Chia-lun, *Biography* [192], I, 137–138. It is not certain whether the students were first notified when Sun was in New York or in London.

[115] Chu Ho-chung, "European T'ung Meng Hui" [157], p. 255.

[116] Yu, *Party Politics* [140], p. 31.

XII

The Founding of the T'ung Meng Hui

The year 1905 marked the point of no return in the affairs of
China. Before it was over, the oligarchy had committed itself to
a reform program which foreshadowed the end of traditional
government. This was only partly and not predominantly the
result of pressure from subversive forces represented by Sun
Yat-sen, K'ang Yu-wei, and the volatile students. Within the
power structure, realistic officials like Yüan Shih-k'ai and Chang
Chih-tung exerted their own pressure for modernization. In
memorials, they echoed and re-phrased demands which radical
reformers had been making for almost ten years. Most important,
however, was the throne's new responsiveness. Actually, the
court, urged by these same officials, had encouraged innovation
ever since the Boxer debacle. One of the results of this new
attitude was the student emigration, which now headed the
nationalist movement. By 1905 the court was prepared to make
even greater concessions. At first dictated by the requirements
of sheer survival, selective modernization had subsequently
created a chain reaction which could no longer be contained
within the traditional political and social setting. Projects involving modern industries, railroads, and the renovation of the
armed forces and the educational system had created new functions, roles, and interests, which required institutional change.
The question now was not whether China should modernize, but
how fast she should modernize, and even more pertinently,
who should direct the modernization already underway and
profit by it.

Competing with the throne and also engaging in politics at the capital were ambitious governors-general, whose real power had been revealed during the Boxer episode. There were also provincial gentry who had recently discovered a new source of wealth in modern enterprises. By 1905, this political and economic rivalry between the center of government and the provincial periphery had created the key issue in Chinese politics. The issue would be further complicated by the presence of foreign bankers with the ready cash which no one in China was able or willing to expend for large-scale industrialization and development.[1]

For its impact upon the changing mood of China, perhaps the most dramatic event of the year was Japan's victory over Russia in a war which had been fought mainly within Chinese territory.[2] For the first time in modern history, Asians had defeated a European power. To the Chinese rulers the lesson seemed clear. The Japanese monarchy, having promulgated a constitution over fifteen years earlier, had built a powerful, modern state based upon centralized power. With this example in mind, the throne responded to Yüan Shih-k'ai's memorial of July 1905 calling for the establishment of constitutional government within twelve years.[3] The Empress Dowager consented to send a commission abroad to investigate foreign constitutional systems. In August Yüan proposed the abolition of the traditional examination system and by September the throne had acted by ordering that it be terminated the following year.[4] This decree signified the end of the Confucian system. In the meantime, the provinces were exhorted to send more students to Europe and America.[5]

The circumstances therefore present a classic revolutionary situation: the bankrupt and ineffectual central government at-

[1] See Fairbank, Reischauer, and Craig, *East Asia* [40], pp. 613–631, for a summary of the late Ch'ing reform movement.

[2] Y. C. Wang, *Chinese Intellectuals* [129], p. 254.

[3] Kuo, *Daily Record* [184], II, 1231. The memorial, dated July 2, was sent by two other governors-general, Chang Chih-tung and Chou Fu, along with Yüan.

[4] Franke, *The Chinese Examination System* [42], pp. 69–71. Five other governors-general joined Yüan in sending the memorial on August 31.

[5] Kuo, *Daily Record* [184], II, 1237.

tempts to recoup its losses in power and prestige by sponsoring those changes which it had previously resisted.[6] The Manchus now hoped that, as in Japan, modernization would facilitate centralization. However, the regime's glaring weaknesses, especially its vulnerability to foreign pressure and the unprecedented financial deficit which had resulted therefrom, made the aggregation of power exceedingly difficult if not impossible. Instead of reviving imperial power, reform invited more demands upon the center. It strengthened the various foci of competition and encouraged open opposition. Moreover, as alien conquerors bent upon reinforcing their dynastic privileges, the Manchus could not easily identify themselves with the nationalist motivation for reform. They had lost prestige and power, and fundamentally they lacked the talent, the knowledge, and the inspiration to lead a national renaissance.

These weaknesses of the throne and the governmental structure as a whole were revealed in 1905. The year of reform was also a year of unusual turbulence. Nationalism, centrifugal pressures, and widespread social misery aggravated by the financial demands of a bankrupt treasury precluded orderly reform. Reports of bandit outrages, tax riots, secret society uprisings, strikes in modern mills, and anti-foreign outbursts flooded Peking.[7] Thus, orders for repressive measures and bans on subversive literature were interspersed with lofty edicts encouraging modern industry and education. Anti-foreignism, for which the government was held responsible, broke out again as economic imperialism spread to the interior. Native entrepreneurs and investors resented foreign competition and the masses found the foreigners a convenient target for their own grievances. In the summer, Chinese merchants and students launched the anti-American boycott which had been advocated in the nationalist press.[8] This protest against American exclusion laws was the first instance of the traditional boycott weapon being used as a modern, nationalist weapon. A Shanghai merchant leader declared: "When our

6 See Brinton, *The Anatomy of Revolution* [12], pp. 40–41.
7 See the items listed for 1905 in Kuo, *Daily Record* [184], II, 1219–1245.
8 See Field, "The Chinese Boycott of 1905" [41], pp. 63–98.

government proves itself unable to protest, then the people must rise up to do so."[9] In October, the massacre of five Presbyterian missionaries at Lienchow in Kwangtung further aggravated relations with America.[10]

The students overseas, the new educated elite upon whom successful reform depended, repudiated the official reform effort. In January the Tokyo students demanded that the throne grant a constitution.[11] But in September, a student nationalist, inspired by Tsou Jung's *Revolutionary Army* and Liang Ch'i-ch'ao's earlier writings, threw a bomb at the five imperial commissioners as they departed on their study tour of foreign governments.[12] The gap between revolutionary nationalists and imperial authorities had become too wide. It could no longer be bridged by hasty reform measures. The student-intellectuals had drawn their own conclusions from Japan's achievement, and before the year was over, they had the example of revolution in Russia.

In brief, this was the setting which gave Sun Yat-sen his great opportunity. By mid-1905, he had created a new revolutionary combination out of the disparate elements which no longer accepted Manchu rule under any conditions.

Sun Yat-sen was in Europe making a flank approach to the students at the beginning of this crucial year. While in London, residing in Holland Park Gardens with his British comrade-in-arms, Rowland Mulkern, Sun received money and an invitation from Chu Ho-chung and from Ho Chih-ts'ai, a student in Brussels.[13] He was met at Ostend and taken to Brussels, where he shared a student's lodgings.[14] After Chu arrived from Berlin, Sun began discussions with the five leading activists of the approximately one hundred Chinese students on the continent.[15]

[9] *Ibid.*, p. 68.
[10] *Ibid.*, pp. 87–88.
[11] Kuo, *Daily Record* [184], II, 1221.
[12] Y. C. Wang, *Chinese Intellectuals* [129], pp. 254, 300.
[13] See Ho's account in Feng, *Reminiscences* [160], II, 136; and Chu Ho-chung, "European T'ung-meng hui" [157], p. 255. Chu erroneously refers to Mulkern as Sun's "teacher."
[14] Lo Chia-lun, *Biography* [192], I, 140.
[15] This is Hsüeh's estimate in *Huang Hsing* [66], p. 37.

There was no need to argue the merits of revolution with this group. Products of the nationalist turmoil in Hupeh, Chu and his friends had in fact been "exiled" to Europe because of their extremism.[16] It was up to Sun, however, to prove his qualifications for leading the wide revolutionary movement they desired. He explained his ideas concerning nationalism, democracy, and socialism. He also unfolded his plan for a "five-power constitution."[17] This consisted of the American three-fold separation of powers plus adaptations of two traditional Chinese institutions—examination and censorial bodies. Although apparently satisfied with Sun's theoretical presentation, the students disagreed with his strategy. Chu held that the intellectuals, meaning the students, were indispensable. He argued that the subversion of the New Army, many of whose officers were returned students, provided the best chance for revolution. The successful agitation of his friend, Wu Lu-chen, an officer in the Hupeh New Army, was a case in point. Yet Sun insisted that degree-holders and officers could not make a revolution. He argued for giving priority to the secret societies and transforming them into revolutionary vehicles. Chu countered with the example of T'ang Ts'ai-ch'ang's unfortunate experience in the Hankow plot of 1900. Like other supporters of the plot, including Liang Ch'i-ch'ao, Chu had concluded that the Ko Lao Hui was entirely undependable for political action and was merely interested in plunder.[18] He also suggested that Sun's past failures were due to a lack of intellectual support. After arguing for "three days and nights" and after tentatively deciding to give equal weight to secret societies and students, Sun finally accepted the student approach. If they devoted themselves wholeheartedly to revolution, he agreed that they were fit to be leaders.[19]

16 Chu Ho-chung, "European T'ung-meng hui" [157], p. 254.

17 Lo Chia-lun, *Biography* [192], I, 140.

18 Chu Ho-chung, "European T'ung-meng hui" [157], p. 256. On the intellectuals' doubts concerning the secret societies, see Wang Te-chao, "Sun's Thought During the T"ung Meng Hui Period" [221], pp. 71–72. See Liang's letter to K'ang, November 18, 1903, in Ting, *Biography of Liang* [214], I, 190.

19 Cho Ho-chung, "European T'ung-meng hui" [157], p. 256. See also Yu, *Party Politics* [140], pp. 36–37.

No one knew better than Sun how badly student support was needed. Yet there were reasons for his seeming reluctance to offer them leadership status and for his high appraisal of secret societies. In order to emphasize his own prowess as a revolutionary leader and strategist, he had to justify the tactics which he had followed for the past ten years. At both Canton and Waichow he had made alliances with the Triads, and during the previous year, he had joined them in Hawaii and campaigned with them in America. If he could establish their importance, it would follow that he, as the Triad specialist, would be the natural supreme leader. But if the New Army were the main arena, Sun's qualifications would be inferior to those of the student activists, especially the Tokyo group. Though Sun wanted students to join him, he wanted to attract them with strength, not weakness. Despite his obvious financial troubles, he did not want to admit that he was helpless without them. Given his betrayal by the previous generation of intellectuals, Sun probably took pleasure in telling the young students that they were not as important as they thought, that the Triads and Ko Lao Hui, whom they, as gentry, had been accustomed to scorn, were equally vital to revolution. Moreover, since in Europe Sun was not yet dealing with the older and more famous student nationalists, he could take a more independent attitude and strongly assert himself as the senior revolutionary.

Yet fundamentally his presentation to the European students was characteristic of his method of reconciling heterogeneous and widely separated elements. Whenever Sun appealed to a particular group, he usually cited the importance of others which he claimed to control. He tried to prove that these other forces were gathering strength and that the addition of the new group would quickly tip the balance. What he offered each audience was a share of the triumph, which he claimed to be imminent. He told the students about the secret societies, and soon he would tell the overseas Chinese about the students as well as the secret societies. With *hua-ch'iao* money and intellectual organizers, he could promote uprisings based upon the Triads and thus attract more funds from abroad. As for the foreigners, the other group he wanted to cultivate, he had long been telling them that he

personally represented all progressive and anti-dynastic agitation, including the intellectuals and the army. The circle would
be completed when he impressed intellectuals with his foreign
connections. Despite a measure of glaring deception in this technique—Sun tended to prematurely translate anticipations into
concrete achievements—it was nevertheless true that no one else
was so persistent in pursuing such diversified contacts.

Thus, at a subsequent meeting with a larger student group in
Brussels, Sun was accepted as the leader of a new revolutionary
movement. He did not propose a name for the organization because he knew that anything accomplished in Europe would have
to be tentative and not binding. What he had to prove here was
that he could succeed in a non-Cantonese, intellectual milieu.
Above all, success in Europe could strengthen his bid for leadership in Japan. In effect, it was a dress rehearsal for his first major
role.

At this Brussels meeting, Sun took about thirty students into
what was loosely called the "Revolutionary Party."[20] He wrote
out the four-plank oath he had developed since 1903 and surprised the students with his knowledge of Chinese characters.
Until then they had believed that he was illiterate in Chinese as
K'ang Yu-wei and Liang Ch'i-ch'ao had charged.[21] He now appeared to be a man of parts. Dressed as a European, he showed
the long-gowned students that he was familiar with the latest
Western political currents. Yet he also demonstrated his expertise in secret society conspiratorial technique. He invested the
swearing-in ceremony with a host of traditional, esoteric devices,
which he had probably picked up the previous year. In dating
the oath, signed by each student on a separate sheet of paper, he
borrowed the Triad practice of using the characters *T'ien-yün*
(heavenly cycle) in place of the reign periods used in ordinary
Chinese dating. The significance of *T'ien-yün* lies in its symbolic
repudiation of the incumbent dynasty. It meant that the Manchus had lost the "Mandate of Heaven" and that a new, Chinese
cycle had been inaugurated. Sun had never used *T'ien-yün* in

20 Lo Chia-lun, *Biography* [192], I, 140.
21 *Ibid.*, p. 141.

Hsing Chung Hui documents but did so when he wrote the American Triad constitution in 1904. Sun also taught the students secret handshakes, passwords, and a catechism, all based upon Triad ritual. However, he inserted the names of his martyred followers, Lu Hao-tung and Shih Chien-ju, in place of traditional Triad heroes.[22]

After posing for a photograph with his new recruits Sun returned to London, where he gained only one student convert. Wu Chih-hui, whom he now met for the first time, still hesitated although he too joined soon after Sun's success in Tokyo.[23]

Resuming the continental campaign, Sun devoted twelve days to long discussions with Chu Ho-chung's fellow-students in Berlin. One student objected to "equalization of land rights" and another, impressed with the Prussian model upon which the German constitution was based, balked at the "five-power constitution." However, since Germany was a monarchy and therefore a less desirable model, Sun's argument prevailed. Twenty students joined, all but two of those present.[24] At his next stop, Paris, Sun enlarged upon his program and strategy. He spoke about *yüeh-fa*, the provisional constitution, which would prepare the masses for full constitutional rights. He also stressed the need for regulating capital. This, together with the "equalization of land rights" method of preventing speculation in land values, ultimately constituted his socialist program. After signing up ten students, Sun asked for funds. He said that a rising in Kwangtung-Kwangsi was imminent but that he needed money for arms. One student pledged half of his monthly government allotment, 200 francs, and others also contributed.[25] They were impressed as Sun related anecdotes of his youth and his revolutionary adventures.

Having recruited about half of the students in Europe, Sun decided that the time was ripe for returning to Japan. He had

[22] Feng, *Reminiscences* [160], II, 137. On *T'ien-yün*, see ibid., III, 208–210.

[23] Lo Chia-lun, *Biography* [192], I, 141.

[24] *Ibid.*

[25] *Ibid.*, p. 142.

definite results to show. And thanks to student generosity, he had money for the trip.[26] Yet typically, he used the opportunity to probe an additional possibility. The previous year he had written the *True Solution* for the American public; now he tried for French support. Paul Doumer, with whom he had negotiated three years previously, was no longer governor-general of French Indo-China, but it was probably through Doumer that Sun got a lead to the new governor-general as well as to the Colonial Minister.[27] While staying in a Paris hotel and awaiting the outcome of his negotiations (his improved financial situation obviated the need for sharing a student's room), Sun received a serious blow which shook his faith in the new recruits and threatened to upset all his plans for capturing the student movement.[28]

After pledging themselves to revolution, two Berlin students had misgivings and came to Paris to make amends with their government sponsors. Two other backsliders invited Sun to lunch, and during his absence, the pair from Berlin stole into Sun's room. They ripped open his briefcase and removed all the European membership pledges plus an important letter of introduction from the French government to the governor-general of Indo-China. Then they went to the Chinese minister in Paris, Sun Pao-ch'i, kotowed, confessed, and handed over the stolen documents as an expiatory gesture. To their surprise, Sun Pao-ch'i told them to return the pledges to the students and sent them on their way. The minister apparently felt that the Chinese government had enough trouble without making a scandal in France. The French document hinted that Sun had high connections, and remembering what had happened in London in 1896, the minister wanted to avoid an embroilment and possible international repercussions. Though he had the letter copied and informed Peking of its contents, he instructed a messenger

26 According to Chu, "European T'ung-meng hui" [157], p. 257, students in Belgium raised ten thousand francs. See also Feng, *Reminiscences* [160], II, 139.

27 Lo Chia-lun, *Biography* [192], I, 143.

28 On Sun's request for money for his expenses in Paris, see Chu Ho-chung, "European T'ung-meng hui" [157], p. 260.

to return the original to Sun Yat-sen.[29] This cautious, almost timid, reaction was a far cry from the audacious kidnapping plot of nine years earlier. Such was the loss in prestige and confidence which the Manchu government had suffered in the intervening years.

Meanwhile Sun assumed that the entire student group had betrayed him and that he was in serious danger. He moved to a different hotel and wrote a scathing letter to Chu Ho-chung. Chu telegraphed one of the Brussels students, who rushed to Paris and located Sun after a long search. Sun was in a bitter mood and declared that he had always known that "literati could not make a revolution" and were inferior to the secret societies. Placated when he learned that there had been only four traitors and that a new registration would be undertaken, the loss of the letter from the French government still bothered him. But at that very moment the Legation's messenger arrived returning it. Though Sun's secret negotiations were exposed, the student, Hu Ping-k'o, realized that the Legation was unwilling to take action. He in fact paid a visit to the minister, who asked whether his pledge had been returned and advised him to concentrate on studies before mixing in politics.[30]

Given a second chance, most of the students took this advice. "Are we essentially students or bandits?" asked one of the traitors and another said that they would make their own revolution without the stigma of Triad and Ko Lao Hui leadership.[31] Only fourteen renewed their membership. Among these were a third of the Brussels group, which had been the most radical from the beginning, Chu Ho-chung, two others in Berlin, and only one in Paris.[32]

By retaining the loyalty of these activists, however, Sun still achieved his major objective. He wrote Feng Tzu-yu that he had succeeded in forming a revolutionary network in London, Brus-

[29] Lo Chia-lun, *Biography* [192], I, 143.
[30] Chu Ho-chung, "European T'ung-meng hui" [157], pp. 262–263.
[31] *Ibid.*, pp. 263–264.
[32] Feng, *Reminiscences* [160], II, 139; Yu, *Party Politics* [140], pp. 37–38.

sels, Berlin, and Paris.[33] The Hupeh activists in Europe also passed the word on to their friends in Tokyo and urged them to give Sun full support.[34] The European students were in turn advised by Sun to complete their studies and get official posts under the Manchus. This would place them strategically for leading the masses when the revolution broke out. If he needed them sooner, he would wire them, though the students in Japan, he declared, were in a better position for launching the revolution.[35] Thus when he left Marseilles on the S.S. *Tonkin* on June 11, Sun was confident that he could finally capture the main student bastion in Tokyo.[36]

He also used the trip to widen his contacts. Traveling on this same ship for part of the way was Chang Jen-chieh (Chang Ching-chiang, 1876–1950), scion of a Chekiang gentry family having business interests in Shanghai. Chang had served as a commercial attaché to Sun Pao-ch'i's Paris Legation and later went into business in the French capital. Chang sympathized with the revolutionary efforts and soon became associated with an anarchist group in Paris.[37] He had heard of Sun's exploits (in fact, he may have helped convince Sun Pao-ch'i to take a lenient stand in the student escapade) and offered to subsidize the revolution.[38] Whenever Sun required money, Chang declared, all he had to do was send a wire. They arranged a code in which the letter "A" would signify a $10,000 request, "B", $20,000, etc. He was prepared to go as high as "E" or $50,000. According to Sun's reminiscences, Chang kept his promise and became one of his strongest financial supporters during the period between 1905 and 1911.[39] That a person of Chang's background was ready to invest

[33] Feng, *Reminiscences* [160], II, 147.

[34] *Ibid.*, p. 139; Chu Ho-chung, "European T'ung-meng hui" [157], p. 257.

[35] Lo Chia-lun, *Biography* [192], I, 142–143; Chu Ho-chung, "European T'ung-meng hui" [157], p. 257.

[36] See Sun's letter to Miyazaki on June 4 in Sun, *Collected Works* [205], V, pp. 27–28. Sun explained that his delay in returning to Japan was due to financial difficulties.

[37] Feng, *Reminiscences* [160], II, 227–230. See also Scalapino and Yu, *The Chinese Anarchist Movement* [100], pp. 2–3.

[38] Feng, *Reminiscences* [160], II, 139.

[39] *Ibid.*, II, 227–238; Lo Chia-lun, *Biography* [192], I, 146.

in Sun was another indication of the changes which had occurred since Sun had begun selling revolution ten years earlier.

When his ship reached Colombo, Sun wired his old friend, Yu Lieh, to arrange for a meeting with Singapore supporters. Remembering his last visit, the ill-fated expedition to K'ang Yu-wei in 1900, Sun was not sure whether he would be allowed to land. At any rate he hoped that Yu and his local recruits could visit his ship. Actually, the Singapore authorities had not issued an order of banishment against him, and Yu got police permission for Sun to leave the ship while it remained in port for one day.[40] Yu introduced him to the three *hua-ch'iao* who had helped him found the revolutionary journal, *T'u-nan jih-pao*: Ch'en Ch'u-nan, Chang Yung-fu, and Chang's nephew, Lin I-shun, a Singapore-born mission graduate.[41] There was no time for extensive discussion, but Sun told them of his success in Europe and his plans for Tokyo. This was Sun's first meeting with these wealthy merchants, and he was encouraged by their promise to support his new organization. Sun later developed this lead and turned Singapore into a major base for infiltrating the Malay Peninsula and Southeast Asia as a whole, an area which later rendered crucial financial assistance.

On July 7 his ship reached Saigon, and Sun wrote Ch'en Ch'u-nan that he found the local Chinese sponsoring reading clubs—*pao-kuan*—a sign of awakened political interest.[42] Though he had written Miyazaki that he might linger in the Nan-yang (Southeast Asian) ports, his Tokyo mission retained precedence and he kept to his original schedule. He arrived in Yokohama on July 19, 1905.[43]

Like their European counterparts, the Tokyo activists were looking for someone to organize the final push against the Man-

---

[40] Lo Chia-lun, *Biography* [192], I, 145–146. According to this source, Sun thought that there was a five-year banishment order against him in Singapore.

[41] On Lin, see Feng, *Reminiscences* [160], I, 175–178. During the *Su-pao* episode in the summer of 1903, Lin distributed copies of Tsou Jung's *Revolutionary Army* in Kwangtung and Fukien.

[42] See Sun's letter of July 7 to Ch'en in Sun's, *Collected Works* [205], V, 28.

[43] Lo Chia-lun, *Biography* [192], I, 147.

chu dynasty. Sun's record was known to most of them, and Feng Tzu-yu and Miyazaki, with whom he had corresponded while abroad, paved the way for a triumphant return. However, at a time when Japanese prestige was soaring, it was Miyazaki's intervention on behalf of his comrade and protégé which was decisive. The day Sun landed in Yokohama, Sung Chiao-jen, who with his fellow-Hunanese, Huang Hsing, carried the most weight with the students, visited Miyazaki. Ch'eng Chia-ch'eng, the Anhwei student who had previously been attracted to Sun, accompanied Sung. Eight years before, Miyazaki himself had anxiously waited for his first glimpse of this Chinese hero, and now he told Sung of the treat which was in store for him. Sun Yat-sen, he declared, was a leader with an "enlightened mind" and "pure ambition" and was unmatched in the entire world. Thinking of the great opportunity which lay before them, Miyazaki expressed regret at not being Chinese.[44]

When Sun arrived in Tokyo, anxious to meet key student leaders, Miyazaki first took him to Huang Hsing with whom he quickly established rapport. The two engaged in a long discussion of their common interest, revolution. On July 28, Miyazaki again accompanied Sun for a meeting with Huang and his lieutenants, Sung and Ch'en T'ien-hua, at the offices of *Twentieth Century China*, the newly formed journal of the Hunanese nationalists.[45] After the Hunanese activities had been outlined, including the Changsha plot of 1904, Sun discussed his own strategy.

His main thesis was that the anti-dynastic effort must be unified. Separate risings by isolated provincial groups would not only lead into the chaotic interregnum which usually followed dynastic overthrows, but would offer foreigners a pretext for intervening and partitioning China. Sun had long foreseen the danger of an internecine power-struggle and had discussed it with Miyazaki at their first meeting in 1897. In 1905 he again

---

[44] Hsüeh, *Huang Hsing* [66], p. 40; Lo Chia-lun, *Biography* [192], I, 147–148.

[45] The magazine had been founded on June 3, 1905. See Yu, *Party Politics* [140], p. 47. Kuo, *Daily Record* [184], II, 1231, gives June 25.

argued that the foreign threat could be neutralized by a concerted, decisive blow against the dynasty. As in Europe, Sun also stressed the growing belligerency of his own bailiwick, Kwangtung-Kwangsi. He pointed out that the secret societies of Kwangsi had been battling the Manchu armies for over ten years and were as yet unquelled. These Triads, he declared, had tremendous destructive power, but without intellectuals they lacked adequate leadership. Hinting at his own special standing with these fighters, Sun said that they had tried to contact him in Hong Kong during the last year, but being in America, he could not respond. This, according to Sun, was where the students came in. If they united, they could inject positive values into the destructive upsurge of the Triad masses. As leaders guiding the secret societies, they would ensure that revolution would lead to the establishment of "civilized government."[46] In other words, Sun was proposing to continue with the strategy of the Hsing Chung Hui and to extend and intensify it with the addition of a larger, more effective, intellectual echelon.

As to the relative importance of secret societies and intellectuals, the Brussels debate was repeated, and for the same reason.[47] Though Sung Chiao-jen and his friends convinced him that the intellectuals were the key factor, Sun made his point: the secret societies would be the operative force through which the students would exert their influence.

Unity of course meant acceptance of Sun's leadership, and the Hunanese took time out for a discussion among themselves the next day. Ch'en favored complete amalgamation and Huang Hsing proposed a formal alliance with Sun while retaining the "unique spiritual characteristics" of their own organization, the Hua Hsing Hui. Others had even greater reservations, and it was finally decided that each individual should choose for himself.[48]

[46] Sung Chiao-jen, *My Diary* [210], pp. 68–69. See also Hsüeh, *Huang Hsing* [66], pp. 40–41.

[47] See Wang Te-chao, "Sun's Thought During the T'ung Meng Hui Period" [221], I, 74, for an account of this argument, which may not have taken place at this first meeting but at a subsequent discussion in 1905.

[48] Sung Chiao-jen, *My Diary* [210], p. 69; Hsüeh, *Huang Hsing* [66], pp. 41-42.

But their most influential leaders were already swinging in Sun's direction.

A larger meeting was held with Sun the next day, July 30. Huang, Sung, Ch'eng Chia-ch'eng, and Feng Tzu-yu notified their friends and the news rapidly circulated among the militants, who represented every province in China except Kansu, which had not yet sent any students abroad. Seventy students gathered in Uchida Ryōhei's home, which also served as an office of the Black Dragon Society. The location of the meeting and the presence of Miyazaki, Uchida, and Suenaga Setsu were visible proof of Sun's Japanese support.[49]

The procedure followed the pattern developed by Sun in Europe. After he made a lengthy presentation, other speakers followed and the meeting approved Sun's call for a new organization.[50] The name finally chosen was Chung-kuo T'ung Meng Hui (Chinese United League). Since T'ung Meng Hui was a common secret society name, the choice reflected Sun's preference for a secret society model.[51] Sun then proposed the membership oath, which, except for minor changes in wording, was the same that he had recently introduced in Europe. The first three goals, "expulsion of the Manchus, restoration of Chinese rule, and the establishment of a republic," encountered no opposition. But as in Europe, Sun's fourth plank, "equalization of land rights," required further elucidation before being accepted. Huang Hsing, the junior partner in the merger which Sun had proposed, called for volunteers to sign the oath. With Miyazaki supplying the paper, Ts'ao Ya-po, a recent arrival from Hunan, took the lead and others followed suit. Again as in Europe, Sun taught each member the conspiratorial paraphernalia, handshakes and pass-words, which he had adopted from the Triads. The Triad custom of using the characters *T'ien-yün* was

[49] Hsüeh, *Huang Hsing* [66], pp. 42–43; Jansen, *Sun Yat-sen* [69], p. 118. On Suenaga, a Fukuoka *shishi*, see Jansen, p. 242, note 27.

[50] Accounts of this meeting appear in Lo Chia-lun, *Biography* [192], I, 142–150; Hsüeh, *Huang Hsing* [66], pp. 42–43; and Yu, *Party Politics* [140], pp. 42–43.

[51] Comber, *Chinese Secret Societies* [27], p. 270.

likewise retained in dating the oaths.[52] A committee was chosen to draft regulations, and election of officers was postponed until the next meeting, which would be considered the formal inauguration of the new organization. However, in a practical sense the movement was already launched according to the format proposed by Sun Yat-sen. In addition to having his slogans accepted, he had also fastened on his favorite Triad symbols.

In the meantime, Sun's new comrades arranged a large student celebration in his honor. On August 13, over seven hundred students filled a Japanese restaurant and hundreds pushed at the doors to give him a rousing welcome.[53] This was Sun's first public appearance in Tokyo, and he fascinated his audience with a display of nationalist rhetoric.[54]

Sun took social progress as his major theme and discussed its application to China. He said that he had seen all of the modern world as well as its now decadent predecessors—Greece, Rome, and Egypt. He had learned that change was the law of life. Some countries changed sooner, others later, like Japan and Russia. Though for many years his call for a nationalist awakening had been directed toward the secret societies, his reception in Tokyo indicated that it had now penetrated the middle and upper classes (from which the students stemmed). The students' new interest proved that China was still alive and ready for change.[55]

In plotting the pace and direction of China's future progress, Sun claimed that nothing less than the highest and most advanced form of government was within her reach. This was so, he argued, first of all because of her innate capacities. Her civilization was much older than that of the Aryan race; her territory was immense. One province, Szechwan, was larger than Japan, and her population was the largest in the world, greater than Russia's or America's and greater than all of Western Europe put together. The second reason was that she already possessed

[52] Feng, *Reminiscences* [160], III, 209.

[53] Lo Chia-lun, *Biography* [192], I, 150–151.

[54] I have used both versions of this speech which appear in Sun, *Collected Works* [205], III, 1–6; and 6–8.

[55] *Ibid.*, pp. 1, 6.

the potential leaders who were capable of transplanting the most modern European institutions from abroad. In Japan, at the time of the Meiji Restoration, there was only a relatively small number of "men of determination" (*shishi*) to provide the motive force for change. In China, however, acknowledgement of foreign material advantages was much more widespread. If the students assumed the responsibility and chose superior models from abroad, China could easily outstrip Japan. What Japan accomplished in thirty years China could achieve in twenty or even fifteen years. Japan, Sun asserted, had to undergo a "natural progress," but China was capable of achieving "artificial progress."[56]

To those who claimed that progress nevertheless had to be sequential and that republicanism had to be deferred until the realization of the intermediate stage of constitutional monarchy, Sun repeated the locomotive analogy which he had used in Hawaii. As with mechanical devices, so with government it was not necessary to recapitulate all the stages of invention and improvement. Everyone else had borrowed from whatever models had been superior and then went on to improve them. Japan had begun by using the once superior Chinese model and later adopted European examples. America, with only "a hundred-year old civilization," learned from England and became the "fatherland of republics." Only recently, Sun declared, America had been a wilderness, but at the St. Louis Exposition of the previous year, he had seen proof of her material achievements which left Europe far behind. If the gradualist argument were true, Sun asserted, Chinese patriots could not even hope to emulate the Hawaiians and the American Negroes. A hundred years ago, he declared, the Hawaiians were head-hunters but through contact with foreigners they made a "leap from savagery" and became a republic. The same was true of the Negro slaves who had recently become a free people.[57]

In referring to foreign affairs, Sun spoke in the ultra-nationalist vein which he reserved for Chinese audiences. He argued that if the Chinese proved their vigor and belligerency

[56] *Ibid.*, pp. 2–4; 7.
[57] *Ibid.*, pp. 4–5.

by overthrowing the Manchus, foreigners would no longer dare infringe upon their sovereignty. Given China's intrinsic physical strength, foreigners would fear and respect them. He pointed out that the current anti-American boycott had not only terrified the United States but all the Western Countries. And if they "tremble" when the Chinese have been only slightly aroused, "how much more so if we were greatly aroused!"[58]

In this first major appearance in Tokyo, Sun captured the mood of young China. His optimism, his appeal to elemental nationalist feelings, and his repudiation of half-way, moderate solutions struck a responsive chord among youngsters who had no patience for learned discourses on China's backwardness and vulnerability. Neither Yen Fu nor Liang Ch'i-ch'ao with their concern for universal laws of evolution or for the preponderance of foreign power could promise the quick restoration of Chinese greatness. This was exactly what Sun supplied. His theory of "artificial progress" postulated that China, with her unique heritage and latent power, could take a unique path, and progress so fast that soon the rest of the globe would sit at her feet. He promised that the world would once more have to learn from the Chinese model.[59]

Above all, Sun's theories gratified the elitist aspirations of young men whose families had ruled traditional China. All of China's problems, inadequate education of the masses, institutional barriers, the foreign threat, would be swept aside by "men of determination" whose intervention would change the course of Chinese and world history. This was the role which Sun offered to the students, who greeted his speech with a tremendous ovation. And again, the speeches of two Japanese "men of determination," Miyazaki and Suenaga, endorsed his claim to speak for an awakened China.[60]

The rest was a formality. A week later, August 20, the T'ung Meng Hui was officially established at a large meeting at the

[58] *Ibid.*, p. 3.
[59] *Ibid.*, p. 5. The contrast between Sun and Yen is illustrated by their conversation in London in 1905. See Schwartz, *Yen Fu and the West* [105], pp. 146–147.
[60] Lo Chia-lun, *Biography* [192], I, 151.

home of Sakamoto Kinya, a member of the Japanese Diet who had interests in Chinese coal mines.[61] Sun's triumph was confirmed with his election as *Tsung-li* (director) of the organization. Over three hundred members were sworn in. Again there were some doubts concerning "equalization of land rights," which perhaps sounded too much like agrarian reform. But Sun won acceptance of this land-value taxation scheme which was in accord with his determination to surpass Europe, not merely emulate her. The group accepted Huang Hsing's draft regulations and chose over thirty officers to head three departments, which were modelled after the three branches of the American government. Tokyo was designated the headquarters, and branches were to be set up in Chinese provinces under five regional offices. The Hunanese offered their own magazine, *Twentieth Century China*, as the organ of the new party. Thus the T'ung Meng Hui was groping toward all the attributes of a modern political party—a hierarchical structure, a program, a propaganda arm, and a plan for action.[62]

For the first time in his life, Sun commanded the manpower and talent for an organized, national political effort. As he attained his goal, few of his old Hsing Chung Hui comrades shared power with him. The T'ung Meng Hui was a student-intellectual movement, and only those of his colleagues, like Feng Tzu-yu, who had participated in the student ferment joined the leadership. Sun's new lieutenants came mostly from the former Hua Hsing Hui, whose leaders, Huang Hsing and Sung Chiao-jen, had given decisive approval to his call for unity. Soon the other parallel organization, the Kuang Fu Hui, also joined. By 1906, almost one thousand recruits had signed Sun's oath, and of these, close to nine hundred were in Tokyo.[63] Though the total student population was then as high as 15,000, the T'ung Meng Hui claimed the loyalty of the most politically conscious and national-

---

[61] Jansen, *Sun Yat-sen* [69], pp. 118, 251, note 39.

[62] On the organization and composition of the T'ung Meng Hui, see Hsüeh, *Huang Hsing* [66], pp. 43–48; and Yu, *Party Politics* [140], pp. 43–49.

[63] Hsüeh, *Huang Hsing* [66], p. 44.

ist elements. The leading figures in the rise of militant nationalism since 1900, intellectuals like Chang Ping-lin, Ch'en T'ien-
hua, Yang Shou-jen, Chang Chi, Ts'ai Yüan-p'ei, Wu Chih-hui,
veterans of the *Su-pao* case and a dozen other clashes with the
authorities, joined its ranks. Hundreds of returned students
eventually spread the revolutionary message throughout China
and infiltrated the modern educational and military institutions
which the government was creating. At the same time, Sun
retained and expanded his influence in Hong Kong and the
treaty ports, in the Nan-yang as well as in more distant *hua-
ch'iao* communities.

Thus in 1905, the year the dynasty embarked upon reform, the
nationalist, revolutionary alternative had found its leader. Sun
Yat-sen finally wore the mantle which he had claimed for over
ten years. If he were to accomplish no more, he had made his
mark in history as one of the few peasant-born leaders of Chinese
intellectuals. However, the conditions under which he was accepted and the nature of his leadership deserve further consideration.

What is most striking is the suddenness with which Sun
achieved his triumph in 1905. For years when he had been in
nearby Yokohama, Sun had rarely ventured into the student
camp. Now he burst into Tokyo like a whirlwind. Only ten
days after his arrival, prominent student leaders, who had just
met him for the first time, agreed to accept his command. In a
matter of days, if not hours, a political community discovered
a leader. The swiftness of Sun's acceptance, after the briefest personal contact and deliberation, testifies to his force of personality.

The quick decision also reflected the sense of urgency which
prevailed among the young intellectuals. They were in a desperate hurry for action and chose a leader who fit their mood. And
they chose him mainly because of his reputation as a revolutionary strategist and tactician. Endorsement by the Japanese, the
recommendations of their friends in Europe, and Sun's impressive performance in Tokyo confirmed what they had been hearing for years, namely, that this was a man whose life was dedicated
to revolutionary action. And when they discovered that he was

not the illiterate ruffian that they had assumed, there was no reason for lengthy deliberation. They wanted a job done and here was the man with the contacts and tools and confidence to perform it. If he mentioned the anti-American boycott, he had merchant friends in Hong Kong who were in the midst of the agitation.[64] If he spoke of the Triads, he had been working with them for a decade. Not only was he ten to fifteen years older than most of the student leaders, but he had been fighting the dynasty longer and more openly than anyone else. No one had so thoroughly canvassed the wide spectrum of potential anti-Manchu forces.

Most important, Sun possessed the one attribute which was crucial to student calculations. They not only wanted a swift revolution but one which would forestall foreign intervention. Fear of the foreigners was uppermost in their minds as they prepared for a showdown with the dynasty. We have already seen that the initial wave of nationalist fervor had been stimulated by anti-imperialism. Now, however, priority was given to anti-Manchuism in the hope that a direct clash with foreigners could be avoided or postponed until China was stronger. It was therefore important that revolution should somehow gain respectability in foreign eyes, that it should proceed so smoothly and efficiently that foreigners would have no pretext for intervening. This was the line which Sun took in his first meeting with the Hunanese. Moreover, Sun was the only revolutionary leader who could speak with authority concerning foreign attitudes. The students only knew Japan. But Sun, as he so strongly emphasized, had been all over the world including Europe and America and their colonies and territories. If anyone could possibly provide the "civilized" or respectable image which the revolutionists hoped to project overseas, it was Sun Yat-sen. Earlier, rejection by the literati had hastened Sun's overtures to foreigners. At this point, his acceptance by intellectuals was largely predicated upon his reputed aptitude for foreign relations.

[64] Li Yü-t'ang, father of Li Tzu-chung, was one of the leaders in the boycott in Hong kong. Ho Kai and Ch'en Shao-pai were also involved. See Feng, *Reminiscences* [160], I, 70; *ibid.*, III, 230.

Therefore, the leadership which Sun attained in 1905 was highly conditional. It was not the kind of ideal intellectual leadership which claimed the full respect of these heirs to the Confucian literary tradition. The young intellectuals chose Sun not so much for his knowledge as for his assumed competency in action. This was entrepreneurial leadership in the sense that the leader provides no original ideas, only the means for achieving what everyone feels is required. Though the T'ung Meng Hui adopted his slogans, its student members did not have to learn about nationalism and democracy from Sun Yat-sen. And those ideological innovations in which he took pride, the land-value taxation method of achieving socialism and the "five-power constitution," were the ones which evoked the least enthusiasm.

Though Sun's lack of ideological authority can only be demonstrated adequately in a subsequent study treating the T'ung Meng Hui in action, it is sufficient to point out that less than two months after its formation, Sun was again traveling to Hanoi and Singapore in search of funds while his new lieutenants launched the ideological struggle with Liang Ch'i-ch'ao and the constitutional monarchists.[65] Sun had assured his followers that the three revolutions, nationalist, republican, and social, could be carried out simultaneously. While they debated this theory with his rivals, Sun discharged the practical, conspiratorial tasks for which he had been chosen. Even so, the students' doubts, in both Europe and Tokyo, of the secret societies' importance indicate that they were not wholly enthused about Sun's strategy but were merely giving it a trial.

Finally, the fragility of this leadership resulted from its having promised too much. The leader's authority was subject to his ability to produce fast results. But given Sun's social disability, his personality, and his style, there were no other terms under which he could assume command. These terms were demanded both by his self-confidence and by his vulnerability.

This bond of leadership eventually had to meet more than the demands of the anti-Manchu struggle. In China, as in revolutionary situations elsewhere, a distinction was made between

---

[65] Lo Chia-lun, *Biography* [192], I, 155.

the active process of revolution and the final seizure of power. As noted earlier in this chapter, officially sanctioned reform had spawned new political and economic interests which were not yet overtly revolutionary. However, the new competitors with dynastic power—local gentry and militarist politicians—were in strategic positions for the contest over the fruits of revolution. They were to provide the severest test of Sun Yat-sen's prestige and authority in the next phase of his career.

Glossary
Bibliography
Index

Glossary

Ai-kuo nü-hsüeh　愛國女學

Ai-kuo hsüeh-she　愛國學社

Chang Chi　張繼

Chang Chih-tung　張之洞

Chang Ching-lu　張静廬

Chang Huang-ch'i　張篁溪

Chang Jen-chieh (Chang
　Ching-chiang)　張人傑 (張静江)

Chang Nan　張枏

Chang P'eng-yüan　張朋園

Chang Ping-lin (Chang
　T'ai-yen)　章炳麟 (章太炎)

Chang Shih-chao　章士釗

Chang Yin-huan　張蔭桓

Chang Yung-fu　張永福

Chang Yü-ying　張於英

Ch'ao-chou　潮州

Che-chiang ch'ao　浙江潮

Chen-lung　鎮隆

Ch'en Ch'ien-ch'iu　陳千秋

Ch'en Ch'ing　陳清

Ch'en Chiung-ming　陳炯明

Ch'en-chou　辰州

Ch'en Ch'u-nan　陳楚楠

Ch'en Ch'un-sheng　陳春生

Ch'en Chung-yao　陳仲堯

Ch'en Fan　陳範

Ch'en Hsi-ch'i　陳錫祺

Ch'en I-k'an　陳儀侃

Ch'en Nan　陳南

Ch'en Pai-sha　陳白沙

Ch'en Shao-pai　陳少白

Ch'en She　陳涉

Ch'en T'ien-hua　陳天華

Ch'en Ting　陳鼎

Ch'en T'ing-wei　陳廷威

Ch'en Tsai-chih　陳載之

Ch'en Ts'ui-fen　陳粹芬

Cheng An　鄭安

Cheng Ch'eng-kung (Koxinga)
　鄭成功

Cheng Kuan-i　鄭貫一

Cheng Kuan-ying　鄭觀應

Cheng Shih-liang　鄭士良

Cheng Tsao-ju　鄭藻如

Ch'eng Chia-ch'eng　程家檉

Ch'eng K'uei-kuang　程奎光

Ch'eng Pi-kuang　程璧光

Ch'eng Yao-ch'en　程耀臣

Chi I-hui　戢翼翬

ch'i-i　起義

Ch'i-lieh　奇列

Ch'i-lieh yang-hang　奇列洋行

Ch'i-pu wei-yüan　緝捕委員

Chia　嘉

Chia-ting (Kiating)　嘉定

Chiang Kai-shek (Chiang
　Chieh-shih)　蔣介石

Chiang-su　江蘇

Chiang Wei-ch'iao　蔣維喬

Chiang Ya-erh　江亞二

Ch'ien-heng hang　乾亨行

Chih-hsin pao　知新報

Chih Kung T'ang　致公堂

Chih-shuo　直説

Chin Ch'ung-chi　金沖及

Chin P'ing-ou　金平歐

chin-shih　進士

Chin Sung-ts'en　金松岑

Ch'in Li-shan　秦力山

Ch'in Yü-liu　秦毓鎏

Ching-chung jih-pao　警鐘日報

Ching-hai ts'ung-pao　鏡海叢報

Ching-hu　鏡湖

Ch'ing　清

Ch'ing-i pao　清議報

Ch'ing-nien Hui　青年會

Ch'iu Feng-chia　邱逢甲

Ch'iu shu　訄書

Ch'iu Shu-yüan　邱菽園

Ch'iu Ssu　丘四

Chou Fu　周馥

Chou Hung-jan　周弘然

Chu Ch'i　朱淇

Chu Ho-chung　朱和中

chu-hsi　主席

Chu Hsi　朱熹

Chu Hsiang　朱湘

Chu Kuei-ch'üan　朱貴全

chu-sheng　諸生

Chu Yüan-chang　朱元璋

Ch'u-pao an-liang　除暴安良

Chung-ho t'ang　中和堂

Chung-hsi hsüeh-hsiao　中西學校

Chung-hsi jih-pao　中西日報

Chung-hua ko-ming chün
　中華革命軍

Chung Kun Ai
　(see Chung Kung-yü)

Chung Kung-yü (Chung
　Kun Ai)　鐘工宇

Chung-kuo ho-chung cheng-fu
　she-hui　中國合眾政府社會

Chung-kuo jih-pao　中國日報

Chung-kuo mi-shih　中國秘史

Chün kuo-min chiao-yü hui
　軍國民教育會

Chung-kuo pai-hua pao　中國白話報

Chung-kuo T'ung Meng Hui
　中國同盟會

Chung-shan　中山

chung-tsu　種族

Ch'ü Feng-ch'ih　區鳳墀

chü-jen　舉人

Chüeh-min　覺民

ch'üan　權

erh mao-tzu 二毛子
Fan Wen-lan 范文瀾
Feng Ching-ju 馮鏡如
Feng Kuei-fen 馮桂芬
Feng-ling 鳳凌
Feng Tzu-yu 馮自由
Fu-jen wen-she 輔仁文社
fu-kuo ch'iang-ping 富國強兵
Fu Ping-ch'ang 傅秉常
Fu-yu shan-t'ang 富有山堂
Fukumoto Nichinan 福本日南
Genyōsha 玄洋社
Gotō Shimpei 後藤新平
Hai-feng 海豐
Han-chien 漢奸
Han-sheng 漢聲
Haraguchi Bunichi 原口聞一
He-ch'in 赫欽
Hei-nu yo-t'ien lu 黑奴籲天錄
Heng-chou 衡州
Hino Kumazō 日野熊藏
Hiraoka Kōtarō 平岡浩太郎
Hirayama Shū 平山周
Ho Ch'ang-ch'ing 何長清
Ho Chih-ts'ai 賀之才
Ho-chung cheng-chih 合衆政治
ho-chung cheng-fu 合衆政府
Ho Fu-t'ang 何福堂
Ho Hsiang-ning 何香凝
Ho Kai (Ho Ch'i) 何啓
Ho K'uan 何寬
Ho Shu-ling 何樹齡
Ho Tung (Sir Robert
　Ho Tung) 何東
Ho Yu 何祐

Hou Ai-ch'üan 侯艾泉
hsi-wen 檄文
Hsiang-shan 香山
hsiao-ch'ou 小醜
Hsiao Kung-ch'üan 蕭公權
hsien-ch'eng 縣丞
Hsin-an 新安
Hsin cheng chen-ch'üan 新政眞詮
Hsin Chung-kuo pao 新中國報
Hsin-hsüeh wei-ching k'ao
　新學僞經考
Hsin Hu-nan 新湖南
Hsin Kwang-tung 新廣東
Hsin-min ts'ung-pao 新民叢報
Hsin-wen pao 新聞報
Hsing Chung Hui 興中會
Hsing Han Hui 興漢會
Hsü Chih-ch'en 許直臣
Hsü Ch'in 徐勤
Hsü Chün-mien 徐君勉
Hsü Ta 徐達
hsün-cheng 訓政
Hsün-huan jih-pao 循環日報
Hu Chang 胡璋
Hu Feng-chang 胡鳳璋
Hu Han-min 胡漢民
Hu I-sheng 胡毅生
Hu Li-yüan (U Lai-un)
　(Hu I-nan) 胡禮垣 （胡翼南）
Hu-pei hsüeh-sheng·chieh
　湖北學生界
Hu Pin 胡濱
Hu Ping-k'o 胡秉柯
Hu Sheng-wu 胡繩武
Hu Shih 胡適

hua-ch'iao　華僑
Hua Hsing Hui　華興會
Hua-tzu jih-pao　華字日報
Huang Chung-yang　黃中央
Huang Fu　黃福
Huang Fu-luan　黃福鑾
Huang Hsing　黃興
Huang Hsü-sheng　黃旭昇
Huang Lung-sheng　黃隆生
Huang San-te　黃三德
Huang Sheng (Wong Shing)　黃勝
Huang Ti Hun　黃帝魂
Huang Yao-t'ing　黃耀庭
Huang Yung-shang (Wong Wing-sheung)　黃詠商
Hui-chou (Waichow)　惠州
hui-tang　會黨
Hui-yang　惠陽
Hung Ch'üan-fu　洪全福
Hung Hsiu-ch'üan　洪秀全
hung-kun　洪棍（紅棍）
Hung-men　洪門
i　義
I-ching　易經
I-hsing Hui　義興會
I-shu hui-pien　譯書彙編
i tai chao　衣帶詔
I-yen　易言
Ichiko Chūzō　市古宙三
Idogawa Tatsuzō　井戶川辰三
Inukai Ki (Tsuyoshi)　犬養毅
Itagaki Taisuke　板垣退助
Itō Hirobumi　伊藤博文
jen　仁

Jen-han　任厂
Jen-kung　任公
jen-tao　人道
K'ai-chih lu　開智錄
K'ai-p'ing　開平
Kaji Ryūichi　嘉治隆一
kakumei　革命
Kang-i　剛毅
K'ang Kuang-jen　康廣仁
K'ang sheng　康聖
K'ang Yu-wei　康有為
Kao-chou　高州
Kiating (see Chia-ting)
Kitamura　北村
Kiyofuji Kōshichirō　清藤幸七郎
Kōbun　弘文
Ko-chih shu-yüan　格致書院
ko-jen ch'üan-li　個人權利
Ko Lao Hui　哥老會
ko-ming　革命
Ko-ming chün　革命軍
Ko-ming Tang　革命黨
Kodama Gentarō　兒玉源太郎
Kokumin Shimbun　國民新聞
Kōtoku Shūsui (Kōtoku Den-jirō)　幸德秋水（幸德傳次郎）
K'o hsüeh pu-hsi so　科學補習所
Kuan-tzu　管子
Kuan Yü　關羽
Kuang fang-yen kuan　廣方言館
kuang-fu　光復
Kuang-fu Hui　光復會
Kuang-hsü　光緒
K'uang Hua-t'ai (Walter N. Fong)　鄺華汰（泰）

K'uang Ju-p'an 鄺汝盤
Kuei-shan 歸善
Kung Chao-yüan 龔照瑗
Kung Pao-ch'üan 龔寶銓
kung-sheng 貢生
kung-shih 貢士
kuo-min 國民
Kuo-min jih-jih pao 國民日日報
Kuo-min pao 國民報
Kuomintang 國民黨
Kuo T'ing-i 郭廷以
Kwang-chou-wan 廣州灣
Kwangtung 廣東
Lai Hsin-hsia 來新夏
Lan T'ien-wei 藍天蔚
Li Ch'ang 李昌
Li Chi-t'ang 李紀堂
Li Ch'i 李杞
Li Chia-ch'ao 李家焯
Li-chih Hui 勵志會
Li Chih-sheng 李植生
Li Han-chang 李翰章
Li Hung-chang 李鴻章
Li Li-t'ing 李立亭
Li-pu 禮部
Li Sheng-to 李盛鐸
Li Tzu-chung 李自重
Li Wen-hai 李文海
Li Yü-t'ang 李煜堂
Li Yün-piao 李雲彪
Liang Ch'i-ch'ao 梁啓超
Liang-kwang 兩廣
Liang Mu-kuang 梁慕光
Liang T'ieh-chün 梁鐵君
Liang Yin-nan (Liang Yum-nam) 梁蔭南
Liao Chung-k'ai 廖仲愷
Liao P'ing-tzu 廖平子
Lien Ta-ch'eng 練達成
likin 釐金
Lin Hsieh 林懈
Lin I-shun 林義順
Lin Kuei 林圭
Lin Shu 林紓
Lin Tse-hsü 林則徐
Lin Wen-ch'ing (Lim Boon Keng) 林文慶
Ling-nan 嶺南
Liu Ch'eng-yü 劉成禺
Liu Chin-chou 劉錦州
Liu Hsiang 劉祥
Liu Hsüeh-hsün 劉學詢
Liu K'uei-i 劉揆一
Liu K'un-i 劉坤一
Liu Li-ch'uan 劉麗川
Liu Shih-p'ei 劉師培
Liu Ta-nien 劉大年
Liu Yung-fu 劉永福
Lo Chia-lun 羅家倫
Lo Feng-lu 羅豐祿
Lo Hsiang-lin 羅香林
Lo Kang 羅剛
Lu-feng 陸豐
Lu Hao-tung 陸皓東
Lu Hsün 魯迅
Lu Mu-chen 盧慕貞
lu-shih 戮尸
Lung-chi pao 隆記報
Lung Hua Hui 龍華會
Lung-t'ou 龍頭

Lung Tse-hou (Lung Chi-chih)
龍澤厚（龍積之）

lü-lin 綠林

Ma Chün-wu 馬君武

Ma Fu-i 馬福益

Ma-lung-t'ou-shan 馬籠頭山

Mai Meng-hua 麥夢華

Mao Tse-tung 毛澤東

Mao Wen-ming 毛文明

Mei-li-chien ho-chung-kuo
美利堅合衆國

Mei-lin 梅林

men 汶

Meng hui-t'ou 猛回頭

min-ch'üan 民權

min-kuo 民國

Min-pao 民報

min-tsu chien-kuo chu-i
民族建國主義

Ming 明

Miyazaki Tamizō 宮崎民藏

Miyazaki Torazō (Tōten)
宮崎寅藏 （滔天）

Miyazaki Yazō 宮崎彌藏

Nakano Tokujirō 中野德次郎

Nakayama 中山

Nan-hai 南海

Nan-t'ou 南頭

Nan Yang 南洋

Nan-yang kung-hsüeh
南洋公學

Narita Yasuteru 成田安輝

neng 能

*Niju Seiki no Kaibutsu Teikoku
Shugi* 廿世紀之怪物帝國主義

Nippon Maru 日本丸

Niu Yung-chien 鈕永建

Nozawa Yutaka 野澤豐

Nung-kung 農功

Nunobiki Maru 布引丸

O-shih ching-wen 俄事警聞

Ōkuma Shigenobu 大隈重信

Ou Ch'ü-chia 歐榘甲

Ozaki Yukio 尾崎行雄

Ozaki Yukimasa 尾崎行昌

pai-hua 白話

Pai-mang-hua 白芒花

pai-shan 白扇

pai-tsei 白賊

Pao-an (Powan) 保安

Pao-an 寶安

pao-chiao 保教

Pao Huang Hui 保皇會

pao-kuan 報館

Pao Kuo Hui 保國會

Pao-yang, mieh-Man 保洋滅滿

P'ei-ying shu-yüan 培英書院

Peng-kang hsü 崩岡墟

P'eng P'ai 彭湃

Pi Yung-nien 畢永年

pien-fa 變法

pien-ko 變革

p'ing-chih chang-ch'eng
平治章程

p'ing-chün ti-ch'üan 平均地權

Po K'ang Yu-wei cheng-chien shu
駁康有爲政見書

Po-li-hsi-t'ien-te 伯理璽天德

Po-lo 博羅

Po Pao-huang pao shu 駁保皇報書

Sado Maru 佐渡丸

Sakamoto Kinya 阪本金彌

Samchautin (See San-chou-t'ien)

San-chou-t'ien (Samchautin)
三洲田

San-to-chu 三多祝

Sanetō Keishū 實藤惠秀

Sanjū-sannen no yume
三十三年の夢

Sha-wan 沙灣

Sham Chun (see Shen-ch'üan)

shan-huo yü-min 煽惑愚民

Shen Chin (Shen K'e-ch'eng)
沈藎 （沈克誠）

Shen-ch'üan 深圳

Shen Hsiang-yün 沈翔雲

Sheng-chiao shu-lou 聖教書樓

Sheng Hsuan-huai 盛宣懷

Sheng-shih wei-yen 盛世危言

Shih-ch'i 石歧

Shih Chien-ju 史堅如

Shih K'o-fa 史可法

Shih-wu hsüeh-t'ang 時務學堂

Shih-wu pao 時務報

shishi 志士

Shuang-men-ti 雙門底

Shun 舜

Shun-pao (Shen-pao) 申報

Shun-te 順德

Soejima Taneomi 副島種臣

Soong, Charley (see Sung
Yüeh-ju)

Ssu-t'u Nan-ta 司徒南達

Su Fu-sheng 蘇復生

Su-pao 蘇報

Suenaga Setsu 末永節

Sugawara Den 菅原傳

Sui-yao pi-chi 隨帕筆記

Sun Ch'iu-sheng 孫秋生

Sun Mei 孫眉

Sun Pao-ch'i 孫寶琦

Sun Ta-ch'eng 孫達成

Sun Ts'ui-ch'i 孫翠溪

Sun Ti-hsiang 孫帝象

Sun Wen 孫文

Sun Yat-sen (Sun I-hsien)
孫逸仙

Sung Chia-shu 宋嘉樹

Sung-chiang 松江

Sung Chiao-jen 宋教仁

Sung Chih-t'ien 宋芝田

Sung Chü-jen 宋居仁

Sung Yüeh-ju 宋躍如

Sung Yüeh-lun 宋越倫

Ta-kuang kuan-shu-lou
大光觀書樓

Ta-lu 太陸

ta-ni pu-tao 大逆不道

Ta-t'ung 大同

Ta-t'ung 大通

Ta-t'ung hsüeh-hsiao 大同學校

Ta-t'ung jih-pao 大同日報

Tai Chi-t'ao 戴季陶

Taiping (T'ai-p'ing) 太平

Taiwan Min-chu kuo
臺灣民主國

T'ai-yüan 太原

Takahashi Ken 高橋謙

T'an Chung-lin 譚鍾麟

T'an Pi-an 譚彼岸

Tan-shui 淡水

T'an Ssu-t'ung 譚嗣同

T'an Yu-fa 譚有發

T'ang Erh-ho 湯爾和

T'ang Fu-ch'eng 唐紱丞

T'ang Ts'ai-ch'ang 唐才常

tao-tsei 盜賊

T'ao Ch'eng-chang 陶成章

Te-shou 德壽

Teikoku shugi 帝國主義

Teng Mu-han 鄧慕韓

Teng T'ing-chien 鄧廷鏗

Teng Wan-liṇ 鄧萬林

Teng Yin-nan 鄧蔭南

Ti Ch'u-ch'ing 狄楚青

T'ien-yün 天運

Ting Wen-chiang 丁文江

Tōa Dōbun Kai 東亞同文會

Tōyama Mitsuru 頭山滿

Ts'ai Chün 蔡鈞

Ts'ai Yüan-p'ei 蔡元培

tsao-fan 造反

ts'ao-hsieh 草鞋

Ts'ao Ya-po 曹亞伯

Tse Tsan-tai (Hsieh Tsuan-t'ai)
  謝纘泰

Tseng Chi-tse 曾紀澤

Tseng Kuang-ch'üan 曾廣銓

Tseng Kuo-fan 曾國藩

Tseng Yu-hao 曾友豪

Tso Tou-shan 左斗山

Tsou Jung 鄒容

Tsou Lu 鄒魯

Ts'ui-heng 翠亨

Ts'ui T'ung-yüeh 崔通約

Tsung-li 總理

Tsungli Yamen 總理衙門

tsung-pan 總辦

tsung-t'ung 總統

Tu Ch'eng-hsiang 杜呈祥

t'u-fei 土匪

T'u-nan jih-pao 圖南日報

Tuan-fang 端方

Tui-O t'ung-chih hui
  對俄同志會

Tung Chung-shu 董仲舒

Tung-kuan 東莞

T'ung Meng Hui 同盟會

T'ung-wen Kuan 同文館

Tzu-li Hui 自立會

U Lai-un (see Hu Li-yüan)

Uchida Ryōhei 內田良平

Ukita Kazuomi 浮田和民

Waichow (see Hui-chou)

Wan Fu-hua 萬福華

Wan-kuo kung-pao 萬國公報

Wan-mu ts'ao-t'ang 萬木草堂

Wang Chao 王照

Wang Chih-ch'un 王之春

Wang Chih-fu 王質甫

Wang Ch'ung-hui 王寵惠

Wang I-sun 汪詒蓀

Wang Jen-chih 王忍之

Wang T'ao 王韜

Wang Te-chao 王德昭

Wang Wen-shao 王文韶

Wang Yü-ch'u 王煜初

Wei-hsing 闈姓

Wei Yuk (Wei Yü) 韋玉

Weng T'ung-ho 翁同龢

Wu Chien-chang (Samqua)
吳健彰

Wu Chih-hui (Wu Ching-heng)
吳稚暉 （吳敬恒）

Wu Hsiang-hsiang 吳相湘

Wu-hsü cheng-pien chi 戊戌政變記

Wu Lu-chen 吳祿貞

Wu P'an-chao 伍盤照

Wu Shou-i 吳壽頤

Wu T'ing-fang (Ng Choy)
伍廷芳 （伍叙）

Wu Tsung-lien 伍宗濂

Wu Ya 無涯

Wu Yü-chang 吳玉章

Yamada Junsaburō 山田純三郎

Yamada Yoshimasa 山田良政

Yamagata Aritomo 山縣有朋

Yang-chou (Yangchow) 揚州

Yang Ch'ü-yün 楊衢雲

Yang Ho-ling 楊鶴齡

Yang Hsiang-fu 楊香甫

Yang Hsin-ju 楊心如

Yang Hsiu-ch'ing 楊秀清

Yang Hung-chün 楊鴻鈞

Yang Ju 楊儒

Yang Shou-jen (Yang Tu-sheng)
楊守仁 （楊篤生）

Yang Wen-na 楊文納

yang-wu 洋務

Yao 堯

Yawata Maru 八幡丸

Yeh Hsiang-nan 葉湘南

Yeh Lan 葉瀾

Yeh Ming-ch'en 葉名琛

Yen Fu 嚴復

Yin Wen-k'ai 尹文楷

Yo Fei 岳飛

Yu-hsüeh i-pien 遊學譯編

Yu Lieh 尤列

Yung-hu 永湖

Yung Wing (Jung Hung) 容閎

Yü ch'en tzu 雨塵子

Yü Man-tzu (Yü Tung-ch'en)
余蠻子 （余棟臣）

Yü Yü-chih 余育之

yüan 圓

Yüan Shih-k'ai 袁世凱

yüeh-fa 約法

yüeh-fa san-chang 約法三章

Bibliography

This Bibliography is in two parts: an alphabetical numbered list of Western sources; and an alphabetical numbered list of Chinese and Japanese sources, which begins on page 387. Characters for all authors' names in Part II are given in the Glossary, pages 369–377.

I. WESTERN LANGUAGE SOURCES

[1] *The Antiforeign Riots in Szchuan: Report of a Meeting of the Missionary Body Held at Hankow, July 12th, 1895, in Connection with the Szchuan Riots.* (n.d.), consulted at Morrison Collection, Tōyō Bunko, Tokyo.

[2] Beard, Charles A. and Mary R. Beard. *A Basic History of the United States.* Philadelphia, 1944.

[3] Bennett, John W. and Robert K. McKnight. "Approaches of the Japanese Innovator to Cultural and Technical Change," *The Annals of the American Academy of Political and Social Science,* 305 (May 1956), 101–113.

[4] Beresford, Lord Charles. *The Break-Up of China.* New York and London, 1899.

[5] Biggerstaff, Knight. *The Earliest Modern Government Schools in China.* Ithaca, 1961.

[6] Bland, J. O. P. *Li Hung-chang.* ("Makers of the Nineteenth Century Series," ed. Basil Williams) London, 1917.

[7] —— and E. Backhouse. *China Under the Empress Dowager.* London, 1910.

[8] *Bolshaia Sovetskaia Entsiklopediia (Great Soviet Encyclopedia),* Vol. 12. Moscow, 1928.

[9] Boorman, Howard L. (ed.). *Men and Politics in Modern China* (preliminary). New York, 1960.

[10] Boulger, Demetrius C. *The Life of Sir Halliday Macartney K. C. M. G.* London, 1908.

[11] Brinton, Crane. *English Political Thought in the Nineteenth Century.* London, 1933.

[12] ———. *The Anatomy of Revolution.* New York, 1957.

[13] Britton, Roswell S. *The Chinese Periodical Press, 1800–1912.* Shanghai, 1933.

[14] Brunnert, H. S. and V. V. Hagelstrom. *Present Day Political Organization of China,* translated by A. Beltchenko and E. E. Moran. Shanghai, 1912.

[15] Bruun, Geoffrey. *Nineteenth Century European Civilization, 1815–1914.* New York, 1960.

[16] Bunker, Gerald E. "The Kidnapping of Sun Yat-sen in London, 1896." Seminar paper, Harvard University, 1963.

[17] Cantlie, James and C. Sheridan Jones. *Sun Yat-sen and the Awakening of China.* London, 1912.

[18] Cantlie, Neil and George Seaver. *Sir James Cantlie.* London, 1939.

[19] Chan, Mary Man-yue. "Chinese Revolutionaries in Hong Kong, 1895–1911." Master's thesis, University of Hong Kong, 1963.

[20] Chapin, Frederick L. "Homer Lea and the Chinese Revolution." Unpublished A.B. honors thesis, Harvard University, 1950.

[21] Cheng, Shelley H. "The T'ung-meng-hui: its organization, leadership, and finances: 1905–1912." Ph.D. dissertation, University of Washington, 1962.

[22] ———. "A Bibliographical Note on Recent Works Dealing with the Chinese Revolution of 1911." Mimeographed, n.d.

[23] *China Mail.* File for 1895–1900 consulted. Hong Kong, daily.

[24] *The China Mission Hand-Book.* Shanghai, 1896.

[25] Chow Tse-tsung. *The May Fourth Movement: Intellectual Revolution in Modern China.* Cambridge, Mass., 1960.

[26] Chung Kun Ai. *My Seventy Nine Years in Hawaii.* Hong Kong, 1960.

[27] Comber, L. F. *Chinese Secret Societies in Malaya.* Monographs of the Association for Asian Studies, No. VI. Locust Valley, New York, 1959.

[28] Coulter, J. W. and C. K. Chun. "Chinese Rice Farmers in Hawaii," *University of Hawaii Research Publications,* 16 (March 1937), 7–27.

[29] Culin, Stewart. "Chinese Secret Societies in the United States," *Journal of American Folklore* (January–March 1890), pp. 39–43.

[30] de Bary, Wm. Theodore, Wing-tsit Chan, and Burton Watson (compilers), *Sources of the Chinese Tradition*, Records of Civilization; Sources and Studies, No. LV, Columbia University. New York, 1960.

[31] Delusin, Lev. "Sun Yat-sen—Tribute to a Great Chinese Revolutionary," *New Times*, 44 (Moscow; November 1, 1966), 16–19.

[32] Diplomaticus. "Lord Salisbury's New China Policy," *Fortnightly Review* (New series), 65.388 (April 1, 1899), 539–550.

[33] *Directory of the Educational Association of China.* Shanghai, 1903.

[34] Dubs, Homer (trans.). *The History of the Former Han Dynasty by Pan Ku*, Vol. 1. Baltimore, 1938.

[35] Elvin, Mark. "The Mixed Court of the International Settlement at Shanghai (until 1911)," *Papers on China*, 17:131–159. Harvard University, East Asian Research Center, 1963.

[36] Endacott, G. B. *A History of Hong Kong.* London, 1958.

[37] Eto, Shinkichi. "Hai-lu-feng—the first Chinese Soviet Government," *China Quarterly*, 8 (October–December 1961), 161–183 and 9 (January–March 1962), 149–181.

[38] Fairbank, John K. *Trade and Diplomacy on the China Coast: The Opening of the Treaty Ports, 1842–1854.* 2 vols. Cambridge, Mass., 1953.

[39] ———. "China's Response to the West: Problems and Suggestions," *Journal of World History*, 3.2 (1956), 381–406.

[40] ———, Edwin O. Reischauer, and Albert M. Craig. *East Asia: The Modern Transformation.* Boston, 1965.

[41] Field, Margaret. "The Chinese Boycott of 1905," *Papers on China*, 11:63–98. Harvard University, East Asian Research Center, 1957.

[42] Franke, Wolfgang. *The Reform and Abolition of the Traditional Chinese Examination System.* Harvard University, Center for East Asian Studies, 1960.

[43] *Free Russia*, No. 2 (London, September 1890). Monthly.

[44] Fung Yu-lan. *A History of Chinese Philosophy*, translated by Derke Bodde. 2 vols. Princeton, 1952, 1953.

[45] Gluckman, Max. *Custom and Conflict in Africa.* Oxford, 1955.

[46] Great Britain. Documents in Public Record Office, London. Foreign Office Records: Series FO 17 (1895–1905); FO 371 (1911). Colonial Office Records: Series CO 129, CO 273 (1896–1900).

[47] Great Britain. Parliamentary Papers (Blue Books). *China,*

No. 3 (1900). Correspondence Respecting the Insurrectionary Movement in China.
China, No. 1 (1901). (Continuing No. 3, 1900.)

[48] Griswold, A. Whitney. *The Far Eastern Policy of the United States.* New York, 1938.

[49] Hackett, Roger F. "Chinese Students in Japan, 1900–1910," *Papers on China*, 3:134–169. Harvard University, Committee on International and Regional Studies, 1949.

[50] Hager, Charles R. "Dr. Sun Yat Sen: Some Personal Reminiscences," *The Missionary Herald* (Boston, April 1912). Reprinted in Sharman, *Sun Yat-sen*, pp. 382–387.

[51] Hahn, Emily. *The Soong Sisters.* New York, 1945.

[52] Hao, Yen-p'ing. "The Abortive Cooperation between Reformers and Revolutionaries," *Papers on China*, 15:91–114. Harvard University, East Asian Research Center, 1961.

[53] Harrison, Brian (ed.). *The University of Hong Kong: The First 50 Years.* Hong Kong, 1962.

[54] *Hawaiian Almanac and Annual for 1881.* Honolulu, 1882.

[55] Hildebrand, George H. (ed.). *The Idea of Progress: A Collection of Readings Selected by Frederick J. Teggart.* Berkeley and Los Angeles, 1949.

[56] Hobson, J. A. *Imperialism: A Study.* 3rd rev. ed. London, 1938.

[57] Hofstadter, Richard. *Social Darwinism in American Thought.* Revised ed. Boston, 1955.

[58] *Hongkong Telegraph.* File for 1895–1900 consulted. Hong Kong, daily.

[59] Howard, Richard C. "K'ang Yu-wei (1858–1927): His Intellectual Background and Early Thought," A. F. Wright and D. Twitchett (eds.), *Confucian Personalities*, pp. 294–316. Stanford, 1962.

[60] Hsiao, Kung-ch'üan. "K'ang Yu-wei and Confucianism," *Monumenta Serica* 18 (1959), 96–212.

[61] ———. *Rural China: Imperial Control in the Nineteenth Century.* Seattle, 1960.

[62] Hsieh, Winston. "The Ideas and Ideals of a Warlord: Ch'en Chiung-ming (1878–1933)," *Papers on China*, 16:198–252. Harvard University, East Asian Research Center, 1962.

[63] Hsiung, S. I. *The Life of Chiang Kai-shek.* London, 1948.

[64] Hsu Pao-chu. "A Short Biography of Dr. Sun Yat-sen," Mao Tse-tung, Soong Ching-ling, et al., *Dr. Sun Yat-sen: Commemorative Articles and Speeches.* Peking, 1957.

[65] Hsüeh, Chün-tu. "Sun Yat-sen, Yang Ch'ü-yün, and the Early

Revolutionary Movement in China," *Journal of Asian Studies,* 19:3 (May 1960), 307–318.

[66] ———. *Huang Hsing and the Chinese Revolution.* Stanford Studies in History, Economics, and Political Science, XX. Stanford, 1961.

[67] Hu Sheng. *Imperialism and Chinese Politics* (English translation). Peking, 1955.

[68] Hummel, Arthur W. (ed.). *Eminent Chinese of the Ch'ing Period.* 2 vols. Washington, D. C., 1943, 1944.

[69] Jansen, Marius B. *The Japanese and Sun Yat-sen.* Harvard Historical Monographs, XXVII. Cambridge, Mass., 1954.

[70] Kerr, John, *The Canton Guide.* 5th ed. Hong Kong, 1891.

[71] Kosaka, Masakata. "Ch'ing Policy Over Manchuria (1900–1903)," *Papers on China,* 16:126–153. Harvard University, East Asian Research Center, 1962.

[72] Kuykendall, Ralph S. *The Hawaiian Kingdom, 1854–1874.* Honolulu, 1953.

[73] Langer, William L. (compiler and editor). *An Encyclopedia of World History.* 3rd rev. ed. Boston, 1960.

[74] Lasswell, Harold D. *Politics: Who Gets What, When, How.* New York, 1958.

[75] Lauterpacht, Hersh (ed.). *L. F. L. Oppenheim, International Law: A Treatise.* 8th ed. London, 1957.

[76] Levenson, Joseph R. *Liang Ch'i-ch'ao and the Mind of Modern China.* Harvard Historical Monographs, No. XXVI. Cambridge, Mass., 1953.

[77] ———. "The Suggestiveness of Vestiges: Confucianism and Monarchy to the Last," D. S. Nivison and A. F. Wright (eds.), *Confucianism in Action,* pp. 244–267. Stanford, 1959.

[78] Li Chien-nung. *The Political History of China, 1840–1928,* translated by Ssu-yu Teng and Jeremy Ingalls. Princeton, New Jersey, 1956.

[79] Liang Ch'i-ch'ao. *Intellectual Trends in the Ch'ing Period,* translated by Immanuel C. Y. Hsü. Cambridge, Mass., 1959.

[80] Lin Yu-tang. *A History of the Press and Public Opinion in China.* Chicago, 1936.

[81] Linebarger, Paul. *Sun Yat-sen and the Chinese Republic.* New York, 1925.

[82] Lo, Jung-pang. "The Overseas Chinese and Chinese Politics, 1899–1911: Some Historical Sidelights on their Political Behavior." Unpublished paper delivered at the Association for Asian Studies Annual Meeting, Boston, 1962.

[83] Lu Hsun. *Selected Works of Lu Hsun* (English translation). 4 vols. Peking, 1956, 1957, 1959, 1960.

[84] Malone, Dumas (ed.). *Dictionary of American Biography.* London, 1933.

[85] Mao Tse-tung, Soong Ching-ling, et al. *Dr. Sun Yat-sen: Commemorative Articles and Speeches.* Peking, 1957.

[86] Morse, Hosea Ballou. *The Trade and Administration of the Chinese Empire.* London, 1908; reprinted in Taipei, 1966.

[87] Muramatsu, Yuji. "Some Themes in Chinese Rebel Ideologies," Arthur F. Wright (ed.), *The Confucian Persuasion*, pp. 241–267. Stanford, 1960.

[88] Nivison, David S. and Arthur F. Wright (eds.). *Confucianism in Action.* Stanford, 1959.

[89] *North China Herald.* File for 1900 consulted. Shanghai, weekly.

[90] Norton-Kyshe, J. W. *The History of the Laws and Courts of Hongkong.* 2 vols. London and Hong Kong, 1898.

[91] *Overland China Mail* (Overseas edition of the *China Mail*). File for 1895–1900 consulted. Hong Kong, weekly.

[92] Png Poh Seng. "The Kuomintang in Malaya, 1912–1941," *Journal of Southeast Asian History*, 2 (March 1961), 1–41.

[93] Purcell, Victor. *The Boxer Uprising.* Cambridge, 1963.

[94] Restarick, Henry B. *Sun Yat Sen, Liberator of China.* New Haven, 1931.

[95] Richard, Timothy. "The Secret Sects of China," *The China Mission Handbook*, pp. 41–45. Shanghai, 1896.

[96] ———. *Forty-five Years in China.* New York, 1916.

[97] Ride, Lindsay. "The Antecedents," in Brian Harrison (ed.), *University of Hong Kong: The First 50 Years, 1911–1961*, pp. 5–22. Hong Kong, 1962.

[98] Russ, William. *The Hawaiian Republic.* Salingsgrove, Penn., 1961.

[99] Sakai, Robert K. "Ts'ai Yuan-p'ei as a Synthesizer of Western and Chinese Thought," *Papers on China*, 3:170–192. Harvard University, Committee on International and Regional Studies, 1949.

[100] Scalapino, Robert A. and George T. Yu. *The Chinese Anarchist Movement.* University of California, Center for Chinese Studies, 1961.

[101] Schiffrin, Harold. "Sun Yat-sen's Early Land Policy: The Origin and Meaning of 'Equalization of Land Rights'," *Journal of Asian Studies*, 16 (August, 1957), 549–564.

[102] ——— and Pow-key Sohn. "Henry George on Two Continents: A Comparative Study in the Diffusion of Ideas," *Comparative*

Studies in Society and History, 2 (October 1959), 85–108.

[103] Schlegel, Gustave. *Thian Ti Hwui, The Hung-League or Heaven-Earth-League.* Batavia, 1866.

[104] Schwartz, Benjamin. "Some Polarities in Confucian Thought," D. S. Nivison and A. F. Wright (eds.), *Confucianism in Action*, pp. 50–62. Stanford, 1959.

[105] ———. *In Search of Wealth and Power: Yen Fu and the West.* Cambridge, Mass., 1964.

[106] *The Shanghai Sedition Trial.* Reprinted from the *North China Herald.* Shanghai, 1904.

[107] Sharman, Lyon. *Sun Yat-sen: His Life and its Meaning.* New York, 1934.

[108] Skinner, G. William. *Chinese Society in Thailand.* Ithaca, 1957.

[109] Smythe, E. Joan. "The Tzu-li Hui: Some Chinese and their Rebellions," *Papers on China*, 12:51–68. Harvard University, East Asian Research Center, 1958.

[110] Song Ong Siang. *One Hundred Years' History of the Chinese in Singapore.* London, 1923.

[111] Soothill, William E. *Timothy Richard of China.* London, 1924.

[112] Stevens, Sylvester K. *American Expansion in Hawaii, 1842–1898.* Harrisburg, Penn., 1945.

[113] Stillman, Edmund and William Pfaff. *The Politics of Hysteria: The Sources of Twentieth-Century Conflict.* New York, 1964.

[114] *Straits Settlements Government Gazette*, July 20, 1900. Singapore.

[115] Sun Yat-sen. *Kidnapped in London.* Bristol, 1897.

[116] ———. "China's Present and Future: The Reform Party's Plea for British Benevolent Neutrality," *Fortnightly Review* (New series), 61:363 (March 1, 1897) 424–440.

[117] ———. *The True Solution to the Chinese Question.* New York, 1904. Reprinted in *Tang-shih shih-liao ts'ung-k'an* (Serial Publication of Historical Materials on Party History), 1:1–10. Chungking, 1944?

[118] ———. "My Reminiscences," *The Strand Magazine*, March 1912, pp. 301–307.

[119] Sun, Zen E-tu (trans. and ed.). *Ch'ing Administrative Terms.* Cambridge, Mass., 1961.

[120] Tan, Chester C. *The Boxer Catastrophe.* Columbia Studies in the Social Sciences, No. 583. New York, 1955.

[121] Teng Ssu-yu and John K. Fairbank. *China's Response to the West: A Documentary Survey, 1839–1923.* Cambridge, Mass., 1954.

[122] Tse Tsan Tai. *The Chinese Republic: Secret History of the Revolution.* Hong Kong, 1924.

[123] ———. *Tse Tsan Tai.* Hong Kong?, n.d.

[124] Venturi, Franco. *Roots of Revolution: A History of the Populist and Socialist Movements in Nineteenth Century Russia.* London, 1960.

[125] Wakeman, Frederic Jr. *Strangers at the Gate: Social Disorder in South China, 1839–1861.* Berkeley and Los Angeles, 1966.

[126] Wang Gung-wu. "Sun Yat-sen and Singapore," *Journal of the South Seas Society,* 15 (December 1959) 55–68.

[127] Wang, Y. C. "Intellectuals and Society in China, 1860–1949," *Comparative Studies in Society and History,* 3.4 (July 1961), 395–426.

[128] ———. "The Su-pao Case: A Study of Foreign Pressure, Intellectual Fermentation, and Dynastic Decline." Unpublished paper, Wentworth-on-the-Sea Conference on the 1911 Revolution. August 1965.

[129] ———. *Chinese Intellectuals and the West: 1872–1949.* Chapel Hill, 1966.

[130] Weale, B. L. Putnam. *The Fight for the Republic in China.* New York, 1917.

[131] Woodside, A. B. "T'ang Ching-sung and the Rise of the 1895 Taiwan Republic," *Papers on China,* 17:160–192. Harvard University, East Asian Research Center, 1963.

[132] Wright, Arnold (ed.). *Twentieth Century Impressions of Hongkong, Shanghai, and other Treaty Ports of China: Their History, People, Commerce, Industries, and Resources.* London, 1908.

[133] Wright, Arthur F. (ed.). *The Confucian Persuasion.* Stanford, 1960.

[134] ——— and Denis Twitchett (eds.). *Confucian Personalities.* Stanford, 1962.

[135] Wright, G. H. Bateson. "Education," Arnold Wright (ed.), *Twentieth Century Impressions of Hongkong, Shanghai, and other Treaty Ports of China,* pp. 121–128. London, 1908.

[136] Wright, Mary Clabaugh. *The Last Stand of Chinese Conservatism: The T'ung-Chih Restoration, 1862–1874.* Stanford Studies in History, Economics, and Political Science, XIII. Stanford, 1957.

[137] Wu Yu-chang. *The Revolution of 1911* (English translation). Peking, 1962.

[138] Young, Ernest P. "Ch'en T'ien-hua (1875–1905): A Chinese Nationalist," *Papers on China,* 13:113–162. Harvard University, East Asian Research Center, 1959.

[139] Young, G. M. *Victorian England: Portrait of an Age.* New York, 1954.

[140] Yu, George T. *Party Politics in Republican China: The Kuomintang, 1912–1924.* Berkeley and Los Angeles, 1966.

II. *CHINESE AND JAPANESE SOURCES*

[141] Chang Ching-lu (ed.). *Chung-kuo chin-tai ch'u-pan shih-liao ch'u-pien* (Initial Compilation of Source Materials on Publications in Modern China). Shanghai, 1953.

[142] Chang Huang-ch'i. *"Su-pao an shih-lu"* (A Record of the Su-pao Case). Reprinted in *Hsin-hai ko-ming* [167], I, 367–386.

[143] Chang Nan and Wang Jen-chih (eds.). *Hsin-hai ko-ming ch'ien shih-nien chien shih-lun hsüan-chi* (Selected Articles on Current Events Written During the Ten Year Period Preceding the 1911 Revolution). Vol. I, 2 *ts'e.* Hong Kong, 1962.

[144] Chang P'eng-yüan. *Liang Ch'i-ch'ao yü Ch'ing-chi ko-ming* (Liang Ch'i-ch'ao and the Revolution in the Late Ch'ing Period). Publications of the Modern History Section of the Academia Sinica, No. 11. Taipei, 1964.

[145] Chang Ping-lin. *"Po K'ang Yu-wei shu"* (Letter Refuting K'ang Yu-wei), 1903. Reprinted in *Hsin-hai ko-ming ch'ien shih-nien chien shih-lun hsüan-chi* [143], I, *ts'e* 2, 752–764.

[146] Chang Shih-chao. *"Shu Huang Ti Hun"* (Commentary on *Huang Ti Hun*). Reprinted in *Hsin-hai ko-ming hui-i lu* [168], I, 217–304.

[147] Chang Yung-fu. *"Sun hsien-sheng ch'i-chü chu"* (Notes on Sun Yat-sen's Behavior), *Nan-yang yü ch'uang-li min-kuo* (The South Seas and the Founding of the Republic). Shanghai, 1933. This chapter reprinted in *Ko-ming chih ch'ang-tao yü fa-chan* [178], IX, 93–97.

[148] Chang Yü-ying. *"Hsin-hai ko-ming tsa-chih lu"* (List of Periodicals of the 1911 Revolution), *Chung-kuo chin-tai ch'u-pan shih-liao ch'u-pien* [141], pp. 97–103.

[149] ———. *"Hsin-hai ko-ming shu-cheng"* (List of Books of the 1911 Revolution), *Chung-kuo chin-tai ch'u-pan shih-liao ch'u-pien* [141], pp. 140–183. This and previous article originally appeared in *Hsüeh-lin*, No. 6, 1941.

[150] Ch'en Ch'un-sheng. *"Keng-tzu Hui-chou ch'i-i chi"* (An Account of the Waichow Uprising of 1900), *Chien-kuo yüeh-k'an* (Reconstruction Monthly), Vol. 5, no. 3. Reprinted in *Hsin-hai ko-ming* [167], I, 235–244.

[151] Ch'en Hsi-ch'i. *T'ung-meng-hui ch'eng-li ch'ien ti Sun Chung-shan* (Sun Yat-sen Prior to the Founding of the T'ung Meng Hui). Canton, 1957.

[152] Ch'en Shao-pai. *Hsing-chung-hui ko-ming shih-yao* (Outline of the Revolutionary History of the Hsing Chung Hui). Nanking, 1935; reprinted Taipei, 1956.

[153] Chiang Wei-ch'iao. "Chung-kuo Chiao-yü-hui chih hui-i" (Reminiscences of the Chinese Educational Society), *Hsin-hai ko-ming* [167], I, 485–496.

[154] Chin Ch'ung-chi and Hu Sheng-wu. "Lun Sun Chung-shan ko-ming ssu-hsiang ti hsing-ch'eng ho Hsing-chung-hui ti ch'eng-li" (The Formation of Sun Yat-sen's Revolutionary Ideas and the Establishment of the Hsing Chung Hui), *Li-shih yen-chiu* (Historical Research), V (Peking, 1960), 49–58.

[155] Chin P'ing-ou (ed.). *San-min chu-i tz'u-tien* (Concordance of the San-min chu-i). Taipei, 1956.

[156] Chou Hung-jan. "Kuo-fu 'Shang Li Hung-chang shu' chih shih-tai pei-ching" (Background to the Period of 'Sun Yat-sen's Letter to Li Hung-chang'), *Ko-ming chih ch'ang-tao yü fa-chan* [178], IX, 270–280. Reprinted from *Ta-lu tsa-chih* (Continental Magazine), Vol. 23, no. 5, 1961.

[157] Chu Ho-chung. "Ou-chou T'ung-meng-hui chi-shih" (A Record of the European T'ung Meng Hui), *Ko-ming wen-hsien* [179], II, 251–270.

[158] Fan Wen-lan. *Chung-kuo chin-tai shih* (Modern Chinese History). Vol. I. Peking, 1961.

[159] Feng Tzu-yu. *Chung-hua min-kuo k'ai-kuo ch'ien ko-ming shih* (History of the Revolution Prior to the Founding of the Chinese Republic). Vol. I. Shanghai, 1928.

[160] ———. *Ko-ming i-shih* (Reminiscences of the Revolution), Vol. I, Changsha, 1939; reprinted Taipei, 1953. Vol. II, Chungking, 1943; reprinted Taipei, 1953. Vol. III, Chungking, 1945; reprinted Shanghai, 1945–46. Vol. IV, Shanghai, 1946. Vol. V, Shanghai, 1947.

[161] ———. *Hua-ch'iao ko-ming k'ai-kuo shih* (History of the Overseas Chinese, the Revolution, and the Establishment of the Republic). Chungking, 1946; Shanghai, 1947; reprinted Taipei, 1953.

[162] ———. *Hua-ch'iao ko-ming tsu-chih shih-hua* (History of the Overseas Chinese Revolutionary Organizations). Taipei, 1954.

[163] Hirayama Shū. "Hirayama Shū t'an shang chieh Fei-li-pin so kou hsieh t'an shih" (Hirayama Shū Discusses the Negotiations for Utilizing the Arms and Munitions Purchased by the Filipinos), from "Ma Pai-yüan yü kuo-fu Jih yu t'an-hua chi-lu" (Record of Ma Pai-yüan's Conversations with Sun Yat-sen's Japanese Friends). *Ko-ming chih ch'ang-tao yü fa-chan* [178], IX, 602–606.

[164] Ho Ch'i (Ho Kai) and Hu Li-yüan. "Hsin-cheng chen-ch'üan" (excerpt), (The True Meaning of Modern Government), Shanghai, 1901. Reprinted in *Ko-ming chih ch'ang-tao yü fa-chan* [178], IX, 149–173.

[165] Ho Hsiang-ning. "Wo ti hui-i" (My reminiscences), *Hsin-hai ko-ming hui-i lu* [168], I, 12–59.

[166] Hsiao Kung-ch'üan. *Chung-kuo cheng-chih ssu-hsiang shih* (History of Chinese Political Thought). 6 vols. Taipei, 1961.

[167] *Hsin-hai ko-ming* (The 1911 Revolution), Chung-kuo shih-hsüeh hui (Chinese Historical Association) (eds.). Compiled by Ch'ai Te-keng et al. 8 vols. Shanghai, 1957.

[168] *Hsin-hai ko-ming hui-i lu* (Recollections of the 1911 Revolution). Chinese People's Political Consultative Conference (eds.). 5 vols. Peking, 1961–1963.

[169] *Hsin-hai ko-ming wu-shih chou-nien chi-nien lun-wen chi* (Collected Essays Commemorating the Fiftieth Anniversary of the 1911 Revolution). Hupeh Philosophical Society and Scientific Society (eds.). 2 vols. Peking, 1962.

[170] Hu Han-min. "*Min-pao* chih liu ta chu-i" (*Min-pao*'s Six Great Principles), *Min-pao*, III (April 1906) 1–22. This issue appears in Volume I of the four volume edition of *Min-pao* reproduced in Peking in 1957.

[171] ———. *Tzu-chuan* (Autobiography), *Ko-ming wen-hsien* [179], III, 373–442.

[172] ——— (ed.). *Tsung-li ch'üan-chi* (Collected Works of Sun Yat-sen). 5 vols. Shanghai, 1930.

[173] Hu Pin. *Wu-hsü pien-fa* (The Reforms of 1898). Shanghai, 1956.

[174] Hu Sheng-wu and Chin Ch'ung-chi. "Hsin-hai ko-ming shih-ch'i Chang Ping-lin ti cheng-chih ssu hsiang" (The Political Thought of Chang Ping-lin during the Period of the 1911 Revolution), *Hsin-hai ko-ming wu-shih chou-nien chi-nien lun-wen chi* [169], ts'e 1, 323–353. Reprinted from *Li-shih yen-chiu* (see [154]), IV (1961).

[175] Huang Fu-luan. *Hua-ch'iao yü Chung-kuo ko-ming* (The Overseas Chinese and the Chinese Revolution). Hong Kong, 1954.

[176] Ichiko Chūzō (chief ed.). Chūgokubun shimbun zasshi sōgo mokuroku (Comprehensive Catalogue of Chinese Newspapers and Magazines). Tokyo, 1959.

[177] Kaji Ryūichi (ed.). *Dai ichi nin sha no kotoba* (Words of the Number-One Men). Tokyo, 1961.

[178] *Ko-ming chih ch'ang-tao yü fa-chan* (The Advocacy and Development of the Revolution). Kuomintang (eds.). First series

of *Chung-hua min-kuo k'ai-kuo wu-shih nien wen-hsien* (Documents on Fifty Years of the Founding of the Chinese Republic). Vols. IX and X. Taipei, 1963.

[179] *Ko-ming wen-hsien* (Documents on the Revolution). Kuomintang (eds.). Vols. I-III. Taipei, 1953-1958.

[180] Kōtoku Shūsui. *Teikoku shugi* (Imperialism). Tokyo, 1901; reprinted Tokyo, 1952.

[181] Kuomintang (eds.). See *Ko-ming chih ch'ang-tao yü fa-chan* [178]; *Ko-ming wen-hsien* [179]; *Kuo-fu ch'üan-chi* [205].

[182] —— (eds.). "Tōa Dōbun Kai chih i-p'ieh" (A Glance at the Tōa Dōbun Kai), *Ko-ming chih ch'ang-tao yü fa-chan* [178], IX, 534-535.

[183] —— (eds.). "Shih Chien-ju chuan" (Biography of Shih Chien-ju), *Ko-ming chih ch'ang-tao yü fa-chan* [178], IX, 620-627.

[184] Kuo T'ing-i. *Chin-tai Chung-kuo shih-shih jih-chih* (Daily Record of Events in Modern Chinese History). 2 Vols. Taipei, 1963.

[185] Lai Hsin-hsia. "Shih-lun Ch'ing Kuang-hsü mo-nien ti Kuang-hsi jen-min ta ch'i-i" (Inquiry into the Great Popular Risings in Kwangsi During the Last Years of the Kuang-hsü Reign of the Ch'ing Period), *Li-shih yen-chiu* (Historical Research), XI (Peking, 1957), 57-77.

[186] Li Wen-hai. "Hsin-hai ko-ming yü hui-tang" (The 1911 Revolution and the Secret Societies), *Hsin-hai ko-ming wu-shih chou-nien chi-nien lun-wen chi* [169], I, 166-187.

[187] *Liao Chung-k'ai chi* (Collected works of Liao Chung-k'ai). Academia Sinica, et al. (eds.). Peking, 1963.

[188] Liao P'ing-tzu. "Shih Chien-ju an shih-i" (Notes on the Case of Shih Chien-ju), *Chien-kuo yüeh-k'an* (Reconstruction Monthly), X, 6. Reprinted in *Hsin-hai ko-ming* [167], I, 249-250.

[189] Liu Ch'eng-yü. "Hsien tsung-li chiu-te lu" (Sketches of Sun Yat-sen's Character), *Kuo-shih-kuan kuan-k'an* (Bulletin of the National Historical Bureau), I, 1 (Nanking, December 1947), 44-56.

[190] Liu Ta-nien. "Hsin-hai ko-ming yü fan-Man wen-t'i" (The 1911 Revolution and the anti-Manchu question), *Li-shih yen-chiu* (Historical Research), V (Peking, 1961), 1-10.

[191] Lo Chia-lun. *Chung-shan hsien-sheng Lun-tun meng-nan shih-liao k'ao-ting* (A Critical Study of the Official Documents Concerning Sun Yat-sen's Kidnapping in London). Shanghai, 1930.

[192] —— (ed.). *Kuo-fu nien-p'u ch'u-kao* (Chronological Biography of Sun Yat-sen, First Draft). 2 vols. Taipei, 1958.

[193] ——— (ed.). *Kuo-fu mo-chi* (Facsimile Copies of Sun Yat-sen's Calligraphy). 2 vols. Taipei, 1961.

[194] Lo Hsiang-lin. "Kuo-fu yü Wei-li-shih chu-chiao" (Rt. Rev. Alfred Willis) (Sun Yat-sen and Bishop Willis), *Kuo-fu yü Ou-Mei chih yu-hao* (Sun Yat-sen and His Western Friends). Taipei, 1951. This chapter reprinted in *Ko-ming chih ch'ang-tao yü fa-chan* [178], IX, 180–190.

[195] ———. *Kuo-fu chih ta-hsüeh shih-tai* (Sun Yat-sen's University Days). Taipei, 1954.

[196] ———. *Liu Yung-fu li-shih ts'ao* (Draft History of Liu Yung-fu). Taipei, 1957.

[197] Lo Kang, *Lo pien kuo-fu nien-p'u chiu-miu* (Correcting the Errors in the Chronological Biography of Sun Yat-sen Edited by Lo Chia-lun). Taipei, 1962.

[198] Mao Tse-tung. *Mao Tse-tung hsüan-chi* (Selected Works of Mao Tse-tung). 4 vols. Peking, 1958, 1960.

[199] *Min-pao* (People's Journal), (Tokyo, monthly; 26 nos. 1905–1910).

[200] Miyazaki Tōten (Torazō). *Sanjū-sannen no yume* (The Thirty-three Years' Dream). Tokyo, 1902, 1926, 1943.

[201] Nozawa Yutaka. *Son Bun* (Sun Yat-sen). Tokyo, 1962.

[202] Sanetō Keishū. *Chūkokujin Nihon ryūgaku shi* (A History of Chinese Students in Japan). Tokyo, 1960.

[203] Sun Ch'iu-sheng. "Hsiang tso huang-ti ti Liu Hsüeh-hsün" (Liu Hsüeh-hsün; The Man Who Wanted to be Emperor), *Hsin-wan pao* (Hong Kong, daily), (date unknown). From the collection of Dr. T. C. Lau.

[204] "Sun Kung Chung-shan tsai T'an shih-lüeh" (Outline of Sun Yat-sen's Activities in Hawaii) from *T'an-shan hua-ch'iao* (The Overseas Chinese of Hawaii). Honolulu, 1929. This chapter reprinted in *Ko-ming wen-hsien* [179], III, 278–284.

[205] Sun Yat-sen. *Kuo-fu ch'üan-chi* (Collected Works of Sun Yat-sen). Kuomintang (eds.). 6 vols. Taipei, revised edition, 1957.

[206] Sun Yat-sen. "Shang Li Hung-chang t'ung ch'en chiu kuo ta chi shu" (Urgent Presentation to Li Hung-chang of a Grand Plan to Save the Country), 1894. Printed in *Kuo-fu ch'üan-chi* [205], V, 1–12.

[207] ———. "Chih-na pao-ch'üan fen-ko ho-lun" (The Arguments for Preserving or Dismembering China), *Chiang-su*, no. 6 (November 1903). Reprinted in *Hsin-hai ko-ming ch'ien shih-nien chien shih-lun hsüan-chi* [143], I, ts'e 2, 597–602.

[208] ———. "Ching-kao t'ung-hsiang lun ko-ming yü pao-huang chih fen-yeh shu" (A Letter Respectfully Warning My Fellow

Countrymen To Distinguish Between 'Revolution' and 'Protect the Emperor'), *Lung-chi pao* (Honolulu, 1904). Reprinted in *Kuo-fu ch'üan-chi* [205], V, 23–25.

[209] ———. "Po pao-huang pao" (Refuting the Protect the Emperor Newspaper), *Lung-chi pao* (Honolulu, 1904). Reprinted in *Kuo-fu ch'üan-chi* [205], VI, 226–232.

[210] Sung Chiao-jen. *Wo chih li-shih* (My diary). Reprinted Taipei, 1962.

[211] Sung Yüeh-lun. *Tsung-li tsai Jih-pen chih ko-ming huo-tung* (Sun Yat-sen's Revolutionary Activities in Japan). Taipei, 1953.

[212] T'an Pi-an. "O-kuo Min-ts'ui-chu-i tui T'ung-meng-hui ti ying-hsiang" (The Influence of Russian Populism on the T'ung Meng Hui), *Li-shih yen-chiu* (Historical Research), I (Peking, 1959), 35–44.

[213] Teng Mu-han. "Shih Chien-ju shih-lueh" (A Sketch of Shih Chien-ju), *Chien-kuo yüeh-k'an* (Reconstruction Monthly), Vol. II, no. 6. Reprinted abridged in *Hsin-hai ko-ming* [167], I, 245–248.

[214] Ting Wen-chiang (ed.). *Liang Jen-kung hsien-sheng nien-p'u ch'ang-pien ch'u-kao* (Preliminary Draft of Sources for a Chronological Biography of Liang Ch'i-ch'ao). 2 vols. Taipei, 1962.

[215] Tsou Jung. *Ko-ming chün* (The Revolutionary Army). Shanghai, 1903. Reprinted in *Hsin-hai ko-ming* [167], I, 331–364.

[216] Tsou Lu. *Chung-kuo Kuo-min-tang shih-kao* (Draft History of the Kuomintang). Changsha, 1938.

[217] Ts'ui T'ung-yüeh. "Wo chih ko-ming ching-kuo" (My Revolutionary Past). From *Ts'ang-hai sheng-ping* (Shanghai, 1935). This chapter reprinted in *Ko-ming chih ch'ang-tao yü fa-chan* [178], IX, 629–638.

[218] Tu Ch'eng-hsiang. "Tsou Jung ti ssu-hsiang yen-pien chi ch'i tsai Chung-kuo hsien-tai ko-ming shih-shang chih ti-wei" (The Development of Tsou Jung's Thought and Its Place in Modern Chinese Revolutionary History), *Chung-kuo hsien-tai-shih ts'ung-k'an* [224], ts'e 1, pp. 189–208.

[219] Ukita Kazuomi. *Teikoku shugi to kyoiku* (Imperialism and Education). Tokyo, 1901.

[220] Wang I-sun. "Hsin-hai ko-ming shih-ch'i tz'u-ch'an chieh-chi yü nung-ming ti kuan-hsi wen-t'i" (Problems Concerning the Relations Between the Bourgeoisie and the Peasants during the Period of the 1911 Revolution), *Hsin-hai ko-ming wu-shih chou-nien chi-nien lun-wen chi* [169], I, 115–146. Reprinted from *Hupeh Daily*, October 21, 22, 1961.

[221] Wang Te-chao. "T'ung-meng-hui shih-ch'i Sun Chung-shan hsien-sheng ko-ming ssu-hsiang ti fen-hsi yen-chiu" (An Analytical Study of Sun Yat-sen's Thought during the T'ung Meng Hui Period), *Chung-kuo hsien-tai-shih ts'ung-k'an* [224], *ts'e* 1, pp. 65–188.

[222] Wu Ching-heng (Wu Chih-hui). "Wo i i-chiang Chung-shan hsien-sheng" (I Also Expound on Sun Yat-sen). From *Wu Chih-hui ch'üan-chi* (Complete Works of Wu Chih-hui). Shanghai, 1927. Reprinted in *Ko-ming chih ch'ang-tao yü fa-chan* [178], IX, 11–13.

[223] ———. "Tsung-li hsing-i" (Sun Yat-sen's Righteous Behavior). Lecture (1939). Printed in *Ko-ming chih ch'ang-tao yü fa-chan* [178], IX, 1–11.

[224] Wu Hsiang-hsiang (ed.). *Chung-kuo hsien-tai-shih ts'ung-k'an* (Serial Publication on Modern Chinese History). *Ts'e* 1. Taipei, 1960.

[225] Wu Shou-i. *Kuo-fu ti ch'ing-nien shih-tai* (The Period of Sun Yat-sen's Youth). Taipei, 1959.

[226] Wu Ya (pseud.). "Sun Chung-shan tsai Ao-men so Ch'uang-pan ti pao-chih" (The Newspaper Founded by Sun Yat-sen in Macao), *Ta Kung-pao* (Hong Kong, daily), (January 29, 1965). From the collection of Dr. T. C. Lau.

[227] Wu Yü-chang. *Hsin-hai ko-ming* (The 1911 Revolution). Peking, 1961.

[228] Yamada Junsaburō. "Shina kakumei to Son Bun no Chūnichi remmei" (The Chinese Revolution and Sun Yat-sen's Sino-Japanese Alliance), *Dai ichi nin sha no kotoba* [177], pp. 259–282.

Index

Agricultural operations. *See* "Nung-kung"

Agricultural Study Society, 66, 84, 148; manifesto of, 63, 64

Aguinaldo, Emilio, 168, 334

Ai-kuo Hsüeh-she (Patriotic School), 264

Ai-kuo Nü-hsüeh (Patriotic Girls' School), 265

America: missionaries of, 14, 16, 18, 22, 172, 250, 267, 347; and Sun's education, 15; and Hsing Chung Hui oath, 43; and Chinese exclusion, 185, 255; and discrimination against Chinese, 186n; and Waichow Triads, 244; Declaration of Independence of, 276; Anti-Imperialist League of, 284; anti-imperialists' influence Chinese, 284, 285; imperialism of, 286; Chinese boycott of, 291, 346, 361, 364; as democratic model, 315; Liang Ch'i-ch'ao in, 323; influence of K'ang Yu-wei and Liang Ch'i-ch'ao in, 332, 333; appealed to by Sun, 334–337. *See also* American, Hawaii, *Hua-ch'iao*, Sun Yat-sen

American Consul, 89, 250, 270, 316

American Revolution, 258, 268, 335

Amoy, 235–237, 245, 246; Japanese designs upon, 237

Amur region, 57

Anarchism: and Ts'ai Yüan-p'ei, 278; and student nationalists, 296, 297

Anglo-Japanese Alliance (1902), 260

Anhwei, 57, 340, 341; uprising of, 220, 223

Annam, 19

Aoyama military school, 307

Bache, Victor, 103

Bagehot, Walter, 266n

Balaarat, S. S., 191n

Barère, Bertrand, 297n

Basel Mission, 228, 242

Beresford, (Lord) Charles, 212n, 216

Big Sword Society, 222

Black Dragon Society, 358

Blake, (Sir) Henry, 189, 192, 211, 221, 244, 247, 253; mediator between Sun and Li Hung-chang, 198–200; interview with Li Hung-chang, 202–204; and Sun's representatives, 206; desire to negotiate with revolutionaries, 210; and Waichow rebels, 242, 247

Bocca Tigris: and Waichow uprising, 229, 232, 234

Boer War, 285, 292; tactics influence Sun, 302, 307. *See also* Krueger, South Africa, Transvaal

Borneo, British North, 227, 227n

Boxers, 196, 208, 242, 244, 287; and Sun, 6, 309, 312, 335, 336; rebellion of, 179, 180, 185, 200, 250, 283, 285, 345; rehabilitation of, 291

Boycott, Chinese. *See* America

Braga, J. M., 32n, 33n, 87n

Brenan, (Consul) Byron, 90, 95, 242n

British: education of Sun, 13; preferred over Japanese in Canton, 59; and Canton plot propaganda, 71, 72, 79, 80; and Hsing Chung Hui, 81; China policy, 130–132, 223; and Tsungli Yamen, 134; interest in China, 203; fear violence in South China, 205, 206; and Tzu-li Hui, 221; and Hankow plot, 222, 223; imperialism, 285, 286. *See also* British Colonial Office, Brit-